The
Tarnished Dream

The Tarnished Dream :
THE BASIS OF AMERICAN ANTI-SEMITISM

Michael N. Dobkowski

Contributions in American History; Number 81

GP GREENWOOD PRESS,
WESTPORT, CONNECTICUT•LONDON, ENGLAND

Library of Congress Cataloging in Publication Data
Dobkowski, Michael N
    The tarnished dream.

    (Contributions in American history ; no. 81 ISSN 084-9219)
    Bibliography: p.
    Includes index.
    1. Antisemitism—United States. 2. Jews in the United States—
Public opinion. 3. Public opinion—United States. 4. United
States—Politics and government. I. Title.
DS146.U6D6   301.45'19'24073   78-67655
ISBN 0-313-20641-4

The author wishes to thank the following publisher for
permission to quote from the source listed:
    "Burbank with a Baedeker: Bleistein with a Cigar." From
    Collected Poems 1909 – 1962 by T. S. Eliot, copyright 1936
    by Harcourt Brace Jovanovich, Inc.; copyright © 1963, 1964
    by T. S. Eliot.

Library of Congress Catalog Card Number: 78 – 67655
ISBN: 0-313-20641-4
ISSN: 0084-9219

First published in 1979,

Greenwood Press, Inc.
51 Riverside Avenue, Westport, Connecticut 06880

Printed in the United States of America

10   9   8   7   6   5   4   3   2   1

To Monik Dobkowski (1914– 61),
Bronia and David Kalt

*They inspired this work
through their suffering and
survival with purpose.*

Contents

Acknowledgments

In the course of preparing this book, I have incurred many debts, some of which I am at last able to acknowledge publicly. Without the financial and emotional support of my parents, I would never have been able to devote the time needed for this undertaking. Words are inadequate to describe my gratitude. A generous grant from the Memorial Foundation for Jewish Culture enabled me to carry out a major part of the research. Additional grants from New York University and from the Southern Fellowships Fund were of invaluable aid during my years of graduate study. A Faculty Research Grant from Hobart and William Smith Colleges facilitated the completion of the work.

The staff members of the libraries and manuscript depositories I visited were unfailingly helpful in making materials available. I would like to offer special thanks to Dr. Leonard S. Gold of the Jewish Division, John Miller of the American History Division, Paul R. Rugen of the Manuscripts and Archives Division, and Maud D. Cole of the Rare Book Division of the New York Public Library. These individuals were consistently cooperative and good-natured despite my compulsiveness. I would also like to express my appreciation to Dr. Stanley F. Chyet and the staff of the American Jewish Archives; to Harry J. Alderman and his wonderful assistant Syma Horowitz of the American Jewish Committee Library; to Dr. Nathan M. Kaganoff and the staff of the American Jewish Historical Society; to Stephen D. Riley and the staff of the Massachusetts Historical Society; to the staffs of The Houghton Library, Harvard University, and the Library of Congress; and to Gretchen Gross, the energetic and dedicated reference librarian of New York University's Bobst Library.

I owe a particular debt of gratitude to James Marshall for permission to consult the Louis Marshall papers, and to Milton Himmelfarb and Harry Alderman for permission to use the American Jewish Committee

Archives. Dr. Jacob Marcus graciously allowed me to look at his personal materials on American anti-Semitism and opened his home as well as his mind to a young scholar in a strange city. He has been a continuous source of intellectual inspiration. I would like also to recall the words of encouragement and spiritual strength given to me by the Rebbe "Shlita," Menachem Mendel Schneerson.

As for guidance, I want especially to thank my mentor and friend Dr. David Reimers for his insightful commentary as well as for his warm support, advice, and concern. I would also like to acknowledge Dr. Irwin Unger and Dr. Paul Baker for their helpful suggestions for improving the manuscript, and Dr. Bayrd Still for the personal and scholarly counsel he has provided me both in this undertaking and throughout my years of study. To my department colleagues at Hobart and William Smith Colleges—Richard Heaton, Valerie Saiving, Mary Gerhart, and Lowell Bloss—and to my other friends and students in the College community who facilitated this work by their example and quiet encouragement, many thanks. A special acknowledgment to Dr. Herbert A. Strauss for his friendship, guidance, and teaching.

Credit for typing and good-humored advice goes to Ann Hovey. I, of course, assume full responsibility for any errors and all interpretations.

Finally, but not least, my thanks to my wife, Karen, who in this, as in all my work, has been an integral part. Her remarkable patience, sensitivity, good humor, and support created the conditions that made the writing of this book possible. And to Batsheva, the new joy of my life who kept me going when things were rough.

The
Tarnished Dream

Introduction

There is a startling contrast between the neglect of anti-Semitism by students of American history and the intense fascination it has held for scholars of European history. The latter assigned to anti-Semitism an extraordinary importance, arguing that critical attitudes toward Jews are indicators of the basic health of any society. Anti-Semitism in this view is not just a serious problem in human relations; it is the very archetype of prejudice and is caused largely by stereotyping.[1]

To American historians, in contrast, anti-Semitism has never seemed a subject of major importance. No political or social movement, no religious development, no deep social crisis, has been associated with, or is significant because of, anti-Semitism. Accordingly, scholars have rarely taken more than a passing interest in studying it. In keeping with this neglect, they have for the most part de-emphasized the importance of literary and social stereotyping as indices of prejudice. This is unfortunate, for conceivably, ideology drove a wedge between Jews and gentiles simply by sharpening negative stereotypes. Minds were often made up before any personal encounter with Jews could transpire. This ideological assault, which is traced in this book, left a deep imprint on its victims, even if it did not otherwise affect the course of American history.

Not until the 1920s did American scholars—prodded by the nativism of the preceding decades, Henry Ford's campaign, and the fulminations of quasi-fascist groups—begin to recognize the existence of anti-Semitism as a significant development in American history.[2] Walter Lippmann, Frank Boas, Robert E. Park, and Horace Kallen made their studies of racial prejudice and ethnocentricity in the United States in response to the racial and ethnic xenophobia that overcame American society during and following World War I.[3] Their perspectives based on a faith in cultural relativism were joined a decade later to the theories of social psychologists Gardiner Murphy and Richard Crutchfield, who responded to the demagogic madness of the 1930s and identified anti-Semitism with the illiberal attitudes of groups who supported militarism, imperialism, economic conservatism, and isolation.[4]

After the Holocaust, American scholars again returned to this question. Prominent social scientists and psychologists attempted to analyze and understand those social, economic, religious, and psychological factors that predispose some individuals to reactions of hostility to racial and religous groups. The writings of Theodor Adorno, Bruno Bettelheim, Morris Janowitz, Seymour Martin Lipset, Alan Davies, Gordon Allport, Charles Stember, Daniel Bell, Charles Glock, and Rodney Stark, all nationally known specialists in this field, are indicative of the vast social science research that has been done on this question. There is, however, little historical orientation in these works, and the problem remained how to account for earlier and specifically American manifestations of anti-Semitism.[5]

In the late 1940s with the prestige of Marxian economics high, Carey McWilliams developed the thesis that racial prejudice was primarily the product of economic factors. According to McWilliams, the industrial barons fomented anti-Semitism to provide "a mask for privilege" enabling them to exploit without detection the society that professed democratic ideals. It was a rationalization for their elite social order that came into being with the rise of industrial capitalism in the late nineteenth century.[6]

McWilliams' use of Marxist economic determinism to explain American anti-Semitism, although provocative, lost favor in the following decade to another intellectual deity—consensus. Historians in the late 1950s carried out an extensive grading process to smooth over America's social convulsions. They emphasized the continuity and homogeneity of American history, the stability of basic institutions and the nonideological, conservative nature of political and social life. They minimized the importance of the myths and stereotypes that have exacerbated the differences between competing groups and idealized instead their surface uniformity and agreement. This is essentially the historical tendency that has characterized the most accepted scholarship on American anti-Semitism. Although porous and not definitive, it has succeeded in generating a sense of well-being and tolerance that has not done justice to the evidence. A close reading of the data may reveal that negative imagery deserves more than patronizing attention.

John Higham, for example, a careful historian who was cognizant of the weaknesses inherent in the panoramic approach of consensus historiography, nevertheless emphasized a causal relationship that if followed to its conclusion would belie the significance of the nativist phenomenon once certain social ingredients were removed.[7] He argued that the first great acceleration of American anti-Semitism occurred in the post-Civil War period and continued until the turn of the century when a rapidly aspiring first- and second-generation Jewish community began to impinge upon the social preserve of its native American neighbors. Discrimination developed where and when Jews participated in the general middle-class scramble for prestige and status; it developed "where and when a hectic pace of social climbing made the guardians of distinction afraid of being invaded."[8] American anti-Semitism, Higham contended, owes little to ideological sources. Nor does stereotypic thinking play a decisive role. Actual and everyday conflict situations in the social and economic arenas provided the patterns of exclusion that gradually restricted the opportunities of American Jews.[9]

Higham denied the contention of Oscar Handlin and Cary McWilliams that discrimination grew as reactionary leaders imposed their undemocratic values on the innocent masses. He also criticized Richard Hofstadter and Handlin for focusing too much attention on the role of ideas and images and not enough on economic forces.[10] But even Handlin, who admitted the relationship between ideology and American anti-Semitism, generally de-emphasized the scope of the problem in the nineteenth century and argued instead that by 1900 there existed a prevailing temper of tolerance and a great willingness to accept the Jew.[11] America's brief escapade in Judeophobia was only a decade in duration and rather insignificant according to the Harvard University historian. Handlin writes as if the stereotype of the Jew took on negative definition only in the 1890s. He would have us believe that it was only then that the Jew was identified to his detriment "as a peddler, as an old-clothes dealer, and as a pawnbroker." He further asserts that "the American stereotype involved no hostility, no negative judgment."[12] Handlin argues that the renderings of the Jew on the stage, in literature, and in magazine caricatures were not meant as "anti-Semitic insults" and "were not taken as such at the time."[13] Comments in the American Jewish press suggest this was not the case. As early as the 1850s, Rabbi Isaac M. Wise, the spiritual leader of Reform Jewry, stated that one reason for publishing his magazine, the *American Israelite,* was to counteract the current stream of abusive stereotypes. "A rascally Jew," he explains, "figured in every cheap novel, every newspaper printed some stale jokes about Jews to fill up space, and every backwoodsman had a few jokes on hand to use in public addresses; and all this called forth not one word of protest from any source."[14]

Richard Hofstadter, the great synthesizer, agreed with Handlin that a qualitative change took place in anti-Semitism in the late nineteenth century, although he saw this as a specific aftereffect of the anti-Jewish agitation of the Populists. "It was chiefly Populist writers," he argued, "who expressed that identification of the Jew with the usurer and the 'international gold ring' which was the central theme of the American anti-Semitism of the age." Although the movement "did not lead to exclusion laws, much less to riots or pogroms...," yet it essentially "activated most of what we have of popular anti-Semitism in the United States."[15]

In other words, Handlin, Hofstadter, and Higham, the three historians most closely identified with this question, contend that the new level of overt and articulate anti-Semitism that developed at the end of the nineteenth century was either relatively insignificant, or rested primarily with the anti-Semitic rhetoric of the Populist movement, or was precipitated by social conflict as Jews moved out of the "ghetto" and into the Fifth Avenues and Riverside Drives of America. These theories are misleading oversimplifications. All three scholars display an inclination to deny the anti-Jewish character of the most obvious and flagrant stereotypical expressions that appeared frequently in literature, on the stage, and in print. Evidence indicates that there were many misconceptions and falsehoods, including conspiracy theories, circulating in America well before the 1890s that had nothing to do with the agrarian protest or social claustrophobia. Their error thus lies in overlooking the presence of another significant source of anti-Semitism—the ideological—and in underestimating the quality and quantity of prejudice present decades before the century came to a close. The pervasiveness of this negative imagery is one more indication that America was not as tolerant in this fluid and turbulent age as some of its apologists would have us believe; it is one more index of the continued presence of anti-Semitism in American society. Despite all professions of equality, prejudice persisted, and it was expressed, consciously or unconsciously, through the stereotyping of the American Jew.

The major acceleration of this negative imagery, although present before on a smaller scale, began essentially in the 1870s and continued through the Henry Ford crusade of the 1920s.[16] The historiography of American anti-Semitism, although acknowledging in varying degrees the significance of this phenomenon, has not adequately analyzed its relationship to discrimination and prejudice. In this study I look at this generally neglected aspect of the problem and provide a framework for a reinterpretation of American anti-Semitism. Although this may not reflect positively on certain individuals or on society generally, I hope it will shed a modicum of light on the forces that have shaped human interaction and on the times that may have appeared tranquil to some, but were in essence replete with the revilement of a much abused people. The denouement is yet before us.

NOTES

1. Arthur Hertzberg, *The French Enlightenment and the Jews* (New York: Columbia University Press, 1968), pp. 248 – 314; Edward H. Flannery, *The Anguish of The Jews* (New York: The Macmillan Company, 1965), pp. 3 – 25; Charles C. Lehrmann, *The Jewish Element in French Literature*, trans. George Klin (Rutherford: Fairleigh Dickinson University Press, 1971); Montagu Frank Modder, *The Jew in the Literature of England to the End of the Nineteenth Century* (New York: Meridian Books, 1960); Edgar Rosenberg, *From Shylock to Svengali: Stereotypes in English Fiction* (Stanford: Stanford University Press, 1960).

2. Lee J. Levinger's *Anti-Semitism in the United States: Its History and Causes* (New York: Bloch Publishing Co., 1925) was a popular study of current events.

3. Walter Lippmann, *Public Opinion* (New York: Penguin Books, 1946); Horace M. Kallen, *Culture and Democracy in the United States* (New York: Boni Liveright, 1924). See Ronald A. Urquhart, ''The American Reaction to the Dreyfus Affair. A Study of Anti-Semitism in the 1890s,'' Ph.D. dissertation, Columbia University, 1972.

4. Gardiner Murphy, L.B. Murphy, and Theodore Newcomb, *Experimental Social Psychology* (New York: Harper & Brothers, 1937), pp. 889 – 1046; David Krech and Richard S. Crutchfield, *Theory and Problems of Social Psychology* (New York: McGraw-Hill Book Co., 1948), p. 487.

5. See Theodor Adorno et al., *The Authoritarian Personality* (New York: Harper & Brothers, 1950); Bruno Bettelheim and Morris Janowitz, *Dynamics of Prejudice* (New York: Harper & Brothers, 1950); Seymour Martin Lipset, *The Politics of Unreason* (New York: Harper & Row, 1970); Alan T. Davies, *Anti-Semitism and the Christian Mind* (New York: Herder and Herder, 1969); Gordon Allport, *The Nature of Prejudice* (Cambridge: Addison-Wesley Publishing Co., 1954); Charles Stember, *Jews in the Mind of America* (New York: Basic Books, 1966); Charles Y. Glock and Rodney Stark, *Christian Beliefs and Anti-Semitism* (New York: Harper & Row, 1966).

6. Cary McWilliams, *A Mask for Privilege: Anti-Semitism in America* (Boston: Little, Brown and Co., 1948).

7. John Higham, "The Cult of the 'American Consensus': Homogenizing Our History," *Commentary,* Vol. 27 (February, 1959), pp. 93–100.

8. John Higham, "Another Look at Nativism," *The Catholic Historical Review,* Vol. 44, No. 2 (July, 1958), p. 154.

9. Even Higham's revised essays in *Send These to Me: Jews and Other Immigrants in Urban America* (New York: Atheneum, 1975) continue to de-emphasize the impact of ideology.

10. John Higham, "Anti-Semitism in the Gilded Age: A Reinterpretation," *Mississippi Valley Historical Review,* Vol. 43, No. 4 (March, 1957) pp. 559–78; John Higham, "Social Discrimination Against Jews in America, 1830–1930," *Publications of the American Jewish Historical Society,* Vol. 47 (September 1957-June 1958), pp. 1–33. See Louis Harap, *The Image of the Jew in American Literature* (Philadelphia: The Jewish Publication Society of America, 1974).

11. Oscar Handlin, "American Views of the Jew at the Opening of the Twentieth Century," *Publications of the American Jewish Historical Society,* Vol. 40 (June, 1951), pp. 324–45.

12. Oscar Handlin, "How U.S. Anti-Semitism Really Began: Its Grass-Roots Source in the 90's," *Commentary,* Vol. 2, No. 6 (June, 1951), pp. 542–43.

13. Ibid.

14. Isaac M. Wise, *Reminiscences,* trans. David Philipson (Cincinnati: L. Wise, 1901), p. 272.

15. Richard Hofstadter, *The Age of Reform; from Bryan to F.D.R.* (New York: Alfred A. Knopf, 1956), pp. 78, 80.

16. I chose 1877 as a symbolic date because that was when Joseph Seligman was refused entry into the Grand Union Hotel in Saratoga, New York. In 1927 Henry Ford publicly apologized for his anti-Semitic campaign, thus signaling the close of an era. I do not deal with the anti-Semitism of the 1930s because the issue is clouded by foreign influences and Nazi propaganda.

CHAPTER

1

Yea, what are thou, blind unconverted
Jew/ That with thy idol-volume's
covers two/ Wouldst make a jail to
coop the living God?[1]

JAMES RUSSELL LOWELL

We are not a narrow tribe of men, with
bigoted Hebrew nationality—whose
blood had been debased in the attempt
to ennoble it, by maintaining an
exclusive succession among
ourselves.[2]

HERMAN MELVILLE

Origins of American Anti-Semitism: The Religious Factor

It would be simplistic to attribute American anti-Semitism solely to a bigotry passed down from Europe. But it would be equally naive to assume that class and ethnic differences alone account for the unfavorable attitudes held in many circles. If not for the various stigmas attached to Jews, their cultural characteristics would have received less notice. Herein lies the importance of the religious factor. Even in America the tendency was to think of Jews in terms of unregenerate sinners and Christ killers, especially in the religiously active nineteenth century, and to think of non-Jews in terms of the highest standards of gentility and Christian values. Here the accusations are not as extreme and the emotions not as volatile as in Europe, but the religious issue remains important (if not basic) and is the first to have any recognizable impact.

Bearers of the guilt of the Crucifixion, Jews were perceived in Europe as incapable of spiritual enlightenment. They became the prime symbols of medieval close-mindedness, the rightful inheritors of Pharisaic cruelty. They seemed to be a people enslaved by the proscriptions of the Talmud, the document widely regarded as the most diabolical theological tract ever venerated by a religion. Learning, no doubt, was much respected by Jews, but it was seen as a cold, unappealing learning, a learning that had no relation to reality, that emphasized mental gymnastics beyond reason. Like their ancestors, the rabbis were cruel and narrow individuals and were the major obstacle blocking Jewish entry into the modern age. In their search for the meaning of every dot and dash, they became insensitive to the plight of the masses who suffered under the yoke of the Torah. It seemed that Judaism, and particularly traditional Judaism, had become a mass of meaningless formulas, totally divorced from life, unworthy of the respect and admiration of sincere and sensible men.[3]

The American view of Judaism was not so distinctly defined. In describing the images harbored by Americans, it is necessary to keep in mind and to guard against the categorizing, black or white tendency that distinguishes too sharply between anti-Semites and philo-Semites. Most people waiver between conflicting and often contradictory attitudes and seldom enjoy an undivided state of mind. Stereotyping is an ambivalent emotional response. It may blend feelings of affection and contempt, pity and hostility, praise and envy. In religious perceptions, we also find this manifested. There was a strain of philo-Semitism that in the Colonial period and to some extent until the early nineteenth century served as a beacon, although often weak and flickering, lighting a society otherwise darkened by a proliferating religious prejudice. In this orthodox Christian view, the Jews were God's Chosen People, miraculously preserved and sustained. There is no doubt that the clerical and lay spokesmen for an Old Testament, Puritan culture felt an awestruck sympathy and identification with the "people of the Book." Many Americans in the Puritan tradition in New England regarded themselves as modern Israelites and their contemporary situation as a latter-day version of Old Testament history. They were the new Chosen People who devoutly believed they, too, were a nation in covenant with God—hence, their sympathy for Jews. Moreover, the presence of the Jews, the source of Jesus Himself, was a mirror of the Christian prophecy and a constant reminder that the conversion of the Jews would mark the beginning of the millennium. Still the "chosen and favorite people of the Most High,'' as Ezra Stiles described them, the Jews were destined to be a "glorious nation and a blessing to the world" in the approaching messianic age.[4] In this vein a prominent philo-Semite in the 1880s described the Jews as "descendants of... Him whom we esteem as the Son of God and Saviour of men."[5] When Timothy Dwight composed his epic poem celebrating the American Revolution, he called it *The Conquest of Canaan* and described the Revolution in biblical terms, with Joshua standing for George Washington.[6] The most gifted poet of the Revolutionary period, Philip Freneau, frequently alluded to the biblical Hebrews in a symbolic fashion.[7] Yet within this Christian orthodoxy that honored the portentous ancient patriarchs were embedded the seeds of the prevailing opinion that came to characterize America's perception of Judaism, for in the final analysis it still had to confront the issue—the Jew as rebel against God's purpose.

Thus the Jews who crossed the Atlantic to find new hope in the beckoning land of freedom experienced a greater degree of social acceptance but, for the most part, did not find a corresponding appreciation of their religion. We find this ambivalent attitude first manifested in the Colonial period.

It was during the Colonial period that the basic outlines of the American-Jewish relationship were established. The Colonial period, after all, nearly equals in time the period that stretches from the Revolution to the present. It offered ample opportunity to develop deeply those aspects of national habit and style that often are the major ingredients in shaping intergroup relations. Americans who immigrated to this country brought with them as emotional and cultural baggage many of the prejudices and misconceptions that were prevalent in Europe and added a few of their own. A nation built of many nations did not rid itself so easily of the intolerance and suspicion that were the legacies of Europe. As a consequence, tolerance did not spring fully blown in 1654 when Jews first settled here. It was wrested gradually and with some difficulty from reluctant local authorities over several generations and was won through making common cause with other minorities who also were discriminated against. But it did occur and become a crucial factor in fashioning the conditions under which American Jewry developed and ultimately flourished. Certainly without the growth of such tolerance the sometimes stormy but essentially successful relationship between America and its Jews would not have materialized. Clearly America was different from Europe, was indeed a more open and free society, especially after Independence with the establishment of separation of Church and State, but it would be a profound error to assume that anti-Semitism was unimportant on the American scene. The more we learn about relations between Jews and their fellow countrymen in the early days of the nation, the more the evidence emerges of feelings of both hostility and tolerance.

Religious acceptance had not always been the rule in the early Colonial society. The American Colonies were in fact a seething caldron of religious particularism and prejudice, and only in the final decades of the eighteenth century was some kind of peace established between the various religious groups. The early settlers were frequently religious zealots rather than advocates of religious liberty. Many had found their way to the New World in quest of greater religious freedom for themselves, but paradoxically were not inclined to extend to others the freedom they so courageously sought. One need only recall the cases of Roger Williams and Anne Hutchinson who were forced to flee the Bay Colony because of their religious beliefs. These were not tolerant folk. This was particularly unfortunate for the fewer than three thousand Jews of the Colonies who, needless to say, were non-Christian in an overwhelmingly Christian environment.

The situation of New Amsterdam's Jews is a good illustration of how religious animosity could lead to prejudice and economic restrictions. The twenty-three Jews who landed in the colony faced a series of restrictions that stemmed from the colony's general disapproval of other religious practices and the specific anti-Semitism harbored by Governor Peter Stuyvesant and the colony's church officials. Jews were denied even the most elementary economic and religious rights by the choleric governor and the Dutch West India Company. By the time the Dutch flag was lowered a decade later, the Jews had achieved the right to settle and own land, but it was not until the 1690s, under British rule, that they were accorded the privilege of holding public worship and selling at retail. Fortunately, the problems Jews faced because of the attitude of Governor Stuyvesant were eventually overcome.

In other communities, the degree of religious toleration varied not only with the period but also from colony to colony. In general, some form of religious restriction was the rule rather than the exception in all colonies. Eventually, they were abrogated. In Virginia, for example,

Jews were simply excluded at the outset. In Maryland the Jews were persecuted under the Toleration Act of 1649. Non-Christians were exempted from religious freedom: the death penalty was proscribed for blasphemy, fines and prison for profanation of the Lord's day. Not until 1826 did Maryland pass "An Act to Extend to the Sect of People Professing the Jewish Religion the Same Rights and Privileges That Are Enjoyed by Christians." Because of their concentration in Philadelphia, religious prejudice in Pennsylvania had a more drastic effect on Jews. William Penn's "Holy Experiment" featured greater restrictions against Jews than Catholics, the alternate focus of discrimination. Jews could not legally vote, hold public office, participate fully in business, or hold public worship. Fortunately, in practice these restrictions were often ignored. The Jews who settled in Louisiana in the middle of the eighteenth century did so despite the open hostility of the French government. The Code Noir of 1724 ordered the expulsion of Jews from the colony within three months and forbade the exercise of any religion other than the Catholic. The code remained in effect even after Louisiana became a possession of the United States in 1803 through the Louisiana Purchase. Delaware followed the Swedish precedent of simply barring all Jewish settlement, a situation that did not change until the Dutch took over the colony in 1655. North Carolina in its constitution of 1776 restricted the holding of public office to Protestants. This was not changed until the Reconstruction Constitution of 1868. It would take until 1876 before New Hampshire Jews finally achieved a full political enfranchisement and could vote and run for office like their fellow citizens. As late as 1840 the constitutions of Connecticut, New Jersey, and Rhode Island still had discriminatory legislation on the statute books.[8]

For Jews the thrust of these restrictive provisions and anti-Semitic attitudes was clear—the young nation thought of itself as Christian. Full legal and religious equality would come only after a long and difficult struggle. That it did was a result as much of Jewish effort, skill, and endurance, as of a native spirit of American tolerance.

It is apparent that in some circles Judaism as a faith and as a way of life was not viewed positively. It was perceived as a backward religion that, at its best, underscored the progressive nature of Christianity and, at its worst, presented a direct and serious challenge to the American spirit and character. This predisposition was a real problem for Jews, for if their faith was not understood or valued, prospects for their acceptance as equal and valuable members of society were lessened. But it goes deeper than that. Their very nature and religious essence were interpreted in literature and by social commentators as being anathema to America's Christian heritage. Like the Irish and Italian immigrants, Jews were identified with a foreign religion, but they did not have the advantage of allegiance to the common Savior. They epitomized the anti-Christian elements in the world and were a constant reminder that Christ's mission on earth was still unfulfilled.

The view of the Jews as Christ killers, rejected by God and justly punished for their sins, was widely taught in American Sunday schools in the early nineteenth century and was echoed by religious publications.[9] An 1813 volume, *Sabbath Lessons* by Elizabeth Peabody, spoke of the ''conspiracy of the Jewish rulers against Jesus Christ.'' An 1846 text, *Scripture Lessons for the Young,* forcibly proclaimed that Jews nailed Jesus to the cross and ''reviled Him.'' A Sunday school primer for teachers admonished instructors to ''remark on the willfulness and fickleness of the Jews.'' Another stressed Jewish stubbornness in refusing to accept Christ as Savior. The *Berean Tract and Bible Mission,* a series of tracts published by the Methodist Episcopal Church in the late 1870s, contains numerous examples of this religious antipathy.[10]

Religious books also often accepted the basic image of the Jew as despised Christ killer. In his *A Pictorial Descriptive View and History of All Religions* (1860), the Reverend Charles A. Goodrich noted that the exile of Jews teaches ''the evil and danger of despising divine admonitions.'' Hannah W. Richardson in *Judea in Her Desolations* (1861) wrote that ''the great mass of the Jews... conspired the death of [the] Just One assuring an awful responsibility.'' *An Illustrated History of the Holy Bible* (1868) contained a great deal about ''perverse Jews'' who murdered Christ.[11] These books expressed the view that Judaism is a mere prelude to Christianity and that Jewish suffering is just retribution for their heinous sin.

In the historical novels of the nineteenth century that dealt with the Old Testament and Christian eras, these themes are reiterated, and one searches in vain for the sympathetic and universal Jew created by a Gotthold Lessing or a Richard Chamberlain who occasionally lifted his head above the morass of bigotry and misunderstanding perpetuated by European literature. The Jew of this fictional genre is shackled by a tribal religion that never outgrew its allegiance to the harsh and cruel desert God Yahweh. Jews are a narrow people, bigoted by nature and proscribed by their faith from accepting a more humane and compassionate way of life—Christianity. Always fanatically proclaiming the superiority of Judaism, they are not adverse to bending their knee to the golden calf or participating in the frenzied orgies of Baal worship, if it suits their fancy. A militaristic and materialistic nation, they appeared in these popular works as a negative force impeding the moral progress of mankind.

The specific religious experience of the American people brought forth hundreds of such novels. This was the century that witnessed the great revivals and the general resurgence of religiosity, and writers capitalized on the public's interest. As the Dwight Moodys and Billy Sundays ignited the "Burnt-Over" districts of the nation, fictional writers also inundated the public with a barrage of religious novels. The Jews, however, were not to benefit from this reawakened interest in spiritual matters. The Protestant Episcopal priest Joseph Holt Ingraham, for example, a prolific author of historical thrillers, also spent his time turning out fictional versions of biblical folklore whose confessed purpose was to contribute to the conversion of Jews. He dedicated many of his books to the people of Israel with the hope that they might finally see the light of the cross and "enter at last the Real Canaan, under the True Joshua, Jesus, The Son of Abraham."[12] In his biblical trilogy, *The Prince of the House of David* (1855), *The Pillar of Fire* (1859), and *The Throne of David* (1860), which together sold over five million copies,[13] Ingraham depicts in some detail his view of the gradual disintegration and demoralization of the Jewish kingdom. He traces in a Christological account the decline of Judaism from its prophetic Mosaic period, to the dissipation of the Kingdom of David, until it became, by the time of Christ, a totally narrow and superstitious faith.[14]

Such themes even intruded into a generally balanced treatment like Lew Wallace's best-selling novel *Ben Hur, A Tale of Christ* (1880). It has been translated into many languages and its sales are numbered in the millions. This work did some good by allowing the Hebrew to glory as a member of the "race" that produced Christ; but it also did significant harm by emphasizing a relationship that can never lead to the eradication of anti-Semitism. Jews are depicted in the novel as reverent servants of the law, strongly devoted to their families and friends, but they are also described as proud, insular, and nationalistic followers of a religion that long ago prostituted the spirit of God. They represent the forces of reaction in the work, because they are unwilling to accept the humanistic message of Jesus. To the anti-Semite Messala, "all men and things, even heaven and earth, change; but a Jew never."[15] In fact, most of the Jews who appear in the novel are basically malicious and vengeful types. Malluch believes Ben-Hur is Jewish, for example, because of the intensity of his hatred, and Simonides, a cripple, who owes his broken, deformed body to Roman cruelty, hates while realizing that it is an evil and sinful passion. He rationalizes his behavior and continues to give vent to his emotions anyway, for he knows that "revenge is a Jew's of right; it is the law."[16]

Wallace's general attitude is ambivalent, but probably can best be summed up in the words of Ben-Hur's mother who sees the Jews as fallen and degraded but yet redeemable because their soul has in it "some little of heaven." They retain the potential for salvation if they will but free themselves from the corrupt and power-blind priestly class and open themselves up to the new spirit of the age.[17] Judaism has served its purpose and must now make way for its logical successor, Christianity.

The great popularity enjoyed by *Ben-Hur* was to whet the popular taste for the religious novel and bring forth numerous books in the following years. In 1881 James Freeman Clarke, the prominent transcendentalist and Unitarian clergyman, published his *Legend of Thomas Didymus, the Jewish Sceptic,* which is in the same tradition but is not as conciliatory as Wallace's work. The gulf between Jew and Christian looms large for Clarke and is clearly reflected in the novel. The practices and requirements of Judaism as presented appear reactionary and stifling. Thomas, the protagonist, complains that he no longer receives comfort or gratification from Jewish rituals. "All life seemed to be going away out of my heart."[18] The dietary rules and the Sabbath laws, for example, are oppressive in their demands and take away freedom of movement and individuality. "We were taught that we broke the Sabbath if we took a needle out of cloth in which it was sticking...; if we went out with a reed-pen in our hand"; or even "if we read by candlelight."[19] The very nature and extent of these requirements made lofty thoughts impossible and put Judaism in a straitjacket, according to Clarke. Every act in life was ticketed and marked; this forbidden, that permitted. The only lesson Thomas was able to glean from the complicated and obscure dictates of his creed was the necessity to separate himself from the abominable ''stranger'' who sought always to impinge on Jewish prerogative. ''To hate with a holy hatred the idolatries and idolaters of the world I believed to be a main part of the Jewish faith.''[20]

Similar themes are expressed in Elbridge Streeter Brooks's novel, *A Son of Issachar; A Romance of the Days of Messias* (1890), first published in 1889–90 as a prize story in the *Detroit Free Press*.[21] Brooks presents a rather sophisticated and lengthy discussion of the ''Jewish personality'' with its alleged weakness for extreme and violent solutions for practical and soluble problems and its flights of delusions of grandeur that characterize Jewish madness. The protagonist of the novel is Bar-Asha, a sympathetic but pliable individual who falls under the influence of Judah Bar-Simon, leader of the fanatic Zealots or Knifemen, who believe in the coming of a warrior Messiah who will restore Israel to her former glory. They will not hesitate to commit any atrocity, no matter how heinous, for the sake of their cause and the honor of their God.

Judah embodies the fierce bigotry and cruelty of the men of Judea who remain tribal in their instincts and morality, but are aggressively nationalistic in their commitment to a resurgent Israel. Patriotism is a burning passion that has enveloped them in a false sense of superiority and invincibility and has reawakened their espousal of the biblical ''Chosen People'' concept. This is in sharp contrast to Bar-Asha who represents the typical Semite ''of that mid-Palestinian folk who had bowed the neck to tribute and whose hot anger of the moment gave place, all too soon, to a submissive fear of the heavy heel of Rome.''[22] Elbridge Brooks is contemptuous of both types of Jews. They resurrect the Jehovah of Joshua's time, when they should be preparing themselves instead for the arrival of the ''true'' Messiah. This time the walls of the city crumble before Titus's trumpet, and all Jews, including the vacillating and unprincipled Palestine masses, suffer the fate reserved for unregenerate sinners. Only Christianity can save, Brooks argues. ''Only the Lord Himself whose word brought you back to life can fix your wayward nature firmly to a certain aim and hold you to that faith unfaltering and unmoved.''[23]

The final transgression, according to this fiction, was committed during the time of Christ, for that was the watershed, the turning point, when Judaism chose to forsake the future and retreat instead to the superstitions of the past. Many novels published in the late nineteenth century deal with this topic and present the most detailed and negative evaluation of the creed, in addition to the charge of deicide. Because of their unanimity of interpretation, a few examples will suffice.

The fin-de-siècle popular writer and aesthete Edgar Saltus, who is regarded as an American disciple of Oscar Wilde, tried his hand at the Crucifixion theme in *Mary Magdalen: A Chronicle* (1891). Literary Historian Harry Levin has analyzed this novel as "a typical intermingling of pornography and hagiography, which reads like a collaboration between Flaubert and General Lew Wallace." In it, the Savior's generosity and Mary's humanity are contrasted with the intolerance of Simon Barlevi, a Jew of repulsive appearance who observes the law strictly but has no place in his heart for mercy that is not provided for by the Scriptures or the oral tradition as interpreted by the Pharisees. The High-Priest Caiaphas personifies the relentless cruelty of the Jews who are portrayed as fanatical formalists easily excited into frenzy concerning Christ's guilt. He as well as the Sanhedrin react violently in the face of Jesus's challenge to their authority. Jewish customs and practices are described as part of a complex and illogical system that may offer its followers a degree of security, but also serves to keep them inactive, soporific, and under the oppressive influence of selfish religious leaders.[24]

Mary Elizabeth Jennings's *Asa of Bethlehem and His Household* (1895) and Caroline Atwater Mason's *The Quiet King: A Story of Christ* (1895) parrot many of these stereotypes.[25] Jews are formal; they tend to be exclusive and unassimilable and are vengefully ferocious in their hatred of the gentle Christ and take great satisfaction in his cruel demise. Judaism is decayed and corrupted by materialism and is no longer relevant and functional. It serves as a barrier against future spiritual development. The basic thrust of these novels, their common objective, is to emphasize the wide chasm that separates Judaism from Christianity. The origins of Christianity are developed with sympathy and compassion while, in sharp contrast, the weaknesses of Judaism are underscored.

The tradition of Christian anti-Semitism was further asserted in the popular tetralogy by Florence M. Kingsley: *Titus* (1894), *Stephen* (1896), *Paul* (1897), and *The Cross Triumphant* (1898).[26] In a Christological account, each centered on a great figure from the New Testament, she depicts the stubbornly self-righteous and hateful nature of the Jews who refused to accept Jesus. Her works were published by the New Sabbath Library, sold well over a million copies, and undoubtedly found themselves on many a child's Sunday school desk. They were directed towards an older audience but, at 5 cents a copy, were not prohibitive in either price or style to an impressionable, juvenile public.

The balanced approach is absent also from Elizabeth Stuart Phelps Ward's *The Story of Jesus Christ, An Interpretation* (1898). She achieved great popularity with her fervid religious novels. In this work, heartless Israel is held collectively responsible for the Crucifixion. "Christian love and mercy are alien feelings to a people whose habits of thought were stiff with the selfishness of a race to which self-protection has been for generations foremost in mind."[27] This characteristic is manifested not only in their hatred for all gentiles and the cruelty visited upon Jesus, but also finds expression in Jewish dogma and practice itself. Incessant worshiping and constant concern with the minutiae of every commandment are typical, Ward argues, of a religion that is obsolescent, retains only an artificial, external attachment to ceremony, and uses bigoted, meaningless religiosity as a cloak for hypocrisy.

Other novelists, like Fannie E. Newberry, who also published in the New Sabbath Library series, argued consistently that Jews and Judaism have "become so overloaded with trivial forms and ceremonies as to have all spirituality smothered out of them.'"[28] These writers include, to name only a few, William A. Hammond, Anna May Wilson, the Reverend Enoch Burr, the Reverend George Anson Jackson, Edmund Berry, and Eliza Lee.[29] They saw Jews as proud, narrow, cruel, nationalistic, and bearing a hatred "such as only a Hebrew can cherish."[30] Mary Magdalene, one of the writers suggests, had very little to do with the Jews precisely because they were "narrowminded, obstinate and possessing stronger and more senseless prejudices than any other people on the face of the earth."[31]

These novelists viewed Jews, honored by God in the past, as fit objects of disfavor and derision. From tall ancient patriarchs who exude righteousness and noble dignity, they have shrunk in these works to little cowardly, wizened Jews. Their forthright purpose and commitment have become shrewd manipulation and agility. Their vengefulness and intolerance contrast with the unselfish love and charity of the

Christians they hold so much in contempt. The materialism and externality of their faith, illustrated as far back as the exodus from Egypt, when they were advised by God to take with them all the wealth they could possibly carry, continue to be borne out by Jewish delight in ostentatious display and ornamentation. The accumulation of gold has become the Hebrew's chief raison d'être. The spirit of the Bible with its universal messages of morality, generosity, mutual respect, and discipline was prostituted to the new god, Mammon. The processes of age and ambition have petrified Judaism, these authors maintain, to the point where it no longer can contribute to man's betterment and serves instead as an impediment to progress.[32]

The preachings of Christianity reinforced by historical fiction thus made a fairly consistent statement regarding the bigoted nature of Judaism and its role in the Crucifixion that created an atmosphere, in a religiously active century, that was unconducive to mutual understanding and regard.[33] The justifications for prejudice appeared to be overwhelming and Jews could find little comfort in their tenuous security while literature, as well as Christian doctrine, continued to upbraid their character and faith.[34]

These themes were central also to the popular conversion literature of the period. All the spiteful bigotry and narrowness associated with the Jews who called for Christ's death are found in their descendants who still harbor their traditional antipathy for Christians and are still shackled and blinded, this time from modernity. Emancipated by the French Revolution, the Jew of this literature was still untouched by the Enlightenment and continued to maintain the strains of medieval superstition.

Sarah Baker, writing under the pseudonym Aunt Friendly, treats Jews in a most unfriendly manner in her conversion novel *The Jewish Twins* (1860). She argues that only through the acceptance of Christ can Jews overcome their inherent failings. Jacob Myers and his wife, Naomi, have twin boys, Muppim and Huppim, named after the sons of Benjamin in Genesis, who are strongly attracted to Christianity. When Jacob learns that Muppim has secretly converted, he reacts with characteristic rage and gives his son a harsh scolding, "not to speak of the outward signs of contempt, so marked among the Jews, to which even our Savior himself was subjected."[35] Jacob banishes Muppim, mourns his death, and continues to seek solace in the Talmud that sanctions his greed and love of gain. But times are not good to Jacob and he becomes as poor financially as he has always been spiritually. When Muppim hears of his parents' difficulties, he sends them his own hard-earned money. "This, surely, was a forgiveness of which the Jew knows nothing."[36] Christianity is Muppim's emancipation and the source of his rekindled humanity.

Harriette N. Baker, who first broached the subject of the negative characteristics of Judaism in *Lost But Found; or, The Jewish Home* (1868),[37] makes a more dramatic and serious presentation of her argument in her second novel, *Rebecca the Jewess* (1879).[38] These works achieved great popularity and were republished in several foreign languages. Rebecca Stickney, like Sarah Baker's twins, gradually becomes attracted to Christianity. As she is exposed to the teachings of the faith, she loses her taste for rich jewelry and gorgeous, showy dress and becomes more earnest about life and more dedicated to charity and good works. This is in sharp contrast to her father Aaron who, although a religious leader and a strict Orthodox observer of the 613 "Mitzvot," does not let this interfere with his quest for riches even though his projects often embrace the oppression of the poor and helpless. The more religious he becomes, the more his cruelty and greed manifest themselves. In fact, all the Jews of the novel are described as made angry and uncharitable by their beliefs, and that is why Rebecca finds no solace in Judaism. "There is no vitality in the synagogue," she remarks. "The Rabbies [sic] read and chant as rapidly as possible, as if hurrying to get over a disagreeable task;... the merchants often converse in whispers, relating some profitable investment; and the women... gaze about... weary of the whole service, and consulting their watches to see when it will be through."[39] The experience of conversion frees Rebecca from the spiritual slavery imposed upon her by the past and rids her of the fanatical teachings of individuals like Rabbi Ben Ezra who would rather see Rebecca die than give consonance to her apostasy.

The conversion novel distinguished between the modern Jew, who is as cruel and narrow as his ancestors, and the apostate, who exudes love and mercy as soon as he is liberated by Christ's ministry. In Annie F. Johnston's *In League with Israel: A Tale of the Chattanooga Conference* (1896), we have the Methodist version of this theme. David Herschel comes under the influence of the Reverend Frank Marion who attempts to convert him. He realizes that without concerted action it would be difficult to wean David away from his creed. "As a nation," he remarks, "Israel had stooped so much to the gatherings of dry tradition, had bent so long over the minute letter of the law, that it could not straighten itself to take the crown held out to it."[40] David, in characteristic fashion, is won over by Marion and decides to be baptized. He knows that, like all other converts, he will be ostracized and avoided by his friends and teachers; "that his grave would be dug in the Jewish cemetery...; that the rabbi would read the rites of burial over his empty coffin, and that henceforth his only part in the family life would be the blot of his disgraceful memory."[41] One of Johnston's characters remarks that this was the most that could be expected from the archaic faith. "People who have been living in a ghetto for a couple of centuries are not able to step outside merely because the gates are thrown down, nor to efface the brands on their souls by putting off the yellow badge. Their faults are bred of its hovering miasma of persecution."[42] Johnston's books were meant for young adults and apparently were widely read. In view of the evidence assembled to this point one may doubt the accuracy of Oscar Handlin's assertion that among the many "popular novels with biblical setting... Jewish characters... [are] generally sympathetically portrayed." As Louis Harap reminds us, this is so only if they convert to Christianity.[43]

It was not only the biblical or the conversion novel that pointed to Jewish bigotry and close-mindedness. In a curious reversal of intent, even a favorable treatment was perverted by an anonymous writer into an anti-Semitic work replete with all the stereotypes that have been so harmful to Jews throughout the ages. It will be recalled that the British novelist George Eliot in her work *Daniel Deronda,* published in 1876, provided one of the first full-length expositions of the Jew as an authentic hero. It was clearly written to ennoble Judaism. The protagonist has no trace of Shylock or Fagin and is instead a universalist who turns social prophet and political man and works for the improvement of his people through Zionism. The novel was so acclaimed by Jews that it was eventually translated into Hebrew and became a Zionist tract; in recognition of her contribution to the battle against negative stereotyping, George Eliot even had a street named after her in Tel Aviv.

In the would-be sequel published in 1878 by an anonymous American author, however, Deronda is not a sympathetic character. He becomes disillusioned with his faith, gradually abandons his Orthodox views upon observing Jewish life in "reality," and arrives at the conclusion that "as a nation they [the Jews] had been scattered for cause."[44] As individuals, their personalities and habits were not such as would bring glory or greatness to a people and he therefore relinquishes his Zionist philosophy. Jews are not capable of successfully undertaking industrial or mechanical pursuits. The only hope for the Hebrew, he feels, lies in their complete extirpation through amalgamation with the assiduous and honest people of the world. They have to "strive to do for themselves that which they now allow others to do; and which their unscrupulous minds now feast on."[45]

The barbaric nature of Jewish ways and manners becomes an obsession with Deronda, and he resolves to abjure the faith he believes is now permeated with the rankest vices and dishonesty. This decision is underscored for him after he witnesses a sc3ene of untold cruelty perpetrated by the Jews. A rabbi and his congregation curse and humiliate a helpless but essentially kind man, Schmule, and place him in *cherem* (excommunication), all because his wife refuses to cut her beautiful long hair as dictated by Orthodox ritual. As if this is not enough, they steal into his house, cut off the wife's hair right after she has given birth, thus causing the baby's death, her death, and eventually Schmule's death—all to satisfy an ancient tradition. For this author, there seems to be no limit to Jewish superstition and perfidy, even to the taking of human life itself![46]

Henry Gillman, archeologist and botanist of note and American consul to Turkey who spent a great deal of time in Palestine, wrote a novel entitled *Hassan, a Fellah: A Romance of Palestine* (1898), which similarly degrades and mocks Jewish traditions. He describes in harsh terms the handful of Jews, dark-skinned and poverty-stricken, who have come to spend their last days in the Holy Land and be buried in the soil of their ancestors. They are abjectly impoverished, Gillman advises, living like Arab slum squatters, dependent on *chalukah* (charity from abroad), and adverse to undertaking any meaningful work. A deadly inertia lay on these relics.

No other people are like them, Gillman maintains. They have an individuality of the most pronounced order that separates them from all other members of the human family. The curse that continues to befall them has its origins in the Crucifixion itself, for it was then that they sinned against the light as no others have ever sinned. But the murder of

Christ was just the culmination of a plethora of abominations that have been committed by Jews.

> These are stiff-necked, rebellious, and adulterous people, according to the description of their own prophets. These are they who murmured against Jehovah in the midst of his living kindness and deliverance, longing for the flesh-pots of Egypt, and setting up the golden calf and worshipping it.... These are of the iniquitors and abominable hundred, full of uncleannesses, who defiled the holy place,... turning their backs upon the Shekinah, that they might worship the idol!... These are the people of whom the Lord has made a hissing and a byword and a proverb,... scattering them among all the nations of the earth.[47]

But Jews have learned little from the experience of exile and, if anything, have sunk lower into the depths of ignorance and superstition. The Wailing Wall Hebrews of Palestine, with their sharp piercing eyes, their beaklike noses, and their protruding flabby lips, dressed in their ancient-looking gabardines that are stiff with greasy filth, remain culturally imprisoned by their Talmudic tradition.[48] From their long-standing preoccupation with an "extremely rigid interpretation of the law," Gillman deduces that the Jews have become past masters in the art of evasion and hypocrisy.[49] He emphasizes that it is their religion that contributes to their dishonesty and perversion. As long as they are obedient to the letter of the ritual, they can continue to indulge themselves in their materialistic Saturnalia. This is most evident in Jerusalem, where Jews participate in their petty businesses "with the hovering keenness of vultures," while they subject themselves "to everything even of the most tyrannical character emanating from the head rabbis and pertaining to the Mosaic law and their religion."[50] Gillman, clearly, has no sympathy whatsoever for Jewish customs and beliefs.[51]

A detailed negative presentation of Jewish practice, specifically its opposition to intermarriage, is provided also by Henry Harland in his significant novel *The Yoke of the Torah* (1887).[53] Harland, writing under the pseudonym Sydney Luska, penned a series of works dealing with the Jewish question that always seem to hark back to his basic contention that Judaism is enthralled by its rigid orthodoxy, formalism, and its opposition to intermarriage. These are the factors that make it retrogressive and hinder Jewish assimilation into mainstream American life.

Born in Connecticut, Harland attended Harvard Divinity School for a year before settling in New York and coming under the influence of Felix Adler and the ethical culture movement. He wrote these early novels of New York Jewish life before emigrating to England to edit *The Yellow Book.* The Jews he had come to know through "ethical culture" and as a student at City College of New York appear in his novels as mysterious, exotic, almost occult creatures tied to the yoke of a long ethnoreligious tradition they are unable to throw off. Harland had a message to preach: salvation through assimilation. Yet his characters are unsuccessful in their attempts to escape the past. As a result, the Jew in America is lost, destined to wander eternally on the periphery of society.

The main character of *The Yoke of the Torah* is Elias Bacharach, a young painter, a rather sympathetic man who, while retaining an outward allegiance to his religion, inwardly doubts the validity of much of what he has been taught. He lives with his uncle, Rabbi Felix Gedaza, who is a strict observer of Jewish ritual and who has attempted to instill in Elias a pride of race and a nationalistic attachment to his people that would preclude any contact with gentiles. Unfortunately for the old rabbi, this is precisely what occurs. Elias falls in love with Christine Redwood, a beautiful and kind woman. Mr. Redwood, Christine's father, gladly consents to the marriage and accepts Elias even though he is a Jew, thus demonstrating Christian tolerance. Rabbi Gedaza, however, is not as generous. He warns his nephew that he will do everything in his power to stop the marriage and that, in fact, it will never take place. Elias decides to go ahead with the marriage anyway, and on the day of the ceremony, at the moment when he is to offer his vows, he faints away in an epileptic fit. This is a family illness known to the rabbi but kept secret from Elias. When Elias awakes, Gedaza proclaims it is a sure sign from heaven that the union was never meant to be. Elias accepts this interpretation and concludes that God has actively intervened to forestall him from committing the ultimate sin—marriage with a gentile.

Christine suffers greatly, but Elias, and particularly Rabbi Gedaza, with his "bowels of brass," have little compassion for her.[53] "The Lord desires that she shall receive none," the rabbi declares. "She is a Christian, a Goy, despised and abominated of the Lord."[54] To alleviate the void left in his nephew's life, Gedaza arranges to marry him off to a proper Jewess. He introduces Elias to a very wealthy but parvenu German-Jewish family who are thoroughly obnoxious but acceptable because of their prominent position in the community. Elias does not love Tillie Morgenthau, but is pressured into marrying her although he is obviously unhappy with the arrangement. He gradually comes to the realization that he still loves Christine. He decides to see her one more time before she is to wed a successful Christian engineer. Christine refuses and this greatly pains and agonizes Elias. He dies tragically and alone shortly thereafter in the lonely streets of New York City, the victim ostensibly of an epileptic fit, but in a more profound sense of Jewish intolerance and bigotry. Intermarriage is the chance Harland offers the protagonist to escape the "Yoke of the Torah," but Bacharach was ominously unable to take it.

Henry Harland develops the theme that Jewish cruelty and rigid religiosity will sacrifice happiness, love, and even life itself for the strict adherence to tradition. He admits that, among the better educated and more intelligent Jews of America, orthodoxy of this stripe is not common. Nevertheless, it is a curious circumstance, he maintains, that even the Jews "who have cast quite loose from their Judaism, and proclaim themselves 'free thinkers,' 'agnostics,' or what not, retain their prejudice against intermarriage, and even their superstitions."[55] This remains for Harland Judaism's most dangerous consequence.[56]

Given the theological consensus and the images projected in literature, it is not surprising that other sources of opinion similarly deprecated Judaism. Literature often is a reflection of the culture it represents. As noted, Judaism fared poorly in a nineteenth-century genre of literature that reflected the religious fervor of the age. Beginning in the 1840s and continuing throughout the nineteenth century, a stream of religious novels set in the biblical or Christian periods appeared with the express purpose of spreading the faith, and Jews and Judaism were treated quite negatively in this literature. Even before the mass immigration of the late nineteenth century began, Americans who were exposed to these works, and many of them must have been because of their popularity, met a Jew clothed in the Christological myths accepted in the period. He seemed to be a throwback to a much earlier, darker age and thus a threat to America's Christian experiment. As far as can be determined, these images did not emerge out of any real contact with American Jewry and certainly not from any objective study of the faith. Most of these authors were devout Christians who were expressing in literary form what the churches preached in practice. They were merely adding their voices to the religious consensus. The religious factor is therefore extremely important in the developing American anti-Semitism, especially in the period from approximately 1840 to 1900. Generally after that, with the increasing secularization of American society, these images lost their appeal. But before they did, other vehicles of opinion took up the cudgel.

Many social commentators and intellectuals who grappled with the "Jewish question" with a scholar's eye, or who at least attempted to deal with the issue factually, came to very much the same conclusion. They did not find many universal truths established by its teachings. Judaism, for them, seemed foreign to the nation's religious ethic. In an era of burgeoning nationalism, it represented the very antithesis of Christian unity and was perceived as an alien spirit. It was a retrogressive faith, the epitome of medievalism in an age of democracy, of superstition in an age of science, and of narrow group solidarity in an age that valued assimilation and assembly-line uniformity. As early as 1812, this viewpoint was broached by Hannah Adams, the first professional woman writer in the United States and author of the first history of the Jews written in this country. She underscored this apparent defect in Judaism. Her evangelical history is filled with profound sympathy for Jewish suffering; yet she deplored their stubbornness in refusing to embrace Christianity.

> The history of the Jews exhibits a melancholy picture of human wretchedness and depravity. On one hand we contemplate the lineal descendents of the chosen people of God, forfeiting their inestimable privileges by rejecting the glory of Israel, and involving themselves in the most terrible calamities; condemned to behold the destruction of their city and temple; expelled from their native country; dispersed through the world; by turns persecuted by Pagans, Christians and Moslems; continually duped by imposters, yet still persisting in rejecting the true Messiah.[57]

It is ironic that it was often the professed admirers of Jews who most misrepresented and misunderstood the essence of Judaism and did it substantial harm, all the while proclaiming their respect for its ideals. Senator Zebulon Vance of North Carolina, who delivered his very popular "The Scattered Nation" address in almost every major city of the United States in the 1870s and 1880s, also falls into this category.[58] The principal thrust and objective of his speech aimed at extolling the contributions made by Jews to civilization and of combating the cancer of anti-Semitism that Vance perceived as a threat to the American spirit. Yet there is a negativism in his interpretation that prevails over his noble intentions and that could hardly have elicited sympathy from those who heard his eloquent words. Vance equated, like many of the novelists already discussed, Christian oppression throughout history with the Jewish aversion to social intercourse with gentiles as equal contributors to the growth of anti-Semitism. He did not see any causal relationship between the two phenomena and he made the illogical argument that Jewish suspicion and intransigence were as injurious to mutual respect as Christian life-taking persecution. Prematurely predicting the eradication of prejudice, he eagerly awaited the amelioration of Jewish hatred and hardness of soul that he maintained were the last remaining obstacles blocking total acceptance. The Jews had to incorporate into their value system the one principle of Christian theology that is so foreign to their behavioral outlook and that has impeded their entrance into the community of nations. The concept of "forgive us our trespasses as we forgive them who trespass against us,"[59] found in the New Testament but absent in the Talmud, was the key difference between Jew and gentile.[60] Until Jews rid themselves of their revengeful instincts that were theologically induced, the onus of prejudice would remain with them and not with the perpetrators of anti-Semitism.

There is nothing ennobling in a people that still prides itself on its ability to retain ancient prejudices in the face of modernity. For many influential thinkers, this was precisely the aspect of Judaism that most rankled. Professor John Huston Finley, for example, a political scientist who became president of Knox College and then later of City College in New York City, emphasized in 1888 his belief that there is a danger in Jewish unflinching loyalty to ancient customs and particularly in the rigid commitment to the mysterious and incomprehensible Talmudic obligations. Persecution has "engendered in them a morbid, revengeful and isolated disposition" that prevents Jews from grasping the kind hand of Christianity.[61] Until they do so, there is very little chance that anti-Semitism will dissipate.

Must Jews first abandon their faith before they can live and function as free men? The implication is clear that, to satisfy many Americans, they either had to do that or, as economist Edward Atkinson[62] and lawyer-atheist Robert Ingersoll argued, in 1890, they had to outgrow their superstitions, "throw away the idea of inspiration,"[63] and renounce their hatred of Christians before they would be deserving of equal recognition in the hierarchy of world religions.[64]

Noted historian James Hosmer, who wrote a treatise on Jewish history in 1893, one of the few published in America in the nineteenth century, concurred. Indicating his bias at the outset of the work by presenting the Christian orthodox view that Jews should have accepted Christ rather than crucify him, he saw the remainder of their sad history as a consequence of this heinous sin. Aside from the Diaspora and the persecutions that were a punishment for the deicide, the murder of Christ instilled in Jews a passion and a hatred that is unique in human experience. "The heart of the Jew can be very unamiable," he wrote. "From the mountain of his scorn, the Gentile has seemed to him worthy of contempt more often than of any softer feeling."[65] It is of course true that the Christian cannot be said to have thoroughly relented in his antipathy for the Jew, but at least he has made great strides in his effort to do so. This is not the case with the Hebrew. His heart has lost none of its contempt. Hosmer recounted the story of his visit to a Jewish shop in an old European city and his experiences with the proprietor. During the process of bargaining, the Jew became angered and abusive. "The flash in his dark eye was of the hereditary wrath bequeathed to him from many generations of persecuted fathers...; in the hiss with which his words came forth, I seemed to hear a serpent that had been gathering its poison for a thousand years."[66] It seems that, for Hosmer, Jews and Judaism retain such an aversion to Christian society that the burden is on them for any improvement in relations. Once again the curious circumstance of the oppressed become the oppressor and the victim blamed for his self-protective reaction to persecution.

This view was reinforced by developments in the last decades of the century. As a result of mass immigration, Jews were viewed in some circles as a danger to America's Christian civilization. One minister, the Reverend J.R. Johnson of Detroit, argued that Jews were a "pauper and lawless class" who would "combine with our own worst elements" to undermine Christian traditions. Their seeming preoccupation with religious and business activities led another observer to comment that "the

Jews, particularly those that are orthodox and poor, have but two interests in life: business and religion.'' They are incapable of assimilating the higher Christian sensibilities.[67]

Even the Social Gospelers who in some respects viewed Judaism quite positively were capable of perpetuating these unfortunate religious images. It was in the ancient prophets that Walter Rauschenbusch, the acknowledged theologian of the Social Gospel, sought the inspiration to social justice.[68] ''They are an integral part of the thought life of Christianity,'' he observed in 1907. ''What other nation has a library of classics in which spokesmen of the common people have the dominant voice? It would be hard to find a parallel to it anywhere.''[69] Ministers spoke frequently about the debt Christianity owed to Judaism. One observer remarked that ''nearly everything we have that dignifies us and sweetens and refines us and makes us significant... has come to us from Judaism.'' Edward C. Baldwin, author of *Our Modern Debt to Israel*, was convinced that the Social Gospel movement was simply the rediscovery of Judaism by Christianity.[70]

Notwithstanding these positive assessments, there was also an ambivalence, even a religious antipathy, which was clearly present. ''The judicial murder of Jesus Christ is rightly held up... as the great crime of mankind,'' declared Reverend Morgan Dix of New York in 1890. ''We must teach our children the facts of history.''[71] Solutions presented by clergymen to eliminate anti-Semitism included such suggestions as the hope that Jews voluntarily will ''knock down the barriers set up by your faith which keep you apart''; that Jews ''mingle more... with Gentiles; go to Gentile churches more frequently... cultivate the American idea: move forward into nineteenth century thought.''[72]

Throughout the years of the Social Gospel, leading Christian periodicals, such as the *Bibliotheca Sacra, The Methodist Review, The Homiletic Review, The Missionary Review, The Independent,* and others, deplored anti-Semitism on the one hand, but helped to perpetuate it on the other with references to ''the Judaic sport of separation,'' and to the ''fetish of the Torah and Targum.''[73] Social Gospelers found it difficult to extirpate the prevailing view that Judaism had long since served its essential function and had in fact reached a point of decay and obsolescence. It is interesting that a course in ''Hebrew Sociology'' offered at Tufts College proposed to trace ''the origin and development of social, political and religious institutions from the rise of Judaism to its decay.''[74] Rauschenbusch himself attributes the lingering antisocial characteristics of Christianity to the influence of Judaism, which is "fixed, monotonous, a thing by itself, shut off from the spontaneity and naturalness of the general life." Like many Christians, Rauschenbusch views Jesus as a social revolutionary who challenged the authority of reactionary Jews whose "piety was not piety," whose "law was inadequate" and backward, and was killed for his efforts.[75] Hence the curious ambivalence present even among these reformers.

At the heart of much of this criticism was a basic misunderstanding of Judaism in general and of Talmudic literature in particular. It was quite natural that critics should look for the soul of Jewish persistence in the mysterious pages of the Talmud, that voluminous compilation of the Jewish oral tradition that is laced with allegory and rabbinic disputation. Surely there must be some elixir there that nourished an indomitable spirit. In every century, the Talmud was treated as if it were somehow endowed with life and was excommunicated, vilified, and destroyed. Emperors, popes, and czars throughout the ages condemned the cursed volumes, the contents of which few of them knew or could even read.[76] The great bogey of ignorance, in Europe as well as America, cast its dark shadow over the Jews and kept them in a state of perpetual suspicion.

Much of what was written concerning Talmudic Judaism was a hopelessly confused collection of misquotation and false statements. Professor A. J. Mogyorosi, for example, focused upon the myth that the Talmud countenanced and encouraged Jewish hatred of Christians and even exonerated Jews who killed gentiles. "These traditions were, and are still utterly devoid of all feelings of right, equity, humanity and moral principles.... After this no man will wonder that God rejected the Jewish people.''[77] Mogyorosi was certainly not original in these accusations. He probably was aware of Jacob Brafman's *The Book of the Kahal* or similar works that received wide circulation in Russia and Europe and eventually found their way to America. Brafman, an embittered Russian apostate Jew, recounted in his vitriolic tract that the Talmud was actually a secret document that contained within its obscure and amorphous narrative *Aggada,* the blueprint for Jewish control and the justification for Jewish oppression and exploitation of Christians.[78]

Preposterous as it may appear, similar viewpoints were accepted by other scholars. Goldwin Smith, the prominent English historian and social critic who taught at Cornell University, may have tempered Brafman's argumentation, but was equally as hostile. The Talmud for him "was a vast repository of legalism, formalism, ceremonialism and casuistry. Nothing can be more opposed to the spontaneity of conscience, trust in principle, and preference of the spirit to the letter characteristic of the Gospel."[79] The unfortunate intention of the Talmud is "by multiplying ceremonial barriers, to keep the Chosen People separate from the Gentiles among whom they lived; in other words, to perpetuate a tribe."[80]

Andrew White, the historian, educator, politician, diplomat, first president of Cornell University, and the man who recruited Goldwin Smith from England, expressed similar sentiments. White had been liberally exposed to Jews, but unfortunately, he had witnessed them in their most degraded and impoverished circumstances. As attaché to the United States legation at St. Petersburg in 1854–55 and as minister to Russia in 1892–94, he saw firsthand the oppressions and the disabilities visited upon them in the land of reaction. But, like Charles Emory Smith, George W. Wurts, and other American officials in Russia, he too readily accepted the government position on the Jewish question and took at face value the accusations made by professional Jew baiters such as Pobedonostsev and Ignatiev.[81] Reporting back to Secretary of State Walter Quintin Gresham, White indicated that he believed much of the official propaganda and warned Gresham about the dangers presented by the continuing emigration of Jews. Recent translations of the Talmud published in America demonstrated "that Israelites are educated in bitter and undying hate of Christians, and taught not only to despise but to despoil them."[82] The fact that this kind of instruction has gone on for centuries and the simple laws of heredity made it imperative that the Russian peasantry be protected from the Jews who have been made into "beasts of prey with claws and teeth especially sharp."[83] Not until the Jews of Russia are freed from the "darker features of the Talmud" can they expect to enjoy greater respect and toleration.[84] In more moderate form, White's concern with the emigrating Russian Jews was shared by segments of the already settled and assimilated German-Jewish community.

White, Mogyorosi, and Smith perceived Talmudic tradition as a major impediment to enlightenment. They saw no value in its *Halakah,* which details the basic structure and requirements of Jewish life, nor did they find any inspiration in its *Aggada,* or narrative, with its homilies and obiter dicta that are able to draw out the full consequences of the moral injunctions and admonitions of the Bible for the enrichment of Jewish ethical teaching and the general moral uplift of mankind. This is the opinion that is frequently manifest when one finds any mention of the Talmud in this period. *The Independent,* a liberal Christian journal, wrote editorially that the Russian Jew "is still the exponent of the petrified formalism and traditionalism of Rabbinism and Talmudism."[85] Because he is so imprisoned, he is not touched by the main currents of political, social, and intellectual life and still lives in the Middle Ages. "His faith in his people and in his religion is that of the Pharisee of the time of Christ, whose modern representative he is. The seem and substance of all wisdom, human and divine, is for him the Talmud, and in it and in its teachings he lives and moves and has his being."[86] George Warner, in *The Jewish Spectre* (1905), charged that the Talmud is based on hypocrisy and falsehood and has served to enslave people by introducing the onus of sin.[87] Even Robert Ezra Park, the founder of the Chicago school of sociology and the exponent of realism in the examination of urbanism and ethnicity, could unjustly criticize the nature of Judaism. "As long as Hebrew was the only language of instruction," he wrote, "the masses of the Jewish people remained imprisoned within the walls of the Talmud, knowing nothing of modern science or modern thought.[88] There are still learned rabbis on the East Side of New York, men who have devoted the best years of their lives to sharpening their wits on Talmudic casuistry, who believe that the earth moves around the moon."[89]

It is certain that those who wrote and propagandized against the influences of the Talmud must have been unaware of the many beautiful parables and universal and moral truths contained within its pages. Undoubtedly there are instances where it appears narrow and legalistic, but through it all is contained the message of honesty, faith, and self-control. The rabbis could write tomes about single concepts in the Bible that no longer appear to be relevant, but they also knew how to regulate their lives by a sincere piety, charity, and self-sacrifice. They taught an exalted concept of God, of a Deity who had compassion for the sufferings of man, and they underscored the importance of mercy and human equality. The ideals of the Talmud may often be limited by the world in which it was created, but more often, it soars high above its passions and hatreds. Although the society around it practiced untold cruelties and horrors on those who lived by its faith, the Talmud continued to proclaim the message of ethics and morality.[90]

But whatever the reality is, this was not the prevailing image. Predisposed to a hostile position by their Christian heritage, religious novelists in the midnineteenth century and social commentators later often found Judaism to be an intolerant, narrow, and egotistical faith that kept its followers in darkness, presented a cold face to the world, and impeded enlightened progress. It was a throwback to the Middle Ages and a reminder of the events on Calvary, a constant thorn in the side of those who aspired to Christian unity. Judaism became associated in the minds of many Americans with formalistic adherence to foolish ritual, narrow racial identity, Christian hatred, and delusions of grandeur. The "Chosen People" were often portrayed as intolerant and insensitive, conceited and aggressive, and not adverse to subverting the ideals of Christian society. This negative evaluation of the Jewish faith was the soil from which, as we shall see, a variety of invidious stereotypes were nurtured once millions of Jews began to arrive on these shores. Their very extent and pervasiveness probably affected the actual manifestations of American anti-Semitism. Image and act, thought and deed, are not very far removed.

NOTES

1. James Russell Lowell, *The Complete Poetical Works of James Russell Lowell* (Boston: Grosset & Dunlap, 1896), p. 158.

2. Herman Melville, *Redburn* (New York: Harper & Brothers, 1849), p. 214.

3. See the following basic works on anti-Semitism. Hannah Arendt, *The Origins of Totalitarianism* (New York: World Publishing Co., 1951); Jacques Barzun, *Race—A Study of Modern Superstition* (New York: Harcourt, Brace and Company, 1937); Robert F. Byrnes, *Antisemitism in Modern France: The Prologue to the Dreyfus Affair* (New Brunswick, New Jersey: Rutgers University Press, 1950); Edward H. Flannery, *The Anguish of the Jews* (New York: The Macmillan Co., 1965); Adolf Leschnitzer, *The Magic Background of Modern Anti-Semitism: An Analysis of the German-Jewish Relationship* (New York: International Universities Press, 1956); James Parkes, *Anti-Semitism* (Chicago: Quadrangle Books, 1963); Leon Poliakov, *The History of Anti-Semitism,* trans. Richard Howard (New York: Schocken Books, 1974); Mau-

rice Samuel, *The Great Hatred* (New York: A.A. Knopf, 1940); Jean-Paul Sartre, *Anti-Semite and Jew* (New York: Schocken Books, 1965); Joshua Trachtenberg, *The Devil and the Jews* (New Haven: Yale University Press, 1943).

4. Jacob R. Marcus, *The Colonial American Jew, 1492 – 1776*, 3 vols. (Detroit: Wayne State University Press, 1970), vol. 3, p. 1143. See John Higham, *Send These to Me: Jews and Other Immigrants in Urban America* (New York: Atheneum, 1975), p. 121; see Louis Harap, *The Image of the Jew in American Literature* (Philadelphia: The Jewish Publication Society of America, 1974), p. 3.

5. Zebulon Vance, *The Scattered Nation* (New York: The Rational Publishing Co., 1904).

6. Harap, p. 26.

7. Philip Freneau, *The Poems of Philip Freneau*, ed. Fred Lewis Pattee, 3 vols. (Princeton: The University Library, 1902). See Harap, pp. 30–34.

8. See Stanley F. Chyet, ''The Political Rights of the Jews in the U.S., 1776-1840,'' *American Jewish Archives*, vol. 2 (April, 1958); Jacob R. Marcus, *American Jewry Documents, Eighteenth Century* (Cincinnati: Hebrew Union College Press, 1959); Jacob R. Marcus, *The Colonial American Jew, 1492 – 1776;* Lee Friedman, *Early American Jews* (Cambridge: Harvard University Press, 1934); Morris U. Schappes, ed., *A Documentary History of the Jews in the United States 1654 – 1875* (New York: The Citadel Press, 1952); Henry Feingold, *Zion in America* (New York: Hippocrene Books, 1975).

9. The continued potency of this hostile religious image can be seen in the study by Charles Y. Glock and Rodney Stark, *Christian Beliefs and Anti-Semitism* (New York: Harper & Row, 1966). They found a correlation between fundamentalism and anti-Semitism. Of all Protestants polled, 33 percent unequivocally agreed with the statement: ''The Jews can never be forgiven for what they did to Jesus until they accept Him as the true Savior.'' The figure for Missouri Lutherans was 70 percent and among Southern Baptists, 80 percent. Another sample showed that 21 percent of the American Lutheran, 22 percent of the American Baptist, and 38 percent of the Missouri Lutheran ministers agreed. See pp. 62 – 65.

10. Elizabeth Peabody, *Sabbath Lessons* (Salem, 1813), pp. 32, 49 – 50, 60; H.P. Peet, *Scripture Lessons for the Young* (New York, 1846), pp. 113 – 14, 119; C. Soule Carter, *Questions Adapted to the Text of the New Testament* (Boston, 1865), pp. 42, 69, 81; Mrs. Wilbur F. Crofts, *Lesson Handbook for Primary and Intermediate Teachers* (Boston, 1883), pp. 13, 122; *Berean Tract and Bible Mission,* nos. 17,24,48 (1876); nos. 28,30,42,46,47 (1877).

11. Charles A. Goodrich, *A Pictorial Descriptive View and History of All Religions* (New York: Gilman, 1860), pp. 42 – 44; Hannah Richardson, *Judea*

in Her Desolations (Philadelphia: H.H. Henderson & Co., 1861), pp. 269 – 70; J. Kitto, *An Illustrated History of the Bible* (Norwich: H. Bill, 1868), pp. 496 – 97, 556,560, 574,631 – 32.

12. Joseph H. Ingraham, *The Pillar of Fire; or Israel in Bondage* (Boston: Roberts Brothers, 1888), p. i.

13. Don B. Seitz, "A Prince of Best Sellers," *Publishers Weekly*, Vol. 119 (February 21, 1931), p. 940.

14. Joseph Ingraham, *The Throne of David* (Boston: Roberts Brothers, 1896); *The Prince of the House of David* (Philadelphia: Henry Altemus, 1897). See Harap, pp. 55 – 60.

15. Lew Wallace, *Ben-Hur, A Tale of Christ* (New York: Signet Books, 1962), p. 69; see Harap, pp. 166 – 69; and Abraham H. Steinberg, "Jewish Characters in the American Novel to 1900," Ph.D. dissertation, New York University, 1956, p. 76.

16. Ibid., p. 260.

17. Ibid., pp. 80 – 83.

18. James Freeman Clarke, *The Legend of Thomas Didymus the Jewish Sceptic* (Boston: Lee and Shepard Publishers, 1881), p. 64; see Harap, pp. 169 – 70; Steinberg, pp. 37 – 38.

19. Ibid.

20. Ibid., p. 65.

21. Elbridge Streeter Brooks, *A Son of Issachar: A Romance of the Days of Messias* (London: G.P. Putnam's Sons, 1890); see Harap, p. 178; Steinberg, p. 40.

22. Ibid., pp. 47 – 48.

23. Ibid., p. 269.

24. Edgar Saltus, *Mary Magdalen: A Chronicle* (New York: Belford Co., 1891); see Harap, p. 178; Steinberg, p. 46; Robert E. Spiller et al., ed., *Literary History of the United States* (New York: Macmillan, 1963), p. 1074.

25. Mary Elizabeth Jennings, *Asa of Bethlehem and His Household* (New York: A.D.F. Randolph and Co., 1895); Caroline Atwater Mason, *The Quiet King: A Story of Christ* (Philadelphia: American Baptist Publishing Society, 1896); see Harap, pp. 182,188; Steinberg, p. 46.

26. Florence M. Kingsley, *Titus* (Chicago: D.C. Cook Publishing Co., 1894); *Stephen, a Soldier of the Cross* (New York: Grosset & Dunlap, 1896); *Paul: A Herald of the Cross* (New York: Grosset & Dunlap, 1897); *The Cross Triumphant* (New York: Grosset & Dunlap, 1898). See Harap, pp. 181 – 83; Steinberg, pp. 52 – 54.

27. Elizabeth S.P. Ward, *The Story of Jesus Christ, An Interpretation* (Boston: Houghton, Mifflin and Co., 1898), p. 173; see Steinberg, p. 45. See Spiller et al., 1974 edition, vol. 2, p. 220.

28. Fannie E. Newberry, *The Wrestler of Philippi: A Tale of the Early*

Christians (Elgin, Ill.: D.C. Cook Publishing Co., 1896), p. 132.

29. Anna May Wilson, *The Days of Mohammed* (Chicago: D.C. Cook, 1897); Enoch Burr, *Aleph, the Chaldean* (New York: W.B. Ketcham, 1891); George Anson Jackson, *The Son of a Prophet* (New York: Houghton, Mifflin & Co., 1893); Edmund Berry, *Leah of Jerusalem: A Story of the Time of Paul* (New York, 1890); Eliza Lee, *Parthenia; or, The Last Days of Paganism* (Boston: Ticknor and Fields, 1858); William A. Hammond, *The Son of Perdition* (Chicago: Herbert S. Stone & Co., 1898).

30. George Anson Jackson, *The Son of a Prophet* (New York: Houghton, Mifflin and Co., 1893), p. 31.

31. Hammond, *The Son of Perdition* (Chicago: Herbert S. Stone & Co., 1898), p. 310.

32. See, for example, the novels of Katherine Woods, Florence Kingsley, William Hammond, Anna May Wilson, Enoch Burr, George Anson Jackson, and Eliza Lee, as well as William O. Stoddard's *The Swordmaker's Son* (New York: The Century Co., 1896); *Ulric the Jarl* (New York: Eaton & Mains, 1899), and J. Breckenridge Ellis's, *Dread and Fear of Kings* (Chicago: A.C. McClurg & Co., 1900).

33. See Matthew 27: 17 – 25.

34. The theme of Jews as rebels against God's purpose supplied the thrust for many a sermon. "The Jew," *Yale Literary Magazine,* 12 (August, 1847), pp. 419 – 22; Clarence H. Faust and Thomas H. Johnson, eds., *Jonathan Edwards: Representative Selections* (New York: American Book Co., 1935); Osborn W. Trenery Heighway, *Leila Ada, the Jewish Convert* (Philadelphia: Presbyterian Board of Publication, 1853), pp. 111 – 17, 226.

35. Aunt Friendly [Sarah S. Baker], *The Jewish Twins* (New York: Robert Carter & Brothers, 1860), p. 160.

36. Ibid., p. 201.

37. Harriette N. Baker, *Lost but Found; or, The Jewish Home* (Boston: H.A. Young & Co., 1866); see Harap, pp. 153 – 54; Steinberg, pp. 88 – 89.

38. Harriette N. Baker, *Rebecca the Jewess* (Boston: I. Bradley, 1879).

39. Ibid., p. 132.

40. Annie Fellows Johnston, *In League with Israel* (New York: Eaton & Mains, 1896), p. 34; see Harap, pp. 155 – 56; Steinberg, pp. 93 – 94.

41. Ibid., p. 69.

42. Ibid., p. 141.

43. Oscar Handlin, *Adventures in Freedom: Three Hundred Years of Jewish Life in America* (New York: McGraw Hill Book Co., 1954), pp. 176 – 77; see Harap, p. 541.

44. *Gwendolen: A Sequel to George Eliot's Daniel Deronda* (Boston: Ira Bradley and Co., 1878), p. 28.

45. Ibid., p. 29.

46. See also H.H. Boyesen, *A Daughter of the Philistines* (Boston: Roberts Brothers, 1883).

47. Henry Gillman, *Hassan: A Fellah* (Boston: Little, Brown and Co., 1898), p. 53; see Harap, pp. 325 – 26; Steinberg, pp. 179 – 80.

48. Ibid., p. 55.

49. Ibid., p. 62.

50. Ibid, p. 55.

51. See also Charles F. Stocking's *Thou Israel* (Chicago: The Maestro Co., 1921) for a similar treatment.

52. Sidney Luska [Henry Harland], *The Yoke of the Torah* (New York: Cassell & Co., 1887). See Harap, pp. 454 – 60.

53. Ibid., p. 160.

54. Ibid., p. 171.

55. Ibid., pp. 65 – 66.

56. See also, Adelina Lust, *A Tent of Grace* (Boston: Houghton, Mifflin and Co., 1899); Allan Davis, *The Promised Land* (Cambridge: The Harvard Dramatic Club, 1908); for a humorous treatment, see Anne Nichols's *Abie's Irish Rose* (New York: Harper & Brothers, 1927).

57. Hannah Adams, *The History of the Jews from the Destruction of Jerusalem to the Nineteenth Century* (Boston: J. Eliot, Jr., 1812), vol. 2, pp. 325 – 26. See Harap, pp. 27 – 28.

58. Zebulon B. Vance, *The Scattered Nation* (New York: The Rational Publishing Co., 1904).

59. Ibid., p. 40.

60. This is, of course, erroneous and again points out the consequences of misinformation. The truth is that when Jesus taught his followers to love their fellowmen as they love God, to do unto others as they would have others do unto them, to value humility as the highest virtue, he was repeating the teachings of the great Jewish scholar Hillel, who had preceded him by a generation.

61. John Huston Finley, "The Jew in Modern History," unpublished address, 1886, John Huston Finley Papers, *Speeches* file, New York Public Library, New York.

62. Letter, Edward Atkinson to Philip Cowen, February 13, 1890, Philip Cowen Papers, *American Hebrew* file, American Jewish Historical Society, Waltham, Massachusetts.

63. Letter, Robert Ingersoll to Philip Cowen, February 12, 1890, in ibid.

64. See also Jacob Riis, *How the Other Half Lives* (New York: Hill and Wang, 1957), p. 83.

65. James K. Hosmer, *The Story of the Jews* (New York: G.P. Putnam's Sons, 1893), p. 215.

66. Ibid., p. 358.

67. Quoted in Robert A. Rockaway, "Anti-Semitism in an American City: Detroit 1850 – 1914," *American Jewish Historical Quarterly,* vol. 64, No. 1 (September, 1974), p. 46.

68. See Egal Feldman, "The Social Gospel and the Jews," *American Jewish Historical Quarterly,* vol. 58, No. 3 (March, 1969), pp. 308 – 22.

69. Walter Rauschenbusch, *Christianity and the Social Crisis* (New York: The Macmillan Co., 1907), pp. 1 – 3, 7 – 9, 11 – 13, 21 – 22.

70. See Feldman, p. 310.

71. Quoted in *The American Hebrew* (April 4, 1890), pp. 167,169.

72. Ibid., pp. 168,172 – 73.

73. See Feldman, p. 318. *The Bibliotheca Sacra,* vol. 52 (October, 1895), pp. 756 – 58; *The Homiletic Review,* vol. 61 (June, 1911), p. 470; *The Methodist Review,* vol. 96 (March, 1914), pp. 269 – 70.

74. See Feldman, p. 319.

75. Ibid., p. 322. Walter Rauschenbusch, *A Theology for the Social Gospel* (New York: The Macmillan Co., 1918), pp. 215 – 27, 250 – 52.

76. For discussions of the question of the Talmud and anti-Semitism, see Salo W. Baron, *A Social and Religious History of the Jews,* Vol. II (New York: Columbia University Press, 1951), pp. 215 – 321; Solomon Grayzel, *The Church and Jews in the Thirteenth Century* (Philadelphia: Dropsie College, 1933), p. 340; Hans J. Schoeps, *The Jewish Christian Argument* (New York: Holt, Rinehart & Winston, 1963), pp. 24 – 25; Edward H. Flannery, *The Anguish of the Jews* (New York: The Macmillan Company, 1965), pp. 34, 108 – 9.

77. A.J. Mogyorosi, *The Reprobation of Yisróel* (Allegany, New York, 1886), p. 9.

78. Howard Morley Sachar, *The Course of Modern Jewish History* (New York: Dell Publishing Co., 1958), p. 187.

79. Goldwin Smith, *Essays on Questions of the Day,* ed. Arnold Haultain (New York: Macmillan and Co., 1887), p. 270.

80. Ibid., p. 271.

81. National Archives Microfilm Publications, *Dispatches from United States Ministers to Russia, 1808 – 1906,* Roll 43, Vol. 43 (April 1-November 26, 1892).

82. Andrew White to Secretary of State Walter Gresham, April 11, 1893, in ibid.

83. Ibid.

84. Ibid.

85. *The Independent,* Vol. 43, No. 2221 (June 25, 1891), p. 949.

86. Ibid.

87. George H. Warner, *The Jewish Spectre* (New York: Doubleday, Page & Co., 1905).

88. Here Park demonstrates his basic ignorance of the Talmud for it was written in Aramaic, not Hebrew.

89. Robert E. Park, *The Immigrant Press and Its Control* (Westport, Connecticut: Greenwood Press, 1970), p. 105. This is a reprint of a 1922 edition.

90. Yehezkal Kaufmann, *The Religion of Israel* (Chicago: The University of Chicago Press, 1960); J.Z. Lauterbach, *Midrash and Mishnah* (Philadelphia: The Jewish Publication Society of America, 1941); Isidore Epstein, *Judaism* (Baltimore: Penguin Books Ltd., 1959); H.L. Strack, *Introduction to the Talmud and Midrash* (Philadelphia: The Jewish Publication Society of America, 1931).

In police records of criminality, the Jews take a leading place. The gangmen, the gunmen, the gamblers, drug vendors and white slavers, the bribers of ballplayers, the bond thieves, and loft robbers, are almost exclusively Jews....[1]

The Jewish Question.
Enemies of Christ Must
Withdraw from America.

Gilded Age Images: The Criminal Jew

The imaging of the American Jew was not relegated only to a discussion of doctrinal and theological deficiencies. Americans, beginning essentially in the Gilded Age, were also inundated with a number of Jewish stereotypes that made damaging commentaries on the immigrants' social traits. These became particularly prevalent during the decades of mass immigration when Jews became concentrated in the major Northeast cities and were gradually identified with the problems created by urbanization, including crime. Jews were perceived in some circles as the symbol of urban decay. There was cause for concern. From 1881 to 1910 over 1,560,000 Eastern European Jews arrived in the United States. Highly urban, by 1917 New York City had over 1.5 million Jews, or 30 percent of the population. One popular image identified Jews with robbery, gambling, and, later in the century, violent crime. Conventional wisdom suggests that violent crime was not an area of Jewish activity. Commentators in the early part of the nineteenth century occasionally agreed. As an example, the *Washington Sentinel* wrote in 1854:

This ancient race can boast that there are among them fewer paupers and fewer criminals than any other race can exhibit.... If we enter a penitentiary or prison of any description, the marked face of the Israelite is rarely to be seen within its walls.... Jews seldom commit murder or any of these crimes and offenses that are marked by violence and passion. The offenses committed by them, and they are of rare occurrence, are frauds, and small larcenies.[2]

Yet even this view contained the seeds of prejudice. As the century progressed and as social problems became more acute, stereotypes were brought forward that lent credence to the view that Jews participated in antisocial activities, that they were predisposed to find ways of making money even if illegal, that they undermined the American work ethic, that they did not engage in the legitimate pursuit of wealth but were involved instead, along with the Italian immigrants, in clandestine endeavors masked by the mysterious, subterranean society of Baxter Street and Broadway. The American interpretation of Judaism was one argument against them. If, however, it could also be demonstrated that Jews had little respect for Christian laws, property, or even life, as certain individuals and literary treatments seemed to imply, their status in the popular mind was further seriously compromised.

The spotlight of attention was focused on the connection between Jews and crimes against property in September 1908, when New York City's police commissioner Theodore Bingham claimed that 50 percent of the criminal class in the city was composed of Russian Jews although they numbered less than 25 percent of the population. The allegations appeared in the September issue of the *North American Review* in an article entitled "Foreign Criminals in New York." The commissioner wrote:

It is not astonishing that with a million Hebrews, mostly Russian, in the city... perhaps half of the criminals should be of that race when we consider that ignorance of the language, more particularly among men not physically fit for hard labor is conducive to crime.... They are burglars, firebugs, pickpockets and highway robbers—when they have the courage; but though all crime is their province, pocket-picking is the one to which they take most naturally....[3]

The high position the author held, the reputability of the publication and the statistical data that lent an air of objectivity to his findings, rocked the Jewish world with its bold assertion that the crime rate among immigrant Jews far exceeded that of other groups. The specificity of the accusation and the authority and prestige of Bingham may have been unique, but in essence these ideas and images had been present in the public arena for decades, given expression in fiction and corroborated by social observers who questioned the sober and law-abiding image of the Jew.

The identification of Jews as petty criminals involved in minor thefts, smuggling, pawnbroking, and the like seems already to have been widespread by the middle of the nineteenth century and was also a major theme of European literature.[4] It was assumed that these activities were countenanced by Talmudic Judaism that apparently was able to combine a celestial spiritualism of the angel on pin variety with a crass, aggressive, and dishonest business ethic. Indeed, it was further surmised and was born out substantially by the evidence that the Jew did not commit violent crimes, but only engaged in those that provided profit with minimal risk.[5] This was even used to his detriment, for his avoidance of bloodshed because of assumed cowardice was used to discredit the Jew in an age that admired even illegal public displays of bravery. Thus the *New York City Police Gazette* wrote accusingly as early as 1862 that the Jew was already implicated in crimes against property.

The developments of almost every day serve to show the extent to which the German Jews are acting as receivers of stolen goods.... A very general suspicion prevails against this people, and it is not surprising. Many of them are professional lifters, burglars and swindlers. Those in business find it difficult to effect an insurance upon their stock because of the frequency with which fires occur in their stores and the suspicious circumstances attending them.[6]

The problems that resulted from the charge of arson, financially inspired, influenced a group of Jews to gather in New York City on March 15, 1867, to protest the discrimination practiced by many insurance companies. They agreed to boycott a number of them including the Metropolitan Insurance Company, the Firemen's Home Insurance Company, Germania, as well as a dozen others. Benjamin Nathan, the chairman of this impromptu Jewish committee, communicated his group's grievances to James Larimer Graham, the president of the Metropolitan Insurance Company, but the latter evidenced the persistence of the stereotype.[7]

It is a fact which is abundantly proved by the insurance experience of the last fifteen years, that losses have occurred in the premises of Jews of German origin,... far out of proportion to their numbers as compared with the business community—that they are for the most part persons of no known business antecedents, of no known social standing, or pecuniary responsibility, and... these results... have... created a wide spread—I might almost say unanimous— prejudice against the class named....[8]

It is their perverseness, Graham argues, their mind state that looks for profit in every act but is apparently oblivious to ethical considerations or business accountability, that inevitably brings the weight of criticism down upon them.[9] Fortunately, this position was not held unanimously. The Philadelphia *Sunday Dispatch* wrote on April 21, 1867, that the insurance companies' "implied charge against their [Jewish] character is without the slightest foundation."[10]

Thus even before the flood of Eastern European Jewry inundated America's East Coast cities and offended the genteel sensibilities of reformers and social workers, as well as the uptown Jewish grandees, the belief that Jews were untrustworthy and dishonest was abroad. George Lippard, the author of many sensational exposés of vice for the *Saturday Evening Post,* in *The Quaker City; or, the Monks of Monk Hall* (1844), a novel that was republished in 1876 and enjoyed some success as a best seller, lent literary force to this conception.[11] The work recounts the activities of a group of organized criminals in Philadelphia who come from the best elements of society but nevertheless are involved in evil deeds including robbery, murder, and the seduction and rape of women. Lippard's rather bizarre and sensational novel detailed the corruption permeating the Quaker City. It is a record of crimes that never come to trial, of murders that are never divulged, and of atrocities almost too horrible to believe. Significantly, a Jew, Gabriel von Gelt (Mr. Money), is one of the key characters and negative influences in this novel of urban corruption. He is described as a grotesque hunchback whose face gives "you the idea of a horse's head, affixed to the remnant of a human body." Jew is written all over it "as clearly and distinctly as though he had fallen asleep at the building of the Temple at Jerusalem...; and after a nap of three thousand years, had waked [sic] up in the Quaker City, in a state of perfect Hebrew preservation."[12] His broken English dialect is the trademark of the rascally Jew, and he is generally depicted as the most selfish, eager, and grasping of the criminals. He instinctively seems to be attracted to the most lucrative cache and is often seen rubbing his hands with anticipation and proclaiming that he can hardly wait to "smellish te gooldt already."[13] The Jew is even ruthless enough to betray and blackmail his fellow malefactors. Disparagingly referred to as "Judas" von Gelt, Lippard provides him with no redeeming virtues.[14]

Contemptuous treatment of the criminal Jew is also found in a novel by Charles F. Briggs, a well-known New York editor and associate of Poe's. The Jew in Briggs's *Haunted Merchant* (1843) is a malicious caricature that so resembles von Gelt that one suspects Lippard may have borrowed the idea from Briggs. Jacobs is hired by Tom and Fred Tuck to drug their uncle and destroy his latest will, since they are named benefactors in an earlier one. A drug overdose administered by Jacobs kills the uncle. Jacobs flees, but ultimately is arrested and sent to jail. Because of a lack of evidence, the charges are dropped. When Tom Tuck discovers that the Jew is attempting to extort money from them, he exclaims: "Curse him, the Iscariot wretch; I wish there was an Inquisition for his sake and that I was Grand Inquisitor. I would tear his dog's flesh with hot pincers for this."[15] Jacobs ends his career, like von Gelt, willing to turn state's evidence against his partners in crime.[16]

The Jew as criminal of a different sort is set forth in journalist J. Ross Browne's adventure novel *Crusoe's Island* (1864), which deals with mining life in San Francisco.[17] Racial stereotypes and negative imagery were widespread on the West Coast after the gold-rush days. The charges are generally familiar. Jews are a peculiar people who keep to themselves; they do not drink and mingle socially with other men; they sell shady goods to down-and-out miners, exploiting their weaknesses while demonstrating generosity to poor, needy Jews.[18] To this list of accusations, Browne adds the charge of dishonesty and theft. The protagonist, a poor prospector who makes his way from dry claim to exhausted mine, twice meets a Jew on the trail who steals his stockings and boots that "were valuable beyond gold or silver in this foot-weary land."[19] This was "a miserable wretch at best," Browne writes, who left the miner bootless and alone in the craggy hills of San Francisco, victim of Jewish thievery.[20]

Several early plays expound and develop the image of Jewish monetary malfeasance in equally vivid terms. Melter Moss in Tom Taylor's *The Ticket-of-Leave-Man* (1864) is a counterfeiter, forger, and burglar who has never done an honest day's labor in his life. He roams the streets of New York looking for the easy caper, the one with no risk that requires little courage or originality, since he has neither.[21] In similar fashion, Dion Boucicault, one of the most successful of midnineteenth-century dramatists and actors, who vaunted his talents on both sides of the Atlantic, makes the Jewish character Mo Davis, in his play *Flying Scud* (1867), a crooked, unscrupulous, cowardly scoundrel.[22] The play remained popular for a decade and was retained in the repertory of stock companies until 1900.[23] Mo Davis is meant to be an unmitigated miscreant who speaks in dialect and is involved in shady deals that always fail. He is a perennial complainer who continually laments his misfortunes. "Oh, vy didn't I stick to the cigar and cabbage leaf line? The swindle was small but it was sure."[24] A second play by Boucicault, *After Dark* (1868), presents another version of this stereotype in Dicey Morris, a gambling-house keeper and blackmailer who even attempts murder to accomplish his nefarious purposes.[25]

Melter Moss, Mo Davis, and Dicey Morris are all comparatively simple characters who are unsophisticated in their approach to crime, can appear ridiculous in their fumbling attempts to avoid capture and conviction, and are allied with equally corrupt Christians who aid them in their enterprises. Mordie Solomons, alias Allcraft, in Dublin-born playwright John Brougham's *The Lottery of Life* (1868), is a more complicated and elaborate villain in his various roles as fence, money-lender, counterfeiter, and blackmailer. The play ran for nine weeks and was revived a number of times during the next seven years.[26] Solomons is bent on revenge, on increasing his hoard of money and on victimizing the innocent hero. No crime of treachery is too revolting for Mordie to engage in. When his schemes appear doomed, he threatens "such a sweeping revenge the world will shudder at."[27] To accomplish it, he plans to dynamite those who oppose him while they are aboard ship. He soliloquizes:

Ah! They little know the man whose desperate revenge they have invoked. . . . I'll soon interrupt their complacent security.... The drunkenness of an insatiate vengance fills me with a sense of devilish joy — cries of despair and death are ringing in my ears.[28]

One is reminded of Shylock stripped of the dignity Shakespeare gave him and of the infamous ingenuity and cruelty of Marlowe's Barabas.

Such characterizations were not limited to drama; they also found frequent expression in the popular novels of the period, those hastily written and inexpensive works that reached a wide audience and catered to its fantasies, escapist tendencies, and its appetite for sensationalism and prurience. This fiction generally fell in with the popular mood of the times; it was nationalistic and reflected nativist attitudes towards the immigrant, the Jew, the Indian, and the Negro. In keeping with that tradition, one endlessly meets in these popular novels the Jewish pawnbroker-fence who is involved in crimes against property.

This treatment appears in at least three of Horatio Alger's novels: *Adrift in New York* (n.d.), *Ben, the Luggage Boy* (1870), and *Paul, the Peddler* (n.d.).[29] Alger, the great popularizer of self-help values, found his inspiration in the city. He invested his heroes with all the moral virtues honored by the cult of the rags to riches theme, and his Ragged Dicks and Tattered Toms won success either by steady application or more often by some sudden stroke of fortune.[30] Occasionally, however, they came across some shady individual that indicated to them that all was not right in Gotham. In several instances, this was the dishonest Jewish pawnbroker. In *Ben, the Luggage Boy*, Alger remarks that the Baxter Street shops are so notorious for this illegal trade that the police are frequently involved in surveillance and arrests. Because of the close scrutiny of the authorities, the dealers make certain "as soon as an article comes into their possession, to obliterate all the marks of former ownership.''[31] Or in *Paul, the Peddler*, Alger writes that the pawnbroker Eliakim was fortunate to have "narrowly escaped punishment for thus indirectly conniving at theft.''[32] Although these are minor characters in the novels, they take their place with the other exploiters of the poor and unfortunate whom Alger so harshly criticizes.

Several dime novelists further developed these themes. It should be recalled that some of the most prolific authors of dime novels were nativistic leaders. Edward Z.C. Judson (alias Ned Buntline) and Sylvanus Cobb were leaders of the know-nothing movement. Cobb produced some thirteen hundred short stories and novelettes and was incredibly popular. Judson, who endowed William F. Cody with the name "Buffalo Bill,'' published at least four hundred novels; Prentiss Ingraham, son of J.H. Ingraham, wrote six hundred. Their literary productions inevitably dealt with crime and violence in a simplistic, villain-hero manner. Jews, when they appear, were not the only villains, but they came in for their share of abuse and are generally the only ethnic group so described aside from an occasional opium den Chinese or vendetta-prone Italian. Albert Aiken, for instance, who was one of Erastus Beedle's most prolific practitioners, apparently found in the Jewish character a particular *bête noire* if the frequency of his use of the Hebrew criminal is any indication. In *The White Witch* (1871), Herman Stoll, a German-Jewish Wall Street broker, is corrupt and fraudulent and is involved in various bunco schemes.[33] Aiken's *The Genteel Spotter* (1884) features another despicable Jew, Sheeny Lew, a brigand and "enforcer" who operates out of the notorious "Five Points" district in New York City.[34] A lesser Jew is "Slippery" Moses Cohenson who is a dialect-speaking pawnbroker and fence. He is described as an "oily sort of a chap, with a squeaky voice and a sneaky manner…. Whenever he talked with anybody, he was always rubbing his hands together, as if he was washing them in invisible soap and water."[35] He operates in a pawnbroker shop that has the familiar "three ball sign" displayed outside. It signifies, Aiken suggests, that "two to one you don't take out what you put in."[36] Or then there is Aaron Mosenstein in *Dick Talbot the Ranch King* (1892), a cunning rascal who is involved in a kidnapping venture.[37]

More wicked and perverse are Gilbert Jerome's Jews. Aaron Moses Lachstein of *Dominick Squeek, the Bow Street Runner* (1884) is ostensibly a secondhand clothing dealer, but the police have known him for years as a receiver of stolen property. He has been arrested often, but has somehow managed to escape conviction. It is accepted, Jerome writes, that "the Jew won't fight," or commit murder since they involve a certain degree of risk, but Lachstein, together with another stealthy intriguer, Zobrowski, is willing to participate as an accomplice.[38] Either peripherally or actively, both remain deeply involved in the criminal world.

Israel Isaacson, the nefarious Jew of Jerome's *Old Subtle* (1885), extends the scope of Jewish participation in stolen articles to include kidnapping a young girl, Lizzie Corday, whom he has taken for ransom.[39] When Lizzie finally escapes, Israel becomes disconsolate. "The Jew worked himself into a paroxysm of rage. He tore handfuls of hair from his beard, and rolled over and over upon the floor, like a beast in pain."[40] To the very end he is the inveterate scoundrel. Similarly, Lem Mosher in *Young Weasel, the Detective* (1885) is the fence turned exploiter.[41]

Several other dime novelists introduce Jewish fences who are similar, in feature as well as activity, to the Mosensteins, Lachsteins, and Isaacsons already discussed. Jacob Judah in Prentiss Ingraham's *Duke Despard the Gambler Duellist* (1892) extends his ventures to include fraud and extortion. When his schemes fail, he is willing to resort to violence, is forestalled by his co-conspirator, and salves his disappointment by buying a Negro slave to insure for himself a higher social status.[42] H.P. Halsey, in *Monte-Cristo Ben, the Ever-Ready Detective* (1893), introduces the English-Jewish pawnbroker who operates on New York's lower East Side, but is too shrewd to be caught by the police handling stolen goods.[43] Likewise, the nameless Hebrew pawnbroker in his *Lights and Shades of New York* (1905) pays the lowest price for the merchandise he purchases because it "may have been stolen."[44]

In the 1890s a number of the popular Nick Carter detective stories, created by J.R. Coryell, further perpetuated the stereotype of excessive Jewish involvement in financial crimes. Many of these stories were translated into foreign languages and influenced serious writers including the French Dadaists and Surrealists. The author, who was probably Frederick Van Rensselaer Dey, for example, presents Isaac Arnheim, in *The Book-Maker's Crime,* as the familiar corrupt Jewish pawnbroker.[45] In another episode entitled *Among the Fire-Bugs* (1893), Nick Carter uncovers a scheme that involves the attempted murder of two wealthy Russian-Jewish immigrants. They are the intended victims of a Jew who uses the Christian name Thomas Brown. He decides to burn down the building where they reside, and he hires some men to commit the deed. Typically, Brown, who does not have the courage to do it himself, is compassionless. "I would trample out a thousand lives in order to aid in securing this fortune."[46]

Success bred imitation, and by the beginning of the twentieth century, dime novel publishers were churning out a new brand of thriller, the Wall Street success story or, as *Fame and Fortune Weekly* put it, "Stories of Boys Who Make Money."[47] Beneath the lurid covers of dime novels (that cheaper press and competition drove down to a nickel) were reams of small print that basically amounted to a liberal borrowing of the Horatio Alger formula. The surest way to the top is still through rescuing the boss's son from certain death, but quick wits, perseverance, and honesty also paid off. Money making and business acumen are extolled in this series, but Jews are rarely involved positively in this race for financial achievement. In fact, when they do appear, and this is rarely, they are mostly shady characters, fraudulent stock dealers and thieves who impede, through their actions, the natural economic progression and substantial opportunities for wealth that the publisher, Frank Tousey, found on Wall Street. So we discover in *Dick Dalton, the Young Banker* (1912) the Jew Golding who deals in stolen bonds and is also involved in a burglary ring.[48] Or the brokers Blumm and Einstein in *Beating the Market* (1912) who participate in a number of illegal and unethical transactions that threaten the investments of a young, ambitious clerk who is successfully negotiating the market.[49] Similarly, in *A Mad Broker's Scheme* (1918), we find the Jews on Wall Street acting as a negative force, upsetting the natural course of the investment economy.[50] The Golding crowd is a clique of daring and unscrupulous speculators who take great risks with the market and keep Wall Street unsettled and precariously guessing about what they are really up to. They epitomize the "artificial" instability that Tousey implies is the only factor, aside from financial malfeasance, that might frustrate or hinder economic progress. There is also the perennial Jewish fence so popular in the earlier dime novels in the person of Moses Solomons, the "shark" of Grand Street in *A Rough and Ready Dick* (1918).[51]

It is evident that the themes may have been changed in *Fame and Fortune Weekly* to adapt to the more contemporary interests of the American public, but essentially the stereotype was not basically altered. The Jewish dialect may now be Russian instead of German and Jews may have graduated from the individualistic crimes of Baxter Street to the more sophisticated swindles of Wall Street and the organized thievery associated with smuggling and extortion, but their predilection for crime remains constant. The image developed in the dime novels is basically one dimensional. The Jew is concerned only with the illegal pursuit of wealth, is stripped of the virtues of courage, honesty, sacrifice, and the other positive attributes associated with the hero, and is rarely cast in that role. He is relegated mostly to sinister and mischievous activities in these novels and is part of the conspiracy of evil that this simplistic and popular form of literature relies upon to create its histrionic and sensationalist approach. As a symptom and vehicle of anti-Semitism then, the dime novel is a social phenomenon that cannot be underestimated.

This fictional portrayal projected by the pulp trade is not significantly different from that found in novels of higher literary quality. Henry Harland is a case in point. He did not only concern himself with Jewish opposition to assimilation, but also approached the theme of Jewish instability and criminality.[52] Ernest Newman, the musician in *As It Was Written: A Jewish Musician's Story* (1885), is a schizophrenic, Jekyll-Hyde individual, a sensitive violinist and affectionate lover, as well as a psychopathic murderer, bound by the curse of his deceased father.[53] The protagonist of Harland's *Mrs. Peixada* (1886) is another sensitive, "spiritual" Jew, Judith Peixada, who is married to an extremely cruel, vicious, and criminal pawnbroker in a match of financial convenience. Bernard Peixada is described as an individual with "a hawk's beak for a nose, a hawk's beak inverted for a chin; lips, two thin, blue, crooked lines across his face, with yellow fangs behind them." His hands are shaped like claws, "and, instead of fingers, they were furnished with long, brown, bony talons, terminated by black, untrimmed nails."[54] Despite his physiognomical grotesqueness, he is esteemed by his fellow Jews because he is wealthy and because he meticulously follows Jewish ritual. In reality, he is a complete rogue who is implicated in illegal activities, condones murder, and is immersed in corruption.

Considerable jejune theorizing about this Jewish trait appears also in Brander Matthews's *A Tale of Twenty-Five Hours* (1892).[55] Here we find the first of a number of literary works that seem to reflect the concern felt by some writers and many more Americans over the acute social problems associated with the rapid urbanization of the late nineteenth century, particularly crime. Jews, like other immigrants who were concentrated in cities, were deemed responsible for this corruption. Anti-Jewishness and anti-urbanism are often indistinguishable in these literary commentaries.

Matthews, the prominent Columbia University literary critic, social commentator and novelist, was concerned with the rising crime and pauperism rates in America's cities, which he linked to immigration. In 1899 he made a statistical study of inmates in New York's workhouses, prisons, and asylums, which confirmed for him that the recent East European immigrants represented the greatest number of the city's mendicants and malefactors.[56] He dealt with the issue often and did not exclusively implicate Jews. In *Vignettes of Manhattan* (1894), he focused mostly on Italians whom he depicted as secretive, clannish, and given to violence, as well as the Irish who most often were affable and good-natured when sober, but became meddlesome, unruly, and a nuisance when intoxicated.[57] His Jewish characters were not immune from criticism. Two years earlier, together with Columbia University law professor George H. Jessop, in *A Tale of Twenty-Five Hours,* he presented Mike Zalinski, a fence who worked closely with burglars in their illegal ventures. He was notoriously crooked, "was a receiver of stolen goods" and "quite likely... was in communication with thieves in all capitals of the world."[58] Although he is a relatively minor figure in the novel, the point remains that the principal shady character in the work is Zalinski, a prototype of the image of the sinister Polish Jew that was gradually emerging on the American scene, who refuses assimilation, identifies exclusively with his religion, and transplants his Old World experiences as exploiter, subverter of law, and trafficker in crime to his new environment.

Steele Mackaye, noted dramatist, actor, teacher, and founder of the first acting school in America, offers a dramatic version of this theme in *Money-Mad,* produced in 1890. This play also contains an Italian assassin and other ethnic stereotypes. But Mackaye is merciless in depicting the evil, cowardly Slink who, Fagin-like, has trained a group of criminal disciples to be "the smartest gang of rogues in the whole country."[59] The play is a succession of hackneyed melodramatic situations involving crime. When Slink is finally caught, he pleads for an undeserved amnesty. "Blease, blease, ledt me go... and I vill become a corporal-general in de Salvation Army—so hellup me cracious I vill."[60] Once again the cowardly response appears to be uniquely Jewish.

A dramatic presentation of the archetypical American Jewish fence, who probably inspired much of this literature, was presented by Colonel Edward M. Alfriend and A.C. Wheeler in *The Great Diamond Robbery* (1895).[61] It must be remembered that there was some factual basis for these stereotypes since crime was a serious problem in the immigrant ghettos. This popular play was first performed at the American Theater in New York on September 4, 1895, and ran periodically for over ten years. It deals with the career of Felonious Fredericka, the ineffable Mother Mandelbaum, the "Queen of the Fences," who operated for over two decades on the lower East Side until she was forced to flee to Canada in 1884.[62]

In the play, Alfriend and Wheeler depict the intricacies of Mandelbaum's illegal organization. Her fictional counterpart, Mother Rosenbaum, is the mastermind of the operation and is able to control not only her hirelings who would resort to murder at her command, but also the police and the courts, which are not opposed to accepting her tainted "sheeny" money as a token for their cooperation. She epitomized Jewish involvement in this area and dramatically brought to life for many Americans this legendary woman who became synonymous with crooked pawnshops and the sale of stolen property. The transactions made behind the innocent facade of her small dry goods store on the corner of Clinton and Rivington Streets were broadcast in literature as well as in the press and indelibly implicated her coreligionists with a tainted profession.

Julian Ralph's collection of stories of immigrant life, *People We Pass; Stories of Life Among the Masses of New York City* (1896), also emphasizes the extraordinary, bizarre, and criminal aspects of survival in the "ghetto."[63] For over twenty years Ralph was a police reporter with Jacob Riis on the New York *Sun,* and he knew the area he described intimately. Although the purpose of the vignettes seems primarily to be local color and to depict, often patronizingly, the curious circumstances of these immigrants, he often waxes indignant over their living conditions. As with Riis, there are clearly two voices: the social commentator appalled at the poverty and disease in the "ghetto" and the "intruder," who makes value judgments about the various cultural and ethnic characteristics that appear strange and somewhat menacing. Thus he could describe with compassion the tenements he saw as the "tomb of manly and womanly dignity, of thrift, of cleanliness, of modesty, of self-respect," while criticizing vociferously the rampant crime that was overlooked, if not encouraged, by corrupt Jewish politicians like Moe Eisenstone.[64] In fact, it is the Eisenstones of the city, Ralph implies, who most contributed to the backsliding of their constituents by their influence peddling, bribery of police, and involvement in gambling and prostitution.

The East Side Jews of Edgar Fawcett's *New York* (1898) are detailed even more graphically. This prolific novelist and playwright emphasized in his thirty-five works the debilitation of urban society. This particular novel of New York crime, poverty, and slum existence depicts the Jew fallen to his lowest depths. Mrs. Volatski, the keeper of a boardinghouse, is a miserly hellcat, proud of her religion, who believes that Jews have weathered two thousand years of oppression by virtue of their ability to amass wealth. "We don't go under because we don't never miss a chance to make money. That's why they can't kill us."[65] Her lover John Lynsko is a greedy, bloodless individual who is bitterly cruel to his tenants and was known to have ejected from his miserable hovels more than one helpless soul whom illness had impoverished. "If Lynsko had miraculously shot out a pair of clammy, batlike wings, and had projected a curled horn from either temple, the metamorphosis would hardly have amazed his watcher."[66]

Aside from his avidity, he is also a bank robber, dishonest real estate speculator, and arsonist. He hires individuals to help him set fires to his buildings for the insurance benefits. "His project was loathsome in its villainy," Fawcett writes. "It is worse than mere murder, because it took murder for granted.... To get the insurance money on these buildings whole families would be recklessly imperiled." Lynsko epitomizes the evil, dissolute Jew who comes to America to satiate his materialistic instincts and would undertake any project, however damaging and repulsive, to achieve that objective. "New York is hateful to me. I stay here as long as necessity compels. Then, pouf, I vanish back to Europe."[67] Fawcett implies that America would have been better off if the Lynsko-type Jew had never arrived.

Perhaps the oddest fictional portrait of the criminal urban Hebrew is A.H. Frankel's 1898 novel, *In Gold We Trust,* a loosely constructed and eclectic work in the Dickensian style, dealing with the innocent poor exploited by the sagacious rich.[68] The characters, all immigrants in the East Side of New York, form a gallery of the grotesques, men enslaved by a greed that leads to the most hideous crimes against their immigrant brethren. The melodramatic plot consists of a number of episodes loosely organized, calculated to demonstrate the pervasiveness of man's cupidity. The Jewish army of the greedy are endowed with connotatively suggestive and exaggerated names: Wolf Zamzumewsky, wholesale clothing dealer who feigns being a wealthy merchant to marry rich Jewesses, two of whom he drives to early graves; Balaam Amalik, promoter of land schemes who swindles thousands of Jews in a bunco land investment; Zumri Lachmandritzky, pawnbroker and banker who flees to Europe with his poor clients' money; and Schmandritzki, the "schadchen" or marriage broker whose rapacity gets the better of his conscience as he procures wealthy girls for men he knows to be cruel fortune hunters. The solution Frankel proposes is not immigration restriction, which he deplores, but rather vegetarianism. The unnatural craving for meat is to Frankel a form of cannibalism of a kind with the selfish exploitations of man by his fellowmen. By the end of the novel, the corrupters one by one die ignoble deaths and the virtuous succeed in their younger, meatless generation. A rather deleterious work, *In Gold We Trust* deserves consideration as another fascinating example of how far the treatment of the Jew has strayed in the direction of the bizarre and the sordid.

We find this attraction for the sensational and concern with urban crime evidenced also in several popular plays that achieved some degree of success in the second and third decades of the twentieth century. The crude pawnbroker-fence was now replaced by the Jewish gambler, fraudulent businessman, process server, and crooked lawyer—more subtle and sophisticated criminals. Witness Ira Lazarre in Max Marcin's *Cheating Cheaters* (1916), which ran for 286 performances.[69] Lazarre is a lawyer for a gang of thieves. He financially backs robbers in their burglary activities.[70] The corrupt Jewish lawyer appears also in Bartlett Cormack's *The Racket* (1927), a drama about crime in Chicago.[71] Sam Meyer of Reilly, Platka and Cohen is "an unkempt, shifty little Jew" who "is in a state of perpetual anxiety."[72] He is an attorney who is disbarred because of his questionable ethics and his close association with gamblers.

This theme is further reiterated in drama in *Cristilinda* (1922), by Monckton Hoffe; *Square Crooks* (1928), by James P. Judge; and *Night Hostess* (1928), by Philip Dunning. In *Cristilinda,* Ikey-Mo is not only a gambler, but is also a dishonest art dealer and blackmailer.[73] In *Square Crooks,* we find the familiar portrait of the Jewish fence,[74] and Ben Fisher, in *Night Hostess,* is a more sophisticated practitioner who has moved up from the petty amateurish intrigue of the ghetto to become the operator of a successful prohibition speakeasy and gambling den. He prides himself on the fact that he runs a "respectable highclass... joint."[75]

Finally, a significant literary expression of Jewish criminality is developed in F. Scott Fitzgerald's influential novel *The Great Gatsby* (1925). Meyer Wolfsheim, the fictional representation of Arnold Rothstein, the industrial racketeer and gambler who ostensibly fixed the 1919 Baseball World Series, is used to personify the essentially impersonal forces of urban-Jewish corruption that bring tragedy and death to the "simple" American Jay Gatsby. He contributes to Gatsby's improbity and introduces him to the criminal world. Wolfsheim epitomizes the primary aspect of the myth: the Jew as source of pollution. Nick Carraway, the narrator, thus remarks after hearing of what Wolfsheim did that "it never occurred to me that one man could start to play with the faith of fifty million people—with the singlemindness of a burglar blowing a safe."[76] Yet that is what Wolfsheim and his brethren, in fiction, did with great ease, for they were not concerned with the sensibilities or property of the populace, but only with the materialistic opportunities that crime provides. Racially exclusive, they helped their own, but were impervious to the pain of the "stranger." Always keen after the "gonnegtion," they are not the substance that good citizens are made of.[77]

That is the basic message implicit in the fictional portrayal of the criminal Jew. Prescribed by a formalistic faith, greedy and mercenary by instinct or choice, they slip easily into crime in these literary treatments until eventually some of them even regress to the depths of murderous violence. Along with the Italian immigrants who were also stereotyped in this fashion, the Jews suffered for they became bywords in many circles for lazy, avaricious, irredeemably dishonest people, who are a threat to the social structure and a menace to law.

Aside from the images developed in literature, the assumed moral obtuseness of the Jew received extensive examination in the public sector. This was an issue of some social import, and consequently individuals responsible for law enforcement and reputable analysts, as well as intellectuals and the press, often postulated on the alleged excessive Jewish participation in crime. In the end, after years of reiteration, the charge became a convenient argument for those who sought to develop the idea that the Jewish immigrant presented some real problems of acculturation in the urban environment.

The most accurate test of Jewish morality is not the number of convictions or criminals languishing in prison, the detractors maintained (the statistics would not buttress their case), but rather the nature of the offenses and their permeation throughout Jewish life. Their crimes are characterized by such a shrewd evasion of the law that it is seldom the arm of justice can reach them. The Reverend A.W. Miller, a Presbyterian pastor who wrote several treatises on Jews and Judaism, including *In The Restoration of the Jews* (1887), delineated his perception of the dichotomy between Christian and Jew. "Whereas the moral delinquencies of the Protestant nations are more striking, but limited to comparatively small and neglected sections of the population, who repudiate every religious profession; those of the Jews are less apparent, but almost co-extensive with the whole people, and more or less due to the baneful influence exerted by their creed."[78] Judaism "deadens his moral sensibilities, and blunts his spiritual perceptions," and leads directly to crime.[79]

This view of the Jewish blindspot for Christian standards of legal behavior was further expounded in two books by America's first "professional" anti-Semite, Telemachus T. Timayenis. Within the space of two years there appeared in New York several works that peddled a vicious brand of Judeophobia compounded of ancient lies and contemporary racism. Although published anonymously, *The American Jew* (1888), *Judas Iscariot* (1889), and *The Original Mr. Jacobs* (1888) were written by Timayenis, a self-proclaimed professor, editor, businessman, and controversial figure in Boston's Greek community. Born in Smyrna, Turkey, he emigrated to the United States at the age of sixteen or seventeen and lived in Springfield, Massachusetts, New York City, Boston, and Lowell. When he arrived in New York by 1880, he tutored the children of wealthy families at his own institution, the New York School of Languages, and he also established the Minerva publishing company.[80] It was that venture that became the focal point of his contribution to anti-Semitica, for it was the first publishing company in America that devoted itself primarily to the proliferation of anti-Semitic literature. He attempted through its production to create an American anti-Semitic movement.

Timayenis's approach was sensationalist and was an early expression of the "big lie" strategy. This is reflected in *The American Jew*, which was intended to prepare the way for the establishment of an anti-Semitic monthly to be called *The Anti-Semite*.[81] It pretends to tell the story of the Jew in America, to describe his "racial" and religious characteristics, and to chronicle his participation in the commercial, professional, and criminal life of the country.

According to this account, about one hundred Polish Jews came to the United States in 1825 and since then have multiplied so abundantly and prospered so exceedingly that their offensive racial characteristics are encountered everywhere. What are these repulsive traits? Jews have restless, suspicious eyes, hooked noses, ill-shapen elongated ears, thick lips, sharp ratlike teeth, round knees, long, clammy fingers, and flat feet. These unattractive physical exteriors are encrusted with filth and infested with lice. Yet these Jews, Timayenis maintained, have become successful and prosperous. They did not achieve this by intelligence, invention, or even hard work, because Jews despise labor and grasp only the values others produce. They have gotten along so well only because they are dishonest; they receive stolen goods, set fires, and defraud insurance companies. He argued that Jews furnish a greater number of criminals than any other foreign element in the United States.[82] Even within the crime fraternity they are considered untrustworthy, because of their cunning shrewdness. They would not hesitate to betray their confederates without any remorse "for personal safety, personal profit, or personal gain of any kind." Jews would cheat their employers, lie, steal, murder, and commit the most atrocious acts of incendiarism for money. In fact, the very source of their success is predicated on their illegal inclinations. "The basis of the whole Jewish pyramid," he wrote, "is composed of pawnbrokers, receivers of stolen goods, lewd bawds, and fences of the well-known Mandlebaum type." They go in for these endeavors because there is little personal risk involved, which suits their cowardly temperament; and the profit is large, which accords with their greed for gain.[83] The Jew's mission in America is to rob Christians, "to enter on the inheritance of the Gentile, which Jehovah has promised him.... He cares not for our laws except to escape their penalties for fraud and crime."[84] The Jew is not a useful citizen; he contributes nothing to the betterment of society and is a parasite feeding off the body politic. This is inevitable and unchangeable because of his unregenerate soul.

As he comes from an inferior race, degraded by corrupt blood, his heart full of malice, his brain full of intrigues and tricks, his ideas invariably turn by natural law to deceit, usury, theft, counterfeiting, forgery, embezzling, extortion, blackmailing, and above all to fraudulent bankruptcy. This is the field and compass of Jewish inventiveness, skill and genius.[85]

Timayenis, totally consumed by his hatred of Jews, reached further back into his feverish mind to concoct even more preposterous and untenable accusations. The Jews became for him the most "cold-blooded murderers'' of the world, real ''bloodthirsty savages'' who wait anxiously to pounce upon their gentile hosts. He even resurrected the ancient charge of ritual murder, taking his calumnious treatment to its most illogical extreme. The Jews are the only people upon the globe ''who immolate human lives from fanaticism,'' and they are the only true ''living cannibals.''[86] Murder becomes the perverse extension of their selfish and hateful nature, the ultimate expression of their inveterate greed and the culmination of centuries of circumventing Christian laws.

These stereotypes were not exclusively propagated by individuals with demagogic objectives. The popular humor sheets and graphic magazines of the late nineteenth and early twentieth centuries relied upon similar themes, although with less vitriol, in their quest for commercial success. It is through the medium of comedy that many of a society's prejudices are most clearly delineated, and the caricatured ''Isaacs'' and ''Ikeys'' that were presented to the American public contributed to the development of a deprecating image. *Puck, Judge, Life, Chick, Tid-Bits,* and other humor magazines delighted in presenting full-page color cartoons and sketches of men, women, and children with huge hooked noses, gross lips, and crude ostentatious manners. These unsavory figures spoke with a vaudeville German accent and were perennially concerned with the bargain or with money to be made from some unsuspecting innocent and were characterized as dishonest, unscrupulous, and by implication as unworthy citizens. One of the most frequent charges made against them was that they accepted bankruptcy and arson as a means of gaining profit.

There gradually began to develop in the minds of many Americans an association between the Jew and insolvency and fraud. This probably came about because there was no better way for the common folk to identify the risks of capitalism than to relate them to the classical representative of that system, the Hebrew. The disaffection and frustrations of the masses have historically often been directed at Jews. The Jew had no particular economic function in America, but was felt to be nearer the capitalist economy than any other immigrant group and, consequently, his behavior was more carefully scrutinized and questioned. During the period of economic uncertainty and crisis in the 1880s and 1890s, doubts about the beneficialness and permanence of the system began to grow. It became appealing to deflect fears by focusing on the Jew who ostensibly exploited and weakened the economy, thus explaining, however incorrectly, some of the difficulties the country was experiencing.[87]

One of the most interesting repositories of this emerging anti-Semitic stereotype during the years 1885– 1905 was the New York German-American humor magazine *Puck*. Essentially, it represented the views of the small businessman who was buffeted by the great economic and social changes that were transpiring around him and made to feel helpless in their wake. It reflected the new economic, political, and psychological values and interests of small merchants, shopkeepers, salesmen, clerks, and salaried employees. In this regard, it opposed Catholics, unions, strikes, Tammany Hall, and the high tariff and favored civil service reform, tariff reform, and the emerging middle class.[88] Although it had harsh words to say about the Irish and the Italians, it also focused frequently on Jews with its favorite weapon — the cartoon. Joseph Keppler, the founder and chief developer of the magazine, along with Frederick Opper, Louis Dalrymple, and Syd B. Griffin, developed this into a socially caustic art form. A two-paneled cartoon in April 1886, for example, shows first an old caricatured Jew giving street urchins balls to play with and then the same old man selling glass window panes at exorbitant prices to storekeepers whose windows were broken by the boys. Another one, two decades later, entitled "The American Fagin, Instructor in the Art of Stealing and Getting Away With It," depicts a corporation lawyer in the figure of a Jew who teaches a young, growing corporation the art of picking Uncle Sam's pocket.[89]

The image continually drawn by *Puck* was that of the small entrepreneur, the degenerate middleman, who exists not by force of wealth or hard work like the Christians around him, but by shifting and cheating. His weapon is not the money he controls, but his lack of morality. For many years fire insurance and failure jokes were the vogue, and Burnheimer, Burnstein, Smokenstein, Blazenheimer, and Jews of their kind delighted over this convenient method of making money, even if it was at the expense of property damage or human life. Mr. Burnupsky, for example, is content since "despite hard times, he has had two failures and three fires." Flameski remarks that "there is only one thing our race hates more than pork — asbestos!" Little Isaac asks his father what the expression "Every cloud has a silver lining" refers to. Old Isaac answers: "I dink dot means financial clouds, like fires and failures, mein son."[90]

Along with the Jewish association with criminal activities, one finds in *Puck* the pawnbroker with his insatiable desire for profit, the parvenu who intrudes into society and degrades everything he touches, and, of course, the "typical" Jew who believes that if money does not bring happiness, then certainly "der interest vot you gets on der moneysch vot makes you happy."[91] These few examples provide the flavor of the humor that was a common feature in *Puck*.

A publication that drew a similar stereotype was *Leslie's Illustrated Weekly*. Although *Leslie's* represented different groups politically, was the spokesman for the New York Republicans and big business, and stood for issues like the high tariff, this did not affect its basic antipathy for foreigners and "Yids." In May 1889 it passed under the management of the Judge Publishing Company and from then on it began to parrot the prejudicial sentiments of the parent corporation. It revived the old charges concerning the alleged Jewish predilection for arson with an article in February 1897 entitled "Incendiarism" by Valerian Griboyedoff, a frequent author of articles denouncing Jews. He pictured an "oriental firebug fraternity" haggling over the prices they should receive for their nefarious deeds. He spoke of the Semitic lust for gain, of their cavalier attitude towards the death of innocent people, and of the Talmudic basis for arson and murder. "It would be hard to find," he wrote,

a parallel to the story of organized Polish-Jewish incendiarism in New York and Brooklyn. The business of burning down tenement houses teeming with human lives,... for the sake of insurance money assumed such proportions at one time, and was conducted with such impunity, that the miscreants actually lost all consciousness of its criminality.... The thirst for gain of these wretches increased with their success. Orthodox Jews of strictly Talmudic training, they so forgot the tenets of their faith as to include co-religionists among their victims.[92]

The impetus for these negative images really came from *Judge,* the parent magazine, which deftly relied upon the cartoon as well as sarcastic wit to make its social criticisms. *Judge* began its career as a political rival to *Puck* in 1881 and used a similar style and technique to gain a readership. Under William J. Arkell, a prominent Republican businessman, it succeeded; and by 1891 it achieved a circulation in excess of fifty thousand.[93] Characteristic of the graphic weekly genre, *Judge,* like the other humor sheets, focused on the problems of immigration and urbanization that became a major concern in the 1880s and 1890s. To many Americans, the economic, political, and social difficulties of the Gilded Age were linked to the arrival of ethnic groups who appeared foreign and unassimilable. Like many other commentators, *Judge* pointed to the vast influx of newcomers with their almost instant citizenship and their unfamiliarity with America's legal standards as one of the primary causes of the political and ethical demoralization of society. Several immigrant groups came under severe attack and Jews were not the exclusive targets of its caustic treatment. Yet the frequency of their appearance in its pages and caricatured cartoons as parvenu, materialistic exploiters, as well as questionable businessmen circumventing the law, lent credibility to the growing identification of the Jew with crime. Like *Puck,* it relied heavily on bankruptcy and arson jokes to develop this image. Thus Mr. Goldgraber laments that after twenty-four years in the same building, he has had his fill with economic stagnation. "Ach! If I don'd haf a fire here preddy quig I dik I vill busd up." Or an editor remarks to a reporter who covered a story of a fire that he neglected to say who the losers were. "I said it was in Chatham Street, didn't I? There were no losers; all winners."[94]

Likewise, in the area of failures financially inspired, there is a plethora of gibes and sarcasms linking Jews to this illicit activity. Rosenblum, for instance, advises Cohen that there were eighty-seven failures in New York recently. Cohen replies much aghast: "Mein Gott! such competition as dot will kill buziness endirely." In fact, it might be said that the Jewish business ethic, according to *Judge,* is like an old adage slightly modified. "If at first you don't succeed, fail, fail again."[95] Troubled by the extremes of wealth and poverty, the magazine linked the growth of Jewish prosperity to unsettled commercial conditions and seized upon an anti-Semitic explanation for them.

Life magazine represents the arrival of the university wits to the field of comic journalism. Less politically oriented than either *Puck* or *Judge,* it was primarily a product of *Harvard Lampoon* graduates. Its commentaries were basically social; it opposed Wall Street and the trusts, the vulgarity of wealth, the commercialization of culture, the pretensions of medicine, and the skullduggery of the law.[96] The clever pens of John

Ames Mitchell and Edward S. Martin, along with the artful cartoons and sketches of Charles Dana Gibson, employed the standard Jewish stereotypes. Until 1906– 7, when *Life* began to connect Jews with un-Americanism and conspiracy, it emphasized the caricature of the greedy, materialistic, and criminal German Jew. Thus it wrote in 1898 of ''ten little Israelites standing in a line, one set his store on fire, then there were nine.'' Or it told about Swindlebaum who advertised his fire sales ten days in advance of the conflagration, and Cohen who has never failed but has had numerous fires instead because ''he dinks dey pays better.'' When Police Commissioner Theodore Bingham retracted his 1908 attack, *Life* predicted that when Jews discovered that ''far from showing special talent for firebugs, fraudulent bankrupts, burglars, forgers, and pickpockets, they are not even getting their fair share of the emoluments of these professions, one is loath to conjecture what the effect will be.''[97] *Life,* like the other graphic weeklies, was certain of one thing — that immigrant Jews, infused with criminal instincts, were a poor addition to the American urban scene.

These literary and pulp press expressions of anti-Semitism were eclipsed in importance during the first two decades of the twentieth century by a more factual, if not always accurate and unbiased, approach to the subject. Others in American society began to connect Jewish immigrants with crime. The Progressives, for example, had a penchant for facts and data. They rummaged through the mass of information available to their eager minds in search of the roots of society's maladies, but in the process they often brought forward an unsubstantiated portrait of the Jew not very divergent from the fictional efforts of the nineteenth century. The specific accusations were slightly different and the crimes were now those specifically associated with the plight of the cities, but the general thrust was familiar.

Muckrakers, political reformers, and intellectuals proceeded to attack Jewish immigrants for their alleged political corruption and involvement with gambling and prostitution. The widely publicized Lexow and Mazet investigations in 1894 and 1899, exposing the ties between crime, the police, and Tammany Hall, implicated Jews.[98] Frank Moss, a prominent New York City attorney who was very active in criminal work as reflected by his participation as trustee of the City Vigilance League, as president of the New York Board of Police under reform Mayor William L. Strong, and as counsel to the Society for the Prevention of Crime as well as for the Lexow and Mazet Committees, assigned much of New York's difficulties in this area to Russian Jews.[99] In an 1897 study of New York City, he devoted nearly one hundred pages to a harshly drawn portrait of organized crime in the city's Jewish district. The colony of Jews congregated around Grand, Canal, and Baxter Streets is characterized, he wrote, by a "willingness to pander to vice and crime, and to use the strong racial traits not for godly, moral or humanitarian purposes, but for the making of money out of wicked practices." The East Side is a center of crime. "It is infested with petty thieves and house-breakers, many of them desperate; and the criminal instincts that are so often found naturally in the Russian and Polish Jews come to the surface here in such ways as to warrant the opinion that these people are the worst elements in the entire make-up of New York life."[100] There are schools for thieves in the district[101] that equal Fagin's in perfidity, although "in them the tutor's name generally ends with 'ski.' "Along with burglars and pickpockets, firebugs are a definite feature of life on the East Side. Echoing the portrait developed by the New York graphic weeklies, Moss maintained that "the miserable Poles and Russians make a business of effecting insurance and then setting fire to their stores and homes, and defrauding the insurance companies, regardless of danger to human life." Another large element in "New Israel" is addicted to vice and is involved in gambling and prostitution. A fraternity of Russian and Polish Jewish procurers supervise this activity and are "unmatched for impudence, and bestiality, and... reek with all unmanly and vicious humors."[102] Moss saw the Semitic bogey behind every illegal act, but only exceeded the popular conception by the scope of his accusations and by the nature of his extreme and somewhat histrionic treatment.

The pervasive concern with crime in America's urban centers thus fastened public attention on the East Side as one of the primary recruiting grounds for young criminals and as the center of smuggling, gambling, narcotics, and prostitution. The frequency with which Jews appeared in the well-publicized accounts of crime and corruption gave the section a newly found but unwelcome and undeserved notoriety. The fact that there were Jewish criminals like Yuski Nigger (Joseph Toblinsky), Abe Greenthal, Mike Kuntz, Jack Zelig (William Albert), Sam Schepps, Max Hochstim, and Herman Rosenthal, to name a few of the more notorious, is not surprising, for why should Jews, as part of the human family, be untouched by this type of activity. What is unfortunate is that men of good intentions, and some who were not, spoke with increasing concern about criminality as a phenomenon particularly bred in the ghetto and transformed and handed down to the sons of immigrant Russian Jews.

Muckrakers soon joined the attack. Following closely on Bingham's 1908 accusations, several articles appeared in the June and November 1909 issues of *McClure's* magazine that undertook to uncover vice and crime and that implicated large numbers of Jews in the process. The main target of these exposés was Tammany Hall, which Samuel S. McClure blamed for the iniquity that allegedly thrived on the East Side, raising thereby a generation of procurers, thieves, and gunmen. This was the process he labeled the "Tammanizing of a Civilization," but significantly, for our discussion, it was the Jews, according to McClure, who were given free rein by the Democratic organization to indulge in these endeavors.[103]

The principal contributor to this journalistic treatment was the noted muckraker George Kibbe Turner. For several years, he focused on the demoralization of America's cities, and he determined that the aspect of commercialized crime most debilitating both for the victims and for society was prostitution. He described a highly organized and complex system that fed upon the mass of chaste and defenseless girls and that contributed to the putrefaction of the growing foreign populations. At the core of this festering human cancer was the Jew. In a 1907 article entitled "The City of Chicago: a Study of the Great Immoralities," he wrote that "the largest regular business in furnishing women... is done by... Russian Jews, who supply women of that nationality to the trade. These men have a sort of loosely organized association extending through the large cities of the country, the chief centers being New York, Boston, Chicago, and New Orleans."[104] In June 1909 he broached the subject once again, this time emphasizing political ramifications. He described how "Jewish commercial accumen" contributed to the growth of 50-cent prostitution. Out of the Bowery and red-light districts of New York these organized criminals used their voting power to influence New York politics. This was a particularly unfortunate situation since the Jewish pimp "vitiated more than any other single agency, the moral life of the great cities of America," and was a most compliant tool for Tammany operations.[105]

Turner's major exposition of this theme was developed in his well-known article, "The Daughters of the Poor." He traced the transfer of a vast empire of prostitution from the ghettos of Europe to New York's East Side. Out of this medieval environment "has come for unnumbered years the Jewish kaftan, leading the miserable Jewish girl out of Galicia and Russian Poland."[106] Once in America, he frequents the employment agencies, the dancing academies, and even waits at the docks to lure naive immigrant girls into his net of pollution. This enterprise, Turner maintained, is not exclusively an East Coast or New York phenomenon. These Jewish "cadets" "are strong in all the greater cities; they swarm at the gateway of the Alaskan frontier at Seattle; they infest the streets and restaurants of Boston; they flock for the winter to New Orleans;... and they abound in the South and Southwest and in the mining regions of the West."[107]

While writers and muckraking journalists were taking this position, governmental bodies were also examining Jewish criminality. In December 1909 the United States Immigration Commission, the Dillingham Commission, presented to Congress the report of its special inquiry into the white slave traffic. Directed by the economist Jeremiah Jenks and assisted by officials of the New York City police department, the findings indicated the preeminent role Jews played, according to the commission, in commercial vice. Although some positive legislation, particularly the Mann Act, resulted from its investigations, the accusations levied against this immigrant population added the authority of an ostensibly "scientific" government study to the image that was already quite widespread.[108] The report said that

there are large numbers of Jews scattered throughout the United States, although mainly located in New York and Chicago, who seduce and keep girls. Some of them are engaged in importation, but apparently they prey rather upon young girls whom they find on the street, in the dance halls, and similar places, and whom, by the methods already indicated—love-making and pretenses of marriage—deceive and ruin. Many of them are petty thieves, pickpockets, and gamblers.[109]

A year later, another volume of the Dillingham Commission appeared, this one dealing with immigration and crime. The commission's staff abstracted statistics from a variety of court sources and collected limited data on the relationship between crime and ethnic origin. It reported that "the Hebrews have a larger proportion of alien prisoners committed for larceny and receiving stolen property than any other race."[110] In addition, it extrapolated from the statistics the questionable conclusion that Jews comprise the "largest proportion of alien prisoners under sentence for offenses against chastity."[111] Data can be manipulated to demonstrate almost anything the investigator wants and this is particularly evident in the case of these inquiries. Recent scholarship has shown that the commission's report was neither impartial nor scientific and was influenced by its underlying objective, which was to prove the superiority of the old immigration over the new.[112]

The trail of innuendo and accusation did not end with the issuance of this "authoritative" study. Charles Davenport, the pioneering eugenicist; Frederic Haskins, the prominent journalist; and Edward Ross, the economist and social critic, echoed the sentiments previously expressed and added the weight of their public, academic, and scholarly standings to them. Davenport, repeating the findings of the Dillingham Commission, wrote in 1911 that "statistics indicate that the crimes of Hebrews are chiefly 'gainful offenses,' especially thievery and receiving stolen goods, while they rarely commit offenses of personal violence. On the other hand, they show the greatest proportion of offenses against chastity and in connection with prostitution, the lowest of crimes."[113] Similarly, Haskins argued in 1913 that nearly half of the foreigners involved in the white slave traffic in New York are Jews, and most of the rest are French.[114]

Edward Ross, the University of Wisconsin economist who made a reputation as a supporter of the welfare state at a time when this viewpoint was not very popular, also established himself as one of the principal critics of the new immigration and forthright nativists. Like Frederick Jackson Turner, Francis Amasa Walker, and Richmond Mayo Smith, he believed frontier life had nurtured the solid virtues of the native stock. This pioneering spirit could never become part of the makeup of Eastern Europeans. Somewhat influenced by the Teutonic myth, he was unable to mask his prejudice for the "Nordic" race. The new immigrants were "beaten men from beaten breeds" who had little prospect of ever reaching the high level of their predecessors.[115] This was particularly true in the case of Jews. They arrived in America, according to Ross, "moral cripples, their souls warped and dwarfed by iron circumstance. The experience of Russian repression has made them haters of government and corrupters of the police.... Pent within the Talmud and the Pale of Settlement, their interests have become few, and many of them have developed a monstrous and repulsive love of gain.'' Like the other scholars mentioned, Ross recounted the alleged Jewish predilection for gainful offenses rather than violent crimes that involve considerably greater risk. Shrewdness is a characteristic that even their critics could not take away from them. The fact that Jews are not convicted as frequently as other groups is no consolation, since it ''is harder to catch and convict criminals of cunning than criminals of violence.''[116] His full-length study of ethnic groups, *The Old World in the New* (1914), widely disseminated these stereotypes and furthered the burgeoning restrictionist appeal.

Charges of Jewish criminality found additional exposure on the popular stage and in the nascent movie industry. During the early days of the silent movies and vaudeville, most minority groups were stereotyped in disparaging caricatures. The boorish Irishman was the inveterate drunkard; the Italian spent his time either as an anarchist or as a Black Hand Mafioso; the American Negro, in Stepin Fetchit tradition, was a creature of comic relief. This was also the period of the denegrating ''Jew comedy.'' The new stage figure, first popularized by Frank Bush, replete with eccentricities of dress—hat over ears—and accent, was characterized not only by the traditional obsession with money, but by a peculiar affinity to crime. Standard vaudeville and movie characters included ''Moe-the-fence-Greenstein'' and ''Jew Rosenstein,'' the diamond smuggler. Repeated representations of such eccentrics on the stage and in film reinforced their identification as typical in the public mind.[117] The Anti-Defamation League noted the extent of this practice when it wrote in 1913:

Whenever a producer wishes to depict a betrayer of public trust, a hard-boiled usurious moneylender, a crooked gambler, a grafter, a depraved firebug, a white slaver or other villains of one kind or another, the actor is directed to represent himself as a Jew.[118]

There is no doubt that crime (including prostitution and arson) existed on New York's lower East Side and in the other congested urban centers where Jews congregated. This is the inevitable consequence of the poverty, poor housing, filth, and ignorance that fester in the ghetto environment. It is also true that the ''uprooted'' experience and the weakening of family and religious ties, coupled with the environmental factors, created an atmosphere that was conducive to crime. Indeed many uptown Jews felt at first embarrassed and then threatened by the situation and expressed criticisms in private similar to those that were making headlines in public.[119]

Notwithstanding the reality, what is important is the identification of Jews, especially during the four decades of mass immigration (1882–1927), with an *excessive* participation in illegal acts. What comes through from all the discussion in literature and in the public arena is the viewpoint that the Jew, by experience, heritage, predilection, and even religion, is enveloped by a moral standard that countenances the subversion of law for profit. This is an inaccurate and misleading portrait based substantially on emotionalism, prejudice, and innuendo, rather than hard data. There is little evidence that Jews were more criminally inclined in this period than other groups. In fact, there is a good deal of evidence that indicates the contrary. Commissioner Bingham, who made the issue a *cause célèbre* of sorts, issued a retraction in October 1908, denying the validity of his statistical accusation.[120] Shortly thereafter, a study was issued that demonstrated that of the 2,848 convictions in the Court of General Sessions for New York County in 1907, 460, or 16.1 percent, were Jews. On the basis of an estimated Jewish population in New York County of 750,000, the ratio of convictions per 10,000 Jews was 6:1. For non-Jews it was 12:3, or twice as large as the Jewish rate.[121] Dr. H.S. Linfield further indicated this trend in a study he undertook for the American Jewish Committee in 1927. He found that during the previous ten years, Jews comprised 19.3 percent of the prison population in New York City, while they made up approximately 27.5 percent of the city population. In the state, they were 10.4 percent of the prison community, while comprising 16.1 percent of the total population.[122] In another study in which he examined the national figures, he found even more graphic results. During the period 1920–29, a total of 394,080 convicts were received in the prisons and reformatories of America. This number included 6,846 Jews or 1.74 percent. During the same period, the percentage of Jews to the total population averaged 3.43 percent. The number of Jews in prison was thus 49.27 percent smaller than the percentage of Jews to the total population of the nation.[123]

There are some difficulties with these statistics and they should not be accepted as absolute indicators. The estimates of the Jewish population were crude and general and there is no assurance that among those classified as gentile there might not be Jews. Furthermore, the purely legal test of convictions as well as prison population does not truly reflect the extent of any criminal class. Many others might never have been caught or might have used wealth and influence to avoid conviction. Nevertheless, the limited data does suggest that Jews did not predominate in those illegal activities that their critics accused them of, and that they were no more corrupt or criminally inclined than any other segment of society and possibly statistically less involved.

This, however, was not the image that was broadcast by many writers and social commentators who began to examine the Jewish character during the period of mass immigration. The Jew who walks through the pages of the dime novel or the works of Edgar Fawcett, A.H. Frankel, and F. Scott Fitzgerald, or who leers through the caricatures of Joseph Keppler and Charles Dana Gibson, as well as who garnishes the scholarly treatments of an Edward Ross or Charles Davenport, is an unsavory character consumed by criminality and oblivious to the moral standards of society. He has little appreciation of law and comes out of a tradition that has long sanctioned the subversion of Christian authority. This is an era when Americans were increasingly anxious about urbanization and fearful that their cities would be inundated, degraded, and controlled by the "invading" immigrant. As one critic wrote: "The Jewish immigrants have brought us crime, indecency, immorality, filth, and all the other things that have long been associated with that race." For that reason, they "are to be feared."[124]

This imaging of the American Jew excludes entire areas of Jewish experience and contribution that are significant and socially beneficial. If the culture of the Jew produced, on the one hand, the ostentatious, boisterous model of the parvenu type, it produced also, on the other hand, the understanding model of the poet and thinker. If it created the crass, even cynically materialistic model of the aggressive, dishonest businessman, it also created the socially sensitive and realistic model of the reformer and philanthropist. Judas and Jesus, Rothschild and Marx, Sabbatai and Mendelssohn, and Lepke-Buchalter and Brandeis all had Jewish origins.

NOTES

1. Letter, Mrs. Alexander Kohut to Louis Marshall, October 4, 1922, Louis Marshall Collection, Box 157, American Jewish Archives, Cincinnati, Ohio.

2. Quoted in Morris U. Schappes, ed., *A Documentary History of the Jews in the United States 1654 – 1875* (New York: The Citadel Press, 1950), pp. 342 – 43.

3. Theodore A. Bingham, "Foreign Criminals in New York," *North American Review*, No. 634 (September, 1908), pp. 383 – 84.

4. See George Sand, *The Mississippian*; Charles Dickens, *Oliver Twist;* Anthony Trollope, *The Way We Live Now;* Honoré Balzac, *The Human Comedy;* and Voltaire, *Candide,* for examples of this image in European literature.

5. The *Washington Sentinel* for May 21, 1854, wrote: "Jews seldom commit murder or any of those crimes and offenses that are marked by violence and passion." Before the 1870s there were very few reported cases of Jewish violent crime. Two of the more prominent were the following: Dr. Moses Lowenberg in 1861 killed a patient over nonpayment of fees; Bennet Scop was accused of murdering Jacob Goodman, a fellow peddler in Ohio in 1870. (*American Israelite*, Vol. 8 [1861], p. 182; *American Israelite*, Vol. 17, No. 7 [1870]).

6. Michael Selzer, *"Kike!" A Documentary History of Anti-Semitism in America* (New York: World Publishing Co., 1972), pp. 20 – 21.

7. *The Insurance Monitor and Wall Street Review,* Vol. 15, No. 4 (April, 1867), p. 225.

8. Ibid.

9. In 1890 – 93 there was again an effort by insurers to raise the fire rates on Jews (see *Jewish Tidings,* Rochester, 1890 – 93). One of their investigators found that Jews were involved in arson but that the rate of fire in Jewish areas was lower than in non-Jewish areas of similar economic condition.

10. Quoted in Schappes, p. 514.

11. Frank Mott, *Golden Multitudes: The Story of Best Sellers in the United States* (New York: Macmillan Co., 1947), pp. 247 – 48.

12. George Lippard, *The Quaker City; or, The Monks of Monk Hall* (Philadelphia: Leary, Stuart & Co., 1876), p. 149; see Harap, pp. 47 – 49; Steinberg, p. 115.

13. Ibid., p. 202.

14. Ibid., p. 116.

15. Harry Franco [Charles F. Briggs], *Bankrupt Stories* (New York: John Allen, 1913), p. 316. See Harap, p. 50.

16. See also Theodore S. Fay's *The Countess Ida, A Tale of Berlin,* 2 vols. (New York: Harper & Brothers, 1840) for another conventional treatment of this theme.

17. J. Ross Browne, *Crusoe's Island* (New York: Harper & Brothers, 1864).

18. Norton B. Stern and William M. Kramer, "Anti-Semitism and the Jewish Image in the Early West," *Western States Jewish Historical Quarterly,* Vol. VI, No. 2 (January, 1974).

19. Browne, p. 350.

20. Ibid., p. 423.

21. Tom Taylor, *The Ticket-of-Leave Man* (New York: Samuel French, Publishers 1864).

22. By the time Boucicault died in 1890, he had written approximately 130 plays, some dealing with serious themes like the American Negro, the Civil War, and Irish freedom.

23. Produced on April 24, 1867, at Wallack's Theatre in New York after which it remained popular for about a decade and was retained in the repertory of stock companies until 1900. Odell says "it ran swiftly to success. It was mere melodrama, but it caught the popular fancy." (*Annals of the New York Stage,* Vol. 8. [New York: Columbia University Press, 1927–49], p. 34).

24. Dion Boucicault, *Flying Scud: or, A Fourlegged Fortune* (New York: Photostatic Reproduction of Original Typescript, New York Public Library, 1867), p. 57.

25. Dion Boucicault, *After Dark: A Drama of London Life in 1868* (Chicago: Dramatic Publishing Company, n.d.); see Louis Harap, *The Image of the Jew in American Literature* (Philadelphia: The Jewish Publication Society of America, 1974), p. 215.

26. The play ran for nine weeks after its first performance on June 8, 1868, and was revived a number of times during the next seven years (Odell, Vol. 8, p. 278; Vol. 9, pp. 48–103).

27. John Brougham, *The Lottery of Life* (New York: Samuel French & Sons, 1867), p. 33; see Harap, p. 212; John Bloore, "The Jew in American Dramatic Literature (1794–1930)," Ph.D. dissertation, New York University, p. 110.

28. Ibid., p. 40.

29. Horatio Alger, Jr., *Adrift in New York* (Cleveland: The World Syndicate Publishing Co., n.d.); *Ben, the Luggage Boy; or Among the Wharves* (Boston: Loring, Publishers, 1870); *Paul, the Peddler* (New York: A.L. Burt Co., n.d.).

30. Irving G. Wyllie, *The Self-Made Man in America* (New York: The Free Press, 1954), p. 60.

31. Alger, *Ben, the Luggage Boy,* p. 112.

32. Alger, *Paul, the Peddler,* p. 186.

33. Albert Aiken, *The White Witch or, The League of Three* (New York: Beadle and Adams, 1871). For a discussion of dime novels, see Harap, pp. 334 – 41, and Steinberg, pp. 117 – 35.

34. Albert Aiken, *The Genteel Spotter; or the Night Hawks of New York,* Beadle's Dime Library, no. 320 (New York, 1884).

35. Ibid., p. 11.

36. Ibid.

37. Albert Aiken, *Dick Talbot, the Ranch King,* Beadle's Dime Library, no. 733 (New York, 1892).

38. Gilbert Jerome, *Dominick Squeek, the Bow Street Runner,* Old Cap Collier, no. 80 (New York, 1884), p. 35.

39. Gilbert Jerome, *Old Subtle; or, The Willing Victim,* Old Cap Collier, no. 125 (New York, 1885).

40. Ibid., p. 21.

41. Gilbert Jerome, *Young Weasel, the Detective; or "Piping" a Beautiful Friend,* Old Cap Collier, no. 134 (New York, 1885).

42. Dr. Noel Dunbar [Prentiss Ingraham], *Duke Despard the Gambler Duellist,* Beadle's Dime Library, no. 730 (New York, 1892).

43. Old Sleuth [H.P. Halsey], *Monte-Christo Ben, the Ever-Ready Detective,* Old Sleuth Library, no. 63 (New York, 1893).

44. Old Sleuth [H.P. Halsey], *Lights and Shades of New York,* Old Sleuth Library, no. 101 (New York, 1905), p. 21.

45. J.R. Coryell, *The Book-Maker's Crime; or, Nick Carter's Accidental Clue,* Nick Carter Library, no. 99 (New York, 1893).

46. J. R. Coryell, *Among the Fire-Bugs; or, Nick Carter's Bravest Deed,* Nick Carter Library, no. 110 (New York, 1893), p. 5; see also Steve Shadow [Robert C. Brown], *The Frozen Face or Dick Dobbs Among the Smugglers,* Dick Dobbs Detective Weekly, no. 7 (May 1, 1909), p. 2.

47. Part of the title page of each *Fame and Fortune Weekly* edition.

48. A Self-Made Man (Pseud.), "Dick Dalton, the Young Banker or, Cornering the Wall Street 'Sharkes,'" *Fame and Fortune Weekly,* no. 328 (January 12, 1912).

49. A Self-Made Man (Pseud.), "Beating the Market or, A Boy Broker's Big Deal," *Fame and Fortune Weekly,* no. 342 (April 19, 1912).

50. A Self-Made Man, "A Mad Broker's Scheme or, The Corner that Couldn't Be Worked," *Fame and Fortune Weekly,* no. 680 (October 11, 1918).

51. A Self-Made Man, "Rough and Ready Dick; or, A Young Express Agent's Luck," *Fame and Fortune Weekly,* no. 655 (April 19, 1918).

52. Sidney Luska [Henry Harland], *The Yoke of the Torah* (New York: Cassell & Co., 1887).

53. Sidney Luska [Henry Harland], *As It Was Written: A Jewish Musician's Story* (New York: Cassell & Co., 1885); see Harap, p. 456.

54. Sidney Luska [Henry Harland], *Mrs. Peixada* (New York: Cassell & Co., 1886), pp. 252–53; see Harap, pp. 459–60.

55. Brander Matthews and George H. Jessop, *A Tale of Twenty-Five Hours* (New York: D. Appleton and Co., 1892). See Harap, p. 316.

56. Brander Matthews and George H. Jessop, "A Study in Nativities," *Forum*, Vol. 26 (1899), pp. 621–31.

57. Brander Matthews and George H. Jessop, *Vignettes of Manhattan* (New York: Harper & Brothers, 1894).

58. Matthews and Jessop, *A Tale of Twenty-Five Hours*, p. 136.

59. Steele Mackaye, *Money-Mad*, Typewritten prompt book in Theater Collection, Harvard College Library, n.d., p. 5; see Harap, p. 216.

60. Ibid., p. 14.

61. Edward M. Alfriend and A.C. Wheeler, "The Great Diamond Robbery," in *Favorite American Plays of the Nineteenth Century*, ed. Barrett H. Clark (Princeton: Princeton University Press, 1943), pp. 353–404.

62. Herbert Asbury in an article in *The New Yorker* said the following about her: "Marm Mandelbaum... was probably the greatest and most successful fence in the criminal annals of New York. She is said also to have been a Fagin, and to have maintained a regular school in Grand Street... where small boys and girls were taught by expert pickpockets and sneak thieves." (*The New Yorker*, Vol. 3 [January 7, 1928], pp. 22–24).

63. Julian Ralph, *People We Pass* (New York: Harper & Brothers, 1896).

64. Ibid., pp. 5, 84.

65. Edgar Fawcett, *New York* (New York: F. Tennyson Neely, 1898), p. 61; see Harap, pp. 317–19; Abraham H. Steinberg, "Jewish Characters in the American Novel to 1900," Ph.D. dissertation, New York University, 1956, p. 218.

66. Ibid., p. 82.

67. Ibid., pp. 82, 123.

68. A.H. Frankel, *In Gold We Trust* (Philadelphia: Pile, 1898). See Harap, p. 450; see David Martin Fine, "The Immigrant Ghetto in American Fiction, 1885–1917," Ph.D. dissertation, University of California, L.A., 1969, p. 72.

69. Produced on August 9, 1916, at the Ettinge Theatre in New York where it ran for 286 performances (*The Best Plays of 1909–1919* (New York: Dodd, Mead & Co., 1933], p. 577); see Bloore, pp. 120–28.

70. Max Marcin, *Cheating Cheaters* (New York: Samuel French, 1916), p. 4.

71. Produced on November 22, 1927, at the Ambassador Theatre in New York where it ran for 119 performances (*Best Plays of 1927 – 1928*), p. 62.

72. Bartlett Cormack, *The Racket* (New York: Samuel French, 1927), p. 62.

73. Monckton Hoffe, *Cristilinda* (New York: Samuel French, 1926).

74. James P. Judge, *Square Crooks* (New York: Longmans, Green and Co., 1929).

75. Philip Dunning, *Night Hostess* (New York: Samuel French, 1928), p. 40.

76. F. Scott Fitzgerald, *The Great Gatsby* (New York: Charles Scribner's Sons, 1953), p. 74.

77. Ibid., p. 173.

78. A.W. Miller, *The Restoration of the Jews* (Atlanta: Constitution Publishing Co., 1887), p. 35.

79. Ibid., p. 36.

80. Leonard Greenberg and Harold Jonas, "An American Anti-Semite in the Nineteenth Century," in *Essays on Jewish Life and Thought,* ed. Joseph L. Blau et al. (New York: Columbia University Press, 1959), pp. 265 – 83.

81. Telemachus T. Timayenis, *The American Jew; An Exposé of His Career* (New York: The Minerva Publishing Co., 1888), and ibid.

82. Timayenis, p. 89.

83. Ibid., pp. 89, 90, 216.

84. Timayenis, *Judas Iscariot: An Old Type in a New Form* (New York: The Minerva Publishing Co., 1889), pp. 12 – 13.

85. Ibid., p. 231.

86. Ibid., pp. 273, 284.

87. We see this phenomenon reflected in the Populist identification of Jews with the evils of capitalism, as well as in Europe in reference to the Rothschild myth (Mary E. Lease, *The Problem of Civilization Solved* [Chicago: Laird & Lee, 1895]; James B. Goode, *The Modern Banker* [Chicago: Charles H. Kerr & Co., 1896]; Hannah Arendt, *The Origins of Totalitarianism* [New York: World Publishing Co., 1951]).

88. William F. Lichliter, "Political Reflections of an Age; The New York Graphic Weeklies During the 1880's," Ph.D. dissertation, Brandeis University, 1970, pp. 27 – 32.

89. *Puck*, Vol. 19, No. 475 (April 14, 1886), p. 102; Vol. 62, No. 1596 (1907 – 8), p. 1.

90. Ibid., Vol. 36 (1894 – 95), pp. 232 – 33; Vol. 48, No. 1239 (December 3, 1900), n.p.; Vol. 36, No. 911 (August 3, 1894), p. 3.

91. Ibid., Vol. 44, No. 1121 (1898 – 99), p. 12.

92. Valerian Griboyedoff, "Incendiarism," *Frank Leslie's Illustrated*

Weekly, Vol. 84, No. 2162 (February 18, 1897), p. 102.

93. Lichliter, pp. 32 – 34; George P. Rowell and Company, *American Newspaper Directory* (New York: 1891).

94. *Judge,* Vol. 26, No. 639 (January 13, 1894), p. 23; Vol. 26, No. 642 (February 3, 1894), p. 68.

95. Ibid., Vol. 35, No. 888 (October 22, 1898), n.p.; Vol. 26, No. 648 (March 17, 1894), p. 162.

96. Lichliter, p. 36.

97. *Life Magazine,* Vol. 52, No. 1364 (December 17, 1898), p. 696; Vol. 24, No. 619 (November 8, 1894), p. 301; Vol. 26, No. 670 (October 31, 1895), p. 275; Vol. 52, No. 1354 (October 8, 1908), p. 385.

98. Gustavus Myers, *The History of Tammany Hall* (New York: Boni & Liveright, 1917), pp. 278 – 79.

99. Frank Moss, *The American Metropolis,* 3 vols. (New York: Peter Fenelos Collier, Publisher, 1897).

100. Ibid., pp. 55, 160.

101. Alfred E. Ommen in a 1904 letter to F.H. Ainsworth remarked: "I have been particularly disturbed by the growth of faganism [sic] of children on the eastside" (Ommen to Ainsworth, March 1, 1904, Prescott F. Hall Collection, The Houghton Library, Harvard University, Cambridge, Massachusetts).

102. Moss, pp. 164, 191 – 92, 235.

103. S.S. McClure, "The Tammanyizing of a Civilization," *McClure's Magazine,* Vol. 34, No. 1 (November, 1909), pp. 117 – 28.

104. George Kibbe Turner, "The City of Chicago: A Study of the Great Immoralities," *McClure's Magazine,* Vol. 28, No. 6 (April, 1907), pp. 581 – 82.

105. George Kibbe Turner, "Tammany's Control of New York by Professional Criminals," *McClure's Magazine,* Vol. 33, No. 2 (June, 1909), p. 121.

106. George Kibbe Turner, "The Daughters of the Poor," *McClure's Magazine,* Vol. 34, No. 1 (November, 1909), p. 45.

107. Ibid., p. 52.

108. For a highly critical view of the Dillingham Commission as being biased and statistically misleading, see Oscar Handlin in *Race and Nationality in American Life,* (New York: Little, Brown and Co., 1957), Chap. V.

109. U.S. Congress, Senate, *Importing Women for Immoral Purposes: A Partial Report.* S. Doc. 196, 61st Cong., 2nd sess., Dec. 10, 1909. Washington, D.C., 1909, pp. 23 – 24.

110. U.S. Immigration Commission, *Reports of the Immigration Commission, Immigration and Crime.* Vol. 36 (Washington: Government Printing Office, 1911), p. 30.

111. Ibid., p. 31.

112. Handlin, pp. 197–98; John Higham, *Strangers in the Land: Patterns of American Nativism 1860–1925* (New York: Atheneum, 1971), pp. 309–11.

113. Charles Benedict Davenport, *Heredity in Relation to Eugenics* (New York: Henry Holt & Co., 1911), p. 216.

114. Frederic Haskin, *The Immigrant* (New York: Fleming H. Revell Co., 1913), pp. 157–58.

115. Edward A. Ross, *The Old World in the New* (New York: The Century Co., 1914), pp. 157–58.

116. Ibid., p. 155.

117. Douglas Gilbert, *American Vaudeville, Its Life and Times* (New York: McGraw-Hill Book Co., 1940); Harold E. Adams, "Minority Caricatures on the American Stage," in *Studies in the Science of Society,* ed. G.P. Murdock (New Haven: Yale University Press, 1937).

118. John P. Roche, *The Quest for the Dream, the Development of Civil Rights and Human Relations in Modern America* (New York: Macmillan, 1963), p. 93.

119. Letter, Louis Marshall to "Organization of Orthodox Rabbis whatever the name may be," July 23, 1912, Louis Marshall Collection, Correspondence (Miscellaneous).

120. *The North American Review,* No. 635 (October,3 1908), p. 638.

121. Francis J. Oppenheimer, "Jewish Criminality," *The Independent,* Vol. 65, No. 3120 (September 17, 1908), pp. 640–42.

122. American Jewish Committee Archival Materials, General Correspondence 1906–1932, Folder C, New York.

123. Ibid., Administration Folder.

124. Letter, J.I. Hayes to Rabbi Nathan Krass, December 4, 1923, Louis Marshall Collection, Box 66.

There sat the very Jew of Jews, the distilled essence of all the Jews that have been born since Jacob's time; he was Judas Iscariot; he was the Wandering Jew; he was the worst, and at the same time the truest type of his race...; and he must have been circumcised as much as ten times over. I never beheld anything so ugly and disagreeable, and preposterous, and laughable as the outline of his profile, it was so hideously Jewish, and so cruel, and so keen; and he had such an immense beard that you could see no trace of a mouth until he opened it to speak, or to eat his dinner,—and then, indeed you were aware of a cave.... I rejoiced exceedingly in this Shylock...; for the sight of him justified me in the repugnance I have always felt towards his race.

NATHANIEL HAWTHORNE, 1856[1]

Gilded Age Images: Shylock Resurrected

The underlying characteristic of the criminal Jew portrait is that the Jew, whenever he engages in illegal activities, is more likely to participate in fraudulent business transactions where the motive is profit, rather than violent crime where the motive is senseless revenge. This harks back to what is perhaps the most persistent theme in anti-Semitism from medieval times to the present: that of the Jew as a cheap, miserly, manipulator of money, preoccupied with materialism and characterized by predatory business habits.[2] William Shakespeare created the classic expression of this image of the Jew as the usurer and exploiter, and his character Shylock came to epitomize this accepted aspect of the Jewish personality. Geoffrey Chaucer, Christopher Marlowe, and Martin Luther before him also emphasized the parasitic and usurious nature of the Jew.[3] This depiction was obviously not an American invention, but was one of those unfortunate articles of cultural inheritance that found its way to the New World as part of the folklore as well as visceral baggage of the immigrants.[4] It was articulated here with great frequency in the last decades of the nineteenth century. Shylock brought up to date with his peddler's pack, in his "old-clo'" shop, or in his Broadway emporium may appear different from his Venetian ancestor, but he remained, nevertheless, a familiar figure on the American scene, easily associated with more modern versions of business subterfuge and moral turpitude. Many Americans in this period would probably have agreed with William Cullen Bryant's assessment that the Jews are marked by an "unquenchable lust for lucre," and with Oliver Wendell Holmes's remark that "the principal use of the Jews seemed to be to lend money..."[5]

But even here there is some ambivalence. A duality complicated the economic stereotype of Jews. They epitomized both the capitalist virtues and the capitalist vices. On the positive side, the Jew commonly symbolized an admirable keenness and resourcefulness in business. In this sense, his economic energy seemed very much in the tradition of Yankee America. As *The Evening Telegraph* of Philadelphia remarked in 1872: "Wherever there is a chance for enterprise and energy the Jew is to be found... And Americans should be glad that such is the case for the Jew... brings into every community wealth and qualities which materially assist to strengthen and consolidate its polity."[6] Diplomat John Hay similarly observed in 1867 that "in America we always say, 'Rich as a Jew,' because even if a Jew is poor he is so brisk, so sharp and enterprising that he is sure to make money eventually."[7]

In another mood, however, keenness might mean cunning; enterprise might shade into greed. Along with encomiums of the Jew as a model of commercial skill went frequent references to avaricious Shylocks. The earliest published plays containing Jewish characters (1794, 1823) portrayed Shylock types, and by the 1840s the verb "to Jew," meaning to cheat by sharp practices, was becoming part of American slang.[8] *The Merchant of Venice* was one of the most popular plays performed on the nascent American stage. Edmund Kean toured with it in the 1820s and powerful and popular actors such as Edwin Booth and Henry Irving performed the play around the country later in the century. One reviewer described Booth's Shylock as ''a fierce Jew animated... by personal hatred and greed,... a fiend-like man.'' The greedy, vile Shylock, patterned on Edwin Booth's interpretation, made its rounds across the country. Noah Ludlow took it by wagon and flatboat through the South. Thousands who had never seen a Jew in person saw Shylock in his most extreme form. As ''Sam Slick'' a country ''bumkin'' reported in 1858: ''I once seen a theater play and there was an old Jew in it,... and if ever there was a critter ravin, tarrin mad, it was old mister Shylock....''⁹ In the early nineteenth century the favorable economic images predominated. Later, in an increasingly secularized society marked by mass immigration, the religious image declined in importance and the unattractive elements in the economic stereotype grew more pronounced.

This tendency has a deep psychological basis and reveals some of the doubts and fears that Americans were experiencing concerning their moral worth in an age of industrialization. Accustomed to viewing their experiment in democracy as a ''city upon a hill,'' as a beacon giving direction and inspiration to mankind, they painfully had to reevaluate and face the contradictions intrinsic to some of their assumptions when the abuses of capitalism became manifest. The emotional relief provided by displaced aggression and scapegoating can be appealing when the truth is too difficult to accept. The rise of capitalism in America in the nineteenth century with its frequent economic dislocations may have occasioned such needs. Initially, capitalism was perceived as a positive and inevitable development. Gradually, new values were formed to accord with its requirements. The physiocratic virtues of the Jeffersonian age were replaced by new Hamiltonian societal goals and soon wealth, success, and power were idealized as the uniquely American contribution to the Protestant ethic. Everyone seemed to be on the monetary express. In such a situation it is possible that Americans felt great guilt in the face of these new economic and moral standards and found in the Jew the medieval symbol of Mammon, a likely target through which to relieve their anxieties. By labeling the Jew as the purveyor of greed, the arch example of money's corruptibility, their own gravitation toward blind economic pursuits became less significant. Sensitive to the accusation that idealism and Christian ethics had given way to Wall Street and the Standard Oil Corporation, it was some comfort that the inveterate Jew, conniving, bargaining, and scrapping for every last cent, was always there to receive the criticisms that originated not in his own failings necessarily, but found their source in the depths of the nation's insecurities and doubts.

Be that as it may, Americans began to parrot the timeworn accusation of Jewish excessive materialism. Americans have always put an exceptionally high premium on productivity; on the work of the hand and the sweat of the brow.[10] The tradition of agrarian protest from Jefferson through Jackson and the Populists was predicated on this distinction between the producing classes who cleared the forests and plowed the field and the unproductive creditors and speculators who reaped the rewards of the hard labor of others. The former group comprised the industrious creators of valuable products; the latter, the exploiters and makers of money. Jews were identified as essentially parasitic in function precisely because they appeared to operate on the periphery of the economy, concerned only with the end product of labor—its profits— and were unwilling or unable to lend a hand to the growth of society. Thus *Niles' Weekly Register,* which was generally sympathetic to Jews and abhored their ill treatment in Europe, suggested in 1820 a reason for this oppression. "There must be some moral cause to produce this effect.... They will not sit down and labor like other people—they create nothing and are mere consumers. They will not cultivate the earth, nor work at mechanical trades, preferring to live by their wit in dealing."[11]

The Jewish image in America was slowly changing. With the first substantial immigration of German Jews in the late 1830s and 1840s, the depiction of Jews as the people of the law, as the symbol of freedom and of industrious work, characterized by an admirable "Yankee" keenness and resourcefulness in trade, was modified to include the Jew despised by God, the cunning Shylock and the vagrant peddler and "old-clo'" hawker invading the countryside. In the worst sections of America's cities, the immigrants opened squalid secondhand shops. Commenting on these shops, a popular guide to New York City in 1850 referred to the typical proprietor's hooked nose, "which betrays the Israelite as the human kite formed to be feared, hated and despised, yet to prey upon mankind."[12] Many of the newcomers spread rapidly throughout the country, making their way usually as peddlers. These raw Jewish itinerant Chapmen with their pack of *tsores* (woes) who swarmed southward and westward made a mixed impression. Terribly poor and often not very clean or attractive, they looked unappealingly alien and untrustworthy to some. They wandered into strange and often hostile districts, oblivious to the taunts and stones of unfriendly boys and adults, aggressively and at times offensively pursuing "monish." Jewish peddlers were treated harshly in many cities. In Rochester, New York, they were often physically attacked. Things got so bad in Detroit and in Baltimore that Jewish peddlers established their own self-defense organizations.[13] Resolute before the signs and shouts that proclaimed "no beggars or peddlers allowed," they continued to "handle" and to bargain, as one observer noted, since profit was their only objective.[14] The habit of acquisitiveness was part of their heritage; it was the legacy of oppression they brought with them. Jews have been portrayed the world over, the New York *Sunday Dispatch* wrote in 1854, as usurers, "as a nation treacherous, as a nation so fond of money that it would sell its own mother and its own soul for a dime."[15] Little else could be expected from a people descendent from the traitor Judas, who prostituted his conscience for thirty pieces of coin.

Several early literary treatments expounded upon this theme. James Fenimore Cooper in his 1831 novel *The Bravo: A Tale* depicts Jews as usurers whose shrewdness has enabled them to survive under oppression, but he hardly makes them likeable or sympathetic characters. Mutual hostility and suspicion mark the relationship of Christian and Jew in this society.[16] A no less conventional treatment is found in author, editor, diplomat Theodore S. Fay's widely read *Sidney Clifton* (1839). Fay's Jewish character, Wall Street moneylender Isaac Samuel, is described with most of the grotesque features of the stereotype. He is "a striking illustration of the fearful inroads that ironhearted avarice makes upon the frame and spirit of its worshipers."[17]

At least two of the novels of the phenomenally popular Mrs. E.-D.E.N. Southworth contain the exploiting Jew who vents his greed on unsuspecting Christians.[18] Similarly, the frontier novelist J.B. Jones, in *Border War* (1859), develops the theme of gentile-Jewish conflict made particularly acute because of the latter's avidity. In this novel about the impending Civil War, Sargeant Jack Bim confronts the "bill-broking, sharpfaced, screwflint Jew, Solomon Mouser," who exploits the sufferings and misfortunes of others for financial gain.[19] Bim represents the "true" American who will fight for his convictions, and Mouser epitomizes the sneaky, parasitic Jew who has little concern for ideals and is interested only in his usurious rate of return. Bim, who was cheated by Mouser, remarks on one occasion: "You nosed out my treasure just as naturally as a buzzard finds carrion. Not to eat, like the sensible buzzard, but to watch and starve over for others. What a fool you are, old Tuppenny! You can lie in rags all your life and hug a pile of gold, and when you die you can't even take it to the devil with you."[20]

If evidence were lacking of the almost uncritical projection of the anti-Semitic portrait, one could adduce the play *The World's Own* (1857), by Boston bluestocking and abolitionist Julia Ward Howe. This melodramatic drama, set in early nineteenth-century Piedmont Italy, is a tale of seduction and revenge. The seduced Leonora hires a Gypsy Zingara and the moneylender Jacob to kidnap the vitiator, Count Lothair's child. The Jew throughout threatens ruin to all unless they return borrowed money. "The moneylenders press hard. These vultures circle in the van of ruin, and fan it onward with their eager wings."[21] Even the social conscience of a Julia Howe was blind to the prejudice inherent in the use of this imagery.

The American Civil War added new fuel to these charges when Jews were accused of selfishly exploiting the conflict and of attempting to destroy the national credit for their own materialistic purposes. It was alleged by Senator Henry Wilson of Massachusetts and Generals Benjamin Butler, William T. Sherman, and Ulysses S. Grant, as well as others, that Jews were engaged in profiteering during the war; that they were responsible for the speculation in gold; that they were supplying the South with goods, thus demonstrating their concern for profits over patriotism; that they were engaged in passing counterfeit money; that they fed the inflation by charging outrageous prices; that they were driving well-established Christian firms out of business by using unfair competitive methods and generally were parasites who thrived on the misery of others. Henry Wilson thus described the conflict as a contest between the "curbstone Jew Broker" and his like, men who "fatten upon public calamity," and the "productive, toiling men of the country."[22] Similarly, Sherman warned against the swarm of Jews who "smuggle powder, pistols, percussion-caps" and who will "overrun us" unless impeded.[23] And, of course, there is the infamous Grant General Order Number 11 of December 17, 1862, which expelled all

Jews from the Department of the Tennessee for "violating every regula-
tion of trade established by the Treasury Department."[24] *Harper's
Weekly* took up the campaign and in an August 1863 article by the
"Lounger," criticized the Jew for his alleged predilection for exploitative economics that has blinded him from higher moral and social
considerations.

You are a German and a Jew, and you have come to make your living in a
foreign land, of which Christianity is the professed religion. You have no
native, no political, no religious sympathy with this country. You are here
solely to make money, and your only wish is to make money as fast as
possible.... If quiet can be preserved by massacring the negroes, amen; you
want money, and money requires quiet. If things can be kept still by slaughter-
ing Irishmen, you cheerfully agree.... You are the material out of which
despotisms are made.... The country you left did not regret your coming away;
the country in which you trade will not mourn your departure.[25]

The *New York Tribune,* the *Herald,* the *New York Dispatch,* and the
Detroit Commercial Advertiser were only a few of the newspapers that
also accused the Jew of illegal speculation. As one newspaper said:
These "hooked nose wretches speculate on disasters and a battle lost to
our army is chuckled over by them, as it puts money in their purse."[26]
There was as little truth in this charge as in any other blanket generalization, but it helped to fix in the mind of the reader the myth of the
grasping, materialistic Jew.

Perhaps nothing highlighted this particular personification more
vividly than the dime novels that featured Jewish characters. It must be
emphasized that many Americans were only exposed in their reading
experience to the pulp press and dime novels and, consequently these
mediums must have had a particularly important impact on shaping
attitudes and ideas. As was previously mentioned, Jews invariably
appear therein as secondhand clothing dealers and pawnbrokers, and
their money-centered personalities complement their dialectal speech
and grotesque physiognomies. They are *never* described as producers,
contributors to the economy, or even as workers. Also of some interest
is the recurrent theme of the Jew who is not what he seems to be at first
sight. The appearance he presents is merely a facade designed to hide a
very different reality; the Jew's true nature therefore emerges as something mysterious and incomprehensible. This assumption enabled the

American to invest the Jew with the wildest attributes of his own fantasy world and to give vent to an imagination that often lent credence to the twaddle being spread by the ignorant or the malicious.

It makes little difference whether we look at the Molochs of Joseph Holt Ingraham, who "looked in every lineament the usurer";[27] or the Abrams, Oppenheims, and Solomons of the prolific Albert Aiken, who "always gif half as much as a thing is worth, and never charge more as five hundred per shent interest"[28] and who jackal-like hang "upon the outskirts of business... eager for... plunder";[29] or whether we examine the Isaacs and Alberts of Edward L. Wheeler, the author of the Deadwood Dick series, who exploit their clients and who are "shrewd one[s] to deal with";[30] or those "hook-nosed Israelites" narcotized by the pursuit of a "leetle puzziness"[31] who abound in the works of Prentiss Ingraham of "Buffalo Bill" fame, Gilbert Jerome, H.P. Halsey, and Jesse C. Cowdrick.[32] All these characters are greedy and, as we have seen, often dishonest misers, who cringe and plead poverty although they have achieved substantial wealth through the exploitation of human weakness and misfortune. Enamored by the prospect of gain, living off the labor and afflictions of others, there is very little to recommend them favorably. Considering the mass consumption of these cheap novels, the reiterated portrait of Jews in most of them could not fail to reinforce the traditional stereotype.

If these images were relegated only to popular literature, they could be explained away as examples of authors catering to the passions and escapist interests of the public. But the same rationalization does not apply as easily to those major novelists who also often reverted to this stereotype. Henry James, for example, wrote for an audience that accepted his prolific and often belabored prose and waded through thousands of words of descriptive character development, but yet when they came to the Jew, they found a familiar medieval figure, although this time in Victorian attire.

The Jew is a persistent figure in James's fiction. He appears in ten of twenty novels, in eight short stories, one critical essay, and several travel essays.[33] The Hebrew symbolizes basically the same areas of human experience that James explored in other literary themes—internationalism, bourgeois corruption, social stratification, genteel decline, the conflict between money and manners, and the exploitation of one human being by another for gain. James uses the Jew as a type representing swindling greed and as the factor that epitomized the decline of "proper" society. He also uses the Jew as a standard metaphor for dark and mysterious beauty. He was intrigued by unusual, foreign, or exotic visages because he believed that outward appearance actually mirrored inner personalities. When depicting the Jew, he depends on the conventional description that includes dark hair and eyes, short stature, large grotesque nose, ostentatious dress, and nervous gesticulation: the composite picture that underlines the Jew's foreignness and makes his intrusion into society such an obvious affront.

Henry James made his home in England after 1876, but he continued to express, even while abroad, the anxieties and sentiments of the declining "Brahmin" social class in America and his literary finger always monitored the pulse of that class. There was, especially in the upper strata of society known to the James family in England, as well as among his friends James Russell Lowell, Henry Adams, Edith Wharton, and John Jay Chapman residing in the United States, a fairly general bias against the trading class and a fear that the continuing influx of all immigrants and particularly the aggressive materialistic Jew might threaten the economic standards of the English and American workers and dilute the original Anglo-Saxon stock. Herman Melville's epic poem "Clarel" (1876) reflects an early association of the Jew with these fears.

Old ballads sing
Fair Christian children crucified
By impious Jews; you've heard the thing:
Yes, fable: but there's truth hard by:
How many Hughs of Lincoln, say,
Does Mammon in his mills, today,
Crook, if he does not crucify?[34]

One of the first expressions of this viewpoint in James appears in an early short story, "Impressions of a Cousin" (1884). The Jews therein are either bourgeois, involved in a blind race for wealth, pseudo-artistic, or generally characterized by a vulgar commercial instinct. James created in Caliph the Rothschild stereotype of government influence, lavishness, and parvenu social presence. James sees the ostentatiousness of the business magnate in terms of oriental opulence and this coincides with his idea of the Jew as a mysterious product of Mediterranean civilization and as a dangerous intruder and corruptor of society.

He is forty years old, large and stout, may even be pronounced fat; and there is something about him that I don't know how to describe except by calling it a certain richness.... I don't think he looks like a gentleman; he is something apart from all that. If he is not a gentleman, he is not in the least a bourgeois— neither is he of the Bohemian type. In short, as I say, he is a Jew; and Jews of the upper class have a style of their own.... To say that he has no moral sense is nothing. I have seen other people with no moral sense; but I have seen no one with that impudence, that cynicism, that remorseless cruelty.[35]

The Jew as materialist and vulgar upstart is present in other James stories. Tourists, generally, are anathema to him. He refers to them throughout his fiction as "barbarians" and "invaders" who disturb the peace of gentlefolk in their holiday retreats. Jewish tourists particularly elicit his antipathy for the bounder. In "Glasses" (1896), James describes a scene at Folkestones, a fashionable English resort, as follows: "There were thousands of little chairs and almost as many little Jews; and there was music in an open rotunda, over which the little Jews wagged their big noses."[36]

Although the parvenu Jew offers a repugnant image, the commercial Jew intoxicated by wealth is treated with even less kindness. Jewish sharpers invade the sanctity of the great house in *The Spoils of Poynton* (1897). Mrs. Gereth's economic and social decline is symbolized by the threatened repossession, by Jewish moneylenders, of her precious art collection. The Gereths "had saved on lots of things in life, and there were lots of things they hadn't had at all, but they had had in every corner of Europe their swing among the demons of Jews."[37] Similarly, in *The Awkward Age* (1899), Jews are rich, vulgar, and most often moneylenders. Harold Brookenham, discussing his lack of business acumen, salves his conscience by emphasizing that he never had to resort to the business ethics used by "the Jews." Better to be unsuccessful and genteel than crude and Semitic.[38] In the story "In the Cage" (1898), James refers to Jews who are wealthy, but who are immoral.[39] In *What Maisie Knew* (1897), he presents two commercial Jews, Mr. Perriam and Mr. Tischbein, who are adulterers and who pose a threat to the abused child Maisie. Perriam possesses much the same oriental opulence of Mr. Caliph. He "wore on the hand that pulled his moustache a diamond of dazzling lustre, in consequence of which and of his general weight and mystery our young lady [Maisie] observed on his departure that if he had only had a turban he would have been quite her idea of a heathen Turk.''[40] James sarcastically refers in ''The Pupil'' (1891) to an unruly mob as being ''as good-natured as Jews out the doors of clothing-shops''[41] and he presents Gutermann-Suess (sweet good man) in *The Golden Bowl* (1905) as a satire for a commercial Jew who could neither be good nor sweet.[42] All these characters—Caliph, Perriam, Tischbein, and the stockbrokers, shopkeepers, and money-lenders who appear in ''Professor Fargo'' (1874),[43] ''Adina'' (1874),[44] ''Covering End'' (1898),[45] and ''The Story In It'' (1902),[46] to name but a few—are unmitigatedly corrupted by their obsession with wealth and are made evil by it. In James, the Jew is always the exploiter, never the exploited, regardless of whether he covets money, social position, his neighbor's wife, or even elementary human liberty. He is the ultimate symbol for predatoriness and dissoluteness. As William D. Howels's Mrs. Lapham remarks in another context: ''They've all got... money,'' but they don't know how to use it.[47]

Although James marks the zenith of sophisticated anti-Semitism in American fiction of the century, others were less refined in their anti-Jewish treatments.[48] One of the worst practitioners was Julian Hawthorne, son of the great writer. Jews make brief appearances in several of his novels. In *Beatrix Randolph* (1884), Hawthorne introduces a theater impresario, Moses Inigo. His face ''which was ruddy and broad, with a large nose and a thick mouth, indicated course... shrewdness, tempered by irritability.''[49] Hawthorne has him bemoan his poverty when in reality he is quite wealthy. Complaining that the actors he sponsors earn huge sums, Inigo adds: ''And here am I, a poor man today, and they rolling in riches!'' Another character responds: ''Yes, for a poor and virtuous man you've done pretty well.''[50]

In an earlier novel, *Sebastian Strome* (1880), the story centers on the heiress Mary Dene, who is courted by both Strome and Selim Fawley, the son of a Jewish banker. Selim's father adheres to the basest pecuniary values. ''A true friend,'' he advises his son on one occasion, ''is the man that owesh you money on good security, or money'sh worth!... There's two times when I know I can trust a man: when I can beggar him, and when I can shame him; and shaming is twenty per cent better than beggaring any day.''[51]

A similarly crude portrait is presented in the works of Francis M. Crawford, one of the most successful novelists of the late nineteenth century, who in his day was an even greater celebrity than James. In *A Roman Singer* (1894), he develops his version of the Wandering Jew. Baron Ahasuerus Benoni is described as a tall, thin, bearded old fop with a mystifying, almost ageless, youthful complexion, eagle nose, and oriental eyes. Benoni is a master violinist, a skilled healer, and a successful banker. Despite his great talents to do good, he prefers the life of pleasure and consumption. "Pleasure and money, money and pleasure" are the only things "in this world worth having."[52]

A Jewish infatuation with the bon marché is also central to Crawford's *A Cigarette-Maker's Romance* (1893). He describes his view of Jewish pawnbrokers in Munich. A man and a woman perform their tasks with oily efficiency and with a sinister sense of pleasure. "Either one of them would have undertaken to name the precise pawning value of anything on earth and, possibly, of most things in heaven, provided that the universe were [sic] brought piecemeal to their counter."[53]

A more pernicious image is developed in *The Witch of Prague: A Fantastic Tale* (1891). The Jews of this city are set forth as

crooked, bearded, filthy, vulture-eyed... hook-nosed and looselipped,... a writhing mass of humanity, intoxicated by the smell of gold, mad for its possession, half hysteric with the fear of losing it, timid, yet dangerous, poisoned to the core by the sweet sting of money, terrible in intelligence, vile in heart, contemptible in body, irresistible in the unity of their greed.[54]

His portrait of the Prague ghetto is hardly an improvement. He describes this social prison as an area wherein the Israelite "directs great enterprises and sets in motion huge financial schemes," and where he "sits, as a great spider in the midst of a dark web, dominating the whole capital with his eagle's glance and weaving the destiny of the Bohemian people to suit his intricate speculation."[55] Shades of a conspiracy theory that became more popular as the decade progressed, Crawford's Jews combine a monetary urge with a desire to control, to pose a threat to Christian dominance.

Equally perverse are the Jews in George Gossip's anti-Semitic novel *The Jew of Chamant* (1898). Gossip, in the preface, advises the reader what his intentions are. "My object in the present work is to paint the rich Jew in his true colors, as the enemy of society."[56] He does this through his main character, the French Jew Lefevre, who is committed to the infiltration and destruction of the Gallic polity.

Utterly devoid of moral sense, his was the most

sordid, contemptible nature conceivable.... Unscrupulous, selfish, vicious, mean, avaricious and depraved, with only one aim or object in life, i.e., the acquisition of wealth.... He was a past master of fraud and finance; both being synonymous from his point of view, as in fact from that of all Israelites—a brute in human form—the very incarnation of greed, lust and rascality.[57]

Representing the fictional marriage of Barabas and Shylock, Lefevre epitomizes the possible consequences of Jewish rapacity.

Less traitorous but nevertheless tainted by an acute materialistic disposition are the Jews in the works of Evelyn Johnson, Clyde Fitch, Hall Caine, Richard Henry Savage, and E.S. March, all popular writers of the period. Little Pansey, in Johnson's *An Errand Girl: A Romance of New York Life* (1889), pays a maximum price for the calico she purchases from a "crafty Jew," but when it is her turn to sell, she is cheated by another greedy Hebrew.[58] Mr. Abrahams, in Fitch's well-received play *Beau Brummell* (1890),[59] which was revived several times, is depicted as "the typical Jew money lender," exaggerated in dress and manner.[60] He advances money to Brummell, the dissipate prince of dandies, who has great difficulty in paying it back. Abrahams becomes overwrought at the possibility of delay and remarks in typical fashion: "I will have my money. I will have my money."[61]

A more articulate expression of this desire is made by the "Shylock of Amsterdam" in E.S. March's *A Stumbler in Wide Shoes* (1896). "I like the element of chance in everything," he soliloquizes. "To consider the law of chances, to stake my opinion on the value of a particular work or gem, to acquire it and wait to see if I have rightly judged, this gives to my mind an interest.... We Jews are merchants born; we do not strive to be rich only; it is not wealth, but the pleasure of acquiring, which fascinates us."[62] Israel Ben Olliel, of Hall Caine's *The Scapegoat* (1891), is the "oriental" Shylock who has the ability of "turning the very air itself into money."[63] The story is set in Morocco, and Israel is the financial adviser to the sultan. He is portrayed as a "self-centered and silent man absorbed in getting and spending, always taking care to have much of the one, and no more than he could help of the other."[64] The prolific Richard Henry Savage, who like F. Marion Crawford wrote romantic adventure novels set in exotic locales, in *The White Lady of Khaminavatka* (1898), presents Russian Jews this time as the "cringing, cajoling, and insinuating" vultures "who trafficked in usury and, with glib cunning, fattened upon the toil of the flaxen-haired, thick-headed

Russian peasantry.'"[65] Their peculiar ability to garner wealth is an inherited trait and is passed on through the generations. Even Jewish children, in his *Delilah of Harlem* (1893), are infected by this "Judaic" business interest.[66]

A more forthright example of this racist image is found in Frank Norris's *McTeague* (1899), one of the most anti-Semitic portrayals in American fiction. He included among his nastiest characters Zerkow, the rag-picking and scavenging Polish Jew who is consumed by petty greed. Zerkow is introduced as follows:

> He had the thin, eager catlike lips of the covetous; eyes that had grown keen as those of a lynx from long searching amid muck and debris; and clawlike, prehensile fingers—the fingers of a man who accumulates, but never disburses. It was impossible to look at Zerkow and not know instantly that greed— inordinate, insatiable greed—was the dominant passion of the man. He was the Man with the Rake, groping hourly in the muck heap of the city for gold, for gold, for gold. It was his dream, his passion; at every instant he seemed to feel the generous solid weight of the crude fat metal in his palms.[67]

It was the opportunity of hearing about great wealth, not even possessing it, that led him to wed Maria Macapa, an old Mexican cleaning woman. She used to tell Zerkow about the gold dishes her family owned long in the past and the Polish Jew would relish with delight over the story. It became an obsession with him, a mania. Enveloped by a ravenous avidity and blinded by the illusory treasure, he murdered Maria in a fit of passion. He then committed suicide by drowning himself, but even in death he held to those symbolic possessions that had shaped his life and that proved to be the cause of his demise. "Clutched in both his hands was a sack full of old rusty pans, tin dishes—fully a hundred of them—tin cans, and iron knives and forks, collected from some dump heap."[68] He ended his life, where he began it, surrounded by the offal of society.

By 1900 Jewish stereotypes had become more clearly delineated and the latent conflict between favorable and unfavorable attitudes came visibly into the open. Occupationally, the Jew is more distinctive than ever. He has by then been identified as a peddler, old clothes dealer, pawnbroker, and a nascent entrepreneur. The three-ball sign and the title "uncle" were synonymous with him. His appearance was also familiar, lumbering with his cumbersome pack, or pushing a cart, or hawking before a store draped with secondhand garments. His clothes were either old and shabby or ludicrously new and ostentatious. His physiognomy was stamped with the Jewish hooked nose trademark and was bearded and he spoke with the crudely heavy vaudeville accent, accentuating "monish." Finally, he was invariably concerned with wealth and was stingy and grasping. The noted historian Paul Leicester Ford's *Janice Meredith* (1899), a Revolutionary war novel, exploits the stereotype for "comic" relief. In a tavern, the protagonist John Brereton wants to buy a razor. A Jewish peddler conveniently has one for sale. "You've a sharper to deal with now," says one of the customers. "Now ye'll need no razor ter be shaved," says another. Opper produces the utensil and claims it is made from "der besd of steel," to which a patron replies: "You can trust Opper to know pretty much everything 'bout steals. It's been his business for twenty years!"[69] Even a likable individual, Old Isaacs, in the popular Charles Blaney novel and play *Old Isaacs from the Bowery* (1900), who essentially is a kind and generous character, tells his daughter: "Vhy I vould trust you mit my life, Rachel. But vid mein money, ach dot vas different."[70]

The question remains, why these negative identifications? Many of these writers used the Jew as a symbol for the rapacity and inhumanity of modern industrial society. The Jew epitomized, in his blind pursuit of wealth and in his sharp business practices, the weaknesses of an aggressive capitalism that seemed to be propelling America to the brink of the moral precipice. These writers resented the onrushing commercialism of Gilded Age America. They had a long tradition of patrician hostility to "trading" and petty bourgeois greed and a strong strain of anti-urbanism. The Jew, because of his immemorial association with the clamor of the Temple money changers, became a likely target to blame for these developments.

There is, of course, another side to this issue. In cartoons and in a good deal of middle-class opinion, the Jew became identified as the quintessential materialistic parvenu glittering with conspicuous and vulgar jewelry and clothes, attracting attention by aggressive behavior, and always forcing his way into society that was above him. The parvenu stereotype held up a distorted mirror to the immigrants' foreignness and cultural limitations. However, if the large Eastern cities were becoming uninhabitable and if America was indeed abusing the privileges of wealth, the fault lay less with the depressed social and cultural standards the immigrants brought with them than with the example set by those who prided themselves on their Anglo-Saxon heritage. Capitalism, Werner Sombart notwithstanding, was certainly not conceived in the ghettos of Europe or in the Pale of Settlement but rather was born in the mind's eye of ambitious men who harnessed the churning wheel and the steam-propelled engine.[71] Although it is probably true that some Jews who after centuries of "ghetto" life in Europe were experiencing wealth for the first time and consequently were more or less uncultivated, loud, and pushy, the nineteenth century in fact saw gentile parvenudom on an unexampled scale. Among the ranks of the upstarts, Jews were by no means the most materialistic or ostentatious. The Newport millionaires who entertained with "monkey dinners" and "black pearl" dinners were not Jews; Jews were not invited to the great fêtes that cluttered the social calendar; the Bradley-Martins and James Hazen Hyde were not Jewish. No Jew went about Europe with the boisterous abandon of a "Bet-you-a-million" Gates, the Chicago magnate. No doubt there were some who endeavored to shine socially by showing off their wealth, but who among them eclipsed the extravagances of Diamond Jim Brady and Jim Fisk? Image once again did not correspond to reality.

Literature had no monopoly on these stereotypes. The Jews' alleged gross materialism afforded many individuals with a convenient explanation of what was ailing America. An early doggerel describing the emergence of Wall Street expressed these feelings as follows: It is

now a street—where brokers meet,
Where Bankers reign and Hebrews cheat,
A Street, too—dearly known to all, and by the
hard-press'd first called Wall.
The Israelitish hosts bowed down
Before a senseless, golden calf;
As you may see a circus clown
Kiss the tanbark or the chaff;
Symbolic that of Wall Street—tastes,
Love of money, love of beasts.[72]

A popular college song in the 1880s gave its interpretation of the inseparable link between a Jew and business. "My name is Solomon Levi/ At my store on Salem Street/ That's where you'll buy your

coats and vests/ And ev'rything that's neat; I've second handed Ulster-
ettes/ And ev'rything that's fine/ For all the boys, they trade with me
at hundred and forty-nine.''[73] Coney Island, debased by the dialectal
speech of the peddler, was celebrated by another poetaster in 1880.[74]

On ev'ry path by almost every turn,
Industrious Israelites a living 'earn!
By selling colored specs to screen the eyes
Which would not serve an idiot to disguise.
Purchase by all means—yellow, green and blue
You and one member of a useful crew;
He will not work; he neither starves, nor begs
But peddles healing-salve for wooden legs.[75]

Even old Shylock himself was transformed in 1883 into a pack-
carrying itinerant selling the elusive "pargain" by Richard Harris Bar-
ham, the noted punster. Like his namesake, however, his materialistic
instincts are eclipsed by his desire for revenge. "Just fancy the gleam of
the eye of the Jew, as he sharpen'd his knife on the sole of his shoe.
From the toe to the heel, and grasping the steel/ With a business like
air was beginning to feel/ Whereabouts he should cut, as a butcher
would veal.''[76]

The popular humor sheets and graphic weeklies of the late nineteenth
and early twentieth centuries that achieved wide circulation often relied
on similar depictions in their search for commercial success. One of the
most revealing repositories of this emerging anti-Semitic stereotype
during the years 1885–1905 was the New York German-American
humor magazine *Puck*. It had particularly harsh words to say about the
degenerate Jewish middleman who operates on the periphery of the
economy and who prospers not by hard work or skill, like the Christians
around him, but by shifting, exploiting, and subterfuge. The secret of
his success is not the money he controls, but rather his peculiar talent to
reap the benefits of cupidity. The Jew who frequents the pages of *Puck*
is the inveterate materialist who strives his entire life for pecuniary
advantage, receives his greatest satisfaction from a particularly profitable business transaction, and looks out upon the world with cash-
register eyes riveted to the possibilities of a quick profit. Thus *Puck* tells
of a Mr. Isaacs who is resigned to his impending death since "dere vas
no moneys in der cloding peesiness nowatays.'' What else is there to

live for? Or then there is Mr. Hochstein who decides to punish his son
by the cruelest method he can devise. "I vos going to put him on der
gounter and make him vatch me vile I scharge der next gustomer only
six per cent." In the same spirit, Isaacs asks Cohenstein whether the
Anglo-Saxons will rule the earth. "Vell mey be dey mighd, but dot
von't brevent der Hebrews from owning id!"[77]

Two magazines that drew a similar stereotype were *Tid-Bits,* which
changed its title to *Time* in June 1888 and eventually merged with
Munsey's Weekly in 1890, and *Texas Siftings.* Basically, they were less
politically oriented than *Puck* and were more exclusively concerned
with comedy for comedy's sake; but that little affected their position on
immigrant groups and little modified their caustic commentary on Jews.
Thus *Tid-Bits* writes of the greedy Mr. Isaacstein who remarks: "Ach,
Sir, you rentered my poy a Goot Service, Sir, in Pulling Him out of De
Vater, Und I shall Nefer Forget It, Sir, Nefer.... Did you know mine
poy Had on Vun of Mine Twenty-Five Dollar Suits?"[78] Or *Time* tells of
Mr. Eisenstein who had a hard-luck day even though he received news
of a $20,000 inheritance. "Dey scharge me extra postage on dot letter. I
vas out zwei cents." In a more serious vein, *Time* describes Jews as
possessing "a reputation of greed second to none," whose mission in
life "is to advance the smallest possible amount of money on the largest
possible value."[79]

Another major source of these negative images was *Judge,* which
skillfully relied on the cartoon, as well as sarcasm, to make its social
commentaries. Like the other graphic weeklies, it emphasized the dangers inherent in the growing commercialization of society and it pointed
to the disintegration of moral values that this headlong race for wealth
left as an unfortunate by-product. Jews, historically linked with the evils
of excessive materialism, became a likely target for its caustic criticisms. Thus *Judge* writes in 1881: "Our Israelite friends have sometimes been accused of lugging the idea of money into every sort of
conversation. This is not always the case. In front of a Lexington
Avenue residence, one evening this week, a young man said tenderly to
his girl: 'Well, we are at last enkaget. And it is so sweet that I do not
even look at the cost!'" The Jewish concern with money is evidenced in
another gibe. Rubenstein, shedding tears of grief, explains the source of
his suffering to Moses. "S'elp me gracious, Moses, I lose more as
feefty tollar yesterday. Dot son Yacob of Mein, he vas tress himself up

in dot feefty tollar show suit, vot hangs in de window, und goes on dot oxgursion und gets drount.'' Similarly, Levi responds after hearing of his son's accidental death, ''Oh, bless dot poy! He had a goot head on him. He knows his fader could get damages. He alvays had an eye fer pizness.''[80] Troubled by the extremes of wealth and poverty in America made acute by immigration and urbanization and concerned with the misuse of that wealth, *Judge* linked the growth of Jewish prosperity to unsettled economic conditions and seized upon an anti-Semitic explanation—Jewish materialism—to account for it.

A parallel type of humor was used by the popular almanacs published by the Ayers and Hostetter Companies. James Harvey Young, in his study of the patent medicine trade in America, *The Toadstool Millionaires,* argues that these almanacs ''may have helped form social attitudes in the American grass-roots mind of the late nineteenth century.'' The humor presented in these almanacs probably reflected the prejudices of the masses to whom they were directed, ''for certainly the patent medicine proprietors... would hardly have repeated in issue after issue stereotypes offensive to the main body of their potential customers....'' Other ethnic groups were caricatured, but Young believes these stereotypes did not have ''the bitterness displayed in the sketching of the Jew. Tramps, peddlers, or pawnbrokers, Jews were always after money and slow to yield it up....'' Caricatures supporting this assessment can be found in *Hostetter's Illustrated.* As an example, when a crab grabs hold of Mr. Hermbetter's toe as he is swimming, he urges his wife, despite the pain, not to pull it off since ''dey vos vort a dollar a dozen in Nye Yorick.''[81]

This stereotype, popularized by the humor sheets of the period, was also part of the vocabulary of intellectuals and appeared in the press. In fact, we begin to discern a shift in the source of this image from the popular mediums that predominated in the Gilded Age to the more sophisticated journalistic and intellectual voices that began to project it in the Progressive Era. The Philadelphia *Evening Telegraph,* in 1872 for example, described the Jew as ''perhaps more inoculated with the love of money-getting than is the average Christian, and hence a little keener and closer in his business transactions.''[82] *The New York Times*, evaluating reports of persecution of Romanian Jews in the 1870s, saw the issue in terms of greed. '''Maudlin sympathy' had been wasted on the Jew who was... non-producing; he earns and hoards, but he does not spend.'' They are ''inferior socially and morally'' and are ''pariahs who... eat up the substance of a country like a swarm of locusts.''[83] About the same time, the Chicago *Post* was editorially denouncing the Polish Jew as ''speculative, carping, ugly, and mean,'' and thoroughly undesirable as citizens either in this country or any other.[84] A decade later, the Fall River, Massachusetts, *Labor Standard* harshly criticized the Jewish merchants in the town for oppressing their Christian employees by refusing a shorter work day. It is a disgrace, they advised, that these ''hoggish Jews who have neither sympathy nor sentiment with anything but a dollar'' shall wreak their selfish interests on the welfare of others. They should be taught forcefully if necessary that ''they will not gain anything by this indecent rush for their pound of flesh.''[85] The *Illustrated American* in 1890 described the Jews who bargained and haggled over pennies on New York's lower East Side as a ''great congregation of malodorous creatures,'' endowed with extraordinary vitality who are moved by a greed that ''is expressed in every motion of their unclean, nervous, clutching fingers.''[86] *The Quarterly Sentinel* noted in 1899 that ''rapacity is a passion, which has become the Jew's second nature.... The lust for gain is so strongly rooted in his organism, that it extinguishes every other feeling, every other passion.''[87] It was the specter of Jewish greed that initiated so much negative commentary.

Goldwin Smith, the transplanted Englishman turned occasional Cornell University historian who graced the pages of British, Canadian, and American magazines with his witty and facile pen harbored an intense antipathy for Jews, based largely on his understanding of this aspect of Jewish life. Smith's aversion did not rest on any concept of racial or physical inferiority; nor was he concerned particularly with religious factors, although he did have some harsh things to say about Judaism. He objected instead to what he called Jewish *tribalism,* or unwillingness to assimilate, and to Jewish commercialism and avidity, the triumph of which over the spiritual character and aspirations of Christian communities would ring the deathknell of his nontrading class. He wrote in 1878 about medieval Jews whom he felt were as much oppressors as oppressed and probably deserved the violence directed at them because ''they were cruel usurers, eating the people as if it were bread, and at once agents and partners of royal and feudal extortion.''[88] He was grateful for ancient Judaism that gave the world its first glimpse of spirituality and of course gave birth to Jesus Christ and Christianity. Yet he was certain that "the Judaism of the Stock Exchange... bore no moral relation whatever" to its Galilean predecessor.[89] "The intense love of gain and the addiction to the money trade are ingrained," Smith argued in 1891, "and it is probable that many generations will pass before the balance of the Hebrew intellect and character is restored by a community of pursuits with other men."[90] Nevertheless, he was confident that a solution would eventually be found. He was certain that his class would not bend its knee to the power of "Coheleth." The Jew would be taught in due time that "civilization is not to be the pedestal or the gambling table of any Self-Chosen People."[91]

Many reputable intellectuals and clergymen fell victim to a similar damaging oversimplification.[92] Social Gospelers like Washington Gladden and R. Heber Newton talked about the "over-development of mercantilism" inherent in the Jewish psyche.[93] The Reverend Chas. Deems, in the same spirit, assigned the commercialism of the Jew as the primary cause of anti-Semitism.[94] W.M. Thornton, president of the University of Virginia, remarked in 1890 that Jews "are immersed in business and money-getting. They look at all questions from the commercial side." That is why they "care less for what is embraced in the term of culture than Christians who are equally well off."[95] Even Presidents J.M. Taylor of Vassar College and Charles W. Eliot of Harvard University, men of stature and erudition who were generally sympathetic to Jews, indicated some willingness to acknowledge the validity of the charge that Jewish businessmen engage in questionable practices to gain an unfair advantage.[96]

Parallel sentiments were harbored by Mark Twain who wavered between generous goodwill and latent prejudice, characteristic of the ambivalence of some of American opinion. Twain, in his essay "Concerning the Jews" (1899), which was written as a stirring denunciation of anti-Semitism, betrayed an unconscious antipathy when he asserted that Judeophobia originates in the uncanny ability of Jews to amass riches. In his efforts to refute the malicious rumors that had recently sprung up concerning the Jew, he unwittingly confirmed some of them. Christianity or fanaticism are not the cause of anti-Semitism. Jews are oppressed and disliked, Twain conjectured, because the average gentile is unable to compete successfully with them in commerce.

The Jew is a money-getter, and in getting his money he is a very serious obstruction to less capable neighbors who are on the same quest. . . . In estimating worldly values the Jew is not shallow, but deep. With precocious wisdom he found out in the morning of time that some men worship rank, some worship heroes . . . , but that they all worship money; so he made it the end and aim of his life to get it. He was at it in Egypt thirty-six centuries ago; he was at it in Rome when that Christian got persecuted by mistake for him; he has been at it ever since.[97]

This is what has generated the world's envy and mistrust and has made the Jew the recipient of its unleashed cruelty. As Finley Peter Dunne's Mr. Dooley so aptly remarked: "Tis th' histhry iv th' wurruld that th' Jews takes our watches fr'm us be tin per cint a month, an' we take thim back be means iv a Jimmy an'a piece iv lead pipe.' "[98]

Many of these accusations were also echoed by individuals who undertook to study the foreign populations firsthand, and who attempted to reform the evils associated with the urban experience. Some of these nascent social reformers, unfortunately, appealed to prurience behind a mask of outraged respectability, and nearly all of them catered to a public interested in the details of the vice, crime, and greed that festered in the "ghetto" environment. By far the most influential of the popular writers on slum life was Jacob Riis, the Dane who came to America in 1870 to become a well-known police reporter. The best received of his books, *How the Other Half Lives* (1890), and some lesser known ones, like *The Battle with the Slums* (1902), are basically journalists' sketch-books that delineate in rather sensational style the poverty, disease, and frustration that bred in the tenements and ghettos of America's cities. When describing the various immigrant groups, however, he was often quite patronizing and he displayed little sympathy or appreciation for their culture or for the social and economic factors that have consigned masses of people to live mean lives. His was not an unselfish cry for social justice, but rather a call to the propertied classes to bestir themselves before they were overwhelmed by the crime and materialism of the immigrant hordes. Consequently, he often relied upon the traditional stereotypes. "Thrift is the watchword of Jewtown," he wrote,

as of its people the world over. It is at once its strength and its fatal weakness, its cardinal virtue and its foul disgrace. Become an overmastering passion with these people who come here in droves from Eastern Europe to escape persecution,... it has enslaved them in bondage worse than that from which they fled. Money is their God. Life itself is of little value compared with even the leanest bank account.[99]

Frederick A. Bushée who studied the Russian Jews who settled in the South End of Boston in the 1890s found within them a tradition that did not recommend them well even in comparison to the hated Irish who were also the subject of stereotyping. "The occupation of the Jew is the reality of his life. He enters it heart and soul" to the exclusion of those amenities that are esteemed by society.[100] The generosity and good fellowship of the Irish contrast sharply with this Jewish trait. "Surely the modern Jew must have been the 'economic man' upon which the 'dismal science' was founded."[101] Business is his only concern and politics. charity, and social conscience are made subsidiary to it. Their "inborn love of money-making," as Jessie F. Beale and Anne Withington. two prominent Boston social workers, put it, make them the inveterate slum dwellers, for they are reluctant to abandon the bargain rents of these dismal hovels even when they have achieved wealth.[102] More lightly, Robert A. Woods, the most distinguished professional social worker in Boston, discussed "the Jewish passion for the unearned increment" as a factor in real estate operations.[103] Emily Green Balch, a scion of an old Boston family who studied under the Columbia University sociologist Franklin Giddings and eventually taught budding social workers at Wellesley College, also exhibited a blind spot when it came to Jews. In 1905 she researched the much maligned Slavic immigrants, and her book *Our Slavic Fellow Citizens* refuted many restrictionist assumptions about these Eastern Europeans. Yet when it came to the Jew, she corroborated much of what they said and likewise focused on the alleged Jewish materialistic urge. Thus she described the Jews who come from Galicia as always "alert to find every profitable penny!"[104]

In general, the image of the Jew projected by individuals like Balch and Woods was mild rather than hostile and was not meant to be part of an overt attack or to generate antipathy. It was merely a reflection of the polite anti-Semitism that had long been a part of the American tradition, particularly among the genteel classes.[105] But by the late nineteenth century, the signposts of a possible anti-Semitic future were being erected. The European Jew baiters were becoming louder and more vociferous in their denunciations and, buttressed by the "scientific" justifications of Houston Stewart Chamberlain, Joseph Arthur de Gobineau, William Z. Ripley, and Dr. Alfred P. Schultz who gave a genetic meaning to the survival of the Jew, their counterparts in the United States took up the tune. In 1885 a four-page pamphlet, "Down with the Jews," by Hananel Marks, cautioned the American people not to have business dealings with the Jews because of their Shylockean propensities. A.C. Baker, a New Jersey anti-Semite who published a hate sheet entitled *The Silhouette* in 1906–7, followed suit. "The violent and exclusive pursuit of gold has made of the Hebrew a human structure of one story and that floor a basement.... Behind his smiling mask of craft he hides a grasping, avaricious hook for the main chance. He is the 32nd degree despoiler of trade and professional methods throughout the world."[106] John C. Van Dyke, noted art historian at Rutgers College from 1891 to 1929, in *The Money-God* (1908), also placed the blame for the commercialization of society and the lowering of business standards at the doorstep of the "shark-like Jews." They are a nation of money getters, he argued, who are interested only in accumulating wealth, "sending it back to Europe, hoarding it, or slipping away with it. They have no notion whatever of helping the country, while helping themselves."[107]

Rupert Hughes, the well-known biographer of George Washington, in a book describing *The Real New York* (1904), raised the familiar cry of Jewish materialism. "Thrift becomes vicious" among the Jews in the "ghetto." "They grow wealthy without advantaging themselves of the graces which wealth can bring and ought to buy. The men, with their treasures hoarded away, look like beggars and live like vermin."[108] They represent the opposite extreme from the English and Scandinavian immigrants who came to these shores with a commitment to community, family, God, and hard work.[109] Similarly, in Theodore Dreiser's novel *The Titan* (1914), we find Isadore Platow, a wealthy furrier who is the father of the beautiful and sensuous Stephanie who attracted the protagonist Frank Cowperwood. Isadore is described with no redeeming values as "a large, meaty, oily type of man—a kind of ambling, gelatinous formula of the male, with the usual sound commercial instincts of the Jew, but with an errant philosophy which led him to believe first one thing and then another so long as neither interfered definitely with his business." The other Jews of the novel, Haeckelheimer and Gotloeb, are international bankers who are crude and uncultured, but who wield tremendous corrupting influence because of their great capital. They decide to invest in the "elefated roats of Chicawkgo," and they fund Cowperwood's monopolistic empire.[110] Dreiser was an anti-Semite who, coming from Terre Haute, probably had known few Jews when he wrote *The Titan*.

By the eve of World War I, then, the image of the Jew with an extensive "closeness in money matters" and "shrewdness," as the prominent psychologist G. Stanley Hall put it, or as a money-crazed, aggressive, and unprincipled individual, loyal only to wealth as the less generous commentators described him, was certainly widespread.[111] As the decade progressed and as the waves of immigrants once again reached these shores with the conclusion of the conflict, the shrill cry of Jew baiting fed by the fuels of postwar xenophobia took on added significance. Many critics saw the possibility of enacting total restriction, and they quickened the production of their scurrilous accusations to help make this a reality. G. Frank Lydston, a Missouri physician, published a book, *That Bogey Man the Jew* (1921), that contributed to this nativist crusade. What particularly offended him about these people was his conviction that "every Jew is a Shylock—that the Jew lives, eats, drinks, and thinks money—money, nothing but money."[112] Literary critic and biographer Ralph Boas, writing in the prestigious *Atlantic Monthly* in 1921, although more tempered in his remarks, also pointed to Jews and their contribution to the headlong commercialization of society, both of which he was unhappy about. They have introduced into the business ethic "chicanery," "cutthroat competition," "pettiness," and "reaction."[113] Everything they touch is degraded. The theater, movie, and clothing industries are controlled by their insatiable passion for wealth. All artistic standards have been compromised on the font of profit. "It is the bald commercialism of the whole business that is so discouraging," he maintained, epitomized by New York City itself with its "meretricious glitter, its premium upon material success..., its boastfulness, its suspicious and sophisticated isolation."[114]

Kenneth Roberts, the best-selling novelist, expressed a similar sentiment in 1922. Jews emigrate not because of oppression or penury in Europe—that has always been part of their experience—but because these "long-whiskered Galician grandfathers... still hope to choke a few diamond lavalieres out of American hens before they leave this vale of tears."[115] They are not accustomed to hard work and live by their wits alone and, consequently, constitute one of the most "undesirable" races of people that have ever crowded into America's cities.[116] If the Jew engages in any labor at all, "he is either a usurer, a peddler, a liquor-dealer, a... food profiteer, or a small shopkeeper." They are "human parasites" who live on other individuals "by means which too often are underhanded."[117] That is why they are objectionable and should be excluded, as Clinton Burr the historian argued, before they manage to break down American institutions and destroy honorable business methods. "It is a matter of debate whether the business trickery of these lower class elements is the cause or the result of centuries of class or religious persecution. But the fact is that this trait has become so ingrained that one may doubt whether it could be eradicated for generations. Many are, or always have been devoid of any sense of obligation to the community that shelters them."[118] They have only one allegiance, and that is to the prospect of gain. All else is merely chaff to be discarded once the glittering kernel has been harvested.

This view of vitiating Jewish economics is present also in several of the early William Faulkner novels. In the beginning of Faulkner's first novel, *Soldiers' Pay* (1926), we meet a salesman named Schluss who says to some returning soldiers of World War I: "I would have liked to fought by your side, see. But someone got to look out for business while the boys are gone."[119] In his second book, *Mosquitoes* (1927), another sad-eyed Jewish salesman is made to remark: "You can't ignore money.... It took my people to teach the world that."[120] Faulkner does not use this major character's name, calling him "the Semitic man" and "fat Jew." It is as if this anonymous entity—the Jew—represents something mysterious and pernicious that has infiltrated into American society. When his surname is finally disclosed towards the end of the novel as Kaufmann, the reader is informed that his grandfather came to the South during the Civil War, along with the rest of the carpetbaggers, to make money illegally by exploiting the defeated Confederates.[121] Other anti-Jewish characterizations can be found in later novels like *Sanctuary* (1930), *The Sound and the Fury* (1929), and in short stories like "Death Drag."[122]

This evaluation of the Jewish personality, developed in literature and further explored by intellectuals and social commentators, lent credence in the United States to a timeworn stereotype that has been associated with the Jew since the early Middle Ages. It contributed to his difficulties in medieval Europe and it did little to alleviate suspicion and envy in America. Prejudice against the country's latecomers had become habitual by the turn of the century and Jews took their place with the Irish, Italian, Chinese, and so forth on the list of those who were maligned. So the Italian murdered, the Irishman drank, the Chinaman smoked opium, and the Jew bargained and connived. Yet the fact that the Jew emerged as an exploiting economic functionary consumed by greed who would not work, but thrived off the labor of others as the middleman par excellence, was particularly unfortunate since many Americans were traditionally suspicious of the financial wizard and idealized instead productive labor as the very key to their successful experiment in democracy. The Jewish peddler, "old clo'" merchant, pawnbroker, Broadway entrepreneur, and Wall Street speculator seemed to be operating at cross-purposes with this ideal. Willing to take unfair advantage of Christian customers and competitors, they were projected in the era of mass immigration as an unsettling and unfortunate factor in the economy. In fact, the phrase "to Jew" came to represent these sharp business practices that the Hebrew had ostensibly mastered over the centuries. For more than fifty years *Roget's Thesaurus* thus gave sanction to the use of the word "Jew" as a synonym for usurer, extortioner, cunning, lickpenny, harpy, schemer, craft, and shifty.[123] The *Encyclopaedia Britannica* lent the weight of its scholarly reputation to this stereotype in 1922 when it described the Eastern European Jew as "essentially a business or commercial man, but rarely a producer. He is usually a middleman or intermediary."[124] Even American children were exposed to this degrading depiction in the fairy tales they read. This extract from *Mother Goose*, for example, was not removed until the late 1930s.

Jack sold his egg
to a rogue of a Jew
Who cheated him out
of half of his due.
The Jew got his goose,
Which he vowed he would kill,
Resolving at once
His pockets to fill.[125]

There seemed to be no area untouched by the shadow of misrepresentation. In this development of the living xenophobia, Jews became "figures" merely, generalized and compartmentalized, stripped of their uniqueness and depersonalized to fit the stereotyped roles expected of them. As one individual expressed it: "They ain't folks, they're nothin' but a parcel of images."[126] Often these were tinged by a less than judicious application of the truth. The fact that no major anti-Semitic movement was occasioned by this stereotype is a function of the more tolerant traditions of the United States, the ambivalence mentioned above, the unobstructed sway of the capitalist way of life, the fact that Americans respect success, and the presence here of great religious, ethnic, and racial diversity, meaning that Jews did not stand out, as in Europe, as a solitary body of nonconformists. Since the fire of American nationalists was scattered among many adversaries, no one minority group bore the brunt of the attack. Hatred of Catholics, of Chinese, of the new immigration as a whole, overshadowed specifically anti-Jewish agitation. Nevertheless, a good deal of distinctively anti-Semitic sentiment also emerged and the fact that it did not flare into mass violence does not lessen the potential dangers attendant to this imagery.

NOTES

1. In 1856 Hawthorne was a guest at a formal dinner given by David Solomons, Lord Mayor of London. The excerpt is his description of the mayor's brother. Nathaniel Hawthorne, *The English Notebooks,* ed. Randall Stewart (London: Oxford University Press, 1941), p. 321.

2. Charles Y. Glock and Rodney Stark, *Christian Beliefs and Anti-Semitism* (New York: Harper & Row, 1966); Edgar Rosenberg, *From Shylock to Svengali: Jewish Stereotypes in English Fiction* (Stanford: Stanford University Press, 1960).

3. Edward H. Flannery, *The Anguish of the Jews* (New York: Macmillan, 1965), pp. 152–53.

4. The long list would include Charles Dickens' *Oliver Twist,* Anthony Trollope's *The Way We Live Now,* Edward Bulwer-Lytton's *My Novel,* George DuMaurier's *Trilby,* Maurice Donnay's *The Return from Jerusalem,* Albert Guinon's *Decadence,* Emile Zola's *L'argent,* Guy de Maupassant's *Mont Oriol,* and Paul Bourget's *Cosmopolis,* to name only a few (Rosenberg, *From Shylock to Svengali; M.J. Landa, The Jew in Drama,* [Port Washington, New York: Kennikat Press, 1926]; Michael N. Dobkowski, "The Jew in 19th Century French Literature: Shylock up to Date," *Patterns of Prejudice,* Vol. 8, No. 1 [January-February, 1974]).

5. William Cullen Bryant, "Bryant's Criticism on Shylock as Portrayed by Edwin Booth," *American Israelite,* Vol. 12, No. 52 (June 29, 1866), p. 410; Oliver Wendell Holmes, *Over the Teacups* in *The Writings of Oliver Wendell Holmes,* Vol. 4, (Cambridge: The Riverside Press, 1871), pp. 194–97.

6. Quoted in Morris U. Schappes, ed., *A Documentary History of the Jews in the United States 1654 – 1875* (New York: The Citadel Press, 1950), pp. 557 – 58.

7. William Roscoe Thayer, ed., *The Life and Letters of John Hay,* 2 vols. (Boston: Houghton, Mifflin and Co., 1915), Vol. 1, pp. 293 — 94; see also, *New York Ledger,* September 3, 1858, and *Harper's Weekly,* November 19, 1859, for images of industrious Jews.

8. Stephen Bloore, "The Jew in American Dramatic Literature (1794 – 1930)," *Publications of the American Jewish Historical Society,* No. 50, Part 4 (June, 1951), pp. 345 – 60; Mitford M. Mathews, ed., *A Dictionary of Americanisms on Historical Principles,* 2 vols. (Chicago: The University of Chicago Press, 1951), Vol. 1, p. 905; see John Higham, *Send These to Me: Jews and Other Immigrants in Urban America* (New York: Atheneum, 1975), pp. 121 – 22.

9. T. Allston Brown, *A History of the New York Stage* (New York: Dodd, Mead and Co., 1903); Toby Lelyveld, *Shylock on the Stage* (Ann Arbor, Michigan: University Microfilms, 1951); William Winter, *Life and Art of Edwin Booth* (London: Macmillan and Co., 1893), pp. 198 – 200; Samuel Hammett, *Pineywoods Tavern or Sam Slick in Texas* (Philadelphia: T.B. Peterson, 1858), p. 37.

10. Henry Nash Smith, *Virgin Land* (New York: Vintage Books, 1950); Leo Marx, *The Machine in the Garden* (New York: Oxford University Press, 1964).

11. Editorial, *Niles' Weekly Register,* October 21, 1820, p. 114.

12. George G. Foster, *New York by Gas-Light* (New York: Dewitt & Davenport, 1850), pp. 58 – 59. See also, Foster, *New York in Slices* (New York: W.F. Burgess, 1849).

13. See Stuart Rosenberg, *The Jewish Community in Rochester, 1843– 1925* (New York: Columbia University Press, 1954), p. 67; Robert Rockaway, "Anti-Semitism in an American City: Detroit, 1850 – 1914," *American Jewish Historical Quarterly,* Vol. 64, No. 1 (September, 1974), pp. 47 – 48.

14. William A. Bell, *New Tracks in North America* (London: Chapman and Hall, 1869), p. 227.

15. Editorial, "Characteristic Traits of the Jews," *Sunday Dispatch,* May 28, 1854.

16. James Fenimore Cooper, *The Bravo: A Tale* (Philadelphia: Carey & Lea, 1831). See Louis Harap, *The Image of the Jew in American Literature* (Philadelphia: The Jewish Publication Society of America, 1974), pp. 189 – 90.

17. Theodore S. Fay, *Sidney Clifton,* 2 vols. (New York: Harper & Brothers, 1839), Vol. 1, p. 143; see Harap, pp. 68 – 70.

18. E.D.E.N Southworth, *The Bridal Eve* (Philadelphia: T.B. Peterson &

Brothers, 1864); Southworth, *Allworth Abbey* (Philadelphia: T.B. Peterson & Brothers, 1865).

19. J.B. Jones, *Border War: A Tale of Disunion* (New York: Rudd & Carleton, 1859), p. 157. See Harap, pp. 53 – 54.

20. Ibid., p. 159.

21. Julia Ward Howe, *The World's Own* (Boston: Ticknor and Fields, 1857), p. 104. See Harap, p. 211.

22. Undated and unnamed newspaper column reporting a February 13, 1862, speech found in the Isaac Leeser Papers, American Jewish Historical Society, Waltham, Massachusetts.

23. Bertram W. Korn, *American Jewry and the Civil War* (New York: Atheneum, 1970), p. 149.

24. Ibid., pp. 122 – 43.

25. *Harper's Weekly*, Vol. 8, No. 344 (August 1, 1863), p. 482.

26. Korn, p. 161; and *Israelite*, March 6, 1863, p. 277.

27. Joseph H. Ingraham, *Moloch, the Money-Lender* (New York: Robert M. DeWitt, 1869), p. 8.

28. Albert Aiken, *The California Detective*, Beadle's Dime Library, no. 42, (New York, 1878), p. 8.

29. Albert Aiken, *The Wolves of New York*, Beadle's Dime Library, no. 161 (New York, 1881), p. 12. See also Aiken's *The Phantom Hand*, Beadle and Adams, Twenty Cent Novels, no. 23 (New York, 1877); *The Lone Hand in Texas*, Beadle's Dime Library, no. 490 (New York, 1888); *Lone Hand the Shadow*, Beadle's Dime Library, no. 562 (New York, 1889); *Old Benzine the Hard Case Detective*, Beadle's Dime Library, no. 607 (New York, 1890).

30. Edward L. Wheeler, *Apollo Bill, the Trail Tornado*, Beadle's Half Dime Library, no. 236 (New York, 1882), p. 4. See also Wheeler's *Jim Bludsoe, Jr., the Boy Phenix*, Beadle's Half Dime Library, no. 53 (New York, 1878); *Boss Bob the King of Bootblacks; or, The Pawnbrokers Plot*, Beadle's Pocket Library, no. 111 (New York, 1886); *Canada Chet, the Counterfeiter Chief*, The Deadwood Dick Library, no. 22 (Cleveland, 1899); and his *Deadwood Dick of Deadwood*, The Deadwood Dick Library, no. 17 (Cleveland, 1899).

31. Prentiss Ingraham, *Gold Plume, the Boy Bandit; or, the Kid-Glove Sport*, Beadle's Half Dime Library, no. 204 (New York, 1881), pp. 9, 12.

32. Prentiss Ingraham, *The Mad Mariner; or Dishonored and Discovered*, Beadle's Dime Library, no. 162 (New York, 1881); Dangerfield Burr [Prentiss Ingraham], *The Phantom Mazeppa; or, The Hyena of the Chaparrals*, Beadle's Dime Library, no. 188 (New York, 1882); Ingraham, *The Cowboy Clan; or, The Tigress of Texas*, Beadle's Dime Library, no. 658 (New York, 1891); Noel Dunbar [Prentiss Ingraham], *The Detective in Rags*, Beadle's Dime Library, no. 604 (New York, 1890); Ingraham, *The Jew Detective; or, The*

Beautiful Convict, Beadle's Dime Library, no. 662 (New York, 1891); Noel Dunbar [Prentiss Ingraham], *Duke Despard the Gambler Duellist,* Beadle's Dime Library, no. 730 (New York, 1892); Ingraham, *The New Monte Cristo; or, The Wandering Jew of the Sea,* Beadle's Dime Library, no. 399 (New York, 1886); Gilbert Jerome, *Isaac Lazurus; The Egyptian Detective,* Old Cap Collier, no. 114 (New York, 1884); Old Sleuth [H.P. Halsey], *On Their Tracks Being the Continuation of "The American Monte-Cristo,"* Old Sleuth Library, no. 95 (New York, 1903); J.C. Cowdrick, *The Detective's Apprentice; or, A Boy without a Name,* Beadle's Half Dime Library, no. 420 (New York, 1885).

33. The most important of these are the following: *Watch and Ward* (1871), *The Golden Bowl* (1904), *The Tragic Muse* (1890), *The American Scene* (1907), *The American* (1877), *The Reverberator* (1888), *The Spoils of Poynton* (1896), *What Maisie Knew* (1897), *The Awkward Age* (1899), *The Ambassadors* (1903), "Impressions of a Cousin" (1884), "Adina" (1874), "Professor Fargo" (1874), "The Pupil" (1891), "Glasses" (1896), "Covering End" (1898), "In the Cage" (1898), and "The Story in It" (1903). For some secondary material on James's anti-Semitism, see the following: Leona Davis, "A Certain Blindness in Henry James: A Study of the Treatment of Jewish Characters in His Fiction," M.A. thesis, University of Pittsburgh, 1961; Leo B. Levy, "Henry James and the Jews," *Commentary,* Vol. 26, No. 3 (September, 1958), pp. 243 – 49.

34. Herman Melville, *Clarel* (London: Constable and Co., 1924), pp. 192 – 93.

35. Henry James, "The Impressions of a Cousin," in *Watch and Ward...* (London: Macmillan and Co., 1923), p. 382, p. 434.

36. Henry James, "Glasses," in *Embarrassments* (New York: The Macmillan Co., 1896), p. 86.

37. Henry James, *The Spoils of Poynton* (London: Macmillan and Co., 1922), p. 12.

38. Henry James, *The Awkward Age* (New York: Harper & Brothers, 1899), Chap. IX, p. 70.

39. Henry James, "In the Cage," in *The Complete Tales of Henry James,* ed. Leon Edel, Vol. 10 (Philadelphia: J.B. Lippincott Co., 1964), pp. 139 – 242.

40. Henry James, *What Maisie Knew* (New York: Herbert S. Stone & Co., 1897), pp. 116 – 17.

41. Henry James, "The Pupil," in Edel, *The Complete Tales,* Vol. 7, p. 492.

42. Henry James, *The Golden Bowl* (London: Methuen & Co., 1905).

43. Henry James, "Professor Fargo," in Edel, *The Complete Tales,* Vol. 3, pp. 259 – 98.

44. Henry James, "Adina," in ibid., pp. 211 – 57.

45. Henry James, "Covering End," in ibid., Vol. 10, pp. 243 – 350.

46. Henry James, "The Story in It," in ibid., Vol. 2, pp. 307 – 26.

47. William Dean Howells, "The Rise of Silas Lapham," *The Century Magazine* Vol. 29 (November, 1884), p. 25.

48. Positive portrayals of Jewish characters appear in William Gilmore Sims, *Pelago* (1838); J. Richter Jones, *The Quaker Soldier* (1866); Amelia Barr, *Bow of Orange Ribbon* (1886); Stuart Cumberland, *The Rabbi's Spell* (1888); Cecily Sidgewick, *Lesser's Daughter,* among others. However, these did not appear as frequently or as forcibly as the popular image of the evil usurer.

49. Julian Hawthorne, *Beatrix Randolph* (Boston: James R. Osgood and Co., 1884), p. 28. See Harap, pp. 308 – 10.

50. Ibid., p. 31.

51. Julian Hawthorne, *Sebastian Strome* (New York: D. Appleton and Co., 1880), pp. 79, 80, 83.

52. F. Marion Crawford, *A Roman Singer* (Boston: Houghton, Mifflin and Co., 1884), pp. 174 – 75; see Harap, pp. 311 – 14; Abraham H. Steinberg, "Jewish Characters in the American Novel to 1900," Ph.D. dissertation, New York University, 1956, pp. 173 – 84.

53. F. Marion Crawford, *A Cigarette-Maker's Romance* (New York: Macmillan and Co., 1893), p. 231.

54. F. Marion Crawford, *The Witch of Prague* (London: Macmillan and Co., 1891), p. 227.

55. Ibid., p. 199.

56. George Gossip, *The Jew of Chamant; or, The Modern Monte Cristo: A Romance of Crime,* Vol. III (New York: G.M. Hausauer, 1898).

57. Ibid., p. 10.

58. Evelyn Johnson, *An Errand Girl: A Romance of New York Life* (New York: G.W. Dillingham, 1889), p. 115; see Harap, p. 315.

59. Produced on May 17, 1890, at the Madison Square Theatre in New York, where it was a brilliant success. On April 24, 1916, it was revived for twenty-four performances at the Cort Theatre in New York (G.P. Sherwood, J. Chapman, eds., (*The Best Plays of 1899 – 1900*[New York: Dodd, Mead & Co., 1944], p. 574).

60. Clyde Fitch, *Beau Brummell* (New York: John Lane Co., 1908), p. 13.

61. Ibid., p. 15.

62. E.S. March, *A Stumbler in Wide Shoes* (New York: Henry Holt & Co., 1896), p. 131.

63. Hall Caine, *The Scapegoat* (New York: Lovell, Coryell & Co., 1891), p. 52.

64. Ibid., p. 30.

65. Richard Henry Savage, *The White Lady of Khaminavatka* (Chicago: Rand, McNally & Co., 1898), p. 13; see Harap pp. 327–33; Steinberg, pp. 142–48.

66. Richard Henry Savage, *Delilah of Harlem* (New York: The American News Co., 1893), pp. 39–40.

67. Frank Norris, *McTeague* (New York: New American Library, 1964), pp. 37–38.

68. Ibid., p. 247.

69. Paul Leicester Ford, *Janice Meredith* (New York: Dodd, Mead & Co., 1899), pp. 31, 32; see Harap, pp. 197–98.

70. Charles Blaney, *Old Isaacs from the Bowery* (New York: J.S. Ogilvie Publishing Co., 1900), p. 19; see Oscar Handlin "American Views of the Jew at the Opening of the Twentieth Century," *Publications of the American Jewish Historical Society* No. 40 (June, 1951), pp. 323–45.

71. Werner Sombart, *The Jews and Modern Capitalism* (Glencoe, Illinois: The Free Press, 1951).

72. *The Bulls and the Bears or, Wall St. Squib no. 1.* (New York: Pub. at 128 Nassau Street, 1854), p. 9.

73. Rochester, New York, Chamber of Commerce Song Book for 1923, Song Number 8, American Jewish Committee Archives, General Correspondence 1906–1932, Folder Anti-AZ, New York.

74. This image manifested in overt discrimination. Austin Corbin, the owner and developer of Manhattan Beach, made public his intention in 1879 to exclude the area from Jewish patronage (*New York Herald*, July 22, 1879).

75. *A Day on Coney Island* (New York, 1880), p. 11.

76. *The Household Book of Wit and Humor* (Philadelphia: Crawford & Co., 1883), p. 292.

77. *Puck,* Vol. 27, No. 683 (April 9, 1890), p. 100; Vol. 32, No. 828 (January 18, 1893), p. 349; Vol. 43, No. 1116 (July 27, 1898), p. 11.

78. *Tid-Bits,* Vol. 4, No. 99 (July 1, 1886), p. 328.

79. *Time,* Vol. 8, No. 212 (September 1, 1888), p. 4; Vol. 9, No. 274 (November 9, 1889), p. 2.

80. *Judge,* Vol. 1, No. 3 (1881), p. 5; Vol. 10, No. 240 (May 29, 1886), p. 418; Vol. 23, No. 582 (December 10, 1892), p. 418.

81. James H. Young, *The Toadstool Millionaires* (Princeton: Princeton University Press, 1961), p. 141; *Hostetter's Illustrated,* 1901, p. 31; see also 1891, p. 15, and 1898, p. 15.

82. Editorial, "The Jew as a Citizen," *Evening Telegraph,* October 19, 1872.

83. *The New York Times,* March 23, 1872; January 13, 1873; October 19, 1874; June 6, 1879; September 14, 1879; January 25, 1880.

84. Quoted in *The American Israelite,* September 6, 1872, p. 8.

85. *Labor Standard,* Vol. 8, No. 39 (September 24, 1881), n.p.

86. *The Illustrated American,* Vol. 3, No. 29 (September 6, 1890), p. 444.

87. *The Quarterly Sentinel,* Vol. 6, No. 1 (May, 1899), p. 6.

88. Goldwin Smith, "England's Abandonment of the Protectorate of Turkey," *The Contemporary Review,* Vol. 31 (February, 1878), p. 1618.

89. Goldwin Smith, "Can Jews Be Patriots," *The Nineteenth Century,* No. 15 (May, 1878), p. 887.

90. Goldwin Smith, "New Light on the Jewish Question," *The North American Review,* No. 417 (August, 1891), p. 141.

91. Goldwin Smith, "The Jews," *The Nineteenth Century,* No. 69 (November, 1882), p. 709.

92. Many of these letters were published in *The American Hebrew* in its April 11, 1890, issue.

93. Reverend Washington Gladden to Philip Cowen, February 14, 1890; Reverend R. Heber Newton to Philip Cowen, February 13, 1890, in Philip Cowen Papers, American Jewish Historical Society, Waltham, Massachusetts.

94. Reverend Chas. Deems to Philip Cowen, February 28, 1890, in ibid.

95. W.M. Thornton to Philip Cowen, February 25, 1890, in ibid.

96. J.M. Taylor to Philip Cowen in *The American Hebrew,* Vol. 42, No. 9 (April 4, 1890), p. 192; Charles W. Eliot to Philip Cowen, n.d., Philip Cowen Papers.

97. Mark Twain, "Concerning the Jews," *Harper's New Monthly Magazine,* Vol. 99, No. 592 (September, 1899), n.p.

98. Finley Peter Dunne, *Mr. Dooley in the Hearts of His Countrymen* (Boston: Small, Maynard & Co., 1899), pp. 260–61.

99. Jacob Riis, *How the Other Half Lives* (New York: Hill and Wang, 1957), p. 78.

100. Frederick A. Bushée, "Population," in *The City Wilderness, A Settlement Study,* ed. Robert A. Woods (Boston: Houghton, Mifflin and Co., 1898), p. 42.

101. Ibid., p. 43.

102. Jessie F. Beale and Anne Withington, "Life's Amenities," in ibid., p. 240.

103. Robert A. Woods, "Work and Wages," in ibid., p. 91.

104. Emily Greene Balch, "Slav Emigration at Its Source," *Charities and the Commons,* Vol. 40, No. 21 (February 24, 1906), p. 836.

105. See E. Digby Baltzell, *The Protestant Establishment: Aristocracy and Caste in America* (New York: Vintage Books, 1964); John Higham, *Strangers in the Land: Patterns of American Nativism 1860–1925* (New York: Atheneum, 1971); Barbara Miller Solomon, *Ancestors and Immigrants* (Chicago: The University of Chicago Press, 1972).

106. *The Silhouette,* Vol. 1, No. 3 (January, 1906), p. 73.

107. John C. Van Dyke, *The Money God* (New York: Charles Scribner's Sons, 1908), p. 47.

108. Rupert Hughes, *The Real New York* (New York: The Smart Set Publishing Co., 1904), p. 334.

109. See also, Charles Benedict Davenport, *Heredity in Relation to Eugenics* (New York: Henry Holt & Co., 1911), p. 216.

110. Theodore Dreiser, *The Titan* (New York: Simon and Schuster, 1925), pp. 202, 472.

111. G. Stanley Hall, "Yankee and Jew," *The Menorah Journal,* Vol. 1, No. 2 (April, 1915), p. 87.

112. G. Frank Lydston, *That Bogey Man the Jew* (Kansas City: Burton Publishing Co., 1921), p. 45.

113. Ralph Boas, "Jew Baiting in America," *The Atlantic Monthly* (May, 1921), p. 663.

114. Ibid., pp. 663, 665.

115. Kenneth L. Roberts, *Why Europe Leaves Home* (New York: The Bobbs-Merrill Co., 1922), p. 11.

116. Ibid., p. 48.

117. Ibid., p. 15.

118. Clinton Stoddard Burr, *America's Race Heritage* (New York: The National Historical Society, 1922), p. 195.

119. William Faulkner, *Soldiers' Pay* (New York: Liveright Publishing Corp.), pp. 17 – 18.

120. William Faulkner, *Mosquitoes* (New York: Boni & Liveright, 1927), p. 325.

121. Ibid., p. 327.

122. See also Amy McLaren's *With the Merry Austrians* (New York: G.P. Putnam's Sons, 1912).

123. These definitions remained part of the text from the late nineteenth century until the 1937 edition. See John Lewis Roget, *Thesaurus of English Words and Phrases* (Philadelphia: J.B. Lippincott Co., 1909), and Roget, *Thesaurus of English Words and Phrases* (New York: Theo. E. Schulte, 1925) as examples.

124. Jeoffrey Drage, "Poland," *Encyclopaedia Britannica,* 11th ed., Vol. 32, p. 123.

125. Quoted in Sigmund Livingston, *Must Men Hate?* (New York: Harper & Brothers, 1944), p. 18.

126. Sarah O. Jewett to Miss Louisa Dresel, June 14, 1898, *Letters of Sarah Orne Jewett,* ed. A. Fieldo (Boston: Houghton Mifflin Co., 1911), pp. 153 – 54.

From impious Babylon festering in
decay, where all God's gifts are basely
turned to gain; Mother of error; shelter
of greed and pain; as life's last hope, I
too have fled away.[1]

HENRY ADAMS

Patrician Anti-Semitism: The End of Confidence

As we have seen, many Americans were critical of Jews and Jewish
traits, but they expressed some confidence in the nation's ability to
modify them in time. Others, particularly in the patrician classes, were
not so sanguine. For them, the ascendancy of Jews and their values was
a symptom of modern social disintegration. Hating the nouveaux riches
and the rising masses, whom they held responsible for the decline of
genteel society, they focused, by way of explanation, on the Jew, the
symbol of all they disliked about the new industrial America.

The impact of industrialization and technology, immigration and
urbanization, in shifting the center of gravity in the nineteenth century
from Europe to America and in reshaping the face of that world, brought
about fundamental changes in human attitudes that greatly affected
United States society. America in the years preceding and directly
following the Civil War experienced the growth pangs of a slumbering
economic giant on the verge of transforming itself from the pastoral,
rural nation idealized by the myth makers, into the brawny and powerful
industrialized society that soon caught the world's imagination by its
efficiency, innovation, and seemingly endless productive capacity.[2] The
promises and opportunities of this "Age of Energy" may have inspired
new wellsprings of optimism and activity for some, but it augured the
rise of a new, bewildering civilization that was foreign and threatening
to others. The increasing secularity, loss of individualism, faceless
anomie, and insecurity that were the inevitable by-products of Vulcan's
forge contributed to the intensification of the fear of status loss and the

disintegration of values and diminution of deference for a class that had watched over America's welfare since its birth.

The patrician merchant princes and Brahmins who lorded over the economy and who set the social and intellectual standards of the nation for its first two centuries were witness to a changing of the guard that they looked upon with great trepidation. These descendants of the early Puritans had a deep sense of destiny that was rooted in a feeling of continuity with the traditions shaped by their American forebears over the past two hundred years. The first settlers in the seventeenth century, like the ancient Jews with whom they often compared themselves, were cast upon the seas by intolerance and were convinced that they, too, were a "Chosen People." Designated by God to found a "City upon a Hill," these immigrants were imbued with a sense of mission and purpose. Although no longer religiously orthodox, the descendants of the Puritans kept a lingering faith in their leadership role. None doubted that their class and the values and culture that it represented were morally superior to the rest of society. They had served as the rudder of the ship of state since its inception and for good reason, since they were certain they were the best America had to offer. Consequently, the Brahmins looked upon the great transformations of the midnineteenth century with some anxiety. No longer transcendent either culturally or politically, they saw themselves and their children being gradually eclipsed by the new industrial barons and immigrant populations with their pragmatic and materialistic goals, their denigration of the genteel virtues, and their invasion and despoilment of the few remaining patrician asylums. Were they merely to become a vestige of that once influential class that ruled over congressional halls, State Street, and Harvard Square? This rude realization jostled their sense of rectitude, tainted their democratic tradition, and drove many of them down the path of scapegoating, intolerance, and intellectual isolation.[3]

Aside from the economic instability created by the Machine Age and the challenges presented by mass immigration, the patrician classes were influenced by the penetration into the mainstream of their thought modes of new patterns from Europe that significantly affected their attitudes toward other groups in society. Among the most far-reaching of these ideas introduced into America after the Civil War were those that conceived of national character in racial terms; for the ideology of Arthur de Gobineau was reintroduced and given new currency and exposure through the teachings of Charles D. Meigs, Samuel G. Morton, Dr. Josiah C. Nott, and George R. Gliddon.[4] Edouard Drumont's racial-mythical tale of untruths was similarly having its impact while being devoured eagerly by some individuals.[5] At the same time, Ernest Renan's romantic, nationalistic formulations were being read with great interest in imperialistic circles.[6] Arnold White, the English author and social reformer whose books and articles were sold and republished in America in the 1880s, likewise propagated this "scientific" argument that Jews, in particular, should be excluded from Anglo-Saxon countries because they are racially and socially inferior and politically ungovernable.[7] In addition, there was Social Darwinism, which had a great impact on the patrician mind.[8] Although it did not lead directly to racial nativism, or to ideas of hereditary determinism, it did invigorate racial consciousness among a group that was rapidly becoming déclassé. For some intellectuals, a struggle for existence was underway between the old American stock and the "new" immigrants, and the former could well be destroyed in the process. In this changing intellectual milieu, the Brahmins adopted a defensive posture that stemmed from their fear of being overrun by the economic and social revolution taking place in an industrializing society. One finds it in the writings of James K. Hosmer, Edith Wharton, Henry James, Barrett Wendell, Lafcadio Hearn, Henry and Brooks Adams, and James Russell Lowell.[9] Grasping at straws, they looked for the source of their decline. In desperation, they focused upon the Jew who became the symbol of the diseased, crass, and parvenu society that was displacing them to pursue instead the promise of unleashed wealth. The simplistic solution once again surfaced during times of crisis and alienation to kindle the flame of anti-Semitism.

James Russell Lowell, in his changing attitudes toward the Jew, demonstrates how this shift in the tide of fortune transformed a vibrant and youthful optimism into a cynical and somewhat paranoiac interpretation of circumstance. In the flower of his youth in the 1840s and 1850s, he expressed an unbounded faith in the future of America. Inspired by the reformist spirit characteristic of the age, Lowell became a champion of the "American idea" of human capacity and was one of the extremists among the antislavery Bostonians. He even raised his voice in the 1840s against the persecution of Jews in the Balkans and the Middle East. At that point in his life, he deplored the forced status of the

Jew, the degraded itinerant vendor of old clothes, and the money changer of Europe.[10] The reformer Lowell wanted to emancipate the victim and liberate him from a restrictive ghetto mentality.

As with many others of his generation, he had a particular affinity for the noble ancient Jews and an uncanny ability to completely divorce them from their modern counterparts. Although not religious, Lowell, a minister's son, retained the Puritan's admiration for the "Chosen People" of the Old Testament. As a learned philologist in his own right, he took great pride in his fluent command of Hebrew and recalled the importance of this biblical language to the Harvard College of his ancestors.[11] Surely the Jews were the predecessors of the Puritans whose search for perfectibility and knowledge he so admired. Yet his spiritual love affair was tempered by his belief that the Jew, since the Middle Ages, had come out of the ghettos as a wretched, usurious, street hawker—as a harbinger of something evil and ugly. It was this image that soon became an obsession with Lowell.

In the decades that followed, while Lowell traveled through Europe, he developed a repugnance for the new, rich Jews who emerged from the Pale into polite society. During his diplomatic missions, he was more than ever conscious of and disturbed by them. In Spain there was "a very large infusion in the upper and middle classes of the most intense, restless, aspiring, and unscrupulous blood of all, the Jewish."[12] They seemed to be invading and controlling the last bastions of society. In England he labeled Henry James's heroine in *The Tragic Muse* a Jewess. "All roads lead to Jerusalem at last."[13] In fact, they seemed to be everywhere one looked in this strange, modern world. This debilitating monomania became a recurring theme in his conversations and it drove the once dynamic sage into a fearful obfuscation. "On a map of the world you may cover Judea with your thumb," he wrote in the early 1890s, "but they still Lord it in the thought and action of every civilized man."[14] One of Lowell's hobbies in the last years of his life was looking up the family trees of Knickerbocker people to trace the influence of Semitic ancestry on the development of America.[15] He soon "detected a Jew in every hiding place and under every disguise."[16] In an interview with an *Atlantic Monthly* reporter in 1897, Lowell insisted that the Jewish blood strain flowed in the veins of European royalty and nobility; in addition, all bankers, most brokers and financiers, were Jewish. He climaxed his discussion with the prediction of their "absolute control of finance, the army and the navy, the press, diplomacy, society, titles, the government, and the earth's surface.'"[17] He revealed his deepest anxieties when he queried what Jewish control would mean for his class and its values. That, he remarked, "is the question which will eventually drive me mad."[18]

To Lowell, as to many of his colleagues in decline, the visibility of Jews added another dimension to an already unrecognizable globe. The participation of a few prosperous Jews in the affairs of state and their intrusion into society represented a loss of fixed social distinctions. Significantly, during the last years of his life, these images became a means through which he expressed his loss of inner confidence in an unstable environment. When he felt out of place in New England, Lowell likened himself to the Hebrew Joseph who also lived among a younger generation who recognized him not.[19] When he felt in a mood of self-ridicule, he would describe himself as the stereotyped, pork-hating Semite who existed only for the sharp trade.[20] Possibly he instinctively knew that his class *was* the new Jew of the age, pariahs in their own nation, scorned, dishonored, and, worst of all, neglected. In that sense, his insistence that he in fact had some Jewish blood in his veins has some logic, for in perception at least, the ascendancy of the Jews cast out from the promised land a new Diasporic people, the expatriate Brahmin Wandering Jew.

Beginning his life as the passionate defender of the sufferers of the Damascus Blood Libel, by the end of his career in the 1890s, he was almost pathologically ambivalent toward the peddlers in the street who offended his sense of propriety and especially the rising class of Jews who were upsetting his idea of what a homogeneous upper class should be. Nevertheless, he was yet incapable of the intense anti-Semitism that eventually overtook his younger friend Henry Adams.

Of all the New England families, the Adamses felt the most intense possessiveness about the destiny of the United States. As long as there had been a nation, an Adams had served in some responsible national capacity as president, congressman, or ambassador. The four able sons of Charles Francis Adams assumed that they, too, would share in this inherited pattern of service.[21] By their own admission they failed and were unable to continue to be the torchbearers of the Quincy tradition. Henry and Brooks reacted to this "failure" most severely. It instilled in them a dark pessimism about the future of their class and the nation and, in fact, they equated their own disappointments with the end of the era of viable democracy that their forefathers had helped to shape and the beginning of the disintegration of Western civilization. As they lost their way in the maze of late nineteenth-century America, a society they did not build and had little influence over, they abandoned the idealism of their youth and retreated instead into a defeatist indifference. The internal crises of their lives, both personal and societal, hardened their already stoic New England souls and set their minds against those aliens who seemed responsible for their decline in fortune.

Henry's life, like many other gifted Brahmins of his generation, began on a note of promise and optimism, and it seemed that he, too, would possibly put his familial stamp on the White House. Born in Boston in 1838, he knew his grandfather John Quincy Adams during early impressionable years; and the legends of John Adams, who died finally in 1826, and the irrepressible Abigail were still fresh in his mind. After attending Boston Latin School, Mr. Dixwell's, and Harvard College, he went to Germany to broaden his education, study civil law, and learn German. Not at all successful in these ventures, he was rescued from the "frightful"[22] Prussians and an early preoccupation with failure by the onset of the Civil War. Writing to his brother Charles in 1859, he rejected the idea that his was to be the closet existence of lyceums, college lecture halls, and dry intellectual endeavors, the pursuit of which he "would rather die" than accept.[23] He wanted action; he wanted to be an architect of events, a moulder of history. "I mean to come home prepared as well as I know how.... In America the man that can't guide had better sit still and look on.... If all goes right, the house of Adams may get its lease of life renewed."[24]

The war seemed to provide an ideal opportunity for the useful contributions that he hungered for, but unfortunately, it only served to whet his appetite for a leadership role that he was never to enjoy. Traveling to the Court of St. James to assist his father, the ambassador, he was a participant and a witness to the diplomatic negotiations that eventually secured the neutrality of England. He yearned to escape from the restrictive shadow of his father's authority and use the Adams's razor-sharp intellect for the realization of his own historical destiny. Henry felt vicariously the stimulus and invigoration of the momentous events transpiring around him in Europe and the excitement of his friends dying in a great cause at home. Anxious to be a part of it, he anticipated the war's end as the moment of real action when he would join the survivors in controlling America's fate.

On his return home in 1868, he turned his back on provincial Quincy and Boston and gravitated instead to Washington, the center of power, and offered his talents to the country. Not only was he not accepted and not welcomed with the enthusiasm that he, in delusion, expected as birthright, but he also found a society that very little resembled the one he had left a decade before. He discovered the machinery of government created by his ancestors breaking down under the impact of industrialization. Shocked and disoriented, the young Adams realized he was defeated before he even began. The corporate forces of the railroads, banking, land interests, and Wall Street posed problems too great for his generation to solve. Industry's seemingly endless wealth and its willingness to deposit a little of it in the halls of congress to insure the expeditious approval of its objectives made reform a quixotic dream. What was worse, the American people seemed indifferent to the vulgar and obvious corruption of the Grant government and deaf to the ministrations of those who were not tainted by graft. Furthermore, Adams was not willing to make those compromises required by the changed political environment and would not stoop to soil his patrician hands in an effort to alert the populous to the festering evil eating away at the body politic. "I will not go down into the rough-and-tumble, nor mix with the crowd.... My path is a different one."[25] This path of aristocratic disdain and patronizing criticism did not project him into the limelight that he had been led to expect as his legacy. He found instead, to his frustration, that the nineteenth-century businessman had usurped his birthright. Writing in the *Education* in 1905, he recalled, in a revealing image, that as early as 1868 he already sensed his irrevocable alienation from the contemporary scene.

What could become of such a child of the seventeenth and eighteenth centuries, when he should wake up to find himself required to play the game of the twentieth?... Not a Polish Jew fresh from Warsaw or Cracow—not a furtive Yacoob or Ysaac still reeking of the Ghetto, snarling a weird Yiddish...—but had a keener instinct, an intenser energy, and a freer hand than he—American of Americans, with Heaven knew how many Puritans and Patriots behind him.[26]

Nevertheless, although his two years as a journalist during the Grant administration shocked and depressed Adams, he refused to give up—his Yankee mettle would not permit total surrender. Reluctantly submitting, in 1870, to a professorship of medieval history at Harvard College, which was to last seven years, and to the accompanying editorship of the *North American Review,* Henry continued to be active in politics. But even his brief escapade in political machinations ended in dismal failure in 1876; his plan to be a maker of presidents collapsed when Carl Schurz deserted the politically inconsequential Adams coterie. This further underscored for Henry the conviction that his class would have to be content with the role of passive spectator and occasional caustic –critic of society—that they would have to swallow the bitter pill of their own insignificance. It was very difficult, however, for Adams to accept his obsolescence without venting his frustration.

After his defeat, Henry and his bride, the former Marian Hooper, left the serenity of Cambridge and moved to Washington, fervently hoping to find some capacity in which to serve the nation. With their intimate friends John Hay, Clarence King, and Elizabeth Sherman Cameron, they settled down to watch the process of government and to determine whether there actually was a future for America. What they discovered, Henry revealed anonymously in his novel ironically entitled *Democracy* (1880). The aristocratic heroine Mrs. Lightfoot Lee, like the author, was bored with the social life she was accustomed to and was restive and uncertain in the changing America. She decided to spend a winter in Washington to "see with her own eyes the action of primary forces; to touch with her own hand the massive machinery of society."[27] What she found was a brutally pragmatic, cynical, and selfish system fed by the prospect of power. Everyone in the capital city seemed bent on his own advancement and would compromise all principle, even honesty, to further himself politically. Courted by the powerful and ambitious Senator Silas P. Ratcliffe, who had his eyes firmly riveted on the White House, she learned that political virtue and idealism, in the Adams sense, no longer existed on the Potomac. She refused to marry the politician who justified bribery in public affairs and who entertained individuals like the shallow and unprincipled Jewish financier Hartbeest Schneidekoupon, who lavishly spread around wealth to advance his own monetary objectives. In a sense, the Philadelphia Jew represented what was wrong with Washington, for he presaged the intrusion of the foreign and corrupting *nouveau riche* into the sanctuary of government.

Written in 1878, this novel reflects Adams's growing sense of isolation from the aims of the political manipulators epitomized by the Jew and, even more poignantly, of his abandonment by the American people.

Still, he had not yet been totally shattered by his negative experiences with democracy. He could summon the confidence to write rather positively at the end of 1877 about the future. "As I belong to the class of people who have great faith in this country and who believe that in another century it will be saying in its turn the last word of civilisation [sic], I enjoy the expectation of the coming day.'"[28] In his major creative work of those years, the *History of the United States,* Adams somehow managed to transcend his despair with the materialistic saturnalia that seemed to have overcome the better instincts of the nation. Like his distinguished grandfather, Adams looked upon the New England way of life as the best. He still retained a flickering ray of hope that the ideals of the Brahmin group would somehow rout the forces threatening its supremacy.[29]

The events of the 1880s were not as kind to Henry and they totally soured the glimmer of assurance that he expressed in his *History*. He no longer retained any illusion about his influence and he retreated into a negativism that colored his perception of the world and its new movers. A series of personally tragic familial deaths transformed Henry into a morose and fatalistic individual, resigned to a life of isolation and unfulfillment. Beginning with his father-in-law's demise in 1885, his wife's suicide in that same year, his father's death in 1886, and his mother's death in 1889, successive tragedies seemed to chip away at his resolve and they left their mark. Particularly crushed by Marian's suicide, he was never able to recover from the calamity. "The world seems to me to have suddenly changed, and to have left me an old man, pretty well stranded and very indifferent to situations which another generation must deal with.'"[30] "The future no longer belongs to us.'"[31] With the loss of his beloved spouse and the completion of his *History* in 1890, the dream that he held onto in desperation turned into a nightmare, and the nightmare increasingly was symbolized by the Jew.

By 1892, twenty years after he had set out to change the face of America, Henry Adams was a "failure" in the sense that he had always feared. Only once in his life—as the class day orator of Harvard College in 1858—had he ever been elected to any office and then by his peers. No president had ever called upon his expertise to serve the nation.

"Give me an office!" he proclaimed to Mrs. Henry Cabot Lodge, and "I should live happily ever after."[32] Politics, the career that he instinctively gravitated towards, was "the single uncompensated disappointment of life."[33] Unrewarded in that province, he complained that his countrymen had not even appreciated the *History* or his other literary productions. "I've wanted to say lots of things, but what is the use! What *do* they understand. Not even their own blossoming interest-tables. Let me be re-born a Jew."[34] He was uncomfortable in his anonymity and felt abandoned by a world that he could no longer call his own.

Drifting along in a morose torpor, Henry was rudely jostled by the depression of 1893. Shocked by a declining revenue and the possibility of bankruptcy, the depression emphasized for Adams the final obsolescence of his class. Looking around for the source of his difficulties, the Jew loomed glaringly as both the symbol of a materialistic society run amuck and as agent of its destruction. "Total ruin appears to be now only a question of time for all of us survivals of a misty past, who know not the tricks of money-making."[35] Henry looked forward in a macabre sort of way to the eventual smashup. "I shall be glad to see the whole thing utterly destroyed and wiped away.... In a society of Jews and brokers, a world made up of maniacs wild for gold, I have no place. In the coming rows, you will know where to find me. Probably I shall be helping the London mob to pull up Harcourt and Rothschild on a lamp-post in Piccadilly."[36] The collapse and America's submission to the gold standard in the same year were sad events for Adams. His lone crusade for the eighteenth century was now over. The depression led to the "nervous breakdown" of the society he cherished.[37] "My generation has been cleaned out."[38] The repeal of the Silver Act meant the acceptance of the power of finance capitalism and with it came corporations, trusts, monopolies, and the like. Financial ruin on top of personal desolation were just too much for him to accept passively. "I am myself more than ever at odds with my time. I detest it, and everything that belongs to it, and live only in the wish to see the end of it, with all its infernal Jewry. I want to put every money-lender to death, and to sink Lombard Street and Wall Street under the ocean."[39] Henry was hurt because he knew the bluebloods had broken their last lance. He extrapolated from his own individual failure the inevitable death of society.

Adams then turned from the change and chaos around him and sought repose in the medieval world of his Norman ancestors and at the shrine of the Virgin Mary, primarily because he could no longer trust modern industrial society that he symbolized with the "Dynamo." Running from reality, Henry became absorbed with a nostalgic craving for his beloved medieval unity and he grew rhapsodic over the chanson, the flying buttress, and the mysteries of stained glass. He became a Mariolatrist and he found in the Christ Mother's purity the nobility and innocence, the serenity, he missed in the financial age. In the Norman era of the eleventh and twelfth centuries, Adams discovered the unity and symmetry his beleaguered soul craved. All forces were formed in one concept, one faith, and one architecture, and everyone was moving in the same direction. Without Jews, science, or business to fragment society and accelerate the disintegration, "vital energy" had its greatest intensity. Jews are referred to throughout *Mont-Saint-Michel and Chartres* (1892) as elements of foreignness and discord. The Jew was an exploiter and *never* a creator of art. Everything he touched, he commercialized and profaned. That is why the Virgin Mary herself, according to Adams, disliked Jews, because they were the archetypes of the economic predators who eventually destroyed the synthesis of the twelfth century. "Like other queens, she had very rudimentary knowledge... of the principles of political economy..., and her views on the subject of money-lending or banking were so feminine as to rouse in that powerful class a vindictive enemy which helped to overthrow her throne."[40] Unfortunately, his retreat into medieval religion, rather than alleviating his anxieties, fed Adams's hatred of the present, particularly his anti-Semitism.

It was during the free-silver debates of the 1890s that his persistent strain of Judeophobia surfaced. The anti-Semitic doctrines that Adams emphatically expressed in his correspondence during the Bryan campaign (which he supported financially) focused on the conspiratorial argument. This was the period when his large inherited wealth was in jeopardy. His reaction was to condemn the capitalism of England and France as Jew dominated. To the Jewish financiers, Henry attributed an all-pervasive force. His propensity for a mechanistic explanation for events led him to accept the current anti-Semitic wisdom making the rounds in Europe and America that pointed to the Jewish banker as the source of the destruction of the world of the small entrepreneur. He added the caveat that they were also responsible for the deterioration of all values, artistic sensibilities, and social distinction. Henry Adams actually thought of three primary sources of pervasive historical energy—the Dynamo for the spirit of technology, the Virgin for the religious impulse, and the International Jew for modern finance capitalism and tottering social decay.

By 1895 Adams was deep in his madness about the Jews. Writing from London to his philo-Semitic friend John Hay, he remarked that Jewish bankers were strangling legitimate British industry. "The Christians are furious. They talk of making a new Ghetto. They secretly encourage the Anti-Semitic movement. After all, the Jew question is really the most serious of our problems. It is capitalistic methods run to their logical result. Let's hope to pull their teeth. Only in this day of dentistry they would have them pulled, painlessly, and put in false ones."[41] As time went on, he increasingly excoriated Jews for all that he disliked about his age. The word *Jew* was in his lexicon synonymous with everything he considered disagreeable, vulgar, and vile. It became interchangeable with "nouveau riche," "businessman," "capitalistic," or British "goldbug;" *Jewish* was his private adjective to describe greed, avariciousness, and materialism. His Jews, the children not of Jehova but of Mammon, were the lowest expression of capitalist morality.

Many of the critics of alleged Jewish avarice failed to recognize the same urge in their ancestors or even in themselves. Thus Henry Adams, ceaselessly railing at Jewish eagerness for money, would forget that he was himself a scion of one of the most exclusive minorities on earth—that of Boston Brahmins—who exhibited a great acquisitive instinct. The confusion in his thoughts is mirrored in his letters; often on the same page he could write a diatribe against Jewish money grubbing and a complaint that his gentile friends were going into nervous collapse over their speculative activities.[42] Nevertheless, Henry was blind to this reality and he fantasized about the personal competition between his family and the Jews. Passing each other on life's escalator with his fortunes on the downward trend and the Jew's looking upward, he reacted with the emotional bitterness of a threatened man.

Jews seemed to be everywhere: in Mayfair, on the Bois de Bologne, in Wall Street—and always in control. "We are in the hands of the Jews. They can do what they please with our values."[43] Everything they touch is degraded. "One does not want it any more. It has become a trade.'"[44] Adams believed they not only dominated the money centers of Europe, but were moving them to New York. "Westward the course of Jewry takes its way!'"[45] They were conspiring successfully against the world and eventually would be triumphant. "For seven years," he wrote in 1900, "I have been preaching, like John the Baptist, the downfall of the Jews, and have figured it up in parallel columns which are proverbially deadly, but, as we are going, all Western Europe will die and howl in Sheol before I can get into my comfortable grave and think it over.'"[46] Frustrated by his inability to obtain power, he imputed a control to the Jews of the kind that he himself dreamed of possessing.

Yet even in defeat, Adams held one trump card. He was convinced that civilization hovered on the brink of disaster—that Jewish victories were Pyrrhic, destined to impel the world toward its fatal end. Tired of America, he withdrew from it and abdicated all responsibility for the course the nation might take. Accordingly, his anti-Semitism, unlike Drumont's and the anti-Dreyfusards whom he admired, was not part of an aggressive program that would substitute a new system for the old.[47] Rather, it was a passive, although reactionary, commentary upon the disintegration of the world. Looking for the reasons that would account for the crumbling of a society he once fondly knew, Adams came upon an anti-Semitic explanation. "I wish I were a Jew, which seems to me the only career suitable to the time.'"[48]

Brooks Adams not only shared his older brother Henry's prejudices against Wall Street and Jewish capital, the source of the inevitable smashup, but also was determined to create a science of history, based—at least in part—on the principle of the dissipation of energy. In 1896 he published *The Law of Civilization and Decay,* an analytical historical work, that began with the downfall of Rome—a tragedy he attributed to capitalistic usury—and traced the conflict of debtors and creditors up to modern times.[49] He wrote of money, associated with Jews, as the instrument of exploitation and domination throughout history; of its effect on the overthrow of the imaginative types in the Middle Ages; of the rise of London as the financial center of the world with its stock exchange controlled by Nathan Rothschild, the "despot of... London," the instrument of exploitation and oppression.[50] He argued that "productive" industrial capitalism had been superseded by "parasitic" financial capitalism, epitomized by the rising Jew—the archetypical usurer.

Brooks was trying to even the score of 1893 by attacking the business system that had destroyed him. Like Henry, he linked capitalistic deterioration to the abandonment of the patrician style of life. Both saw in the gross manners, pervasive materialism, and business ethic of the artless Jew the symbol of the destructive agent weakening the society they represented. "The more I contemplate England," he wrote in 1896, "the sicker I grow.... I can detect no sign that a moral sense exists. The Jew, and the reasoning of the Jew, has so far prevailed.... With it all observe, that for the first time in human history there is not one enobling instinct.... To my mind we are at the end."[51] Anyone who read his book, he advised Henry in 1896, could no longer stand by impassively and witness the spectacle of materialism run wild. The effect of the work, yes, even its purpose, was "to create revolt against the Jews" and the stratagem they are foisting upon an unsuspecting polity.

> I suppose there is more concentrated hate of Wall Street in my last chapter than I could have put into a volume of stump speeches.... I never should have hated Wall Street as I do if I had not first dug the facts out of history.... I tell you Rome was a blessed garden of paradise beside the rotten, unsexed, swindling, lying Jews... who have been manipulating our country for the last four years.[52]

Brooks inherited the family propensity for turning private reverses into cosmic catastrophes. The great tragedy of his life, as in the lives of his brothers and his class, was his failure to receive public plaudits and recognition. Rejection resulted in alienation and anger. "I have for years been preaching disaster," he told his brother in doom, Henry, in 1894, "and I have been suffering under the sting which is hardest to bear, the conspiracy of silence, and the being set aside as a harmless crank."[53]

Brooks matched Henry's bigotry and often unmasked a real personal antipathy toward the Jew. Part of this certainly stemmed from his condemnation of Jewry as the embodiment of the new despised age. In arguing that Jews were supreme, he thereby proclaimed his own displacement by hated business. The passing of his group convinced Brooks that the end was imminent, and he vied with Henry for the most pessimistic formulation of the Second Law of Thermodynamics.

With Henry's death in 1918, Brooks fell deeper into the morass of the conspiratorial mania. His partner in resistance was gone, and he became a lone Jeremiah crying in the Armageddon wilderness. This was the final blow to Brooks and he reacted with characteristic hysteria. Writing to Senator Henry Cabot Lodge in 1919, he advised him of the Jewish objective now that the war was over. "They aim... the capture of this country and the consolidation of its usuries. They mean to own the next presidency.... It all reminds one so of 1893 – 1897.... If they win now they will have it all. I hope they won't and can't, but it is an enormous stake, and it is the old game which has been played over and over again, since Joseph changed the land usurers of Egypt."[54]

Brooks and Henry admitted to being anachronisms, but they never forgave the society that relegated them to that role. Of all human conditions, irrelevance and obsolescence are the hardest to bear. The more the two brothers were ignored in their own lifetimes, the more they professed to scorn the present and fled to the sanctuary of the past. Just as they gave their greatest loyalty to medieval symmetry, they directed their bitterest rancor against the modern preemptors who had so unjudiciously displaced them. The Jew, the banker, the economic man, oftentimes used interchangeably, were responsible for society's miserable state because they typified the vacuousness of contemporary culture. They had driven the Adamses from their perch; they were destroying America's native aristocracy. The Adamses looked on, sometimes in dismay, sometimes in disgust, but always in stubborn defeat.[55]

Barrett Wendell, a Harvard student of Henry Adams and James Russell Lowell, responded in a similar fashion to the ancestral disappointments exuded by the sardonic masters. Born of patrician family, he was the very incarnation of genteel Brahmin culture. Like many others of his generation, he was temperamentally insecure and driven with the ambition that young New Englanders seemingly born too late for the great tradition still felt. At one time, Wendell entertained a curious theory that the early Puritans were largely Jewish in blood. But experiencing the powerlessness of his own life, this literateur who publicized his snobbishness knew as well as Lowell and the Adamses that private society did not give "our time significance."[56] The social facts of 1893 and afterwards that did were hard for Wendell to accept. The opening of the floodgates and the arrival in invasion numbers of Eastern Europeans with what appeared to be bizarre and stunted values presaged the end of his class. "I feel that we Yankees are as much things of the past as any race can be. America has swept from our grasp. The future is beyond us.... Now I find my temper doubtful, reactionary."[57]

In many respects, the immigrant Russian Jew, with his bewildering social and religious code, his frantic activity, aggressiveness, and seeming preoccupation with wealth, symbolized for Wendell the "vanishing into provincial obscurity" of the genteel ideals of his New England forebears.[58] He liked to say with Henry Adams that his "race" was "oppressed" as ever the Jewish one was, and that it did not possess "the vitality to survive the test, nor yet a record which shall assure the future of what we might have been."[59] For Wendell, the Jews were social inferiors who were degrading his idealized America by intruding their standards into society. Concerning the Jewish author Mary Antin, he wrote: "She has developed an irritating habit of describing herself and her people as Americans, in distinction from such folks as Edith and me, who have been here for three hundred years."[60] He knew that although Antin was foreign and Jewish at that, it would be her children rather than those of his stock who would "come to be American in the sense in which I feel myself so."[61] The future was theirs; his days were numbered.

Likewise, the young historian Frederick Jackson Turner expressed a similar foreboding. Although originating from central Wisconsin in a nonpatrician family, he would end his academic career in the same New England environment that nurtured the status fears of the Adamses and the Wendells. The academic profession in the late nineteenth century remained open primarily to the culturally advantaged classes and the native born. The fact that only a small proportion of scholars had urban roots played an important role in determining professional perspectives on the massive changes that America sustained in the century and particularly affected their attitude on immigration. University faculties and intellectuals generally were the privileged who escaped to the ivory towers of the university community as the last refuge of culture and as the bulwark against the rising forces of crass industrialization and urbanization.[62] When they ventured out for an occasional "escapade" into the stranger's camp, they often came back repulsed by what they saw and more resolved in their hostility and isolation. Turner, walking through Salem Street in Boston in 1887, described the experience to his sister Ellen as follows:

I was in Jewry, the street consecrated to "old clothes," pawnbrokers, and similar followers of Abraham. It was a narrow alley, we would say in the west, and was fairly packed with swarthy sons and daughters of the tribe of Israel—such noises, such smells, such sights!... The street was... filled with big Jew men—long bearded and carrying a staff as you see in a picture,—and with Jew youths and maidens—some of the latter pretty—as you sometimes see a lily on the green muddy slime.... At last, after much elbowing, I came upon Old North rising out of this mass of oriental noise and squalor like a haven of rest.[63]

Turner's emotional commitment remained with the old America idealized by the Brahmins. He proudly identified with the pioneer stock he celebrated throughout his research. For Turner, the frontier liberated the immigrants from their historical past, stripped away their European culture, and forced them to reconstruct a society in tune with the patterns of the American scene. The assimilation of the immigrant within the frontier environment posed no problem therefore, for by purging the European of his distinctive heritage, the frontier removed any impediment to facile intercourse. It created "a newer and richer civilization, not by preserving unmodified or isolated the old component elements, but by breaking down the line-fences, by merging the individual in the common product."[64]

In relating this understanding of the greatness of America to the influence of the pioneering experience, Turner found himself in a serious dilemma. The dissolution of European culture patterns could only occur within the context of the national frontier of free land. What would happen now that it was no longer available? Turner felt that with its passing, the nation's capacity to assimilate its immigrants was also dissipating. The foreigners arriving were essentially unaware of America's past and this made them most menacing. Although Turner praised the contributions of the "Old" immigrants from Western Europe, he believed that the "New" immigrants from Eastern and Southern Europe "were a loss to the social organism of the United States."[65] The Italians he found in 1901 "of a doubtful value from an ethical point of view,"[66] but the Jews, "a city people," were the very antithesis of the rugged settler type he admired.[67] Turner was convinced they were "inferior immigrants" who constituted a new phenomenon that the country was incapable of integrating now that the frontier had disappeared.[68] Developing an historical cosmology to account for the unique greatness of America, it held within its corpus the clue to a decline he feared was imminent. The Jew who was "not ready to depart far from the city synagogue and the marketplace," and who was equipped to raise little more than a crop of "pants," symbolized the change in American society that he looked upon with a great deal of misgiving.[69] Reacting twenty-two years later to a Harvard University threatened with the inundation of Jews, still "reeking" from the ghetto, Turner tolled the death knell of his society in a letter to his wife, Mae. "I don't like the prospects of Harvard a New Jerusalem and Boston already a New York. Bad old world and the times out of joint. Rejoice in your Maine Yankee neighbors."[70]

The Lowells, Adamses, Wendells, and Turners, in their varying degrees of emphasis, were not the only upper-class intellectuals who saw in the Jew the representative of a materialistic society unleashed, the despoiler of values, and the agent of destruction. The same patrician pessimism underlay the anti-Semitic outbursts of Vance Thompson's elegantly bohemian and avant-garde magazine *M'lle New York*. It was founded in 1895 by the poet Thompson and the esthete James Gibbons Huneker, who was at that time branching out from his activities as music critic to writing about drama and literature as well.

M'lle New York received its literary ideas directly from France and the Continent. Much of its prose, like its Gallic inspiration, was characterized by a fascination with Jews; the males were represented (in illustration as well as in language) as repulsive physically, yet with oriental lure, and the women were irresistible because they were seductive and sensual and were experienced in the perversities that, it was assumed, commonly suggested themselves to the insidious mind of the Jewish male.

O Ester, daughter of Judea, singer of sweet cantellations, despiser of Christians, lover of diamonds, do you not know that I am fascinated by your face because in it there lurks the sorrowful story of the Semite? You turn your long, full throat and your profile evokes hot, sultry nights and the few large stars of Palestine.... I hold your Oriental hand, browned by the sun and dirt. You are a true Eastern.... You were a splendid mass of fire, and I adored you, adored your crisp, ebon curls, worshipped your slender hips, and maddened for your cruel, cormelion-lipped mouth.

This was Judea seductive and alluring but yet "rotting to the very core"; Judea physically attractive, but yet corrupting and defiling for those Christians who hungered for the sweetness of her Jewish passion.[71]

The magazine's expressed attitude was one of scorn for all lower-class immigrants and the masses in general, but positive contempt for Jews. Aside from its antipathy for the "prurience" of the Hebrew, which may indeed be a projection of the American aristocrat's own sexual fantasies and a reflection of the insecurities of the Victorian era and the decline in Protestant birth rates, it also excoriated the commercialism of a society that apparently was intent on debasing and destroying the few remaining bastions of culture still left intact. The prime villain in this disintegrative process is the Jew. Thompson referred to that quality they possess, "that faculty of decorating and vulgarizing science, philosophy, the arts; the Jewish faculty of being other than onself," as the subversive agent destroying refinement and taste in America.[72] Their materialistic instincts, unfortunate and unseemly even in the realm of business, have had a particularly pernicious impact on the arts. Their intrusion into this area, Thompson argued, has served to prostitute American culture before the requirements of the marketplace. Take, for example, the case of American painting that has become, according to *M'lle New York*, a mass-production venture grinding out a seemingly endless stream of inane excuses for art, all to satisfy the requirements of Jewish business interests. The picture dealers, Thompson advised,

live in houses and have wives, who indulge in the sterile infidelities of diamonds and children—litters of little unbaptized children.... They smoke and breed and export gold—incidentally they frame pictures and sell them to Goyim.... But did you know that there were hundreds of painters who toil along, year in and year out, saying, "Let us paint and paintily paint," lest peradventure the picture-framers starve and their wives die, moaning for diamonds.... Dear Lord! It is all such a monstrous intolerable farce—... it is all the shabbiest sort of commercialism; new and old they nibble at the Yom-Kippured herring of the picture-framers.[73]

Because America was becoming a materialistic nation disinterested in the cultural amenities of life, undeferential and disrespectful of the aristocratic function, Thompson and Huneker found little promise in the future of their class or country. Practicing a patrician disdain made popular by Henry Adams, they looked down from on high and singled out the ascending Jew who most epitomized the advent of the new imbecilic era. Distressed by their ever-loosening grip, they lashed out in an anti-Semitic response and became preachers of doom. "It would be absurd to fancy that this cringing gentility-mad civilization is to last very long." If it does, there will be little to redeem it from the uninspired tyranny of the "huge mob—always mediocre—of fat-witted and unviolent citizens."[74]

A less bohemian and more popular *Life* took up the issue in 1897 when it similarly began to decry Jewish influence on American culture and specifically on the theater. The architect of this campaign was James Metcalfe, the drama critic of *Life,* who from 1897 to 1905 continued to reiterate the libelous charge that Jews were responsible for the deterioration of American culture and that they would bring on an eventual artistic debacle if allowed to continue to use "Baxter Street methods... in theatrical affairs."[75] One of the major theatrical organizations, Klaw and Erlanger—was Jewish owned. It became known as the "theatrical trust" and was much abused in the public press, especially by Metcalfe, for being dictatorial and for allegedly debasing the American theater. In May 1898 he charged that "the entire control of the theatrical business in America rests in the hands of a few Jewish gentlemen, who have decided what the American people want in the way of theatrical entertainment.... To appeal to them, everything must have an absolute commercial rating."[76] This means that the Jew has managed to "contaminate everything in American life that he has touched."[77] Most evident in the theater, Metcalfe interpreted this as a "national calamity."

The insidious pictures of immorality and vice put before the eyes of every girl and woman who goes to the Syndicate theatres have a... penetrating [effect]. They destroy modesty.... It lies quite within *Life's* duty to appeal to American public sentiment against the powerful combination of rich Jews—... who are using their power to search the ... sewers of European capitals for filth to put before the American people.[78]

Left alone to complete their nefarious objectives, there will be little remaining of good taste, respectability, cultural appreciation, and even simple morality. All will have fallen victim to the money maker with his astigmatic perception of the world.

This theme was central also to the works of several of America's major authors and reflected their alienation from an industrial society growing increasingly impersonal. Certain gentile novelists in this period knew only one type of Jew—the bounder. Robert Herrick's novels contain him in contemptuous reference. Willa Cather's do likewise. *The Professor's House* (1925) is one of the most haunting statements of the contrast between the moral purity of a simpler America and the corruption of the present. Two men court the professor's daughter. Tom Outland, a son of pioneers, is a noble, selfless character. Louis Marcellus, a cosmopolitan Jew, makes money from the work of others. He eventually wins the daughter. The antithesis between the two men, like the larger antithesis between the two Americas, is symbolized by a gift each has made to the woman. Tom Outland gave her a "dull silver" Indian bracelet. Marcellus presented her with a gaudy gold necklace. The professor's daughter (America) wears the gold around her neck.[79]

Owen Wister's *Philosophy 4* (1903) presents Oscar Macroni, a symbol of the vacuous, parvenu Jewish immigrant. He had "toiled, traded, outwitted and saved" to enter into Harvard, but not out of sincere, genteel intellectual commitment, rather to satiate his ambition. Oscar's "young days had been dedicated to getting the better of his neighbor...." He possessed few original thoughts, was an intellectual parrot, and got ahead through shrewdness and plodding.[80]

The Jew of vulgar manners who was no longer a ghetto East Sider, although he retained all the characteristics of that genre, had made his way up to Fifth Avenue and Riverside Park and was hobnobbing, or desperately trying to, at least, with the social elites. Edith Wharton described this Jew who epitomized the decadence and purposelessness of contemporary New York society in *The House of Mirth* (1905): "He was a plump rosy man of the blond Jewish type, with smart London clothes fitting him like upholstery, and small sidelong eyes which gave him the air of appraising people as if they were bric-a-brac."[81] He possessed "that mixture of artistic sensibility and business astuteness which characterizes his race." He was a man "who made it his business to know everything about everyone, whose idea of showing himself to be at home in society was to display an inconvenient familiarity with the habits of those with whom he wished to be thought intimate."[82] The luncheon scene in F. Scott Fitzgerald's *The Great Gatsby* (1925), in which Nick Carraway was first informed of Meyer Wolfsheim's fixing of the Baseball World Series, elicited this revealing response from

Wharton in a letter to Fitzgerald. "The lunch with Hildesheim [the name was subsequently changed to Wolfsheim in the second edition] and his every appearance afterward, make me auger still greater things.... Meanwhile, it's enough to make this reader happy to have met your perfect Jew.''[83] It is interesting that Wharton's conception of the Jew should find concurrence in Fitzgerald's Wolfsheim, the personification of the essentially impersonal forces of evil that bring tragedy and ultimate death to the "simple" American, Gatsby.

For these writers, the Jew is a symptom of modern social disintegration. They found Jews everywhere—in the universities and art galleries, in private clubs and exclusive neighborhoods, but above all, in control of the marketplace. Here, they argue in effect, is what modern Christian society is coming to because of the contact with a type that is influencing and corrupting, but that can never truly understand or internalize American values.

These apprehensions did not dissipate as America was propelled further into the technological era, experienced the continuing influx of immigration and the heightened congestion of its cities and was bloodied by the passions of war. In fact, anxieties were compounded by these developments and made some social and intellectual elites more certain than ever that the end of their America was near. Many Jews discovered by the early 1920s that they had entered a period of intense suspicion during which they were scrutinized and tested for their "foreignness." Basically, these xenophobic attitudes derive from the fears then obsessing the established order that it was being threatened by aliens and alien influences of various descriptions. Some of the most important works of the 1920s reflect these concerns and project a posture of opposition to the unhindered intrusion of these outsiders who dare to maintain that they legitimately belong. The Jew, as symbol of the alien forces, represented for some writers not only an economic threat, but a menace to the social structure itself. Like Wharton and Cather before them, they equated the rising fortunes of the Jew with the decline of the cultural and ethical standards of the nation. T.S. Eliot's important poem "Burbank with a Baedeker: Bleistein with a Cigar" (written in 1920) sounded this note pointedly.

Burbank crossed a little bridge
Descending at a small hotel;

Princess Volupine arrived,
They were together, and he fell.

But this as such was Bleistein's way;
A saggy bending of the knees
And elbow, with the palms turned out,
Chicago Semite Viennese

A lustreless protrusive eye
Stares from the protozoic slime
At a perspective of Canaletto
The smoking candle end of time
Declines on the Rialto once.
The rats are underneath the piles

The Jew is underneath the lot
Money in furs. The boatman smiles,
Princess Volupine extends
A meagre, blue-nailed, phthisic hand
To climb the waterstair. Lights, Lights,
She entertains Sir Ferdinand

Klein. Who clipped the lion's wings
And flea'd his rump and pared his claws
Thought Burbank, meditating on
Time's ruins, and the seven laws.[84]

Burbank is the American in Europe, the innocent abroad in profligate Jewish Venice. There he meets Bleistein, the "Chicago Semite Viennese," the epitome of grossness and lack of culture, the representative of modern philistinism. It is significant that he is a Chicago Jew; for Eliot came from St. Louis, the importance of which as a cultural and industrial center declined during his childhood because of the expansion of nearby Chicago. Eliot's anti-Semitism therefore had a specifically American origin with its roots deep in the distaste and dismay felt by displaced intellectuals at this invasion.[85]

Once, of course, things were different when all of Shylock's gold could not buy the old Hebrew honor or respect on the Rialto. But now, Eliot laments, "the rats are underneath the piles. The Jew is underneath the lot. Money in furs." Bleistein typifies the disintegration of Western culture and augurs the approach of barbarism. He represents the new American gawking uncomprehendingly at Europe, the Jew who dares to have pretensions to culture, who frequents the museums to gape at a "perspective of Canaletto." The other Hebrew, Sir Ferdinand Klein, represents the international Jew adventurer who corrupts the European arts by participating in them and financing them; who is welcomed by Princess Volupine with the "phthisic hand," the symbol of that culture in decline. Things are obviously not as they once were in polite circles when "Kleins" became "Sirs."

This obsession with the putrefaction attendant upon Jewish influence is also central to Eliot's poem "Gerontion" (1920). In a cathartic exercise, Eliot describes the death of his obsolescent class. "Here I am, an old man in a dry month/ Being read to by a boy, waiting for rain. My house is a decayed house/ And the Jew squates on the window sill, the owner/ Spawned in some estaminet of Antwerp/ Blistered in Brussells, patched and peeled in London."[86] The points continually emphasized here are that the Jews are a destructive force in Western civilization; that they have no loyalties or roots other than racial allegiance; that they are without artistic sensibility; that they relish in their power over gentiles. The Jew is associated with decay and dilapidation; he is a restless cosmopolitan moving from city to city; he is "spawned" in frightful proliferation like an insect and "squates" like a predator ready to pounce on its victim; he owns the house of the Christian but remains an observer from afar, unassimilated and foreign; he is the creature of the crowded ghetto, not of the physiocratic unity inherent in the land. He is the symbol of deterioration in life, for the closing in of the world as Gerontion (Eliot) stiffens into old age and moves further away from his youthful optimism.[87]

It is probably at this point, in the 1920s, where American and European anti-Semitism (especially in Germany) part ways. For the Europeans, and the Germans in particular, the Great War was the interceding event. Up to 1914 there might have been a shared ideology with America; after 1918, especially in the defeated Axis countries, the racialist aspect in European anti-Semitism emerges as the dominant trend. This is exacerbated by the political dislocations of the decade, the massive inflation, the disappointment of defeat, the vindictiveness of the Versailles Treaty, as well as other social and political factors. Eliot himself will move further down this road of racist anti-Semitism.

Other writers of the 1920s, uncomfortable with the modern social system that deprived their educated superiority of its proper accustomed esteem, asserted their dislike of the bourgeois and vulgar materialistic society by expressing their antipathy toward the Jew—its sterotyped embodiment. They thereby partially asserted their independence and individualism through their anti-Semitism. It demonstrated, to their own minds at least if nowhere else, their fidelity to the "authentic" culture of America as distinguished from the impersonal, parvenu civilization of the ghetto-infected urban scene. For example, there is Theodore Dreiser, who looked upon the changed society with some trepidation. Writing to H.L. Mencken in 1922, he said: "New York to me is a scream—a Kyke's dream of a Ghetto. The Lost tribe has taken the island."[88] Hamlin Garland made a similar observation in a 1922 letter to Senator Henry Cabot Lodge.

The picture you draw... makes me wonder what compensations we are deriving from that flood of Semitic and Schlavonic [sic] immigrants which has made our cities a welter of strange customs and strange tongues. I may be wrong but I feel that they are a menace at this moment not because they are essentially vicious but because they do not know what America means. They have no understanding of our background or our traditions.[89]

Then there is Ernest Hemingway who, in *The Sun Also Rises* (1926), presents a version of the socially ambitious Jewish bounder in Robert Cohn. Cohn's schooling at Princeton and his relations with his class-mates parallel the actual Jewish assault on hitherto sacrosanct institutions. Cohn is not an admirable character. His behavior typifies the pattern of the unwanted outsider trying to identify himself with an "in group" to which he does not and should not belong. Although his background is similar to that of his expatriate friends, he is not at home in their world; he breaks the accepted modes of conduct. He is despised by the coterie he attempts to infiltrate. "Don't you know when you're not wanted?" one of them asks. "I know when I'm not wanted. Why don't you know when you're not wanted?"[90] Another remarks, "I hate him..., I hate his damned suffering."[91] The resentment Hemingway's characters display toward Cohn may be interpreted symbolically as the resentment of an established class against an upstart "alien." Cohn is the ever-encroaching Jew impinging on the preserve and function of the "authentic" American. There is no relief to be had from Cohn, ever clawing to achieve acceptance, never acknowledging defeat or rejection, intent upon making polite society his own. The consequences, Hemingway implies, are unfortunate.

The Lowells, Adamses, Whartons, Wendells, and Eliots began their lives blessed with a patrician opportunity that became, during the course of their adulthood, a trust too heavy to bear. They were never certain whether they could measure up to their past, and they did not find their burden any easier in the hectic, industrial, postwar era that seemed to be rapidly passing them by for a new and bewildering progress. Suffering in temperament and experience, each yielded to xenophobia and anti-Semitism in his own way and to varying degrees.

As they ceased to believe in the principles of their ancestors, their noble ideals and visions degenerated into a reaction against the forces and the people they singled out as the agents of social disintegration. The Brahmin paragon that ignited man's inspiration in the eighteenth century had become a vehicle of brazen prejudice in the nineteenth and twentieth centuries in the hands of those who could not adjust to change. This group that entered the world the inheritors of a vibrant tradition experienced a social shock that altered their minds and hearts and made it difficult for them to have faith in the future. They became the new prophets of doom, the new preachers of hatred and suspicion. They articulated the deepest fears of those in their class who no longer recognized the America that had been conquered and degraded by materialism and cultural insensitivity. Resigned to a life of declining import, they struggled against the approach of their retreat into superannuated oblivion. Like the doomed species of God's kingdom tottering on the precipice of extinction, they reacted in anger and frustration.

NOTES

1. "Petrarch in Kaucluse," Sonnet 91, Henry Adams Papers, Box 1890-June 1891, Massachusetts Historical Society, Boston, Massachusetts.

2. Edward C. Kirkland, *Industry Comes of Age* (Chicago: Quadrangle Books, 1967).

3. See Barbara Solomon, *Ancestors and Immigrants* (Chicago: The University of Chicago Press, 1972); Frederic Cople Jaher, *Doubters and Dissenters; Cataclysmic Thought in America, 1885 – 1918* (London: Collier-Macmillan, 1964).

4. William Stanton, *The Leopard's Spots* (Chicago: The University of Chicago Press, 1960).

5. Thomas T. Timayenis and his circle of sympathizers used *La France Juive* as a virtual textbook treatment of the arguments justifying anti-Semitism.

6. Leivy Smolar, "The Problem of Tolerance and Intolerance in the Work of Ernest Renan," paper presented at the Bloomsburg State College History Conference, Bloomsburg, Pennsylvania, May 1, 1975.

7. Arnold White, *The Modern Jew* (New York: F.A. Stokes Co., 1899).

8. Richard Hofstadter, *Social Darwinism in American Thought, 1860 – 1915* (Philadelphia: University of Pennsylvania Press, 1943).

9. Lafcadio Hearn, *Occidental Gleanings,* Vol. 2, ed. Albert Mordell (New York: Dodd, Mead & Co., 1925), pp. 270 – 89; Lafcadio Hearn, *The Japanese Letters of Lafcadio Hearn,* ed. Elizabeth Bisland (Boston: Houghton Mifflin Co., 1910), pp. 55, 374.

10. James Russell Lowell, "New England Two Centuries Ago," *Prose Works,* Vol. II (Boston: Houghton, Mifflin and Co., 1890), pp. 1 – 2, 13, 32; see Solomon, pp. 17 – 19; James Russell Lowell, review of *Tancred or the New Crusade,* by Benjamin Disraeli, in the *North American Review,* No. 65 (1847), pp. 212 – 14.

11. James Russell Lowell, "The Study of Modern Languages," *Latest Literary Essays and Addresses* (Boston: Houghton, Mifflin and Co., 1892), p. 131.

12. James Russell Lowell, "Lowell's Impressions of Spain," *Century,* Vol. 57 (1898), p. 143.

13. M.A. Dewolfe Howe, ed., *New Letters of James Russell Lowell* (New York: Harper & Brothers, 1932), p. 328.

14. *Harvard Anniversary Literary and Political Addresses,* Vol. VI (Boston, 1892), p. 174.

15. Max Kohler, "James Russell Lowell and the Jews," *The American Hebrew,* February 21, 1919.

16. "Conversations with Mr. Lowell," *Atlantic Monthly,* Vol. 79 (1897), p. 127.

17. Ibid., p. 128.

18. Ibid.

19. Howe, p. 328.

20. James Russell Lowell, "A Moosehead Journal," *Prose Works,* Vol. I (Boston: Houghton, Mifflin and Co., 1890), p. 26.

21. Charles Francis, Jr., John, Brooks, and Henry; See Jaher, pp. 144 – 57.

22. Henry Adams to Charles Francis Adams, Jr., November 3, 1858, *The Letters of Henry Adams,* Vol. I, ed. Worthington Chauncey Ford (Boston: Houghton Mifflin and Co., 1938), p. 2.

23. Henry Adams to Charles Francis Adams, Jr., February 9, 1859, in ibid.

24. Henry Adams to Charles Francis Adams, Jr., November 23, 1859, in ibid., p. 53.

25. Henry Adams to Charles Francis Adams, Jr., May 21, 1869, in ibid., p. 160.

26. Henry Adams, *The Education of Henry Adams* (Boston: Houghton Mifflin Co., 1918), pp. 4, 238.

27. Henry Adams, *Democracy and Esther: Two Novels by Henry Adams* (Gloucester, Massachusetts: Peter Smith, 1965), p. 18.

28. Henry Adams to Charles Milnes Gaskell, November 25, 1877, *The Adams Papers,* Micro. No. 595, Massachusetts Historical Society.

29. Henry Adams, *History of the United States During the Administration of Thomas Jefferson,* Vol. 1 (New York: A and C Boni, 1930), p. 184; *History of the United States of America During the Second Administration of James Madison,* Vol. III (New York: A and C Boni, 1930), p. 225.

30. Henry Adams to Robert Cunliffe, *The Adams Papers,* July 21, 1886, Micro. No. 599, Massachusetts Historical Society, Boston, Massachusetts.

31. Henry Adams to Charles M. Gaskell, April 25, 1886, in ibid.

32. Henry Adams to Sister Anne, November 25, 1891, Henry Cabot Lodge Papers, Folder A, 1891–92, Massachusetts Historical Society, Boston Massachusetts.

33. Henry Adams to Robert Cunliffe, December 16, 1888, *The Adams Papers,* Micro. No. 600, Massachusetts Historical Society.

34. Henry Adams to Holt, January 7, 1899, *The Adams Papers,* Micro. No. 598.

35. Henry Adams to Charles M. Gaskell, November 26, 1893, in *The Letters of Henry Adams,* Vol. II. See Solomon, pp. 36–40.

36. Henry Adams to Elizabeth Cameron, September 15, 1893, in *The Letters of Henry Adams,* Vol. II, p. 33.

37. Henry Adams to Charles M. Gaskell, September 27, 1894, in ibid., p. 55.

38. Henry Adams to Charles M. Gaskell, January 23, 1894, in ibid., p. 35.

39. Ibid.; see Jaher, p. 152.

40. Henry Adams, *Mont-Saint-Michel and Chartres* (Boston: Houghton Mifflin Co., 1933), p. 263; see Jaher, pp. 154–55.

41. Henry Adams to John Hay, October 4, 1895, *Henry Adams and His Friends: A Collection of His Unpublished Letters,* ed. Harold Dean Carter (New York: Octagon Books, 1970), p. 350; see Kenton Clymer, "Anti-Semitism in the Late Nineteenth Century: The Case of John Hay," *American Jewish Historical Quarterly,* Vol. 60 (June, 1971), pp. 344–54.

42. Henry Adams to Charles M. Gaskell, September 27, 1894, in *The Letters of Henry Adams,* Vol. II, p. 55.

43. Henry Adams to Charles M. Gaskell, July 31, 1896, in ibid., p. 111.

44. Henry Adams to Charles M. Gaskell, June, 1899, in ibid., p. 233.

45. Henry Adams to Brooks Adams, October 12, 1899, in *Henry Adams and His Friends,* p. 482.

46. Henry Adams to Elizabeth Cameron, January 29, 1900, in *The Letters of Henry Adams,* Vol. II, p. 258.

47. Henry Adams to Elizabeth Cameron, January 13, 1898, in ibid., p. 144.

48. Henry Adams to Charles M. Gaskell, January 4, 1897, in ibid., p. 120.

49. Brooks Adams, *The Law of Civilization and Decay* (New York: The Macmillan Co., 1896); see Jaher, pp. 158–87.

50. Brooks Adams, p. 383.

51. Brooks Adams to Henry Adams, August 17, 1896, The Houghton Library, Harvard University, Cambridge, Massachusetts.

52. Brooks Adams to Henry Adams, October 10, 1896, in ibid.

53. Brooks Adams to Henry Adams, May 6, 1894, Henry Cabot Lodge Papers, Folder A, 1894–5, Massachusetts Historical Society.

54. Brooks Adams to Henry Cabot Lodge, December 28, 1919, Henry Cabot Lodge Papers, Box 1919.

55. Henry Adams to Anne Lodge, September 26, 1909, Henry Cabot Lodge Papers, Box 1909, Folder A.

56. Barrett Wendell to Colonel Robert Thomson, February 3, 1893, *Barrett Wendell and His Letters,* ed. M.A. Dewolfe Howe (Boston: The Atlantic Monthly Press, 1924), p. 108.

57. Barrett Wendell to Colonel Robert Thomson, December 17, 1893, in ibid., p. 109.

58. Barrett Wendell to Colonel Robert Thomson, February 3, 1893, in ibid., p. 108.

59. Barrett Wendell to Horace M. Kallen, June 5, 1912, in ibid., p. 249.

60. Barrett Wendell to Sir Robert White-Thomson, March 31, 1917, in ibid., p. 282.

61. Ibid.

62. Michael Matthew Passi, "Mandarins and Immigrants: The Irony of Ethnic Studies in America Since Turner," Ph.D. dissertation, University of Minnesota, 1972.

63. Frederick Jackson Turner to Ellen Turner, June 30, 1887, F.J. Turner Papers, The Huntington Library, San Marino, California.

64. Frederick Jackson Turner, "The Contribution of the West to American Democracy," in *Frontier and Section,* ed. Ray A. Billington (Englewood Cliffs, New Jersey: Prentice-Hall, 1961), p. 3.

65. Frederick Jackson Turner, "Studies of American Immigration," *The Chicago Record-Herald,* September 25, 1901.

66. Ibid., September 11, 1901.

67. Ibid., October 16, 1901.

68. Ibid.

69. Ibid.

70. Frederick Jackson Turner to Mae Turner, May 23, 1922, F.J. Turner Papers, Tu Box J, The Huntington Library.

71. "The Shofor Blew at Sunset," *M'lle New York,* Vol. 1, No. 8 (November, 1895).

72. Ibid., Vol. 1, No. 6 (October, 1895).

73. Ibid., Vol. 1, No. 5 (October, 1895).

74. Ibid., Vol. 2, No. 1 (November, 1898).

75. *Life,* Vol. 30, No. 772, (October 7, 1897), p. 292.

76. Ibid., Vol. 31, No. 805 (May 12, 1898), p. 404.

77. Ibid., Vol. 38, No. 987 (October 3, 1901), p. 272.

78. Ibid., Vol. 35, No. 898 (February 1, 1900), n.p.

79. James Schroeter, "Willa Cather and the Professor's House," *Yale Review,* Vol. 54 (1965), pp. 494 – 512.

80. Owen Wister, *Philosophy 4* (New York: The Macmillan Co., 1903), pp. 36 – 38, 57.

81. Edith Wharton, *The House of Mirth* (New York: New American Library, 1964), p. 18.

82. Ibid., p. 19.

83. F. Scott Fitzgerald, *The Crack-Up,* ed. Edmund Wilson (New York: New Directions Paperback, 1956), p. 309.

84. T.S. Eliot, *The Complete Poems and Plays 1909 – 1950* (New York: Harcourt, Brace and Co., 1952), pp. 23 – 24.

85. Hyam Maccoby, "The Anti-Semitism of T.S. Eliot," *Midstream,* Vol. 19, No. 5 (May, 1973); Leo Shapiro, "The Anti-Semitism of T.S. Eliot," *The Chicago Jewish Forum,* Vol. 1, No. 3 (Spring, 1943).

86. Eliot, pp. 21 – 23.

87. See the Maccoby and Shapiro articles (note 85).

88. Robert H. Elias, ed., *Letters of Theodore Dreiser* (Philadelphia: University of Pennsylvania, 1959), p. 405.

89. Hamlin Garland to Henry Cabot Lodge, February 10, 1922, Henry Cabot Lodge Papers, Massachusetts Historical Society; see also, F. Scott Fitzgerald, *The Beautiful and Damned* (New York: Charles Scribner's Sons, 1950) for a treatment of a socially ambitious bounder Jew, Joseph Bloechman.

90. Ernest Hemingway, *The Sun Also Rises* (New York: Charles Scribner's Sons, 1970), p. 143.

91. Ibid., p. 182.

CHAPTER

5

The Jew never becomes a citizen, his posterity never amalgamates with the great mass of people.

THE BOSTON NEWS (1860)

The difference between the Jewish element in natural life and every other racial constituent lies in the fact that... the... Jew... is contemptuous of the people of his adoption.[1]

NEW YORK TRIBUNE (1898)

Don't Send These to Me: The Unassimilable Jew

One of the most historically persistent strains of anti-Semitic imaging portrays the Jew as an ethnic and cultural alien, a mysterious outsider, a stubborn and unassimilable doubter, a nation within a nation, an unsociable entity committed to a separate destiny. This theme, central to classical anti-Semitism as expressed by Cicero and Tacitus, received further exposure in the first-century conflict between the Synagogue and the nascent Christian Church. It was pivotal to the Inquisition as well as to medieval Judeophobia generally and formed an important element in the litany of hatred propounded by variant personalities such as Martin Luther, Voltaire, Edouard Drumont, the Russian czars, the racial mythologists, and the architects of the Final Solution.[2]

Jews remained a most vexatious, puzzling, and contrary people, for although they appeared vulnerable and weak and thus prime candidates for forced assimilation—pallid, impoverished scholars, shabby artisans, bent ghetto dwellers, cautious, Westernized intellectuals—the combined might and influence of Christian society could not break down their identity.[3] Who were these Jews who refused the graces of Christian civilization? Who were these people who clung to their "Yiddishkayt" in the face of the most ominous of circumstances?[4] Could they be "entreated" to forego their allegiance to a desert faith and enter the mainstream of Western society as loyal, contributing participants? The consensus by the nineteenth century, notwithstanding the promises of the Enlightenment, which cast the Jewish people headlong into the modern world, was not very hopeful. The Jew remained the outsider, the alien. This image followed him wherever he went, impugning his motives and objectives. Whether imprisoned behind the Pale of Settlement, liberated in European salons, or seeking succor in the land of opportunity, the Jew was viewed with the side glance of suspicion.

Even before Jewish mass immigration into the United States, this reputation for intransigence and intense solidarity already preceded them and lay the groundwork for an unfriendly welcome. Ever since the patriarchs, the Hebrews had prided themselves on their "Chosen People" distinction, and they used the posture of religious superiority and the sense of unity that resulted to help them weather the storm of oppression. In America their desire to cluster around a cohesive Jewish community created some misgivings, since the nation was the product of a unique nationalistic expression that was not favorably disposed to isolated groups that appeared reluctant to give body and soul to the experiment in democracy. Over one hundred years ago, de Tocqueville suggested that in democracies people put a premium on consistency and sameness rather than upon differences and may indeed become intolerant of the right to be different. The individual loses and society gains in importance, variety disappears, and similar ways of acting, thinking, and feeling are emphasized. Those resistant to amalgamation, those who remain outside the mainstream, become sources of mistrust.

This image of the perpetually alien Jew was an academic concern in the United States, as long as Jews remained relatively invisible. With the advent of mass immigration of Eastern European Jews in the 1880s, however, the charge was heard with greater frequency and urgency, even among the already established German-Jewish Grandees. As the sluice gates opened and tens of thousands of unwashed, foreign and bizarre-looking immigrants flooded into America's cities, the capacity of the nation to absorb them was seriously questioned. Here was a compact, apparently unassimilable mass of human beings, recent residents of the ghettos of Europe, congregating in cities and zealously preserving their religious distinctiveness, their national customs of diet, dress, and prayer, their communal autonomy, their individualism, their predilection for commerce. How were these people to be integrated? How were they to be weaned away from the Talmud, the citadel of Jewish separatism? How were they to be liberated from the Shtetl mentality? How were they to be made loyal and useful American citizens? These concerns sparked the fuse of misunderstanding and resurrected the myth of the eternally Wandering Jew, living everywhere but sinking roots nowhere, a part of humanity, but never a part of any nation.

Anna L. Dawes, an early figure in American anti-Semitica, wrote a short treatise, entitled *The Modern Jew* (1886), to alert her countrymen to this problem and singled out the Polish Jews as the group most unacceptable.[5] Their constant association with their own people combined with their peculiar religious habits make them "the most narrow of bigots." They insist "upon remaining a foreign element in every community, and an indigestible substance" and they are determined "to be always a Jew." This makes wholesale colonization the only solution, Dawes argued, "unless you would contemplate extermination or a war for the supremacy to which the Jew believes himself entitled!"[6]

In 1890 the editors of *The American Hebrew*, troubled by an increase in anti-Semitism reflected in such statements, dispatched a series of questions to a select group of non-Jews who included intellectuals, university presidents, and Protestant ministers of various denominations, requesting reasons for the persistence and intensification of anti-Jewish feeling in America. Some sixty-two individuals responded. Almost all condemned anti-Semitism and disclaimed any personal ill feeling toward the Jew. Interestingly enough, however, a number of those polled were of the opinion that the continuation of Judeophobia was in large part the fault of Jews themselves. The practice of peculiar religious rituals, such as circumcision and keeping the Passover, Jewish snobbishness—"have you not held yourselves apart from the life of this New World in a nook of your own... looking down from your fancied eminence as the chosen race, with a certain disdain and feeling of keep-your-distance?—"[7] and the refusal to intermarry and associate with gentiles were stock objections. The Methodist clergyman and future chancellor of Syracuse University J.R. Day remarked that the Jew "sets himself, by his institutions and social tastes, apart from our citizens, refuses intermarriage..., and will not meet his Gentile neighbors upon a common plane of life.''[8] The Reverend A.H. Lewis found them ''a nation, and yet not a nation,'' ''clannish'' and excessively ''self-defensive.''[9] The Reverend W.H.P. Faunce, the future president of Brown University, discovered within the Jewish people the source of their difficulties. ''There is an indifference to popular opinion, often amounting to open defiance, a want of public spirit, a lack of genuine patriotism, a want of human sympathy and breadth of view, a class spirit in place of real love of humanity.''[10] President E.N. Capen of Tufts College objected to their apparent reluctance to ''assimilate like other aliens; they are always Hebrews.... They never can be Americans, pure and simple.''[11] Prominent naturalist and essayist John Burroughs concurred. ''The Jew will be a Jew; he will not fuse or amalgamate with the other races. He is among us, but not of us.... He is too tough to be digested and assimilated by the modern races, hence the dislike of him.''[12] Music critic and editorial writer Henry T. Finck suggested that ''there ought not to be any Jews at all in America.... Why should not the Jew intermarry with other nationalities and cease to exist as such?''[13] A biased remark, it was voiced by many individuals who saw little inherent value in the perpetuation of an independent Jewish identity. As noted travel writer and illustrator Joseph Pennell, in *The Jew at Home* (1892), warned: ''Make him an Englishman or an American, break up his old customs, his clannishness, his dirt, and his filth—or he will break you.''[14]

This understanding of the Jewish personality probably affected government policy on immigration. One factor that prompted the United States to protest against the inhuman treatment of Russian Jews by Alexander III's regime was that the pogroms and the May Laws forced thousands to emigrate to America. In the decade of 1880–90, 135,000 Russian Jews entered the country. The first catch basin for this new influx was Brody, the frontier station between Russia and Austrian Galicia. There Pennell observed crowds of shabby and penniless Jews bewildered by the spectacle of strange sights and confused and numbed by their trip in third-class railway cars packed with sweating humanity. There and at Eydtkuhnen, Thorn, Ungheni, Hamburg, and Bremen, American consular officials reported to their superiors in Washington of the consequences of this ''invasion.'' These fears, coupled with the panic of 1893, brought covert and overt anti-Semitism into the open and made the stereotype more of an issue.[15] During this temporary phase of shrinking economic opportunity, tolerance for a group reputed to be selfishly concerned with its own welfare and unmindful of the greater good of the nation was at a premium.

Seeing that this stereotype struck a raw nerve in the American threshold of tolerance, the press, of both the popular and more respectable varieties, joined in the attack. *Frank Leslie's Weekly,* for example, a popular sheet that catered to the graphic weekly audience, took up the issue in 1892. The Jews coming from Eastern Europe, it proclaimed, "are among the most undesirable and least welcome of immigrants. The degradation of the average of citizenship, the dangerous strain to the country's power to assimilate and redeem, are constant factors, steadily increasing in importance."[16] *Leslie's* reminded its readers of the perils inherent in the arrival of this teeming mass of humanity who are tied to medieval ways and shielded by a fierce identification with obscurantist Judaism from accepting the liberating influence of American enlightenment and democracy.

There exists on the east side of this town [New York] a great and coherent population of foreigners of a low order of intelligence, speaking their own languages, following their own customs, and absolutely blind or utterly indifferent to our ideals, moral, social and political.... Go and see them swarm in the streets and the houses of the east side if you have doubts on the subject, and form your own conclusions as to the availability of the material for manufacture into the sort of citizen which the founders and fathers of the republic had in mind....[17]

This clarion call of misunderstanding intruded into the otherwise dignified middle-class magazines of the period that prided themselves on their championship of stark honesty. Two of these, the *Independent* and the *Outlook,* were weeklies that descended directly from the powerful religious newspapers of the early nineteenth century. Both were now liberal in religion and reformist in politics; both stood for the family, clean politics, and honest economics; but both, unfortunately, were not as munificent or impartial when it came to evaluating the Jewish personality.

The *Independent* focused on the question of exclusivity and underscored it as the source of Jewish difficulties over the centuries. After the birth of Christianity, it advised in 1889, Judaism refused to expand or idealize itself. It chose to remain "in the narrow limits of racial consanguinity. This has been its coherence, and race consanguinity is about all there is to Judaism today.'' Because of Jewish arrogance, it is not surprising that friction and hostility were generated. ''They regard themselves as a peculiar people, in a sense different from what any other race in the country does. Holding themselves thus distinct and separate, they have no right to object if... it excites a certain amount of social dislike.''[18]

Lyman Abbott's *Outlook* and several more parochial religious magazines sounded a similar note. They reacted negatively to the traditional image of Jewish solidarity. Abbott, a leading spokesman for liberal congregationalism, in a 1903 editorial, wrote: ''Theologically, ethically, sociologically, Judaism was racial.'' Christian theology, in contrast, was human, personal, universal, and open, not narrow, ''not Jewish.''[19] Because the Jew chooses to be a spectator in society, an outsider, *The Methodist Review* postulated, he is unwelcome wherever he resides. ''He is extraneous, original, unassimilable. He may be republican, monarchist, or absolutist—and that conscientiously—but still he is alien in blood, creed, and natural isolation.''[20] *The Catholic Record* endorsed this interpretation. ''Let the Jews be well or ill received; let them be among the plebians or the nobels, rich or poor, scattered or in great numbers, masters or slaves, never do they mingle with them—the legend of the Wandering Jew remains a lasting truth.''[21] *The Boston Pilot,* another Catholic paper, expressed the belief that the refusal of Jews to assimilate had ''cost them dear in money, pain, and blood.''[22]

The *World's Work,* a monthly founded at the turn of the century by Walter Hines Page, like the *Independent* and the *Outlook,* also believed in culture and also believed in reform and also saw in the Jew's isolation much to be criticized. ''Regarded from a sociological point of view only,'' it wrote in 1906, ''the reluctance of the Jews to marry outside their race is a survival of a day of a narrower spirit. They have been willing to take advantage of the toleration and of the opportunities given by a democracy, but to the one essential act of a democratic society they have not consented. They are not willing to lose their identity in the people.''[23] A similar viewpoint was expressed by *Harper's Weekly.* Once a trumpet of moralistic reform, it had been converted by Colonel George Harvey into a conservative rival of these three, full of political vituperation and genteel literary twaddle and pretensions, at once staid and sensational. In that regard, it kept up with the hidebound posture of its more successful competitors. "The chief thing that hinders the disappearance of what anti-Semitic prejudice is left here is the stout preference of the Jews to remain Jews, and so to continue different from the rest of the Americans.... The Jews don't want to merge. They prefer to be a part, belonging to the whole, but not merged into it."[24] The American public, whether it read the popular sheets or the more staid and traditional magazines, was thus presented with a stereotype that, to the misfortune of Jews, has long been associated with the Diaspora experience.

Among the "New" immigrants, then, the Eastern European Jew, who clustered in America's cities with an aversion to amalgamation, provoked interest, comment, and often feelings of misgiving and dislike. As the influx took on massive proportions in the first decade of the twentieth century, the platform of debate was extended from the press to intellectual and patrician circles, even though there had still been no personal intimacy or direct conflict between them in any way comparable, for example, to the daily tensions between the Irish and the Brahmins in Boston. In this transferal, the "scientific" interpretation developed by scholars and reformers gave a new meaning to the persistence and unity of the ancient Hebrew—gave a new meaning to the nineteenth-century definition of assimilation, which in reality meant conversion. It transformed the essentially harmless image of the unacquainted and awkward immigrant Jew into a more serious challenge.

Geologist Nathaniel Shaler, for example, who admired Jews and who thought they were one of the world's ablest types, nevertheless perceived Jews as somewhat anachronistic because they were ruled by religion rather than by science.[25] Shaler became dean of the Lawrence Scientific School of Harvard University in 1891, and as an administrator he had direct contact with many Jewish students. Aware of his prejudices, he strove to override his own doctrinaire concepts. In the interest of harmony, Shaler interviewed his Christian friends to determine what their experiences were with Jews. He found that they confirmed his own encounters with Jewish students who usually responded much more quickly and aggressively to his greetings than those of his own "race." He condoned this quickness, however unpleasant, as an index of their racial capacity.[26] Like the "Aryan," the Jew represented a superior people; unadaptable to environmental influences and unreconciled to Christian domination.

Significantly, Shaler was not satisfied with this state of affairs. He sought to supplant the attitude of prejudice with the "ideal of the neighbor." It was evident to him that the greatest obstacle retarding the advance of all races was ethnocentrism and this was particularly true in the case of the Jews. Among the Jews "there is no trace of a sense of duty to the extratribal neighbor... and no distinct enunciation of the doctrine that all men are brothers until it came from Christ." [27] Despite his own xenophobic reactions, he proposed a union between gentiles and Hebrews to create one common community. Only by the elimination of Judaism through intermarriage, he believed would America benefit from Jewish capacity; and at the same time, the obliteration of the racial type would very conveniently solve the problem of prejudice. [28]

William Graham Sumner, the economist and pioneering Yale sociologist, who attempted to establish a general science of society based on the scholarly investigation of interrelationships and institutions, was also disturbed by Jewish ethnocentrism that he thought was religiously inspired. In his examination of the mores of "primitive peoples," he found that Jews still held onto their ancient customs and this prevented their acceptance by the majority culture. [29] He had few kind words to say about the specific requirements of Judaism and found them naive and antiquated. The laws of Jewish marriage, ritual baths, the dietary requirements, and the Sabbath restrictions were incomprehensible to him and he perceived them as primitive vestiges of a tribal religion that had never freed itself from its nomadic history. Since it was the Jews themselves who divided mankind into two camps, one for the "Chosen People" and the other for the gentiles, they were responsible for their own difficulties. "When Jews conform to the mores of the people amongst whom they live," Sumner argued, "prejudice and hatred are greatly diminished, and in time will probably disappear." [30]

Clichés from William Z. Ripley's *The Races of Europe* (1899) also received wide currency, adding fuel to a nation's imagination already run riot. [31] Ripley, a Columbia University Ph.D., attempted in this book, based on extensive anthropological research, to explode some of the myths about racial theory. He was partially successful in that he demolished the unscientific use of the term *Aryan race,* which European scholars employed indiscriminately, and he reemphasized the importance of social and physical environment in altering ethnic factors. Yet he also fell into the trap that had obfuscated the works of others by attempting to isolate the racial factors that determined national development. With the cephalic index as his guide, he elaborated three European types of the Caucasian race—the Teutonic, the Alpine, and the Mediterranean—and he set up a hierarchy of superiority. Although he denied the purity or permanence of these categories, he could not help believing in his classifications. Scientific racism was thereby provided with a new corpus of "evidence" to buttress its already questionable assumptions.

With scholarly prudence, Ripley negated the existence of a Jewish "race" and even attempted to dispel the notion that there was a peculiar Jewish physiognomy. The ethnic individuality associated with the Jews was "of their own making from one generation to the next, rather than a product of an unprecedented purity of physical descent." Nevertheless, in the visages of Jews he found the stamp of "a people" who had weathered adversity and oppression through their persistent attachment to a common history and religion. Ripley generalized about their "herding" characteristics in such a manner that sociologists and reformers familiar with his influential work knew in advance that Jews were resistant to assimilation even before they encountered them in America's cities. The Jews, he wrote, "have maintained their solidarity in all parts of the earth, even in individual isolation one from another.... Their seed is scattered like plant spores of which the botanists tell us" and they "bunch wherever possible." Residing everywhere and belonging nowhere, they are a source of irritation to their host nation, especially in recent decades. "The nineteenth century... is the age of nationality.... To this,... the Jew is indifferent, typifying still the Oriental tribal idea. As a result he is out of harmony with his environment. It has ever been the Aryan versus the Semite in religion throughout all history...; and today it has also become the people versus the nation, as well as the Jew versus the Christian."[32]

Ripley's text was unfortunately susceptible to xenophobic misuse.[33] Geologist Dr. Alfred P. Schultz, who gave a genetic meaning to the survival of the long-suffering Jew in *Race or Mongrel* (1908), lent credence to the work of his Immigration Restriction League friends.[34] "The Jews are Jews everywhere independent of the environment," he wrote to Prescott Hall in 1909, "and the people among whom they live recognize them as strangers, as differing from them essentially. Environment has not bridged the gulf which separates Aryan from Jew."[35] Dr. J.G. Wilson, an American "authority" on genetics, made a similar assessment.[36] "When the cause of the modern anti-Jewish feeling is analyzed," he postulated in a 1911 article, "it seems to have about the same basis that it had before the time of Christ.... The Jew, as a class, is different from the people among whom he has settled, and he has insisted that he be given certain special privileges which serve to emphasize the difference rather than obliterate it. In other words, he is inherently clannish."[37] That is primarily why J.K. Kingsburg, president of the University of Utah, argued for immigration restriction. He was opposed to admitting any group that was "not willing to amalgamate with the people of the country and become citizens who intend to uphold the government."[38]

Even H.L. Mencken, the disturbing voice of rebellion, the naturalist debunker of myths and pretensions, concurred, although not with the proposed policy but with the underlying character evaluation. In an apologetic style unbecoming the master critic, he asserted the familiar defense made by those insecure about their prejudice that "some of my oldest and most intimate friends... are Jews." Nevertheless, he objected to the fact that "Jews in general... stick together firmly."[39]

In the minds of more committed "racists," Ripley and those who followed his lead provided a jumping-off point for unattractive corollaries to this theme. Richard Hayes McCartney, in a fanatical anti-Semitic treatise entitled *That Jew!* (1905), did not temper his raw and angry narrative by injecting dry scientific justifications. His was a bold and calculated attack on the Jew's suitability for citizenship anywhere on the globe. "They are indeed the children of the restless feet. They seem readily to be acclimated in every land under the sun, but never amalgamated, never lost, never losing identity, never absorbed by the surrounding people; no matter how long they live in any country," they remain "unconquered" and "unvanquished," the ever-present "despicable Jew!"[40] William Williams, commissioner of immigration who was no friend of Jews, agreed in 1912. "It has always seemed to me that there are a great many very estimable Jews who make the mistake... of considering the interests of their race before those of their country."[41] This is most unfortunate since they are "beaten men from beaten races; representing the worst failures in the struggle for existence."[42] Instead of maintaining an acute sense of solidarity, Williams argued, Jews should blend into the mainstream of American society, lose their Jewish mentality in the American spirit, in fact, cease being Jews at all for the benefit of mankind.[43] Robert DeCourcy Ward, one of the Harvard University triumvirate who founded the Immigration Restriction League in 1894,[44] justified the limitation of further Jewish immigration on the ground that Jews "to a considerable extent, hold themselves aloof, socially and religiously, from their fellow men, and thus are with difficulty assimilated."[45] David R. Francis, former governor of Missouri and ambassador to Russia, concurred. Prejudice against Jews has always been evident in every land where they have lived, he wrote in 1916, basically because "they have never thoroughly assimilated with the peoples thereof.... They still consider that eventually they will come into control of the world."[46] The Reverend William Norman Guthrie, Rector of St. Mark's Church in New York City, summarized the problem.

What is at the bottom of this antagonism to the Jew today? In my opinion... it is nothing more nor less than the Chauvinism of the Jew. It is his race-pride, race-conceit, race-exclusiveness, race-aloofness.... The Jew must relinquish forever his race tightness.... He must bury forever all racial self-consciousness, all racial egotism, and be in all things and at all times absolutely and thoroughly American.[47]

In spite of themselves, then, many American intellectuals and reformers, occasionally well-intentioned, were bondsmen to the prejudices of society and their own inherited assumptions. Sharing the *de haut en bas* attitude of an established group facing the bewildering spectacle of an unassimilable mass, some reacted with extremeness and hostility.

Another aspect of this particular imaging of the American Jew is of some import for it extended the category of the clannish and alien Jew to include the charge that Jews are cowardly, unpatriotic, and unwilling to make personal sacrifices for the good of the nation, all falling under the rubric of poor citizenship qualities. In the eyes of these detractors, Jews are not only unassimilable—a trait intrinsically damaging to their position in society—but they are also a weak link in the chain of American nationality that heretofore was forged, in theory at least, on the frontier with its character-building, idealized, rugged individualism. Weak, pallid, ghetto-urban, emasculated people with a propensity to disappear when commitment or courage are required, the Jew, these critics allege, will forever remain an unpalatable force on the American scene.

This stereotype was not unique to the twentieth century or to America. It surfaced here initially during the Civil War when Jews were accused of profiteering, not fighting, and it was an integral thematic component of dime novel literature. Recall the trembling, cowed Jews of Albert Aiken, J.C. Cowdrick, Prentiss Ingraham, and Edward L. Wheeler who are pathetic, unnerved, and impotent characters when confronted by danger, not the resolute, bold, and defiant spirits of the West. Theodore Roosevelt gave currency to this portrait, although with good intentions, when he urged Jews in 1901 to throw off the suffocating miasma of ghetto debilitation and "develop that side of them which I might call the Maccabee or fighting Jewish type."[48] Only by impressing America with the concept that they are more than just thrifty and successful businessmen, "but also able to do their part in the rough, manly work which is no less necessary," will American anti-Semitism be put to its final rest.[49] The implication is that they are presently somewhat less capable of cultivating that attitude. That is also Charles Taft's meaning in a 1908 editorial he wrote for his Cincinnati *Times-Star*, entitled "Ingratitude." The brother of President William Howard Taft referred therein to Russian Jews who come to America to acquire wealth and property but who refuse to pay the price of their success by giving of themselves freely to the American armed services, or who are reluctant to honor its flag or participate in its patriotic functions.[50] The Jew whom the prominent Negro businessman Samuel Scrotten described as perenially "timid," always in "retreat" before any "wild and threatening look," always running to cover to save "his skin," certainly had little to recommend to a nation impressed by the chauvinistic and courageous virtues.[51]

These ideas, abroad in the land, reached a new degree of virulence during the jingoistic years of World War I when the patriotism of many minority groups was impugned. Then Americans were grasping for a homogeneous national unity and were alarmed at the widening rifts of class, race, and religion. Hyphenism came into usage and cast suspicion on any ethnic activity. The Jewish notion celebrating pluralism became increasingly embarrassing and a source of mistrust. The activities of Rabbi Judah L. Magnes and labor leader Morris Hillquit and others in the peace movement brought spotlight attention to the community and raised questions about its patriotism, as did the fact that many Jews generally opposed American participation in World War I on the side of the Allies because Russia, an ally, was a traditional enemy of the Jews.

Jews were publicly attacked throughout the war years for lack of national allegiance. They were portrayed as slackers and draft dodgers in cartoon and musical verse. Edward S. Martin, editor of *Life*, invented an imaginary Washington war correspondent named "Gabriel Samuelson" to satirize this characteristic. A popular California song entitled "Yiddisha Army Blues" was distributed throughout the country, mocking the Jew as a shirker and coward. "Jake tried to sell his business/ But he couldn't give it away/ So he set the place on fire/ In a business way. It's time to save my money/ Till I got a little start/ Now for the battlefields/ I'm going to depart. My head it starts a-reeling/ I got such a sickish feeling/ When I hear them sing that song/ Over there— oi, oi, oi vey, I'm shaking in my shoes."[52] A doggerel distributed around army bases in New York in December 1917 made the point even more forcefully.

The largest mob that the world ever saw/ Trying to beat the conscription Law. Jews in front and Jews behind/ Jews of every conceivable kind. Massed on the steps of the City Hall/ Jews that were big and Jews that were small. Jews that were fat and Jews that were thin/ Prominent noses and receding chin. Socialists, anarchists, slackers and sneaks/ Faces impertinent brazen and weak/ Jews of all station, poor Jews and rich/ Jews that were dirty and Jews with the itch. Eager to marry and hide behind/ Any old skirt of any old kind.[53]

In a more serious vein, Colonel George F. Weeks "informed" Louis Marshall that "the Jew never was and never will be a soldier. The Jew in the present war is nothing, but a dirty malinger of the lowest degenerated speciment [sic], always looking for something easy to which no danger can possibly come. The Hebrew is a disgrace to the flag that protects him from slavery."[54] The Reverend A.E. Potter of Belleville, New York, scene of anti-Semitic activity during the war, expressed a similar sentiment several years later. "Of all my many Jewish acquaintances," he wrote in 1921, "not one *volunteered* for the great war. *Not one* who was drafted went to the colors without fighting strenuously to avoid service."[55] Occasionally, even the wartime profiteer was depicted as a Jew. The *New York Evening News* printed a vicious cartoon representing one of these scavengers as saying: "Me a Goniff, Schnorrer, not me, not me." The caption read: "Some day when caught."[56]

This damaging stereotype encouraged discrimination. The Surgeon General of the Army published a *Manual of Instruction for Medical Advisory Boards* that accused the foreign-born of tendencies to simulate illness. Medical examiners were warned to be particularly on the alert for Jews "who are more apt to malinger than the native-born."[57] In Brooklyn, Samuel H. Cragg was removed from the local Exemption Board 24 for having made the following statement: "There are three epochs in the life of the Jewish boy: first, at birth, circumcision; second, at 13, confirmation; third, at 21, exemption."[58] It is significant that he was discharged only after intense pressure was exerted by Jewish defense groups.

Literature further projected this characterization. John Dos Passos's novel about the war, *Three Soldiers* (1921), presents Eisenstein, a doughboy with "a shiny Jewish nose," who spent the greater part of his time in Europe professing his unsuitability for combat and bemoaning his misfortune at being sent to man the trenches.[59] There was little of the soldier in "that goddam kike Eisenstein." "I'm in the clothing business," he asserted whenever anyone would listen. "I oughtn't to be drafted at all. It's an outrage. I'm consumptive."[60] Or Maxwell Anderson and Laurence Stallings, in their popular play *What Price Glory* (1924), present two Jewish characters, Corporal Lipinsky and Private Lewisohn, both frightened, weak, and cowardly men. Lewisohn is described as the little Jew who is tied to his mother's apron strings. He is portrayed as the pale urban boy who is overwhelmed by catastrophes such as the loss of his identification tag. Both are generally nondistinguishable from the gentiles in the play except that they are poor fighters who attempt to avoid the approaching battle at whatever cost.[61]

With the end of the conflict when the brief hiatus into the area of Jewish disloyalty and pusillanimity had lost its urgency, the nation reverted to its prewar patterns of discussion concerning the Jew. The war had simply suspended these stereotypes while American nationalism vented itself in other directions. Now the nation was free to deal with the social problems that had preoccupied its leaders and thinkers in the years before Sarajevo. One of these was the question of Jewish unassimilability. This issue took on new importance as the trickle of people that entered during the war years was transformed once again into a torrential flow and as the melting-pot debate took on new significance. It was further complicated by the emergence of American Zionism as a political reality.

Virtually halted by the war, immigration had remained at low ebb throughout 1919 and into the early months of 1920. But the tide turned decisively around by the summer of 1920. By early September, an average five thousand arrivals per day, many of them Jews, were pouring into Ellis Island and these numbers generated a new crescendo of public reaction. Some thought that immigration—Jewish immigration specifically—would eventually undermine the American social and political system because of their clannishness and refusal to internalize American values. Wilbur J. Carr, director of the Consular Service, reporting to the House Committee on Immigration and Naturalization in 1920, made this judgment and urged that their movement into the United States be halted before they irrevocably damaged the American ethic and spirit. "The unassimilability of these classes... is a fact too often proved in the past to bear any argument."[62] Another witness, Francis Kinnicutt, founder of the nativist Allied Patriotic Societies, said: "If these Hebrew colonies assimilate with the rest of the population by intermarriage, the result would probably be bad, owing... to the great differences of an ethnic nature. If assimilation does not take place... we have an alien element which is singularly tenacious of its racial and cultural habits of life and institutions."[63] Both men urged no compromise with this encroaching threat.

One of the first sectors of society affected by this sentiment was the university communities, particularly those situated in urban areas. During a period that witnessed a general weakening in democratic values and tolerance, social discrimination against Jews would undoubtedly have occurred even if no concerted ideological attack on them had continued. Nevertheless, the prevalence of the argumentation facilitated and justified the erection of quota barriers that otherwise might have been more difficult to establish. Fearful of being inundated by Jews who staunchly retained their identity, the universities reacted in self-defense. Cultural pluralism was not yet part of their decalogue. A popular college song of the postwar years reflects these sentiments.

Oh, Harvard's run by millionaires,
And Yale is run by booze,
Cornell is run by farmers' sons,
Columbia's run by Jews.

So give a cheer for Baxter Street,
Another one for Pell,
And when the little sheenies die,
Their souls will go to hell.[64]

After the war, the flood of Jewish students into private colleges resulted in restrictions on admission similar to those adopted earlier by preparatory schools and college fraternities. Some colleges set up alumni committees to screen applicants. Others, under the pretext of seeking regional balance, gave preference to students outside the East, thereby limiting the number of Jews who were heavily concentrated in the East. The most common method of exclusion was the introduction of character and psychological examinations. Before the 1920s, scholastic performance was the most important criterion used in admission policies. Now admission committees asked school principals and devised tests to rank students on such characteristics as "public spirit," "fair play," "interest in fellows," and "leadership." These traits were not usually associated with Jews. Here we see the impact of imagery. According to the prevailing opinion, Jews did not use "fair play," but were grasping and excessively ambitious. "Public spirit" and "interest in fellows" were Christian virtues; Jews were excessively clannish and cared only for their group. "Leadership," again, was seen as a Protestant virtue; Jews exhibiting it would be regarded as aggressive and pushy.[65]

Beginning in 1919, New York University instituted stringent restrictions and introduced psychological testing. Chancellor Elmor Brown justified this policy, citing the "separateness" of the Jewish student body.[66] Dean Archibald Lewis Bouton elaborated on the Chancellor's theme. "A grave condition... affects the efficiency of the entire process of training when... the student body is made up of large masses of students who segregate themselves into groups exactly as in the city outside and tend to divide upon matters of undergraduate policy according to racial or national origin."[67] Columbia University, reacting to a similar anxiety, soon cut the number of Jews in the incoming classes from 40 to 20 percent.[68] At Harvard, where elite Protestant students and faculty feared the University was becoming a New Jerusalem, President A. Lawrence Lowell, in 1922 moved, with unseemly frankness, to raise the bars. "There is . . . a rapidly growing anti-Semitic feeling in this country," he wrote in June of that year, "caused by a strong race feeling on the part of the Jews."[69] It has entered the sanctity of the University; hence the numerous clauses as the appropriate solution. Smaller colleges, perhaps more rigidly than some of the large ones, elaborated their applications, required a photograph of the candidate, and enforced a geographic distribution.

Others, both within the intellectual community and on its periphery, agreed with Lowell's evaluation and extended it into a national indictment. Dr. Herbert Adams Gibbons, the prominent journalist, author, and historian, reacting to the rise of Zionism in the United States, responded with vituperation. "If the Jews persist in maintaining a distinct ethnic consciousness and an exclusive community life, anti-Semitism will thrive in America as it has thrived in Europe.... For the Jews it is either into the melting pot or back to the Ghetto."[70] John Punnett Peters, the prominent Episcopal clergyman, archeologist and philologist, sounded a parallel theme in a 1921 article. Zionism will prove to the world the nationalistic character of the Jew and thereby fan the flames of anti-Semitism. That hostility, increasing daily, "results not so much from differences of religion as from the pronounced and obstrusive differences of race, nationality, and political allegiance."[71] Or as Paul Scott Mowrer wrote in *The Atlantic Monthly* in 1921: "It is based on the observation that the Jews... not only have kept their identity as a people, but have opposed a vigorous, if passive, resistance to most attempts at assimilation.... As such, he [sic] is considered to be an enemy of the state."[72]

What was startling about these assessments was not their tone or thrust—these certainly were not unique—but the intensity and frequency with which they appeared. In an America swept along by Red Scares and xenophobia to new degrees of prejudice and in a nation turning its back on world affairs, the question of inner unity and homogeneity took on increased import. The isolationist reaction of the 1920s pressed home the danger not only of world entanglements in a more conscious and articulate manner than ever before, but also underscored for those sensitive to increased immigration the threat of national enclaves within impeding the fortress America concept.

Nativism thus echoed through the halls of the universities; it swayed the policies of the American Legion and rumbled in the "Konklaves" of the Ku Klux Klan; it unleashed a new torrent of interest in restrictive immigration legislation.[73] One of the most widely publicized attacks on Jews during the 1920s was Burton Hendrick's series of articles appearing in *World's Work* in 1922–23 and in book form under the title *The Jews in America* (1923). This well-known muckraking journalist and Yale historian piously deplored anti-Jewish sentiment as something unworthy of the Anglo-Saxon race. Yet his apologetics did not stop him from spreading prejudicial ideas in a book advertised as objective and scholarly. After having some good things to say about the Sephardic and German Jews, Hendrick launched an attack on those of the "New" immigration by assuring his readers that "as candidates for assimilation these Jews, as they land at Ellis Island, are about as promising as a similarly inflowing stream of Hindus or Syrian Druses." Hendrick traced the origins of these East Europeans back to the Khazars of the Crimea, thus enabling him to claim that Polish and Russian Jews have Asiatic blood in their veins. That might explain their stubborn, religious orthodoxy, peculiar mentality, particularism, and resistance to modernization. He asserted that these products of Europe's ghettos "constitute an utterly unassimilable element in our population." The process of Americanization, Hendrick warned, is therefore going to be slower and more difficult with this class of immigrants than with any other. That is why America must close the floodgates before it is inundated by this herding mass. "There is only one way in which the United States can be protected from the anti-Semitism which so grievously afflicts the eastern sections of Europe," Hendrick advised, and "that is by putting up the bars against these immigrants."[74]

Horace Bridges, in an anti-Semitic tract accurately entitled *Jew-Baiting* (1923), agreed. Surveying the course of history, he remarked:

To be a Jew is to be a citizen of the Jewish nation and to cease to be a Jew is a sheer impossibility. Consequently,... wherever Jews are in the world they constitute an alien element, irreducibly different from,... and antagonistic to their hosts.... The inference from the above arguments, is that every oath of allegiance ever made by Jews was a deliberate and conscious lie. Every act of patriotism performed by Jews in the service of these lands has been... hypocritical.... Jews may die in battle, participate in government and attempt to become integral parts of their adopted community, but the cause can *never* become part of their own.[75]

Gino Speranza, a fellow-traveler in the fraternity of restrictionists and proponents of Nordic superiority who served as the New York State immigration commissioner before the war, continued this strain of argumentation in his articles in *World's Work* and in his book *Race or Nation* (1923). Speranza, throughout the 1920s, in fact, undertook a personal campaign to alert the nation to the dangers of unlimited immigration. Considering his own background, this was a rather droll effort, but yet he was a nuisance to those charged with defending minority group rights. As Louis Marshall of the American Jewish Committee explained: "He is a renegade Italian, who for some years past has befouled his own nest. I have a rod in pickle for him."[76]

Speranza argued that American civilization was fundamentally Protestant, Anglo-Saxon, and racially Nordic and that Jews were an unabsorbable mass who were "alienizing" it.[77] The "self-assertive" Jews, exhilarated by the momentum of their expanding numbers, have become "aggressive in their resistance" to integration "until they gradually reach a point where they actually attempt to impose their views and their principles and their interpretations and their standards upon the historic American majority."[78] Noting that immigrants from Northern and Western Europe possessed an affinity for catching hold of the democratic spirit, Speranza warned that "hardest and perhaps impossible will be the spiritual assimilation of Israel."[79] There is a real danger, for the Jew, "is engaged in an elemental struggle to remain alien," in an elemental struggle, in fact, "to make America Alien."[80] Specious as Speranza's fears were, they reflected the growing concern of an embattled nation confronted by a changing environment and a strange resilient population.

Intellectually, the resurgent racism of the early twenties projected by these commentators drew its central inspiration and "scientific" justification from Madison Grant's *The Passing of the Great Race*. Grant, a lawyer, Yale class of 1889, was a prominent amateur zoologist and eugenicist, whose name graced the rolls of many elite social organizations. For Grant, eugenics destroyed the "pathetic and fatuous belief in the efficacy of American institutions and environment to reverse or obliterate immemorial hereditary tendencies" of the "poor helots" who migrated here.[81] Of these, the Polish Jews were the worst. They "adopt the language of the native American; they wear his clothes; they steal his name; and they are beginning to take his women, but they seldom adopt his religion or understand his ideals.' "[82] The book caused very little comment when first published in 1916, but a decade later it enjoyed a substantial vogue in certain intellectual circles. Although Grant never became widely known, his emotionally charged theories of racial development stirred the imagination of many literate people. He inspired a bevy of popular writers like Speranza and influenced a number of scholarly ones like Henry Pratt Fairchild and Lothrop Stoddard.

Stoddard, a lawyer in Brookline, Massachusetts, with a Ph.D. in history, was Grant's leading disciple. His main preoccupation was the rapid multiplication of the yellow and brown races and the danger— spectacularly stated in 1920 in *The Rising Tide of Color*—that they would soon overwhelm the white civilized world.[83] Yet in a later book, *Re-Forging America* (1927), he focused his overgeneralized attention on the problem specifically affecting the United States and echoed the stilted evaluations made by his colleagues in scientific nativism. Talking about Eastern European Jews, he remarked that they are

as thoroughly "alien" to America as it is possible to conceive. For instance: we set great store by our ideal of national life. But to the mass of Eastern Jews the very phrase "national life" was not only meaningless but was positively distasteful. They had never been a nation; nor had they ever formed part of a nation. From time immemorial they had led a closed life as a persecuted tribal sect.[84]

Hence their incompatibility with Stoddard's notion of a homogeneous American populous.

But there was another side to the Jewish personality besides historical exclusivity disturbing to Stoddard and that was its predilection to accept a philosophy that challenged the very essence of American democracy as he conceived it. Their alienism predisposed Jews, he argued, to support cultural pluralism propagated by people like Horace M. Kallen, the Harvard-educated student and disciple of William James. True democracy, Kallen insisted, demands an imaging of America other than the Melting Pot. Each group must be permitted to express the vitality and legitimacy of its own unique cultural life and through the interweaving of the ethnic tapestry, the fabric of the nation will be strengthened and enriched.[85]

Perceptively, the last paragraph of Kallen's essay, "Democracy versus the Melting Pot," opens with: "But the question is, do the dominant classes in America want such a society?"[86] Certainly Stoddard did not. He perceived pluralism as a threat to that national symmetry and homogeneity that became the hallmark of his intellectual coterie. Reacting to Kallen's concept, he wrote: "We find an arch-champion of 'hyphenism' who exemplifies the alien spirit better than any other of its spokesmen! Doctor Kallen is a striking example of what we have already emphasized: that high intelligence in immigrants may be combined with a temperamental make-up so different from ours that assimilation is absolutely impossible."[87] Kallen's thesis is a frank expression of that aggressive alienism that is chipping away at the very foundation of national existence. In fact, it "strikes at the very vitals of American life.... For surely, the disintegration of national unity into anything like a 'Pluralistic America' would mean, not an orchestration of mankind, but a hellish bedlam." The presence, therefore, of this "vast nondescript mass, with no genuine loyalties, traditional roots, or cultural and idealistic standards, is a real menace" to the country's future.[88]

The noted New York University sociologist Henry Pratt Fairchild hewed to a parallel concept of Anglo-Saxon nationalism and pointed accusingly at Jewish clannishness. In his *Melting-Pot Mistake* (1920), which proved to be as much an epitaph to this school of thought as a qualified summation of it, he echoed earlier sentiments graced, however, with less intemperate generalizations. America, he argued, is indeed a "spiritual reality." It is composed of a body of "ideals," "ideas," "traditions," "standards" and "loyalties" that make up a consistent and logical "complex of cultural and moral values."[89] The true Americans, Fairchild advised, "are those who embody most completely in their individual characters... the spiritual traits and qualities that make up the American nationality." Essentially, this disqualifies the Jew who has no home or nation to which he can devote his "restless activities" and dedicate his "ardent aspirations." "Consequently they are driven to seek to perpetuate their own nationality in the midst of other nationalities." This trait is most unfortunate in the United States, where Jews on high intellectual and cultural grounds, oppose assimilation because of the inroads it makes into the strength of their own original nationalities.... Cases have been numerous... where Rabbis and other prominent Jewish leaders have urged their people to remain distinct, and to strive to become constantly more Jewish.... Such persons... constitute an undeniable menace to American national stability.[90]

For Fairchild, as for the others previously mentioned, the Jew thus remained the perennial alien, the stranger at the gate, the visible mutation defiling the panorama of an illusory national unity.[91]

This, then is the charge that resounded even in America, a country that historically has been more receptive and tolerant of Jewish peculiarities and traditions. As one American commentator noted: "You can kill a Jew, ten, a hundred, a thousand, but you can't kill the Jews. They cannot even be absorbed."[92] In the nineteenth century, this sentiment resulted from Jewish refusal to convert; in the twentieth century, it was substantially a reaction to mass immigration, ghetto enclaves, and the burgeoning Zionist movement. In both periods, the Jew was abused as the unassimilable mass, the aloof, unpatriotic outsider who is resistant to total ethnic erasure. It was finally brought forward in the second and third decades of the twentieth century as a major argument for immigration restriction. As prominent New York lawyer William W. Cook summarized the issue: they are "Jews first and Americans second"; they are "an alien race in the nation" that proposes "to maintain their separate identity and social existence"; a "Jewish block of portentious proportions," dangerously situated on the periphery of society, never totally committed to its goals or in tune with its aspirations and traditions.[93] This perception contributed greatly to the aura of suspicion that surrounded the American Jew during the era of burgeoning nationalism.

NOTES

1. Quoted in *American Israelite,* June 22, 1860; *New York Tribune,* June 19, 1898.

2. Edward H. Flannery, *The Anquish of the Jews* (New York: The Macmillan Co., 1965); Samuel Sandmel, *The First Christian Century of Judaism and Christianity: Certainties and Uncertainties* (New York: Oxford University Press, 1969).

3. Mark Zborowski and Elizabeth Herzog, *Life Is with People* (New York: Schocken Books, 1962).

4. The Jewish soul or heart or ethic.

5. Anna Laurens Dawes, *The Modern Jew* (Boston: D. Lothrop and Co., 1886).

6. Ibid., pp. 11, 41 – 42.

7. Reverend Robert Collyer, "Letter," *The American Hebrew*, April 4, 1890, p. 167.

8. Reverend J.R. Day, "Letter," in ibid., p. 173.

9. Reverend A.H. Lewis, "Letter," in ibid.

10. Reverend W.H.P. Faunce, "Letter," in ibid., p. 172.

11. E.N. Capen, "Letter," in ibid., p. 192.

12. John Burroughs, "Letter," in ibid., p. 192.

13. Henry T. Finck, "Letter," in ibid., p. 195.

14. Joseph Pennell, *The Jew at Home; Impressions of a Summer and Autumn Spent with Him* (New York: D. Appleton and Co., 1892), p. 10.

15. For James G. Blaine's attitude, see Letter, James G. Blaine to Charles Emory Smith, February 18, 1891, *United States State Department, Papers Relating to the Foreign Relations of the United States with the Annual Message of the President 1861 – 1931*, Washington, D.C.

16. *Leslie's Weekly*, Vol. 74, No. 1902 (February 27, 1892), p. 57.

17. Ibid.

18. *The Independent*, Vol. 41, No. 2128 (Se3ptember 12, 1889), p. 17; Vol. 42, No. 2158 (April 10, 1890), p. 487.

19. *The Outlook*, Vol. 74, No. 6 (June 6, 1903), p. 312.

20. *The Methodist Review*, Vol. 75 (March, 1893), p. 297.

21. *The Catholic Record*, Vol. 15, No. 44 (April 28, 1898), p. 4.

22. Quoted in *American Israelite*, May 27, 1881.

23. *The World's Work*, Vol. 2, No. 3 (January, 1906), p. 7031.

24. *Harper's Weekly*, Vol. 49, No. 2511 (February 4, 1905).

25. Nathaniel S. Shaler, *The Neighbor* (Boston: Houghton, Mifflin and Co., 1904), pp. 72 – 103; see also Lewis H. Carlson and George A. Colburn, *In Their Place: White America Defines Her Minorities 1850 – 1950* (New York: John Wiley & Sons, 1972), pp. 267 – 68.

26. Shaler, pp. 108, 112; and Barbara Miller Solomon, *Ancestors and Immigrants* (Chicago: The University of Chicago Press, 1972).

27. Shaler, p. 43.

28. Ibid., pp. 325, 328.

29. William Graham Sumner, *Folkways* (Boston: Ginn and Co., 1940), p. 81. This is a reprint of a 1906 edition.

30. Ibid., pp. 14, 110, 399.

31. William Z. Ripley, *The Races of Europe* (New York: D. Appleton and Co., 1899).

32. Ibid., pp. 368 – 69, 384, 395.

33. John Higham, *Strangers in the Land: Patterns of American Nativism 1860 – 1925* (New York: Atheneum, 1971), pp. 269 – 99.

34. Alfred P. Schultz, *Race or Mongrel* (Boston: L.C. Page, 1908).

35. Letter, Alfred P. Schultz to Prescott Hall, February 14, 1909, Prescott F. Hall Collection, The Houghton Library, Harvard University, Cambridge, Massachusetts.

36. See also Sumner, pp. 310 – 11.

37. Dr. J.G. Wilson, "The Crossing of the Races," *The Popular Science Monthly,* Vol. 79 (November, 1911), p. 494.

38. Letter, J.K. Kingsburg to L. Marshall, January 28, 1914, American Jewish Committee Archives, Immigrant Box, General Correspondence 1906 – 1932, New York.

39. Letter, H.L. Mencken to Henry Hurwitz, October 7, 1916, Henry Hurwitz Menorah Association Collection, American Jewish Archives, Cincinnati, Ohio.

40. Richard Hayes McCartney, *That Jew!* (New York: Fleming H. Revell Co., 1905), pp. 9 – 10.

41. Letter, William Williams to Theodore Roosevelt, January 31, 1912, William Williams Papers, New York Public Library, New York.

42. Address delivered before the Senior Class of Princeton University in November, 1904, William Williams Papers.

43. See also Letter, Henry Cabot Lodge to Sturges Bigelow, February 22, 1913, Henry Cabot Lodge Papers, Massachusetts Historical Society, Boston, Massachusetts.

44. The others were Prescott Hall and Charles Warren.

45. Robert Dec. Ward, "The Immigration Problem," *Charities,* Vol. 12, No. 6 (February 6, 1904), p. 144.

46. Quoted in Zosa Szajkowski, *Jews, Wars and Communism* (New York: KTAV Publishing House, 1972), p. 482.

47. Reverend William Norman Guthrie, "Chauvinism Is an Obstacle to a Better Understanding Between Jew and Christian," *The American Citizen,* Vol. II, No. 1 (January, 1913), pp. 4 – 5.

48. Letter, Theodore Roosevelt to editor of The National Encyclopedia Co., May 15, 1901, Jacob R. Marcus Private Collection, xerox copy, Cincinnati, Ohio.

49. Ibid.

50. Cincinnati *Times-Star,* August 21, 1908, Louis Marshall Papers, xerox

copies, Box 1, American Jewish Committee Archives, New York; Cincinnati *Times-Star*, August 18, 1908, in ibid.

51. *New York Age*, August 10, 1905.

52. American Jewish Committee Archives, General Correspondence 1906 – 32, D-Discrimination-E.

53. Ibid.

54. Letter, Colonel George F. Weeks to Louis Marshall, April 18, 1918, American Jewish Committee Archives, General Correspondence 1906 – 32, D-Discrimination-E.

55. Letter, Reverend A.E. Potter to American Jewish Committee, March 17, 1921, American Jewish Committee Archives, Louis Marshall Correspondence, Alliance-Hume.

56. Quoted in *American Israelite*, May 20, 1920, p. 4.

57. American Jewish Committee Archives, General Correspondence 1906 – 32, D-Discrimination-E; and *American Jewish Year Book*, Vol. 21 (1919 – 20), pp. 632 – 36.

58. *New York Times*, August 21, 1917, p. 8, and January 6, 1918, p. 16.

59. John Dos Passos, *Three Soldiers* (New York: The Modern Library, 1932), p. 8.

60. Ibid., p. 42.

61. Maxwell Anderson and Laurence Stallings, "What Price Glory," in *Twentieth Century Plays*, ed. Frank W. Chandler and Richard A. Cordell (New York: Thomas Nelson and Sons, 1934).

62. U.S. Congress, House, *Temporary Suspension of Immigration*, House Report No. 1109, 66th Cong., 3rd sess., December 6 1920, p. 10.

63. Ibid.

64. Quoted in Stephen Steinberg, "How Jewish Quotas Began," *Commentary*, Vol. 52, No. 3 (September, 1971), p. 71.

65. See Steinberg, pp. 71 – 72.

66. *New York University Daily News*, Vol. 1, No. 82 (May 11, 1923), p. 4.

67. *New York University Alumnus*, Vol. 1, No. 2 (November, 1920), p. 24. There were other manifestations of anti-Semitism at New York University. Jewish students complained that they were discriminated against for election to Phi Beta Kappa. Jewish fraternities and organizations were excluded from the yearbook *The Violet*. Only members of non-Jewish fraternities were invited to the annual Junior Prom. Jewish students protested in March 1923, but received no succor from either the administration or the campus press. In fact, two mildly anti-Semitic editorials greeted their complaint. On Monday, March 19, the campus was plastered with the following anti-Semitic poster:

) єɔ

Strictly Kosher—Must not Apply Here
    Scurvey Kikes
Are Not Wanted
At New York University
If they knew
their place they would
not be here.
Make New York
University a White
Man's College.

Sworn Deposition of Mordecai Soltes, July 9, 1919, Louis Marshall Collection, Box 53; Letter of Michael Stavitsky to Liebermann, June 27, 1919, in ibid.; copy of poster in ibid.

68. *Columbia University Bulletin of Information,* December 18, 1920, p. 7, announces the introduction of the psychological examination.

69. Letter, A.L. Lowell to A.C. Ratshevsky, June 7, 1922, American Jewish Committee Archives, General Correspondence 1906–32, D-Discrimination-E.

70. Herbert Adams Gibbons, "The Jewish Problem," *The Century Magazine,* Vol. 102, No. 5 (September, 1921), p. 789.

71. John Punnett Peters, "Zionism and the Jewish Problem," *The Sewanee Review,* Vol. 29, No. 1 (January, 1921), pp. 284–85.

72. Paul Scott Mowrer, "The Assimilation of Israel," *The Atlantic Monthly* (July, 1921), p. 103.

73. Higham, *Strangers in the Land.*

74. Burton J. Hendrick, *The Jews in America* (New York: Doubleday, Page & Co., 1923), pp. 4, 96, 170–71.

75. Horace James Bridges, *Jew-Baiting: An Old Evil Newly Camouflaged* (New York: International Press, 1923), pp. 24, 36.

76. Letter, Louis Marshall to Harry Schneiderman, October 27, 1923, American Jewish Committee Archives, General Correspondence 1906–32.

77. Gino Speranza, "The Immigration Peril," *World's Work* (November, 1924), p. 63.

78. Ibid.

79. Gino Speranza, "Effects of Mass Alienage upon the Spiritual Life of American Democracy," *World's Work* (February, 1924), pp. 408–9.

80. Speranza, "The Immigration Peril," p. 64.

81. Madison Grant, *The Passing of the Great Race* (New York: Charles Scribner's Sons, 1916), pp. 74, 79.

82. Ibid., p. 81.

83. Lothrop Stoddard, *The Rising Tide of Color* (New York: Charles Scribner's Sons, 1927).

84. Lothrop Stoddard, *Re-Forging America* (New York: Charles Scribner's Sons, 1927), p. 130.

85. Horace M. Kallen, *Culture and Democracy in the United States* (New York: Boni & Liveright, 1924).

86. Ibid., p. 125.

87. Stoddard, *Re-Forging America,* p. 246.

88. Ibid., pp. 249, 349.

89. Henry Pratt Fairchild, *The Melting-Pot Mistake* (Boston: Little, Brown and Co., 1926), p. 201.

90. Ibid., pp. 202, 222, 225 – 26.

91. See also Don C. Seitz, "Jews, Catholics, and Protestants," *The Outlook,* Vol. 141, No. 13 (November, 1925), p. 478; Alfred Williams Anthony, "The Jewish Problem" (By the author, 1924), p. 5; Reverend Albert A. Hilleary, *The Jew and the Klan* (Harrisburg, Pennsylvania: The Evangelical Press, 1925), pp. 57, 101.

92. Konrad Bercovici, "The Greatest Jewish City in the World," *The Nation,* Vol. 117, No. 3036 (September 12, 1923), p. 259.

93. William W. Cook, *American Institutions and Their Preservation* (Norwood, Massachusetts: Norwood Press, 1927), p. 122.

Might it not be that the money lenders of London, the magnificent, titled Shylocks of our modern world; who play with Czars, Emperors and Kings as a chess-player with castles, rooks and pawns, in the artificial production of a panic,... may have purposely wrought the ruin of many American banks,... because in America these gamblers of the banking world reap their richest harvests and wish to continue their tightest grip on the people?

THE ILLUSTRATED AMERICAN(July 27, 1895)[1]

Cabinet ministers cannot arrange a budget without consulting Jews, for they govern the money market;... they are the power behind every throne in the world.

WILLIAM TRANT (1912)[2]

The Semitic, is largely international or racial in its interests.

PRESCOTT HALL[3]

A Conspiracy of Evils

The popular notion that Jews were tied together by the invisible but permanent bonds of blood and family and were by instinct clannish and hence alienated from the national culture led, in many minds, to another corollary: that they would use their unity for conspiratorial purposes. This tandem conceptualization has its origins in the misty history of early Christian-Jewish interaction. The fantasy of Jews as a brotherhood of evil was probably first conceived between the second and fourth centuries as a device for immunizing Christians against the attractiveness of Judaism; and seven or eight centuries later, in Western Europe, it developed into a coherent and terrifying demonology. From the Middle Ages onward, Jews were seen as a cabal of sorcerers in league with the devil, working for the spiritual and moral ruination of Christendom.[4] As a result, this was the period when they were massacred by the thousands on charges of killing Christian children, of defiling the consecrated wafer, of poisoning wells, the source of the dread bubonic plague itself.

In the general image the Jew, while retaining all the mysterious, supernatural attitudes that were wished upon him in the Middle Ages, also became the symbol of modernity, particularly of everything that was frightening about the modern world. The industrial revolution brought the emancipation of the Jews. Everywhere, where permitted, they became prominent in those fields for which they had been fitted by their previous history: banking, certain branches of commerce, journalism. There was nothing sinister in any of this, but it did mean that those who suffered helplessly from the modern world and were not able to adjust to it could easily identify the Jew as the embodiment of a civilization they feared and despised. The fateful consequence was that when, for reasons that had nothing to do with the Jewish question, economic and social problems came to the foreground of the political scene, the Jews at once fitted the doctrines and stereotypes that defined a people by blood ties and racial characteristics and took on the shape of a coherent and unified mass working against the public interest.

Beliefs concerning Jewish solidarity and clannishness that were basically benign and were inherited from earlier periods were accordingly reinterpreted. Ideological anti-Semitism in Europe and America condemns the Jew as incapable of assimilation and disloyal to the basic institutions of the host nation.[5] Now, in its more extreme form, it portrays Jews as leagued together in a vast international consortium of evil. The alleged plot usually centers on gaining control of the money supply and destroying the financial system; sometimes it extends to polluting the nation's morals and spiritual resolve through control of communications and entertainment. This image, although originating on the Continent and reaching the greatest expression there, eventually infiltrated into the thought modes of many Americans and was culled during times of crisis and unrest. It was an important factor in the persistence of anti-Semitism in the late nineteenth century and its projection into the twentieth.

The general battle against the supposed nefarious influence of the Jews was waged around certain identifiable storm centers. Of these, the first, and throughout the early period the greatest, was the House of Rothschild. To Christian society, the Rothschild family became a symbol of the working reality of Jewish internationalism in a world of nations and nationally rooted peoples. The amazing financial success of the five brothers born in the Judengasse of pre-Emancipation Frankfurt was inevitably a subject of legend. So much so that *la haute banque juive* became synonymous with high finance, and the Rothschild empire itself was perceived as the center of a vast web that was dedicated to the exploitation of Christian Europe and America.[6] In America, unfortunately, the Rothschilds became involved in one of the most unpopular financial transactions the United States Treasury ever undertook. When President Cleveland's effort to save the gold standard culminated in 1895 in a secretly negotiated contract to buy gold in Europe, the names of August Belmont and Company and N.M. Rothschild and Sons appeared prominently. By singling out the Rothschilds, silverites found all the evidence they needed to demonstrate how Jewish money power profited from American distress.

Although this theme received its greatest expression in the Populist era, it was broached earlier by commentators who presaged the agrarian fever of the 1890s. *Niles' Weekly Register,* during a period of banking controversy in 1835, characterized the family and its enterprise as follows: "The Rothschilds govern a Christian world. Not a cabinet moves without their advice. They stretch their hand, with equal ease, from Petersburgh to Vienna, from Vienna to Paris, from Paris to London, from London to Washington.... They are the brokers and counsellors of the kings of Europe and of the republican chiefs of America."[7] The *New York Times* wrote in 1852 that the Rothschilds control "the decision of war or peace in European countries. A Jew declares empires bankrupt or solvent at will.... The world at last does homage to the... chosen and rejected people." *The Philadelphia Times* remarked in 1856 that "whoever may be king in Europe, Rothschild rules."[8] *Harper's New Monthly Magazine,* on the eve of another monetary crisis in the 1870s, sounded a similar note.

From the first they have been capitalists and amassers. To that every thing has been reduced subservient.... They have belted the globe with their operations and are in the fullest sense universal and cosmopolitan.... Through all their resplendent career they have preserved the heart of the moneychanger, with no fear of fatal consequence from its enlargment. They have been princes in the parlor, and pawnbrokers in the kitchen.... Their monomania has been money mania....[9]

For the Greenbacker Elizabeth Bryant, the Rothschilds epitomized the capitalistic instincts that made the Jew a middleman, a moneylender, and ultimately a monopolistic "Wall Street" banker. Her unbalanced, agrarian anti-Semitism is reminiscent of a later brand of rural extremism. In *Types of Mankind...* (1879), she wrote that the Jew "without a country, with no national existence, owing allegiance to no government,... controls the money power of the world."[10] Overseeing this complex system is the House of Rothschild that acts with the prescience and unity of a solitary omnipotent force. Their autocratic power "outmeasures that of any potentate on the globe." No issue of national policy can be "arranged" without their sanction. "The nations of Europe are but pieces on a chessboard" that they "move at will."[11]

A fictional portrait of this Rothschildean influence is provided by William Macon Coleman in his novel *The Wandering Jew in America* (1875). Written in the tradition of those other works, both in Europe and America, that exploit the legend of Ahasuerus, like George Croly's *Salathiel* (1829), Eugène Sue's *Wandering Jew* (translated into English in 1845), George Lippard's *Nazarene* (1846), F. Marion Crawford's *A Roman Singer* (1883), and Lew Wallace's *Prince of India* (1893), it transforms the mysterious wanderer into a functionary of Jewish international monetary control. Isaacs, the agent of international Jewish wealth, is thus made to expound to Senator Tyrrell, the symbolic exploited American:

Remember that the Jew holds your honorable self and all your honorable colleagues in the hollow of his hand. The wealth and power of this nation is his. Your public securities... and the toil and sweat of this people are... his also. He furnishes the means for your colossal enterprises and holds the mortgages upon them. He makes and unmakes your Senate with a breath. He controls your press.... He permits your nation to exist until it shall suit his purposes to destroy its life.[12]

This image of Jewish monetary control, centered in London and dedicated to the gold standard and working to the disadvantage of agrarians and debtors, received new impetus and exposure through the rhetoric of the Populists in the 1890s. They did not create the portrait, as we have seen, nor did they give it its ultimate expression, but they contributed to its continuation and made it relevant for many who were hopelessly searching for an explanation for seemingly insurmountable difficulties. At a time when Jews and their detractors boasted of their wealth, farmers and workingmen were struggling vainly to curb the accumulation of power and wealth by a business plutocracy. Just as Wall Street provided an institutional symbol of that plutocracy, so the Jews offered an ethnic symbol of the same enemy.

In recent years there has been some historical controversy on the question of Populist anti-Semitism. In the 1950s and 1960s, two "consensus" historians, Richard Hofstadter and Oscar Handlin, put forward the thesis that a qualitative change took place in anti-Semitism in the late nineteenth century that was largely due to the anti-Jewish agitation of the Populists. During the 1890s, Handlin writes,

the injured groups of American society, in agony... scarcely guessed that the source of their trials was a change in the world in which they lived.... Some perceived its instrument, the Jew,... stereotyped, involved in finance, and mysterious.... It was this suspicion that transformed the conception of the Jew after 1900, replaced the older images with that of the Elder of Zion.[13]

A similar, although more cautious, charge is made by Hofstadter. "It was chiefly Populist writers who expressed that identification of the Jew with the usurer and the 'international gold ring' which was the central theme of the American anti-Semitism of the age." Although the movement "did not lead to exclusion laws, much less to riots or pogroms," yet "it is not too much to say that the Greenback-Populist tradition activated most of what we have of popular anti-Semitism in the United States."[14]

Both Hofstadter and Handlin argue that responsibility for the new level of overt and articulate anti-Semitism that developed in America toward the end of the nineteenth century and into the twentieth rested primarily with the anti-Semitic rhetoric of the Populist movement. This is a misleading oversimplification. Both men overlooked the anti-Jewish character of the most obvious and flagrant stereotypical expressions that appeared frequently in literature, on the stage, and in print. Evidence indicates that there were many misconceptions and falsehoods, including conspiracy theories, circulating in America before the 1890s that had nothing to do with the agrarian protest. Anti-Semitism is a phenomenon that is much too complex to have been caused primarily by a movement that, in reality, had limited influence. (Populism could scarcely be blamed for the increasing discrimination in social resorts, private schools, and clubs, for example.) John Higham has suggested some of this complexity by placing the problem in the context of social conflict. Prejudice developed where and when Jews participated in the general middle-class scramble for prestige and status; it developed "where and when a hectic pace of social climbing made the guardians of distinction afraid of being invaded."[15] A pervasive sentiment in America, it could hardly, in justice, be localized to particular segments of the population, be they patrician or agrarian.[16]

This is not to suggest, as have the revisionists Norman Pollack, Walter Nugent, and even John Higham, that Populist Judeophobia was insignificant. As Irwin Unger has reminded us: "Not all Populists were anti-Semites... and neither were all anti-Semites Populists." Yet some elements within the movement "clearly disliked foreigners and Jews, and for reasons... that were uniquely Populistic." To these individuals, "the Jew was a 'nonproducer,' a mere manipulator of money, a parasite, and at the same time representative of the sinister and forbidding power of international finance."[17] To deny that these sentiments existed is rather pointless. There is no doubt that Populism contributed in some degree, along with the Brahmin harbingers of Armageddon, to the formation of an embryonic anti-Semitic ideology when some Populists repeated ad nauseum the conspiracy myth of international Jewish bankers determined to dominate the world. There is no doubt that they helped perpetuate certain thought modes that identified Jews with Shylock, malevolent bankers, and control. All this must be viewed in context, however, since they cannot be held responsible for the previous manifestations and imaging already discussed in earlier chapters. Consequently, they must take their place as a contributing element indeed, but one that enjoyed no degree of exclusivity. Upon examination, some of the factors that propelled a segment of agrarian activists down the road of conspiracy become more evident.

When the economic crises of the 1890s erupted, a stereotype of the

American Jew had already been developed and was available for exploitation. The image recognized the Jew as distinct from the rest of American society and essentially unassimilable. Survivors of all attempts to absorb him indicated superior powers—since he could resist change himself, it was assumed the Jew had the power to change others. Jews, furthermore, had a tendency to transfer their concept of a compact community to urban areas and as such they contributed to a belief among Christians that Jews were indifferent to the patterns of rural American life. Jewish strength was associated with wealth, the East, the city, and business. It drew its sustenance from the power of the mind that used superior cunning to victimize the sturdy but simple yeoman. Jewish isolation and separation from the hinterland encouraged speculation about their mysterious traditions and unfamiliar practices. Folk ballads of "sacred legend," such as "The Jew's Daughter," which reflected visions of darkness and cruelty, found their place in the American Midwest. "She pinned a napkin round his neck/ She pinned it with a pin. And then she called for a tin basin/ To catch his life blood in."[18]

The belief persisted that Jews were constantly involved in money matters and financial maneuvering. Jewish wealth was described as parasitic wealth. As a nonproductive element in society, they were associated with the middleman and wholesaler who, the farmers believed, were robbing them of profits. This meshed with the stereotype of the Jewish financier wielding enormous power through control of the gold supply. Most Americans had heard of the Rothschilds and Lazard Frères. If they had not, translations of Edouard Drumont's *La France Juive* (1886) and the works of Timayenis gave them the elaborate details. The exotic figure of Benjamin Disraeli, the empire builder, was a convenient addition to this growing mythology, as were the prominence of Montefiore Levi and Alfred de Rothschild at the Brussels Monetary Conference, the reputation of Baron Gerson von Bleichröder, the funder of Prussian state loans and confidant of Bismarck, and the influence of Perry Belmont among the Gold Democrats.[19]

In addition to references to the House of Rothschild, the Populists used the image of Shylock to condemn Jews. Many believed in the 1890s that all commerce was corrupt and that trade was foisted initially on the world by the Jews. To these people, every Jewish businessman was the advance guard of a new materialistic civilization. Shylock, concerned with wealth and usurious interest above the plight of humanity, was a perfect allusion for those trying to establish the connection between Jewish financial interests and the economic problems of the farmer. The composite image was a kind of demonic figure who huddled in the darkness ready to manipulate lives and fortunes for his own selfish interest. Since many Americans were reluctant to accept responsibility for their economic decline and were bewildered and uncertain about its cause, they were susceptible to a foreign conspiracy theory that explained the ills of the nation. Only Jews had the craft and will enough to participate in international transactions that squeezed the "ducats" out of unsuspecting Christians; only history's greatest betrayers could commit the greatest of betrayal.

An early exponent of this theory was William M. Stewart, who later became a free-silver senator from Nevada. In 1885, reacting to the "Crime of 1873," he used a familiar imagery to describe the activities of the Anglo-Jewish syndicate. "Every American citizen of ordinary intelligence knows that it would be less difficult to induce Shylock to surrender his pound of flesh than it would be to obtain from Europe a recommendation for the restoration of silver to the place it occupied when the bonded debts of the world were contracted."[20] Thirteen years later, after the defeat of political populism, he was more specific and accusatory. "The Rothschild combination has proceeded in the last twenty years with marvelous rapidity to enslave the human race." The accomplishment of their nefarious scheme, which includes "the final subjection of Europe, Asia, and Africa to the rule of the money power," depends upon "concentrating wealth, building up aristrocracy, and destroying democracy, particularly in the United States."[21]

Tom Watson, the Georgia firebrand, saw this as a *fait accompli* by 1892. Referring to Thomas Jefferson, he queried: "Did he dream that in 100 years or less his party would be prostituted to the vilest purposes of monopoly; that red-eyed Jewish millionaires would be the chiefs of that party, and that the liberty and prosperity of the country would be... sacrificed to Plutocratic greed in the name of Jeffersonian Democracy?"[22] The culprits again were the Rothschilds, working through their lackey August Belmont. G.T. Washburn, a prominent Populist, warned that the gold trust "under the generalship of a European Jew, is capable of anything." C.J. Bradshaw, a Kentucky Populist, called the Jews "hawk-nosed Christ-killers" at the 1896 Michigan State silver convention. A North Carolina Populist identified Jews with Wall Street and Shylock and concluded that "our Negro brethren too, are being held in bondage by Shylock."[23] Sarah E.V. Emery, a Michigan Populist, agreed. She argued that as early as the American Civil War, these "Shylocks" were determined to corner the market on the metallic money supply. They were bent on wrenching "from the government in her distress, such usury as would have put to shame their world renowned ancestor." But they were not satiated with this plunder. "Greed is never satisfied, its ill-gotten gains only serve to sharpen its appeitite, and it is ever crying more, more. Cunning hands, schemeing [sic] brains, degenerate souls, still plot the destruction of this Republic."[24]

One of the central documents of the Populist, bimetalist movement was William Hope Harvey's *Coin's Financial School* (1894). This best seller, in its various editions and versions, sold perhaps one million copies. Harvey's thesis was that the demonetization of silver was slipped over on the American public in 1873 as the result of a subterfuge engineered primarily by the British House of Rothschild. A cartoon in the book, entitled "The English Octopus. It Feeds on Nothing but Gold," tells the whole story. It pictures the Rothschild family as a great octopus with the world in the grip of its tentacles. Harvey published a novel that further dramatized the point. *A Tale of Two Nations* appeared in the same year and also enjoyed considerable success, further underscoring the anti-Semitism in some agrarian circles.

The opening chapters of the novel reveal the conspiracy to demonetize silver, hatched in 1869 by the British Jew Baron Rothe (Rothschild), in part for his own profit, but also to destroy the balance of trade in the United States, thus ruining it economically. To be certain of succeeding, he sends his nephew and ally Victor Rogasner to America. He is truly a figure out of the darkest anti-Semitic tradition. Rogasner mutters statements like: "I will crush their manhood. I will destroy the last vestige of national prosperity among them.... I will set them fighting among each other, and see them cut each other's throats, and carry devastation into each other's homes, while I look on without loss. I am in command of the greatest campaign the world has ever experienced." The scheme is to be accomplished by bribing American legislators to pass antisilver legislation. The plan is consummated when the Coinage Act of 1873 is passed. The implications of this act are only realized later in the decade when the price of silver falls drastically on the world market. By then, it is too late, since Baron Rothe's conspiracy, which includes demonetizing silver in Europe as well, has been irreversibly accomplished. "It was the beginning of a financial movement that was to encircle the globe." Characteristically, given its architects, "its prompting motive was self-aggrandizement."[25]

Harvey clearly presented an anti-Semitic portrait in this novel, Norman Pollack notwithstanding, and contributed to the burgeoning image of a Jewish financial conspiracy. Harvey became sensitive to the fact that he might be so charged and attempted a disclaimer in *Coin's Financial School up to Date* (1895), which revealingly confirms that his thinking about the Jews was prescribed and stereotyped: "Among Jews, many become money changers; it seems to be natural with them, probably on account of their shrewdness. They see that it has advantages not possessed by any other business."[26]

Harvey's conception of the Jews was prevalent at the end of the nineteenth century: that they are both gifted with mental facility and shrewd to the point of unscrupulousness. In Ignatius Donnelly's version of this dualism in the anti-utopian novel *Caesar's Column* (1890), Jews are in control of the world economy, yet are the brains of a ruthless revolution against capitalism. Donnelly, the fiery Minnesota agitator, was a prominent Populist. Active in politics, first as an antislavery Democrat, then as a Republican, he was elected as a Radical Republican congressman from 1863 to 1869. After his defeat, Donnelly turned in the 1870s to agrarian reform. In 1889 he was an organizer of the Minnesota Farmer's Alliance, and in 1890 he became president of the state chapter of the alliance. In that capacity, he was able to wield considerable influence in the Populist movement, and in 1892 he wrote the preamble and much of the platform for the People's party convention in Omaha.[27]

His defeat in the election for senator in 1889 prompted him to write his most successful book, *Caesar's Column,* which sold over 250,000 copies in the first decade of publication.[28] Donnelly's novel claimed that society was controlled by an oligarchy consisting largely of Jews, who, risen from peddlers in a laissez-faire economy, wreak their cruel revenge on Christians for the ancient "sufferings inflicted by their bigoted and ignorant ancestors upon a noble race." Underlying the book's vision is the irrational fear of the growing power of international Jewish bankers and their economic strangulation of gentiles. The novel attempts to project into the future what Donnelly sees as the inevitable result if the prevailing economic arrangements are to go unmodified for the next century. A small group of wealthy, greedy, "Semitic" rulers would reduce the majority of the earth's people to abject slavery. "The world is today Semitized. The children of Japhet lie prostrate slaves at the feet of the children of Shem; the sons of Ham bow humbly before their august dominion."

Gabriel Weltstein describes the advances in technology and science in the New York of 1989, but also the dehumanization, poverty, and suffering of the masses who are ruthlessly controlled by the secret government of Prince Cabano, whose real name is Jacob Isaacs. This hopeless state of affairs, Gabriel is advised by Maximilian Petion, a leader of the International Revolutionary Brotherhood opposed to the oligarchy, did not develop through ignorance, since one hundred years before (1889), warnings were dispatched but went unheeded.

Rebellion is imminent and both sides prepare. The "Brotherhood of Destruction" is led by a triumvirate with Caesar Lomellini, an Italian from South Carolina, in charge; second in command and "the brains of the organization" is a nameless Russian Jew; and the third member is the young American aristocrat Maximilian. Cabano suggests that if a revolt eventuates, a terrible destruction should ensue. "It is our interest to make it the occasion of a tremendous massacre, such as the world has never before witnessed.... If ten millions are slain... so much the better." A holocaust, in fact, is visited upon the world. Caesar becomes mad with victory and drunk with violence and power. He has a pyramid of the dead constructed (Caesar's Column) by pouring cement over a pile of corpses. The Russian Jew absconds with $100 million and "it is rumored that he has gone to Judea; that he proposes to make himself the king in Jerusalem, and, with his vast wealth, re-establish the glories of Solomon, and revive the ancient splendors of the Jewish race, in the midst of the ruins of the world."[29]

For Donnelly, as for other Populists, the apple of discord destroying the Jeffersonian Eden was the existence of money controlled by the international financiers. The unfair interest charges manipulated by these men, so often Jews, tempted people to lust for parasitical wealth. This theme was further complicated by attributing to Jews the brains of the revolutionary opposition to that power. This is an example of the polar stereotyping that was to be heard with more frequency in the twentieth century culminating in the canard that Jews were both the ultimate capitalists, reminiscent of Marx and Gronlund, as well as the archetypical rabid Bolsheviks.

Through centuries of plotting and scheming, the Jews, he feared, had reached the pinnacle of world power. The Semitization of the social order had dark implications for Donnelly. From their financial fortresses in Europe and their offices on Wall Street, Jews appeared to pull the important purse strings and make the important decisions at the expense of the rest of mankind.[30] Denying his anti-Semitism and in fact proclaiming his respect for certain Jewish traits, Donnelly wrote in the *Saint Paul Representative* in 1894 that "we would not persecute the Jews. What we meant was that they have become conspicuous as types of the Plutocrat, because they excel all other people in their capacity to accumulate wealth. We are fighting Plutocracy not because it is Jewish or Christian, but because it is Plutocracy—destructive of the world, eventually even of itself."[31]

A less literary but more colorful version of the conspiracy theory was broadcast around the country by the Kansas "hell-raiser" Mary E. Lease. Fear, hatred, and failure probably had a stronger hold on her than on the other Populists. She grew up after 1860 and did not experience, as many of her colleagues in agitation did, an America of prosperous and respected yeoman farmers. She lived on the edge of poverty most of her life and had to battle not only the economic system, but also the social milieu that shackled her aspirations for greater influence because she was a woman. Frustrated in life and marriage and grieved by the injustice she saw around her, Lease lashed out in anger. Her enemies were bankers, railroads, and devilish Jews who were drawing lifeblood from the toiling farmers. The disadvantaged of the nation, she argued, were "paying tribute to the Rothschilds of England who are but agents for the Jews."[32] They bought their way into a position of dominance in the government until "we are not only a debtor nation, but a nation... of tenant serfs, and our illustrious president—Grover the first—a marvel of profundity and rotundity, the agent of Jewish bankers and British gold." What prospect of a better future can be expected from a government "which allows a company of Jews... to monopolize the measures of value?" She warned that in "the economy of God there is no room for a usurer or a landlord."[33] For individuals such as Mary E. Lease and others nurtured on revivalistic religion, the financial argument against the Jew developed almost into a kind of Christian crusade in which the virtuous downtrodden would once again rout the money changers from the Temple.

Gordon Clark, a Free Silverite who wrote for the American Bimetallic League, presented a similar assessment of mankind's plight in his anti-Semitic pamphlet *Shylock as Banker, Bondholder, Corruptionist, Conspirator* (1894). Referring to the "Crime of 1873," he postulated that "this vampire suck at the daily sustenance of every man, woman and child in the land—was bought and paid for, like the ooze of a slaughter-house, by the Bank of England and the Jews of Frankfort." There is no doubt that America's two political parties "are both little more than the decomposed spoils of London Jews and their New York twins." All virtue and right is sold to the power of the "Anglo-Jew octopus."[34] Ebenezer Wakeley, a People's Silver party candidate for mayor of Chicago in 1892, concurred. In *The Gentile Ass and The Judean Monetary Establishment* (1895), he wrote that "the Rothschild-Great Britain affinity is in complete open control of our financial destinies." The source for this goes back to a biblical injunction proclaimed by Moses that "permitted the Jew to exploit the Gentile race."[35]

Apparently these were widespread sentiments as reported by *The New York Sun* in 1896.

St. Louis, July 22—One of the striking things about the Populist conventions... here and the crowd attending them is the extraordinary hatred of the Jewish race. It is not possible to go into any hotel in the city without hearing the most bitter denunciations of the Jews as a class and of particular Jews who happen to have prospered in the world.

Julius Wayland, a left-wing Populist, editor of the *Appeal to Reason,* reported the same thing, only he approved.[36]

Several fellow travelers of the Populists also engaged in the propagation of the Rothschild myth that, parenthetically, had lost all validity by the late nineteenth century, since by then "the sixth dynasty of Europe" had been eclipsed in power for decades by the joint-stock Berlin "Great Banks" and French and Austrian Christian monetary institutions. As Hannah Arendt has suggested in another context, this wealth without parallel power generated a certain amount of hostility. Society, like nature, hates a vacuum.[37] W. Scott Morgan, in the *History of the Wheel and Alliance and the Impending Revolution* (1891), made many references to Shylock, parasites, and Mammon. He referred to the "great grapple-hook of Shylock" that gathered in "the profits of labor." This modern prototype, a product of Wall Street, Lombard Street, and the devil, "demands not only the pound of flesh, but the life of his debtor and the confiscation of his property."[38] Thomas May Thorpe, in *What Is Money* (1894), sounded a similar note. The world is "now under a despotism meaner than that of the Thirty Tyrants of Athens." It is under the influence of the "Rothschild gold-bugs" who "fasten the shackles upon the limbs of the Goddess of Liberty.... They paralyze the wealthiest nation on the globe... and do it all 'in order' to get 'the poor laboring man's' 'honest money'!" Portending William Jennings Bryan's "Cross of Gold" imagery, Thorpe lamented that "as Judas delivered the Christ into the hands of the Jewish Money changers of that day, so now our 'chosen guardians' have handed us over to the tender mercies of their literal and lineal heirs."[39] James B. Goode charged, in *The Modern Banker* (1896), that Jews control "almost all... banks, of all kinds, and in all nations." This has been "so artfully arranged, and so consummately carried out, that all the people of the world are paying heavy tribute to these same Jews, in interest and exchange, without knowing that they are doing so."[40] Such is the stratagem and cupidity of the Covenant People; such is, as Mary E. Hobart expressed it in 1898, *The Secret of the Rothschilds.*[41]

After the agrarian crusade was beaten, the participants continued to explain their defeat by pointing to the influence of an "invisible empire" centered in the "mysterious money power." One of the reformers, John Clark Ridpath, has Shylock confess the source of his power.

My business is to live by the labor of others. This I have to get under the pretense of patriotic sacrifice. Pity it is that I cannot encourage war any longer; that I am obliged by the unfavorable state of my business to hold back these nations from continuing to cut one another's throats for my benefit.[42]

Clearly, there was a strain of ideological anti-Semitism in the writings and rhetoric of a segment of the Populists and their sympathizers. The mistake of the Handlin-Hofstadter school lies in their overemphasis of this phenomenon, their penchant of putting it in an historical vacuum, and their overlooking and minimizing other significant sources of

Judeophobia. The revisionists err in kind in their apologetic refusal to concede that anti-Semitism could have tainted their apotheosis of American radicalism and rural democracy. Nevertheless, despite the historical debate that has clouded the issue, the Populist experience reveals how deep-seated and refractory the Jewish question is with its centuries of overlay of prejudice so extensive that even those who would sincerely correct the ills of society were susceptible to it. Anti-Semitism erupted even in those sectors of American society that were reformist and libertarian. The democratic impulse was not always resolute enough to overcome the psychological and social momentum of anti-Semitic stereotyping.

Coming at the end of the Populist campaign, several novelists internalized these arguments and lent further credence to the damaging interpretation of Jewish power then circulating. Harold Frederic, the London correspondent for the *New York Times* from 1884 until his death in 1898, who also won some recognition as a realist novelist, devoted a great deal of his creative efforts to Jews. It should be noted that Frederic produced an outstanding series of articles for the *New York Times* that alerted America to the anti-Jewish outrages in Russia in 1890 – 92. But in his last two works, he focused on the question of Jewish influence. In *Gloria Mundi* (1898), he destroys illusions about the British aristocracy and reveals the source of their exploitative wealth. The Jewish branch of the titled Torr family, particularly the young Emanuel, have discovered "the smoothest possible working arrangement of the social system which his class regards as best for itself, and hence for all mankind—the system which exalts a chosen few, and keeps all the rest in subjection."[43] An estimate of the "Jewish" side of Emanuel's character is made by Frances Baily in phrases that seem to echo Frederic's own prejudicial notions. The duke's fortune, she says, was achieved "by stealing the birthright of thousands of dumb human beasts of burden, and riveting the family collar round their necks with no more regard for their wishes or their rights than as if they had been so many puppies or colts." As for the source of their wealth, it was gained by "the most frightful and blood-stained human slavery in the poisonous jungles of the Dutch East Indies—that, and an ancient family business of international usury, every dirty penny in which, if you followed it far enough, meant the flaying alive of a peasant or the starvation of his little children."[44]

Frederic returned to this theme in the last and one of the most successful of his novels, *The Market-Place* (1899). The speculator-hero Joel Stormont Thorpe decides to work for the destruction of a group of Jewish stock-market speculators. Thorpe marvels at their ability

to direct the movement of the greatest force the world had ever known. They and their cousins in Paris and Frankfort, or wherever they lived,... wielded a vaster authority than all the Parliaments of the earth. They could change a government, or crush the aspirations of a whole people, or decide a question of peace or war, by the silent dictum of their little family council.[45]

The members of the cabal were known as ''wreckers'' because ''they had systematically amassed... fortunes by strangling in their cradles weak enterprises which would not have been weak if they had been given a legitimate chance to live.'' The obliteration of the individual in a faceless group stereotype, the archetypical anti-Semitic conception, is clear from Thorpe's comment: ''I don't know them apart, hardly— they've all got names like Rhine wines—but I know the gang as a whole, and if I don't lift the roof clean off their particular synagogue, then my name is mud.''[46] Frederic was sufficiently unsympathetic to Jews to depict them as a people with one function and interest and that quite dangerous to society.

A similar generalized opinion is found in Alexander Craig's utopian novel *Ionia: Land of Wise Men and Fair Women* (1898).[47] Jews, even within an idealized environment of shared labor and property are unequivocally evil and are unable to resist the temptation to control both wealth and people. They take advantage of the freedom and lax supervision to exercise ''their greed and their undoubted genius for business,'' until ''all the banking business of the country was in their hands'' and they even threaten to be ''possessed of all the riches of the community.'' They defy the laws with such impunity and exercise their greedy passions to such an extent that they manage to make Ionian men their servants and women their mistresses and behave ''as if the Greeks were born merely to be the slaves of their luxury.'' Eventually, their encroaching influence becomes intolerable and one forthright ruler decides to deal with the problem. Prominent members of the community are executed and no Jew is permitted to marry or bear children on the penalty of death. This leads to the expected result until ''the whole tribe died out and passed away for ever.''[48] A nineteenth-century bloodless, biological Final Solution!

If there is some ambiguity and restrained hostility in the novels of Frederic and Craig, that is resolved into a deep antipathy in the works of another popular and prolific novelist of the 1890s, Richard Henry Savage, Class of 1868, West Point. In *An Exile From London* (1896), he concentrated with delight on his villainous Jews, each worse than the other. Isador Blum, a German Jew, is the head of a family of brothers who are partners on the Rothschild model, located severally in New York, New Orleans, Fort Worth, El Paso, and Tucson. Blum has risen "from a vicarious cotton-grabber in the Semitic camp following Bank's army, to a New Orleans trader, then, a New York wholesaler, and now,... the proud head of a chain of aggregated Blums, with their tentacles firmly fixed on the... trade" of the aforementioned cities.[49] His brothers and cousins have gathered "since the piping times of the war, from Frankfort, Breslau, Vienna, and Budapest, yea even from Warsaw and Cracow, to aid in distributing all profitably sold articles of use or ornament over that broad zone of the United States, now tributary to the Blums and their international tribesmen." With the aid of his Jewish lawyer, the vulpine Moses Dalman, Isador plans to extend the scope of his empire by plotting to gain control of mine production in the Far West and is determined to stop at nothing—not even murder—to do so. Dalman, a product of New York's public schools who glided "eel-like, through Columbia College," is already rich although he covets his employer's still larger possessions.[50] Not surprisingly for a melodramatic novel, all the cheating, plotting villains are foiled. But not before Savage has helped transplant the Rothschild image to these shores.

This treatment of the Jew, nurtured in the 1890s in agrarian soil and appropriated by several romantic novelists, did not dissipate as the nineteenth century gave way to the twentieth. It continued to have an independent existence and, in fact, took on new significance. There now were additional factors that complicated the issue. The existence of Jewish international organizations, such as the Alliance Israelite Universelle and the World Zionist Congresses beginning with the one in Basel in 1897, became more visible as the years passed and seemed to many people to be a type of Jewish world government. The rallying of the Jewish community to the defense of Alfred Dreyfus and later to Mendel Beilis gave further credence to this sentiment. The rumors leaking out of Russia concerning an elite Jewish establishment directing governments and statesmen, at first nebulous and sketchy but later specific and concrete, were less than helpful. All these bits of "evidence" were absorbed by some American writers, intellectuals, and segments of the public media in their efforts to expose the "Jewish Problem."

The Quarterly Sentinel, based in Chicago, took up the call in an 1899 editorial entitled "Conquest of the World by the Jews." As the heading suggests, this was already a *fait accompli*. The "iron girdle" of Jewish power is at present "drawn across the wealth of the nations, [and] is already fixed so closely and unbreakable, that we may say without exaggeration, that the Jews hold even now in their hands the financial power from one end of the world to the other."[51] Expressions of hostility toward Jews were not absent in American Catholic circles. The Rome correspondent of *The Freeman's Journal* of New York regretted that Jews had "spread themselves all over" and penetrated and often obtained dominant influence in the financial activities of certain European countries.[52] Father Frank McGloin, editor of the *Holy Family*, a weekly Catholic paper published in New Orleans, was passionately anti-Semitic on this theme. Father Walsh, writing in *The Catholic Telegraph* of Cincinnati in 1898, interpreted the Dreyfus case from this standpoint. Before the scandal, "the Jewish influence was paramount" and "their great financial kings dictated political methods to a Catholic country." Now they have been routed from the perch of power but they are unwilling to surrender. "They would pass with pleasure over the ruins of Parliament and the destruction of the Army if by this way only they might regain their lost position."[53] *The Catholic Record* of Indianapolis agreed. The Jew "has the ear of the government; he controls its financial operations; he occupies positions of the highest influence;... he molds public opinion by means of the press, he has money, and money is the sinew of war."[54]

Many intellectuals and commentators were similarly attracted by the magnet of conspiracy theories. James Weldon Johnson, the black author and activist, believed that "the two million Jews have a controlling interest in the finances of the nation."[55] David Graham Phillips, perhaps the most able of the muckraking novelists, influenced by his antibanking bias, described the Rothschild empire as "a nation in itself, compact, patient,... seeking only the advantage of the house," indifferent to society's needs.[56] Journalist E. Alexander Powell warned, in *The Saturday Evening Post* in 1909, against this "unseen" force

> which rules the Europe of today.... Rothschilds come and Rothschilds go, but that Rothschild goes on forever is equally true of any one of the dozen or so great families [Hirschs, Péreires, Sterns, Goldsmids, Gunsburgs, Montefiores, etc.] whose allied fortunes—for they all work together when there is need— form the Invisible Empire of Finance.[57]

Or, as Lincoln Steffens postulated in 1910: "They are powerful financially, both here and abroad.... Slow to enter into a quarrel, once in they make it a war." Because "they join hands all around the earth," they are likely to be successful.[58]

This tendency to foist upon the Jew a supernationalism, occasionally redounded to his misfortune. In Russia, Ambassador Curtis Guild and Consul Jacob E. Connor, influenced by the fabrications contained in the *Protocols of the Elders of Zion,* a document first published in Russia in 1905, referred frequently in their 1912 reports to the Secretary of State and in correspondence with Henry Cabot Lodge to the machinations of "international Jewry."[59] They justified Russia's discriminatory policies, arguing that the Slavic nation had more experience with Jewish subversive and encroaching tendencies and hence "knew" who they were dealing with better than naive Americans did.[60]

Closer to home, Tom Watson came forward again as a public Jew baiter during the Leo Frank case in Atlanta in 1914– 15.[61] In that unfortunate blot on Southern history, the Georgian exploited the interference of influential Northern Jews and urban newspapers in Frank's behalf. His "International Jew" conspiracy was mostly a hobgoblin of the rural imagination, associated with all the insidious influences thought to emanate from faraway eastern cities. After he drew special attention to supposed Jewish physical and moral filthiness, to their supposed practice of extortion and fraud, their sexual depravity, and after he brought up the bogey of ritual murder, he referred to that much traveled theme of Jewish wealth and domination. In the first place, he assured his readers that there was a "gigantic conspiracy of Big Money" organized to corrupt the state's courts, its governor, and its papers to save the life of a "wealthy" murderer. "Is any condemned criminal to be put above the law," he asked in April, 1915, merely "because his family and racial connections can spend millions to defeat justice? Are we to be bulldozed and browbeaten by millionaire Jewish bankers and publishers who act upon the principle that they have the right to say what is a legal verdict in the courts of Georgia?'' Americans must ''sit up and take notice'' and be on guard against the determination and resolve of these people, ''if the repeated campaigns of this Invisible Power seem to mean that Jews are to be exempt from punishment for capital crimes, when the victim is a Gentile.''[62]

Offended by the prodigious efforts made by ''outsiders'' to save Leo Frank from death, Watson culled the depths of his feverish mind for an issue that would appeal to the simple and prejudiced rural Georgians who read his weekly newspaper *The Jeffersonian* and his monthly *Watson's Magazine*. It was primarily these people, many of them barely literate, who were steeped in Christian fundamentalist doctrines that still countenanced the suggestion of the Jew as Christ killer, whom Watson stirred with his diatribes against the financial manipulators invading and exploiting the South. To cater to his followers' need for vicarious excitement, to boost the sales of his publishing ventures, and perhaps to provide some explanation for why the world was ''plunging hellward,'' he broadened his attack to include Leo Frank and his ''Jewish Banker'' defenders who swept down from the North to ravage the yet generally undefiled, Semitic-free South.[63] The result may indeed have been the travesty of justice that transpired in the early morning hours of August 16, 1915, in an oak grove just outside of Marietta, Georgia.

In the minds of less demagogic individuals, the belief in a conspiratorial Jewish power, internationally based, did not necessarily lead to such tragedies, but their acceptance of it did, nevertheless, contribute to the persistence and legitimization of this unfortunate imagery.

David Starr Jordan, the biologist, eugenicist, and president of Stanford University, for example, thought it was true. Referring to E. Alexander Powell's 1909 article in *The Saturday Evening Post* previously mentioned, the eminent scientist remarked: ''It gives... in considerable detail, the way in which the continent of Europe has become mortgaged for about all it is worth to the Jewish bankers in payment of the war expenses of Napoleon and other military heroes.''[64] Later, in 1911, Jordan averred that the rulers of Europe, even the Kaiser, have very little influence ''compared with that of the 'Unseen

Empire of Finance' of which the Rothschilds are the head.[65]... The operations of the nations are held in absolute check whenever the [Jewish] bankers choose to exercise their control.''[66] They are the architects of peace and war. Jordan delineated the source of this awesome power in his book *The Unseen Empire* (1912). Therein he recounted the history of their great fortunes that were "established on national waste,... and in the interest of war,'' until they have succeeded in dividing "the world among them'' for their own selfish purposes.[67]

This question became somewhat of a passion with Jordan, and in his scrapbook he chronicled the various members of the Rothschild family, their financial activities, and particularly their funding of war debts. He did the same with Moses Montefiore, Barney Bernato, Alfred Beil, Baron Hermann Stern, Samuel Oppenheimer, and other historically wealthy Jews. This was not a healthy pastime for an individual already inclined to believe in the permanence of racial characteristics and in an eugenic solution to the immigration problem.

Senator Henry Cabot Lodge, a committed opponent of unrestricted immigration, student of Henry Adams, and confidant of Brooks Adams, was also susceptible to an oversimplified interpretation of Jewish power. As a young senator in April 1898, he discovered Jewish influence at work against the best imperialistic interests of the United States.

The forces which are fighting for Spain and to compel us to peace at any price are the money power, largely represented by very rich Jews in Europe.... England and the United States have not yet been touched by the anti-simetic [sic] excitement, but if this country should be forced to a degradation of its honor and of peace at any price you will see it come here as it has come in France.[68]

Sixteen years later, with the outbreak of war in Europe, he focused on a specific agent of this nefarious "Empire" that managed to intrude itself into a position of financial supremacy in America. The "intrigues'' of Kuhn, Loeb & Company, and Paul Warburg specifically, elicited a great deal of uneasiness and displeasure.[69] In 1919, after the conclusion of the war, he advised Lord Bryce that the real enemies of society came out of the conflict unscathed. "Undoubtedly the... power not only in France but elsewhere rests with the big financiers... who are purely international. Their influence is thoroughly dangerous everywhere and it is as strong here and with our people abroad as in the case of any other nation."[70] In the immediate postwar years, complaining to Brooks Adams, he noted that international Jewry was bringing its weight to bear to help establish the League of Nations. "As you say, they are pursuing the same familiar methods and their skill in using great elements of the population, good people many of them, who have no idea they are being used, is always very interesting."[71] This belief possibly accounts for Lodge's willingness to accept the veracity and authenticity of the *Protocols of the Elders of Zion*, the document that ostensibly identified the sinister forces that were directing world governments and peoples as mere pawns on a chessboard. Writing in 1920 to William Astor Chanler, a fellow patrician who kept him advised of these developments, he assured him that he was up to date on the latest evidence. "'The Protocols' I have. The book was sent to me and it is well worth having—I suppose entirely trustworthy."[72]

A number of twentieth century intellectuals and prominent personages tended then to credit the Jews with supernatural powers, presumably for evil—quite as though these individuals, current as they were on most other matters, found themselves transported back to the Dark Ages on the subject of the Jews. This proclivity also overcame John Jay Chapman—lawyer, reform politician, essayist, classicist, literary critic—who became preoccupied with the Jewish "menace" about the same time that Lodge and Jordan did.

Life, however, did not begin for Chapman on this note of foreboding and phantom watching. The scion of a blue-blood American family—on his mother's side he was related to John Jay, and on his father's, to the abolitionist Maria Weston Chapman—he followed the well-trod path of others of his class from St. Paul's School in New Hampshire to Harvard College and ultimately Harvard Law School. Life was rather simple and uncomplicated; his greatest problems were whether he could win the hand of one of the Lowell daughters, be elected to Alpha Delta Phi, and be chosen as a member of the prestigious Porcellian Club. He numbered among his friends and teachers Charles Eliot Norton, Nathaniel Shaler, Owen Wister, and Henry Adams, and he hobnobbed with his fellow elites at "the Palace," a patrician watering spot. After admittance to the bar in 1888, and his marriage to Minna Timmins in 1889, he moved to New York City to embark on a promising career consistent with his background and to practice the passion of his early life, reform politics.[73]

From the time of his marriage until the illness that downed him at the turn of the century, Chapman gave himself chiefly to this pursuit. His was not the closet and speculative existence of others of his declining generation who retreated to a posture of romantic disdain. Rather, through essays, speeches, work for the City Reform Club and the People's Municipal League, political efforts on behalf of independent candidates, he hurled himself against Tammany, against the alliance of business and politics and against a complacency that celebrated a "keep your hands clean" approach to public affairs. After his wife's death in 1897, he energetically supported the campaign of reformer Seth Low, former mayor of Brooklyn and president of Columbia University, for mayor of greater New York City. The reformers were defeated handily at the polls by Robert A. Van Wyck, Tammany's choice. Chapman brooded over the causes of the political disaster and it gradually began to make some sense to him. It had been a "money fight." "The Jew has it all. The love of money is at the root of all evils! Slavery, bad manners, Howells' novels, the public feeling of contempt for personality which makes the [Hearst] Journal possible—all those terrors which have hitherto been set down to Democracy. In the gross everyone knows it is money."[74] The fault lay not with the inertia of the masses or even with the corrupt politicians. The answer Chapman groped for he summed up in the term *commercialism*. "The hand of commerce has been the brain of the United States. Our public life is debased by it, our literature ruined by it, our social life rendered ridiculous."[75] Herein lies the seed of his future madness about the Jews.

Chapman married again in April 1898, to Elizabeth Chanler, a woman of substantial means and background. Marrying into wealth freed Chapman from economic worries for the rest of his days and allowed him to follow a life of writing and reform. The future seemed full of promise and aesthetic and personal fulfillment. This dream was rudely shattered when, early in the winter of 1901, in his thirty-ninth year, Chapman collapsed from a massive nervous malady that partially paralyzed him. It took him nearly a decade to recover from this physical setback. For a year Chapman was bedridden, practically an invalid. Helpless as an infant, he had to be fed, clothed, and washed. We can only imagine what this vibrant man must have suffered. We can only speculate what thought processes were running through the far reaches of his weakened mind. We do know that he came out of his crisis a profoundly changed man. Although he occasionally participated in his old endeavors (political reform, attacks on business consolidation), he turned his style more and more to the service of those who, like his brother-in-law William Astor Chanler, saw the Jews as the greatest threat to the triumph of civilization. Now commercialism that was a source of contempt in 1897 had become a source of conspiracy a decade later, and this was epitomized by the Jew.

Basically these ideas remained dormant until World War I and its aftermath altered Chapman's world outlook. The change, which began in 1901 when he suffered psychological and physical damage by beating his head uselessly against the gilt of the Gilded Age, was completed from 1914 to 1920. In June 1916 his son Victor, a pilot in the Lafayette Escadrille, was shot down and killed at Verdun behind the German lines. This was a severe personal blow to Chapman, a doting father. More than that, Chapman was horrified at the moral complacency, the apathy, the materialism, and fast living of postwar America. He was terrified by the direction the nation was taking in the pursuit of wild spending, amorality, and the celebration of a tinsel culture.[76] Struggling to understand an age that frightened and perplexed him, he sought solace in the knowledge that the degeneration of society was not an indigenous development but was the product of Catholic and Jewish influences unleashed by the world debacle.

Forgetting old Jewish friends like Isaac Klein, who helped him during the reform years, Chapman, by 1920, was deep in his mania about the international Jewish consortium undermining the public welfare.

The activities of these societies are based on a philosophy of evil, which has been developed by men of enormous intellect in the past, and which has been reduced to practices that have been tested by experience and work toward the destruction of government. The practices of the cabal consist in playing upon the inexperience of the lower classes, exciting their greed and hatred, and at the same time upsetting the purchasing power of their money. The only way to face this peril is to pour light upon it.[77]

This is precisely what Chapman began to do. He informed Louis Marshall in December 1920 that there are "Jewish cliques and a Jewish solidarity amounting almost to a secret society of self interest" that unless disbanded and dissolved will precipitate unfortunate reactions on the part of conscienced Americans. "Such is the constitution of human nature that the Jews will be pounded indiscriminately till some of them take sides with their critics and admit to some portion of blame.''[78] In an article published in the autumn of 1922 in the *London Spectator,* Chapman further elucidated his position. To Europeans, downcast by America's rejection of the League of Nations, he explained that his countrymen had first to put their own house in order. ''Consider the state of America today,'' he invited his foreign readers. She is saddled with similar forces that now beset your capitals. ''She is wrestling with corruptions and is the home of many traitorous cliques. In [President Woodrow] Wilson's day the Jewish peril showed its head. The Jew was behind the wheels of Wilson's intermeddling foreign policy,'' until the nation is currently ''rocking with Bolshevism in every form, from parlor to garret, from pulpit to slum.''[79]

Chapman now became totally consumed by these notions. He began to make overtures to the Ku Klux Klan and, although he never joined it, as far as we know, he certainly was one of its most distinguished supporters.[80] He looked on disconsolately as the world he knew was passing over to foreign hands.

The fact is that after the civil war the old Am. [American] stock *abandoned* its civic duties—and now they are ... likely to be submerged... by a... Irish and a Jewish cabal..., the same set that are working pretty successfully to pull down the British Empire.... There's a wrecking-class of Jews—international—and it is at work in India, and there in Paris, in London, a little everywhere.[81]

Matters, if they proceed along at the same pace, can only get more ominous. ''If England is already in the hands of the Jews and the Jews—as many people believe—are all but in control of the U.S. and if they succeed in their drive on us, why we'll both be consolidated in an unpleasant world governed by financial power.''[82] The only thing left for speculation is whether ''we shall sink into obedience—elect American officials, presidents, judges, etc.—but really be governed by the Jewish control behind.''[83]

The key to an understanding of the anti-Semitism of men such as John Jay Chapman is to be found in the fact that America had not turned out to their liking and expectations. He focused, by way of explanation, on the Jew—that diabolical demiurge who was out to ''murder progress'' as he was fond of saying. The same can be said for his expatriate brother-in-law, the colorful William Astor Chanler who was somewhat of a professional gadfly, warning American leaders about the Jewish plot to rule the world. If nothing else, he certainly had some influence on Chapman's thinking. In midsummer of 1919, the Chapmans traveled to France, chiefly to see Victor's grave. In Paris they met Chanler and apparently he was full of wild stories and "documents" to substantiate them: that the Jewish bankers were the cause of World War I; that Jews controlled the Wilson administration; that the League of Nations was a Jewish scheme to set up a secret Semitic world government; that Wilson's Fourteen Points were written by Untermeyer, Brandeis, Schiff, and the Jews.[84] Amazing deductions, they indicate to what extent the flights of irrational imaginations have swept along this stereotype.

But Chanler became even more hysterical on this question of Jewish power. An avid reader of the *Protocols,* he added a few twists of his own and communicated them to Senator Lodge, one of his favorite sounding boards. He advised Lodge in April 1920 that there is a partnership in destruction to be wary of.

The Catholic Church and the Jews are working hand in hand.... They are both anti-national and international in their plan of politics.... I have nothing against the Catholic Church whatever.... Nor have I anything whatever against the Jews as Jews; but, as an American, I am peculiarly sensitive and watchful... of all movements of an international nature,... and particularly... when the two great international forces—the Roman Church and the Jewish sanhedrim [sic]—are working hand in hand.[85]

The extent of Chanler's belief in a secret network of evil is revealed in another letter to Lodge in November 1921.

Most thinking people are now aware of the existence of a Jewish super-Government (which has its headquarters for the present in London), and that this Jewish super-Government works through Jews disguised under different nationalities throughout the world, their fixed purpose being to advance Jewish interests at the expense even of those nations to which they may claim a certain allegiance.[86]

This is mostly a Jewish threat, he wrote Chapman in 1925, for although there are Catholics who are anti-national, they are dangerous only *"in so far as they are used by the Jews."*[87] Giving a word of advice to his partner in the crusade, Chanler urged Chapman in 1925 to occasionally ''have a crack at the Jews. Try at least to get the papers to print a mild attack on them—a criticism of [Felix] Frankfurter's high position in the Harvard Law School, for instance. Really don't you want our law students taught Blackstone and Chitty... in a straightforward anglo-saxon way, rather than have these good old authors tinted by the Kabbala and the Talmud?''[88] If Chapman was satisfied with a few public jabs at the Jews, others followed the intent of Chanler's exhortations more closely and were more ambitious in their proclamation of conspiracy theories and more successful in attracting an audience.

Anti-Semitism was kept alive in America during the nativist 1920s by the appearance of the *Protocols of the Elders of Zion.* The document comprises a motley array of supposed examples of secret Jewish domination in history and plans for the future, including methods of stupefying gentiles, controlling the press, finance, and government, and fomenting war, chaos, and revolution. The Russian secret police concocted the *Protocols* at the turn of the century on the basis of a novel written anonymously in 1864 by Maurice Joly, entitled *Dialogue aux Enfers,* as part of a campaign against Napoleon III. Joly's work was plagiarized in an 1868 German novel in which the conspiracies originally attributed to Napoleon were transposed and alleged to be the substance of a secret meeting of Jewish elders in Prague. The altered document was brought to the United States during the war by Russian émigrés operating under Boris Brasol, a leader of the Romanov restoration movement who had helped prosecute Mendel Beilis. Brasol was able to enter the good graces of Attorney General A. Mitchell Palmer as an authority on Russian and American radicals. He also found a sympathetic ear in Dr. Harris A. Houghton, a physician who directed the New York section of the Army Military Intelligence Service. Houghton had the *Protocols* translated by Natalie de Bogary, a member of his staff, and the typescript made its way around Washington, in government and social circles, and among 100 percent American organizations like the National Civic Foundation and the American Defense Society.[89] Publisher George Haven Putnam, who was an anti-Semite, used a small firm to publish the first American edition, entitled *The Cause of World Unrest,* a British polemic based upon the *Protocols,* which came out in 1920.[90] Other editions appeared, but it was really Henry Ford and his *Dearborn Independent* that gave the document's message of an international Jewish conspiracy its widest circulation and exposure.

In May 1920 the *Dearborn Independent* launched an anti-Semitic propaganda campaign without precedent in American history. Lasting on and off for about seven years, it was able to graft European anti-Semitic fabrications on native anti-urban and anti-intellectual traditions. It was able to exploit the hard times that struck after 1920, especially among farmers. The rural folk who came out of a heritage of agrarian prejudice built in the late nineteenth century, were ready fodder for the newspaper's xenophobic grist mill. The farmers and their descendents who had followed Bryan and Watson in the 1890s and in 1914 now saw their wartime gains wiped out and the subjugation of their agrarian society confirmed. They were looking for answers, as were Americans generally who had lived through the confusion of the Red Scares and had experienced a resurgent nationalism that was distrustful of the outside world. The isolationist reaction evident in the early twenties pressed home the danger of foreign entanglements in a more conscious and articulate way than ever before. At a time when Americans were painfully aware of disruptive change, it was illuminating to discover that social disintegration had long been the prime method of Jewish intriguers aspiring for universal domination. This is where Henry Ford came in.[91]

The factors that impelled the "Flivver King" into anti-Semitism are unclear. According to Louis Marshall, it entered "what, might for the sake of euphony, be referred to as Henry Ford's mind," when he met David Starr Jordan in connection with the pacifist movement and read the Stanford University president's *Unseen Empire*[92] (1912). Ford's anti-Semitism may have also been caused by the failure of his "peace ship" mission in the winter of 1915–16. Ford himself repeatedly attributed his Jew hatred to something he learned on this ill-fated expedition. As early as December 1919, he muttered privately: "I know who makes wars. The International Jewish bankers arrange them so they can make money out of them. I know it's true because a Jew on the Peace ship told me."[93] The individual referred to, the pacifist Rosika Schwimmer, who actually inspired the peace-ship project, consistently argued in her letters that Ford's anti-Semitic ideas were already evident in November 1915, before the expedition was organized.[94] She recounted how at their first meeting Ford already made reference to "German-Jewish bankers" as the cause of the war. The real culprits, Schwimmer surmised, were the men who surrounded Ford who put these "anti-

Semitic notions in his... head to prevent his starting pacifist work.''[95]

On a more general level, Ford's plunge into Judeophobia may have been inspired by the political disillusion that set in after the collapse of Wilsonian idealism. Or it might have been a result of the economic slump of 1920 that left him with unpaid debts and unsold cars and vulnerable to the wiles and interest rates of eastern bankers. Despite all his wealth, he retained the personal traits, fundamentalist religion, and social ideas typical of his rustic background. A son of Michigan tenant farmers, he looked upon the East and its teeming cities, especially New York City, as dens of iniquity, soul-less, foreign, and menacing. It just is possible that Ford, like others with an agrarian background, turned to anti-Semitism during a time of economic depression, isolation, and blighted hope. Whoever or whatever planted the seed of hatred in Ford's mind, the fact remains that by 1920 he turned his back on reform, became enamored with "Jewish internationalism," and became the standard-bearer and prophet of the new anti-Semitism.

The *Protocols* were a windfall for Ford and his cohorts, and the editors of the *Independent* proceeded to draw heavily upon them. A front-page editorial in the May 22, 1920, issue, entitled "The International Jew—The World's Problem," initiated a series that was published weekly for almost two years and continued sporadically thereafter. The series played endless variations on a reminiscent theme proclaimed in the first article:

In America alone most of the big businesses, the trusts and the banks, the national resources and the chief agricultural products, especially tobacco, cotton and sugar, are in the control of Jewish financiers or their agents. Jews are the largest and most numerous landlords of residence property in the country. They are supreme in the theatrical world. They absolutely control the circulation of publications throughout the country.... There is a super-government which is allied to no government... and yet which has a hand in them all. There is a race, a part of humanity, which has never yet been received as a welcome part, and which has succeeded in raising itself to a power that the proudest Gentile race has never claimed.[96]

In time, the newspaper "exposed" Jewish control of everything from the League of Nations to Tammany Hall, from baseball to agriculture. The fear of Jewish influence was supported by constant reiteration of

Jewish solidarity viewed as a conspiratorial attempt to seize power. The *Independent* claimed that Bernard Baruch ran the country during World War I; that Presidents Taft and Wilson were gentile fronts for the Jewish world plan; that the press was owned, slanted, and muzzled by Jewish money; that Jews were corrupting the labor movement with socialistic ideas; that they were infecting the colleges with Bolshevist propaganda. Borrowing freely from the *Protocols,* the paper sketched how this great, clandestine empire operated. "It is the ancient machinery that the international Jew uses in all those activities which he permits the world to see in part. There are gatherings of the financial, political and intellectual chief rulers of the Jews.... They all appear in one city, confer and depart."[97]

Behind the theorizing about the international Jewish cabal, the *Independent* emphasized the dangers inherent in the tactics used by the modern Svengalis to achieve ascendancy. These included destroying the moral, ethical, cultural, and intellectual fibers of America's hallowed traditions. The newspaper accused the Jews of conspiring to "frivolize" the minds and tastes of the people by intoxicating them with changing styles and fashions and by enticing them to buy vain luxuries. According to this assessment, Jews caused deterioration in literature, amusements, and public standards. They devastated American Theater and substituted instead "frivolity, sensuality, indecency, appalling illiteracy and endless platitude."[98] Controlling the movies, the Jews made them vehicles of sexuality, filth, and crime.[99] "The whole loose atmosphere of 'cabaret' and 'midnight frolic' entertainment is of Jewish origin and importation."[100] Moronic Jewish Jazz was rapidly defiling the finer musical sensibilities—all were seen as part of a diabolical plot to narcotize the moral resolve of Christian America.

Unfortunately, Ford's anti-Semitic campaign did not remain an isolated pastime of a deranged mind. It certainly enjoyed, in its initial stages, a great deal of exposure and generated considerable interest. The circulation of the *Independent* increased from 72,000 in 1919 to 300,000 in 1922 and reached a peak of 700,000 in 1924–25.[101] Ford Motor Company dealers were obliged to buy the paper and distribute it to all new car purchasers. Ford sent thousands of copies free of charge to influential clergymen, educators, and politicians.[102] He also published and distributed hundreds of thousands of pamphlets and books, provocatively entitled: *The International Jew, Aspects of Jewish Power in the United States, Jewish Activities in the United States,* and *Jewish Influences in American Life*. Unable to comprehend the revolutionary times he lived in; frustrated by his failures on the political and peace scenes; fearful of banks, easterners, ideologues and unions, Ford vented his aggression on a traditional target—the Jew. Apparently, he was not alone.

Henry Ford's anti-Jewish agitation excited nationwide attention and met with both sotto voice and more public approval. Herbert Adams Gibbons reported that scarcely a day passed without bringing him letters claiming that Jews were plotting to rule the world.[103] Senator Robert M. LaFollette of Wisconsin introduced a petition in the Senate on March 3, 1923, which cast responsibility for World War I on the international bankers, particularly the Rothschilds. The document also asserted that Wilson, Lloyd George, Clemenceau, and Orlando were surrounded by Jewish advisers who dictated the provisions of the treaty.[104]

Among fanatical anti-Semites, the charge was commonly used. George W. Armstrong, for example, in *The Crime of '20* (1922) and *The Story of the Dynasty of the Money Trust in America* (1923), talked about a Jewish banking conspiracy to control the money markets of America and with that accomplished, eventually world governments.[105] He perceived a sinister cooperation between Jews and Catholics for the purpose of promoting their own supernational interests. Hamilton York, in "The Dawes Report and Control of World Gold" (1925), a pamphlet graced with a swastika and written for Peter Beckwith's anti-Semitic press, described a group of German-Jewish capitalists based in Berlin and working through Paul Warburg who are intent on cornering the world's gold supply. "This is the climax of the program of International Jewish Nationalism. It is the finish of the material side of the movement now centuries old to place Judaism in the position of an international super-nation. The whole is in conformity with the materialistic program as laid down in the 'Protocols of the Wise Men of Zion.'"[106] Almost any page of C. Lewis Fowler's anti-Semitic sheet *The American Standard* reveals an identical dementia,[107] as does the propaganda of Lee Alexander Stone's nativist group, the Military Intelligence Association, that was concerned with "... the political-economic movement of Jewry.''[108] All indicate how deeply the acid of postwar disillusion affected certain groups in American society.

Americans certainly did not originate the belief that cunning Jews were involved in a sinister attempt to monopolize the earth's wealth and power. Like the Order of the Illuminati, the notion of an international Jewish cabal in modern times was the fabrication of European reactionaries whose bitter hostility toward social change became particularly relevant to the mood of bewildered and challenged Americans slipping down the social or economic scale and in search of simple explanations. During the late nineteenth and early twentieth centuries, this was reflected in new anxieties over the seemingly irreversible trends toward modernization and industrialization. Local elites, intellectuals, and writers sensitive to these developments increasingly found themselves and their conception of America displaced or superseded by the corporate structure and unrestrained capitalism. To many Americans who still clung to the Jeffersonian ideal of uncorruptible nature, the simple unvitiated life was becoming dangerously circumscribed by a shadowy ''they''—who might be Wall Street, international bankers, the vested interests of the industrial giants or the mysterious and incomprehensible foreigner.[109]

Some of these fears and accusations were well founded, but they must be distinguished from the more generalized tendency to focus on conspiracy. This is true of the Populist movement in the 1890s that was both a realistic response to acute economic problems and an irrational outburst against the Jewish money power. If Populism was an inspiration for later reforms, it was also a frantic outcry against the emerging technological world and thus anticipated many of the themes of twentieth-century, right-wing hysterics. These surfaced with increasing frequency in the years after World War I, which are probably unmatched in American history (with the possible exception of the 1930s) for xenophobia and paranoid suspicions. The symbols and the themes were basically the same, but they acquired new meaning in the light of an appallingly destructive war that had obviously failed to make the world safe for democracy. The desire for a single, comprehensive explanation for perplexing events encouraged the public discussion of the formerly discrete images of hidden enemies. These revolved around the international Jew who was accused of being the secret force behind recent history. With the aid of the *Protocols*, this conspirator, equally threatening as banker or revolutionary, was superimposed on the earlier stereotypes of anti-Christ, Shylock, and Rothschild.

NOTES

1. *The Illustrated American,* Vol. 18, No. 284 (July 27, 1895), p. 108.

2. William Trant, "Jew and Chinaman," *The North American Review,* No. 675 (February, 1912), p. 250.

3. "Immigration and the World War," undated typed manuscript, Prescott F. Hall Collection, The Houghton Library, Harvard University, Cambridge, Massachusetts.

4. Norman Cohn, "The Myth of the Jewish World-Conspiracy," *Commentary,* Vol. 41, No. 6 (June, 1966), pp. 35 – 42; Edward H. Flannery, *The Anguish of the Jews* (New York: The Macmillan Co., 1965); James Parkes, *Anti-Semitism* (Chicago: Quadrangle Books, 1963); Joshua Trachtenberg, *The Devil and the Jews* (New Haven: Yale University Press, 1943).

5. See chapter 6, this volume.

6. Hannah Arendt, *The Origins of Totalitarianism* (New York: World Publishing Co., 1959), pp. 22 – 23; Michael N. Dobkowski, "The Jew in 19th Century French Literature: Shylock up to Date," *Patterns of Prejudice,* Vol. 8, No. 1 (January-February, 1974), pp. 20 – 23.

7. *Niles' Weekly Register,* Vol. 49 (1835), p. 46.

8. *The New York Times,* May 25, 1852; *The Philadelphia Times,* November 21, 1856.

9. "The Knights of the Red Shield," *Harper's New Monthly Magazine,* Vol. 48, No. 334 (January, 1874), p. 221.

10. Elizabeth Bryant, *Types of Mankind as Affecting the Financial History of the World* (District of Columbia, 1879), p. 6.

11. Ibid., p. 5.

12. William Macon Coleman, *The Wandering Jew in America* (Washington, D.C.: J.G. Hester, Publisher, 1875), p. 49.

13. Oscar Handlin, "American Views of the Jew at the Opening of the Twentieth Century," *Publications of the American Jewish Historical Society,* No. 40 (June, 1951), pp. 343 – 44.

14. Richard Hofstadter, *The Age of Reform; from Bryan to F.D.R.* (New York: Alfred A. Knopf, 1956), pp. 78, 80.

15. John Higham, "Another Look at Nativism," *The Catholic Historical Review,* Vol. 44, No. 2 (July, 1958), p. 154.

16. The question of Populist anti-Semitism has elicited much historical discussion. See the following for descriptions of Populist anti-Semitism: Handlin, "American Views of the Jew at the Opening of the Twentieth Century"; Hofstadter, pp. 77 – 81; William F. Holmes, "Whitecapping: Anti-Semitism in the Populist Era," *American Jewish Historical Quarterly*, Vol. 63, No. 3 (March, 1974), pp. 244 – 61; Victor C. Ferkiss, "Populist Influences on American Facism," in *The American Past*, ed. Sidney Fine and Gerald S. Brown, (New York: The Macmillan Co., 1961); Jeannette P. Nichols, "Bryan's Benefactor: Coin Harvey and His World," *Ohio Historical Quarterly*, Vol. 67, No. 4 (October, 1958), pp. 315 – 16; Irwin Unger, "Critique of Norman Pollack's 'Fear of Man,'" *Agricultural History*, Vol. 39, No. 2 (April, 1965), pp. 75 – 80. But also see the following dissents that deny its importance: Walter T.K. Nugent, *The Tolerant Populists* (Chicago: The University of Chicago Press, 1963); Norman Pollack, "Hofstadter on Populism: A Critique of 'The Age of Reform,'" *Journal of Southern History*, Vol. 26, No. 4 (November, 1960); Pollack, "The Myth of Populist Anti-Semitism," *The American Historical Review*, Vol. 68, No. 1 (October, 1962); Pollack, *The Populist Response to Industrial America* (New York: W.W. Norton & Co., 1966); John Higham, "Anti-Semitism in the Gilded Age: A Reinterpretation," *Mississippi Valley Historical Review*, Vol. 43, No. 4 (March, 1957).

17. Unger, p. 77.

18. "The Jew's Daughter," *Journal of American Folklore*, Vol. 19 (1906), pp. 293 – 94.

19. See Handlin, "American Views of the Jew."

20. William M. Stewart, *Bondholders' Conspiracy to Demonetize Silver* (San Francisco: G. Spaulding & Co., 1885), p. 11.

21. William M. Stewart, "The Great Slave Power," *The Arena*, Vol. 19, No. 102 (May, 1898), p. 581.

22. Thomas E. Watson, *The People's Party Campaign Book, 1892* (Washington, D.C.: National Watchman Publishing Co., 1892), p. 12.

23. Quoted in *American Israelite*, August 10, 1893; July 22, October 15, 1896; Leonard Dinnerstein, "A Note on Southern Attitudes Toward Jews," *Jewish Social Studies*, Vol. 32, No. 1 (January, 1970), p. 60.

24. Sarah E.V. Emery, *Seven Financial Conspiracies which Have Enslaved the American People* (Lansing, Michigan: R. Smith & Co., 1892), pp. 15, 68.

25. William H. Harvey, *A Tale of Two Nations* (Chicago: Coin Publishing Co., 1894), pp. 20, 69 – 70.

26. Quoted in Richard Hofstadter, *The Paranoid Style in American Politics, and Other Essays* (New York: Alfred A. Knopf, 1965), p. 301.

27. Martin Ridge, *Ignatius Donnelly, the Portrait of a Politician* (Chicago: University of Chicago Press, 1962).

28. Ignatius Donnelly, *Caesar's Column* (Cambridge, Massachusetts: Harvard University Press, 1960), p. XIX.

29. Ibid., pp. 32, 98, 127, 155, 248, 283.

30. In fairness to Donnelly, it should be noted that he expressed some sympathy for Jews in *Atlantis* (1882) and *The Golden Bottle* (1892), as well as ambivalence in other editorials of the *Saint Paul Representative*.

31. *Saint Paul Representative*, September 12, 1894, p. 3.

32. *New York Times*, August 11, 1896, p. 3.

33. Mary E. Lease, *The Problem of Civilization Solved* (Chicago: Laird & Lee, 1895), pp. 291, 317 – 20.

34. Gordon Clark, *Shylock as Banker, Bondholder, Corruptionist, Conspirator* (Washington, D.C.: American Bimetallic League, 1894), pp. 55, 60, 111.

35. Ebenezer Wakeley, *The Gentile Ass and the Judean Monetary Establishment* (Chicago: The Mighty Price Quotient Series, 1895), pp. 5, 46.

36. *The New York Sun*, July 23, 1896.

37. Hannah Arendt, *The Origins of Totalitarianism* (New York: World Publishing Co., 1951), Chap. 1.

38. W. Scott Morgan, *History of the Wheel and Alliance and the Impending Revolution* (St. Louis: C.B. Woodward Co., 1891), p. 439.

39. Thomas May Thorpe, *What Is Money* (New York: J.S. Ogilvie Publishing Co., 1894), pp. 21, 24, 66.

40. James B. Goode, *The Modern Banker* (Chicago: Charles H. Kerr & Co., 1896), p. 125.

41. Mary E. Hobart, *The Secret of the Rothschilds* (Chicago: Charles H. Kerr & Co., 1898).

42. John Clark Ridpath, "Plutocracy and War," *The Arena*, Vol. 19, No. 98 (January, 1898), p. 100.

43. Harold Frederic, *Gloria Mundi* (Chicago: Herbert S. Stone & Co., 1898), p. 404; see Louis Harap, *The Image of the Jew in American Literature* (Philadelphia: The Jewish Publication Society of America, 1974), pp. 396 – 99; Abraham H. Steinberg, "Jewish Characters in the American Novel to 1900," Ph.D. dissertation, New York University, 1956, p. 188.

44. Frederic, p. 405.

45. Harold Frederic, *The Market-Place* (New York: Grosset & Dunlap, 1899), p. 344; see Harap, pp. 399 – 400; Steinberg, p. 190.

46. Frederic, *The Market-Place*, pp. 9, 226.

47. Alexander Craig, *Ionia: Land of Wise Men and Fair Women* (Chicago: E.A. Weeks, 1898). See Harap, pp. 412 – 13.

48. Craig, p. 221.

49. Richard Henry Savage, *An Exile from London* (New York: The Home Publishing Co., 1896), p. 8; see Harap, pp. 332 – 33; Steinberg, pp. 147 – 48.

50. Savage, pp. 8, 10.

51. *The Quarterly Sentinel*, Vol. 6, No. 1 (1899), p. 27.

52. *The Freeman's Journal*, April 9, 1898.

53. *The Catholic Telegraph*, Vol. 67, No. 7 (February 17, 1898), p. 1.

54. *The Catholic Record*, Vol. 15, No. 32 (February 3, 1898).

55. *New York Age*, May 9, 1907.

56. David Graham Phillips, "The Empire of Rothschild," *Cosmopolitan*, Vol. 38, No. 5 (March, 1905), p. 507.

57. E. Alexander Powell, "Masters of Europe," *The Saturday Evening Post*, Vol. 181, No. 51 (June 19, 1909), p. 16.

58. Lincoln Steffens, "It: An Exposition of the Sovereign Political Power of Organized Business," *Everybody's Magazine*, Vol. 23, No. 4 (October, 1910), p. 458; see also Andrew White to Simon Wolf, May 12, 1905, Philip Cowen Papers, American Jewish Historical Society, Waltham, Massachusetts.

59. Curtis Guild to Henry Cabot Lodge, November 4, 17, 1911; March 11, 1912; July 9, 1912, Henry Cabot Lodge Papers, Box 1911, Folder G. Box 1912, Folder G, Massachusetts Historical Society, Boston, Massachusetts; Curtis Guild to Philander C. Knox, March 16, 1912, The National Archives of the United States of America, Washington, D.C., Records of the Department of State, 711, 612/110.

60. Jacob E. Connor to Philander C. Knox, February 7, 1912, in The National Archives, 8611, 111/125.

61. See C. Vann Woodward's *Tom Watson Agrarian Rebel* (New York: The Macmillan Co., 1938) for an excellent biography of the man, and Leonard Dinnerstein's *The Leo Frank Case* (New York: Columbia University Press, 1968) for a comprehensive discussion of the history and impact of the case.

62. *The Jeffersonian*, October 15, 1914; passim; April 29, 1915, p. 10; June 10, 1915, p. 1.

63. Oscar Handlin and Mary F. Handlin, *Danger in Discord: Origins of Anti-Semitism in the United States* (New York: Anti-Defamation League of B'nai B'rith, 1948), pp. 22 – 23.

64. David Starr Jordan to Edwin Ginn, February 11, 1910, David Starr Jordan Papers, Correspondence, Microfilm Roll 153, Vol. 64, Stanford University Archives, Stanford, California.

65. D.S. Jordan to Elbert Hubbard, July 18, 1911, in ibid., Roll 74.

66. D.S. Jordan to Henry L. Higginson, February 22, 1912, in ibid., Roll 78.

67. David Starr Jordan, *Unseen Empire* (Boston: American Unitarian Association, 1912), pp. 19, 22.

68. Letter, Henry Cabot Lodge to John [?], April 15, 1898, Henry Cabot Lodge Papers, Letter Books, Vol. 14, p. 135.

69. Letter, H.C. Lodge to Sir George O. Trevelyan, December 12, 1914, in ibid., Box 1914, Folder B.

70. Letter, H.C. Lodge to Lord Bryce, May 27, 1919, in ibid., Box 1919.

71. Letter, H.C. Lodge to Brooks Adams, October 17, 1919, in ibid., Box. 1919.

72. Letter, H.C. Lodge to William Astor Chanler, December 17, 1919, in ibid., Box 1919.

73. Richard B. Hovey, *John Jay Chapman—An American Mind* (New York: Columbia University Press, 1959); Melvin Bernstein, *John Jay Chapman* (New York: Twayne Publishers, 1964).

74. Letter, J.J. Chapman to Elizabeth Chanler, November 25, 1897, John Jay Chapman Papers, The Houghton Library; see Hovey, *John Jay Chapman.*

75. Ibid.

76. See any number of letters written between 1917 and 1919. As an example, see his letters to Charles Armstrong Chapman in those years.

77. John Jay Chapman, review of *The Cause of World Unrest,* by H.A. Gwynne, in *The Literary Review,* Vol. 1, No. 12 (November 27, 1920), p. 4.

78. Letter, J.J. Chapman to Louis Marshall, December 13, 1920, John J. Chapman Papers.

79. John Jay Chapman, "America the Backslider," *The Spectator,* No. 4, 922 (October 28, 1922), p. 589.

80. See unpublished manuscript, "Courage," November 10, 1924, John Jay Chapman Collection; Letter, J.J. Chapman to Robert Nichols, May 18, 1925, in ibid.; Letter, J.J. Chapman to Owen Wister, May 27, 1925 in ibid.; and "Cape Cod, Rome and Jerusalem," May 29, 1925, in ibid.

81. Letter, J.J. Chapman to Emile Legouis, May 6, 1926, in ibid.

82. Letter, J.J. Chapman to E. Legouis, n.d., in ibid.

83. Letter, J.J. Chapman to Samuel Smith Drury, July 25, 1921, in ibid.

84. Letter, J.J. Chapman to Charles Chapman, December 20, 1919, in ibid.; see Hovey, *John Jay Chapman.*

85. Letter, William Astor Chanler to H.C. Lodge, April 10, 1920, Henry Cabot Lodge Papers, Box 1920, Personal A-G.

86. Letter, W.A. Chanler to H.C. Lodge, November 8, 1921, in ibid., Box 1922, A-G.

87. Letter, W.A. Chanler to J.J. Chapman, January 14, 1925, John Jay Chapman Collection.

88. Ibid.

89. American Jewish Committee Archives, General Correspondence, 1906 – 32, New York—Poland A-Protocols/Brasol, Protocols, Ford Folders;

Louis Marshall Papers, folders—P/Minority Rights/Russia, C/Politics; American Jewish Committee Vertical Files, Anti-Semitism, Protocols, Brasol, Ford.

90. The depth of Putnam's anti-Semitism is fully revealed in Putnam to Lee Weiss, March 13, 1922, and Putnam to Harris Weinstock, November 5, 1920, Louis Marshall Collection, Box 56, Box 64, American Jewish Archives; Naomi W. Cohen, *Not Free to Desist: The American Jewish Committee 1906 – 1966* (Philadelphia: The Jewish Publication Society of America, 1972), pp. 127 – 35.

91. Although Ford hired professional journalists like William Cameron to speak for him in the pages of the *Independent*, supplementary evidence indicates that the views expressed therein were in harmony with his own.

92. Letter, Louis Marshall to John Spargo, December 31, 1920, Louis Marshall Papers, xerox copies, Box 3, American Jewish Committee Archives.

93. *Current Opinion*, Vol. 70 (1921), p. 501; *New York Herald Tribune*, January 4, 1921.

94. Letters, Rosika Schwimmer to Nathan Straus, November 22, 1922, to Henry Ford, February 13, 1926, to Norman Hapgood, June 29, 1922, Box F6, Box E50, Rosika Schwimmer—Lola M. Lloyd Collection, New York Public Library Archives, New York City.

95. Letter, R. Schwimmer to Norman Hapgood, June 29, 1922 in ibid.

96. *Dearborn Independent*, May 22, 1920.

97. *The International Jew; The World's Foremost Problem* (Dearborn, Michigan: The Dearborn Publishing Co., 1921), p. 107.

98. *The International Jew; Jewish Activities in the United States* (Dearborn, Michigan: The Dearborn Publishing Co., 1921), p. 192.

99. Ibid., pp. 125 – 26.

100. Ibid., p. 95.

101. Morton Rosenstock, *Louis Marshall, Defender of Jewish Rights* (Detroit: Wayne State University Press, 1965), p. 146.

102. The following is a partial list of the types of groups and individuals that received the *Dearborn Independent* and the number in each group.

Bank presidents	1,900
Rotary clubs	1,100
Academy of Political Science	1,100
American Economics Association	2,300
Women's clubs	4,200
College presidents	757
Heads of churches	265
Congress	500

103. Herbert Adams Gibbons, "The Jewish Problem," *The Century Magazine,* Vol. 102, No. 5 (September, 1921), p. 786.

104. U.S. Congress, Senate, *Justice for Hungary,* S. Doc. 346, 67th Cong., 4th sess., March 3, 1923.

105. George W. Armstrong, *The Crime of '20* (Dallas: Press of the Venney Co., 1922); *The Story of the Dynasty of the Money Trust in America* (Fort Worth, Texas, 1923).

106. Hamilton York, "The Dawes Report and Control of World Gold," in *Documents,* ed. Peter Beckwith (New York: The Beckwith Press, 1925), p. 4.

107. *The American Standard,* Vol. 1 – 2, (1924 – 25).

108. Letter, Ralph E. Duncan to Lee A. Stone, April 7, 1925, Rosika Schwimmer, Lola M. Lloyd Collection.

109. See David Brion Davis, ed., *The Fear of Conspiracy: Images of Un-American Subversion from the Revolution to the Present* (Ithaca: Cornell University Press, 1971), pp. 205 – 10.

The Ghetto in America served as
nursery for many of the loons now at
large in Russia.
CHICAGO TRIBUNE (November 12,
1917)[1]

Jews are leaders of Freemasonry as
well as of the Revolutionary
movements throughout the world.
MOUNT ANGEL MAGAZINE (March 7,
1919)[2]

A General exodus of Russians from
the United States is planned by a group
of radical organizations, Lenine to
supply the ships. If the worst comes to
the worst, Americans must learn to
press their own trousers.
JUDGE, Vol. 78, No. 2009 (May 1,
1920)[3]

From Svengali to Marx: The
Radical Jew

A tandem conceptualization often expressed simultaneously with the
charge of Jewish conspiracy is the theme attributing to Jews a particular
affinity for revolution and radical politics. Both are somehow functions
of his internationalism, his "restless energy." The only difference is
that now Jews were draped in the red flag of radicalism rather than the
escutcheon of the House of Rothschild.

It is true that many Jews, disproportionate to their numbers, were
attracted in nineteenth- and twentieth-century Eastern Europe and
America to liberalism, socialism, and eventually Marxism—probably
for good reason. These movements eschewed anti-Semitism, were radi-

cal in nature, stood in opposition to the state that represented the oppression of Jews and theoretically welcomed all into their folds regardless of race or religion.

On the sociological and intellectual levels of causation, there are other factors that account for Jewish gravitation towards radicalism. Jews in the late nineteenth century were largely urban and many of these movements were born, sprouted, and eventually centered in urban environments. The second-generation Jewish intellectual with a background of Talmudic dialectic and infused with a tradition of Judaic social justice might be seen as intellectually predisposed to Marxism to a degree that he himself rarely appreciated. Marxism with its internationalism and anti-nationalism, to borrow the logic of another stereotype, could be interpreted as eminently fitted to the emotional needs of a people without a fatherland. Marxism, for many Jews, was more than a mere strategy of political action, more than a program of economic and social reconstruction, more even than a comprehensive theory of history and society. As traditional Judaism declined in importance, many Jews diverted their messianic urges into Marxism as a kind of surrogate religion. Marxism became for them an ethic, a theology; it was cerebral, almost Talmudic in its logic; a vast, all-embracing doctrine of man and the universe; a passionate faith endowing life with meaning; an optimistic view of man and the future that jelled very well with the prophetic impulse in Judaism. Some Jews were attracted to radicalism because they very understandably realized that the ''system'' was against them—they were discriminated against in the professions, in academic circles, and in the social sphere—hence many of them turned to a revolutionary response in an effort to attain elementary justice. Whether they embraced these ideologies as a means of escape from oppression and social exclusion, or through loss of faith in their own national-religious traditions, or out of more general ethical and humanitarian considerations, Marxism, for these Jews, represented the ''Promised Land.''[4]

These factors were most operative in prerevolutionary Russia. To one of the most oppressed minority groups, to a group very highly proletarianized, impoverished, subject to violence, discrimination, and virulent anti-Semitism, radicalism seemed the only solution. Jewish participation in Bolshevik politics and the creation of the Jewish Bund are two major manifestations of these developments. As the Russified and

Polonized Jewish immigrants came to the United States, they brought this socialist Weltanschauung with them. Here many of them also found social conditions that fed their radicalism. The shock of immigration, sweatshops, horrible working conditions, child labor, poverty, urban congestion, extremes of wealth and poverty, the strangeness of concrete-skyscraper cities, especially New York City, all contributed to alienation. These conditions tarnished the image of an America of opportunity and influenced many Jews to go the route of working-class protest. There was, by the turn of the century, an immigrant Jewish proletariat of considerable size in the American cities, a proletariat intensively exploited and alienated. The objective conditions for social-ist sentiment surely were ripe.[5]

It is not surprising then that the history of political radicalism in America, from the anarchism of Emma Goldman and Alexander Berk-man through the socialism of Victor Berger, Abraham Cahan, and Morris Hillquit to the communism of Herbert Aptheker, Philip Foner, Howard Fast, Benjamin Gitlow, Mike Gold, and Bertram Wolfe has been largely identified with Jews doubly alienated from Judaism and from capitalism, apostates from the Mosaic dispensation and from the gospel according to Adam Smith. What is unfortunate is that their participation in movements and activities deemed to be subversive, in conjunction with the growing belief that Jews were at the hub of socialism and Bolshevism in Europe, led to the overgeneralized ex-trapolation that Jews as a group are predisposed to radicalism and therefore suspect, if indeed not dangerous to society.

The prominent appearance of Jewish names upon the rosters of labor, Socialist, and Communist groups provided the reactionaries of the nineteenth and twentieth centuries with a most effective weapon. Even those who realized that Jews were a clear minority excoriated them nevertheless for being the noisiest and most influential radical gadflys. Many, internalizing another stereotype, used the popular argument that a few Jews were more important to the movement than the majority of gentile radicals and their sympathizers.[6] Made greater than life and given superior cognitive powers, the implicit threat they posed, despite small numbers, was thereby magnified.

As we have seen, anti-Semitism and negative stereotyping often had little to do with the Jews as such and had little relationship to reality. For some, Jews are all capitalists; for others, they are the secret controllers of the political and economic life of the nation; for still others, they are all Communists. Yet there is an underlying logic to these accusations for they represent a frustrated response to the untrammeled industrialism of the century and its social and political spin-offs that the Jews were supposed to control or exemplify. There were serious moral and social problems created by the rapid progress of industry and commerce. But just as the Jews made up but a small portion of the radical groups and the middle class, so actual Jewish conduct did not justify the onslaught of their critics. The enemy was liberalism, industrialism, secularism, and so on, and the reactionaries found there was no better way of defining and combating these impersonal evils than by labeling them "Jewish." They found that by stigmatizing Marxism (together with the old chestnut of international banking) as a Jewish phenomenon, the changing America, unsettling to a traditional generation, could be explained away as a product of foreign importation.

Although this particular stereotype was mainly a product of the twentieth century, an index of America's increasing concern with the encroaching "Red" menace, it surfaced occasionally in literature and in other sources in the nineteenth century. Edward King, a Comtian positivist who numbered among his friends Abraham Cahan and who was deeply involved in the intellectual life of the East Side, nevertheless presented a rather compromising portrait of the Jew in several of his novels. In his first, *The Gentle Savage* (1883), King describes the anarchist movement in Russia as being largely controlled by Jews. Characters like Stanislas, Vera, and the Polish Jew Ignatius, the "venerable apostle of destruction" and "vengeance," are intent on bringing down the Czarist regime. Ignatius has spent a lifetime inventing an "infernal machine" that will devastate Russian society and make it "relapse into the chaos out of which it sprang." Vera, the "virginal priestess of Bakounin [sic]," dies of tuberculosis; the "ancient mechanic," the "builder of engines of upheaval," along with Stanislas are killed by the premature explosion of the infernal machine; the Jewish nihilists thus meet the violent death they had intended for others.[7]

This novel hardly seems an auspicious prelude to *Joseph Zalmonah* (1894), one of the few fictional works in the period that depicts Jews with sympathy, some insight, and without condescension. Even so, there are within it several stereotypic treatments, particularly of the Jewish Socialist, that are one-dimensional and quite damaging. The action takes place on the East Side of New York City and deals with the career and struggles of labor leader Joseph Barondess. Specifically, it focuses on Barondess's opposition to the Socialists, the difficulties he encounters and his final victory.[8] The story may encompass the entire scope of East Side life—economic, social, cultural, and religious, and that is to be applauded—but it has within it the seeds of misunderstanding.

Since all the characters in the novel are Jewish and since the plot concerns the struggle of labor against oppressive capital, King had the ingredients for a provoking portrait of Jewish exploitation of fellow Jew. The sweaters, landlords, and manufacturers who appear in the novel are without exception cruel, greedy, and totally devoid of simple human sentiments. In fact, the entire system is described in terms reminiscent of Southern slavery. Not always realistic are King's descriptions of a wicked landlord who evicts a dying old woman because she is late with her rent; of charlatan rabbis who are in complicity with heinous crimes against people and property; and of employers and sweaters like Freier who "coined the poor wretch's blood, drop by drop, and when he had it all in good red—yes, blood—red—gold safe in his own pocket, he kicked the useless operator into the street to die!"[9]

This is the system that Joseph Zalmonah (Barondess) had to organize against, but he first had to overcome one more obstacle, Rudolf Baumeister, a stereotyped caricature of a Jewish Socialist. Although the Socialists did oppose Barondess, King did not accurately convey the reason, which was actually an attempt to wrest leadership from the anarchist faction with whom Barondess was allied, rather than an extension of blind Socialist ambition.[10] Rudolf is represented as a satanic villain in the tradition of the European nihilists who are consumed, in image at least, with their violent radicalism. He is portrayed as the product of years of persecution and poverty, and whatever collective cause he may once have embraced has since been perverted into an obsession to destroy his tormentors. His madness—the madness of revolution—is both literal fact and metaphor in the novel. His mania is revealed in every irrational speech and act. On occasion he gives "a mocking laugh, which had a Mephistophelian ring to it."[11] He is, moreover, of "that class of men which is profoundly egotistical, without knowing it—the class which is always serving itself alone, while professing to serve others." His gaze is shifty and demoniac, "and at certain moments the eyes had a wild look, like that of an animal about to attack.''[12] He will stop at neither the murder of Joseph as part of his plan to precipitate the revolution, nor balk at an attempt to burn to death his recently arrived immigrant wife and child when they become cumbersome.

The portrayal of this conventional, wild-eyed Jewish Socialist is a distortion of the truth. For King, Socialists are products of personal defeat who turn their frustrations outward into hatred for all society. They are divested of any trace of humanity and idealism and have become mere creatures of revenge. This is the most serious defect of the novel that otherwise is a vivid, although somewhat blemished, presentation of life in the American Jewish ghetto.

Edward King fictionally exploited a theme that was gradually to press harder on the public consciousness as the turbulence of European politics became more evident and disturbing and as Jewish immigrants from those affected areas flooded into America's cities. The identification of Jews with radical causes both at home and abroad paralleled the rise in importance of Russian nihilism, Bolshevism, and American labor activism. *Puck* thus warned its readers in 1887 not to be foolishly attracted to the economic theories of Henry George that in essence are nothing more than "a few old communistic notions which obtained among the Jews several thousand years ago."[13] Two decades later, it railed against those Jewish Socialists who take a few "red-flag" quotations from Karl Marx and transpose them into a platform for violent upheaval. "It is precisely these isolated utterances that the half-baked Selig Silversteins seize upon. When... Karl Marx writes about 'exciting hatred and contempt for all existing institutions' and about waging war against 'religion, country, state and patriotism,' the low-browed fanatic takes him at his word and manufactures a bomb to throw at the police."[14] The fault lies, according to *The New York Times,* with Eastern European Jews who are prey to "desperate-talking, firebrand flinging poltoons of the [Emma] Goldman kind." Young men "weaned on the pestiferous milk of Nihilism and dynamite throwing long insanely to demolish law and order.... Pamphlets dealing with the murder of police and the assassination of governors are devoured... by hatchet-faced pimply, sallow cheeked rat-eyed young men of the Russian Jewish colony...."[15]

Others in American society inveighed against the impending threat.

The Reverend A.W. Miller, pastor of the First Presbyterian Church, Charlotte, North Carolina, in an anti-Semitic tract, *The Restoration of the Jews* (1887), warned that Jews are undermining the public faith in Christianity and are inaugurating a new crusade to destroy it, crying out once again, "Crucify It! Crucify It!" This is all done in the name of revolution. "The prime movers, the head and front of the Communistick [sic] and Atheistick [sic] movement that now threatens the social upheaval of the Eastern Continent, are Jews.... They are... largely the conductors of the press abroad, and are poisoning the publick [sic] mind with pestilential social and religious heresies...."[16] Arthur Houghton Hyde, writing in *The Popular Science Monthly* in 1898, made a similar analysis. "The anarchist and ultra-socialist parties do not, as is commonly supposed, derive their chief support from the Teutonic element; their ranks are rather recruited from among these members of the Semitic and Slavonic races."[17]

This penchant for associating Jews with radicalism generally declined during the first decade of the twentieth century, as did anti-radicalism itself, while the nation was carried along by the purpose and confidence that characterized the initial stages of the Progressive era.[18] A people with great expectations for improving society could perhaps afford a certain nonchalance toward critics of the present one. At least this was the case when the reform movement was fresh and young. In the last years of the prewar period, the specters of foreign revolution and internal dissent once more grew visible as progressivism showed signs of halting before the mission was completed.[19] A sense of increasing class conflict and unrest evidenced by the birth of the militant unions of the International Workers of the World (IWW) in the West, brandishing the strike as a revolutionary weapon; the growing popularity of Eugene Debs's Socialist party; the violence and unity of American labor as expressed in the International Ladies Garment Workers Union's (ILGWU) Lawrence, and Paterson strikes, and the government's response in the "Ludlow Massacre"; the abortive revolutions in Europe—all these events conjured up old fears and tugged again at the bonds of social unity.[20] Some thought the pace of change too slow; others thought it had gone too far. Regardless, many Americans, losing faith in reform, drifted slowly into an attitude that questioned the very survival of the social order.

This uneasiness began gradually with an occasional comment or literary treatment and reached a crescendo by the eve of war.[21] John Foster Fraser's influential book *Red Russia* (1907), which alerted England to this development, made its way to the United States and was read with great interest here. Fraser advised his audience of the incipient danger of Jewish radicalism. "In the brain of the Jew—though cringing and whining before his oppressors—blazes a clear fire of resentment. So when the revolution began to smoulder and flame in Russia, the authorities knew it was the Jews who were fanning the terror."[22]

Several literary works gave further exposure to the growing identification of Jews with extremism. Although this was not a major fictional motif and authors like Edward Bellamy, for example, did not identify Jews with radicalism, there were occasional treatments in this period that emphasized this association. Isaac Kahn Friedman, an assimilated Jewish author who some consider wrote perhaps the "first radical novel in twentieth century America,"[23] can be included in this discussion because he concerned himself so little with Jews and their problems in his fiction that he can hardly be considered an American Jewish novelist.[24] In his *By Bread Alone* (1901), a strike novel patterned after the Homestead, Pennsylvania, steel-mill warfare, we are given in condemnatory terms the violent foreign radical in the Frenchman LaVette and the Jew Sophia Goldstein (Emma Goldman), ruthless saboteurs who, like King's Rudolf Baumeister, obstruct the peaceful labor agitation of the novel's hero Blair Carrhart.[25] Upton Sinclair's *The Jungle* (1906), a muckraking exposé and a socialist conversion novel, unwittingly perhaps also propagated this image. The protagonist Jurgis Rudkis gets his lessons in socialism from the Polish Jew Ostrinski, a fictionalization of an actual socialist organizer, Bernie Berlyn, who brought his ideology with him from the Old World. A pants finisher in a ghetto sweatshop, he explains the forces at work bubbling beneath the surface, waiting to burst out and engage the capitalist oppressor. "All over the world two classes were forming, with an unbridged chasm between them—the capitalist class with its enormous fortunes, and the proletariat, bound into slavery by unseen chains."[26] It is revealing that Sinclair saw fit to make Ostrinski the transmitter of Marxist dialectic. Although Ostrinski's Jewishness had little to do with stereotyping, and although Sinclair was sympathetically disposed to socialism, his readers may not have been.

On the other hand, anti-radical editor and drama critic John Corbin, in his play *Husband* (1910), is not as optimistic about the impact of these new, "foreign" ideologies. Rather, he sees a great danger in them. This is epitomized in the Jewish character Rebecca Levine, who practices free love, has a child out of wedlock, and is a socialist organizer. She lacks the social graces, is extremely aggressive, and knows exactly what she wants and usually gets it. Levine shocks the other characters of the play with statements such as: "To those who love truly there is only one adultery—to turn from the free kiss of a lover to the enforced embrace of a husband." The "prolific Levine" serves as a warning of what will occur if the restless multitudes of the slums are ever organized by Jews like Levine and her colleagues.[27]

Florence Converse's *The Children of Light* (1912) is another novel that depicts the Jewish Socialist in a disparaging manner. The story traces the development of a young patrician heiress, Clara, from her early utopian days, her college career, her flirtation with socialism, and eventually her decision to live and work among the city's immigrants. Along the way she meets villainous exploiters like Markowsky who literally "sweat" their workers into submission, as well as revolutionary Socialists from Russia like Lazarus Samson and Bertha Aarons who favor the abolition of the marriage tie and the repudiation of Christianity. At first she is attracted to them and she attends a meeting where "the ferret looks of watchful Jews" were much in evidence. But eventually she realizes their "mechanical" radicalism steeped in Judaic hatred and revenge was unsuitable for the American environment and she finds her inspiration instead in the more moderate camp of Christian socialism.[28] The novel ends with a massive strike in the garment industry, patterned after the 1909 labor revolt of New York's working women.

The stimulus for the walkout came at a mass meeting of waist makers at Cooper Union on November 22, 1909. Many prominent labor leaders like Abraham Cahan, Meyer London, Samuel Gompers, and Mary Dreier addressed the crowd, but the workers apparently remained unmoved. Suddenly, an inspired teenaged girl, Clara Lemlich, rose and delivered an empassioned strike plea in Yiddish, and this ignited the crowd and the assembly, which proceeded to vote overwhelmingly for a general strike.[29] This incident seems to have provided Edward Bullard with the idea for his novel about the labor revolt, *Comrade Yetta* (1913), which he wrote under the pseudonym Albert Edwards. A sympathetic and realistic work that deals with the suffering, awakening, and conversion of the proletarian heroine, it nevertheless strengthens the association of the Jew with the radical response, particularly for those not as favorably inclined to labor activism as the Socialist Bullard.

The early chapters treat Yetta's oppressive and dehumanizing sweat-shop experience. The sweater figures in the book are also Jewish, but they are described as pitiful individuals, merely slaves of another sort to the capitalist machine. The balance of the novel deals with her struggle to decide between the three ideological approaches open to her—the claims of trade unionism represented by Mabel Train (Mary Dreier) and the Women's Trade Union League (WTUL); the IWW-type industrial unionism represented by Walter Longman; and the doctrinaire socialism represented by attorney-editor Isador Braun. Braun is described as a man who "with the methodical forethought of his race and the narrow vision of a fanatic,... had arranged his future. He had planned not only each day's work, but his lifework."[30] Yetta decides to give her final allegiance to socialism and she symbolizes this by marrying Braun. Together they edit the Socialist daily *The Clarion,* a counterpart to *The Call,* which Bullard edited with Ernest Poole and Edward Russell; together they struggle to organize all workers who are victimized by unchecked capitalism and human greed.

Comrade Yetta came on the eve of World War I anti-hyphenism and at the very height of the period of mass immigration. Like the other works mentioned, it attempted to depict fictionally the broad outlines of labor's situation, especially in the garment industry of New York City, and the ferment and commitment that characterized the Jewish worker's fight to achieve more livable conditions. That is to be commended, as is the compassion and insight these authors brought to their treatments of this subject. Since Jews were disproportionately represented, at least in leadership capacity, in New York City socialism and unionism, one cannot fault these novelists for spotlighting the Jew. This is certainly true for both Sinclair and Bullard who were writing from a posture of support and for Bullard who was describing an actual incident. Never-theless, what may have seemed a positive trait to individuals attuned to labor's plight could just as easily have been interpreted by others as additional evidence that the Jew is inclined towards radical solutions. Furthermore, even within their generally balanced efforts, the Jew is often unfairly depicted as a rabid anarchist who, like the predatory Jewish capitalist, is seen as an obstacle to genuine labor reform. Marred throughout by sterotyped characters—by stock villain types like the cruel and malicious sweater, the bloodless Jewish landlord, the irrational and sinister anarchist—they contributed to a harmful imaging of the American Jew.

This is particularly unfortunate, because it was divorced from reality. Contrary to the stereotype of Jewish radicalism perpetuated in fiction, the experiences of the immigrant tended to foster moderation. The popular myth of the immigrant as an imported radical blinded many Americans to the fact that organized extremist groups and radical unionism found little support in the nation's ghettos and sweatshops. One is reminded that the IWW and the Western Federation of Miners were not spawned on the East Side, but the Amalgamated Clothing Workers Union and the ILGWU were. Most Jews, indeed, were reluctant even to join unions at first for they saw their jobs as only temporary stopgaps on the road to economic opportunity that they envisioned for themselves and their children.[31] Of course Jews provided a number of prominent labor leaders and organizers, but they were not anarchists advocating blind violence. Clearly, socialism made inroads among New York Jews, and they even elected a socialist congressman; but this was revisionist socialism that advocated gradualism and working within the "system." Abraham Cahan's *Forward* admittedly was a socialist organ read like a bible by thousands of East Side Jews, but its editorials called for reform and self-help, not revolution. Once again, Jewish motives and actions were misread.

This stereotype was further enhanced by the xenophobic passions unleashed by the war, exacerbated by the unpopular efforts of some Jews to keep America out of it. There developed a slackening of confidence, an accumulation of tensions, as the Progressive movement reached its crest in the immediate prewar years. This was complicated by a general disillusion with reform as the crusading spirit seemed to come to a halt by 1916 when idealistic leaders had nearly exhausted their capacity to move Congress and the president. Americans were groping again for national purpose and were alarmed at widening rifts of race, class, religion, and ideology. The war provided a new unifier—patriotism—and as Americans were increasingly moved by its magnetic influence, they began to look with critical eyes on that one group that did not join the effort—the radicals. This interacted with the anti-hyphenism and, specifically, with the anti-German hysteria of the period and formed an important outlet for "100 Percent Americanism."

When the conflict came, the conditions that had discouraged fears of revolutionaries during the Progressive era were erased. Then the commitment to social change had given radicalism some legitimacy. Since a great part of America was responding to various reform impulses and reform rhetoric abounded, the line between progressivism and radicalism dimmed. The war, however, reversed this effect. It put a premium on stability and demanded total immersion in the campaign, thereby isolating the radicals from the rest of society. They alone remained unregenerative and relatively organized and outspoken in their opposition to the war effort. The result was that anti-radicalism became fashionable; indeed, it was considered a barometer of one's patriotism.[32] Obviously, many groups suffered, including the pacifists, the IWW, and the Socialists. But for our purposes, it was the revolutionary Jew canard that once again was broadcast throughout the land.

Several magazines, harbingers of things to come, expeditously took up the issue. Elbert Hubbard's *The Philistine,* an avante-garde "little magazine" in the tradition of *The Chap-Book, The Lark,* and *M'lle New York,* initiated a campaign against Louis Brandeis in 1913 that lasted until the publication ceased its operations late in 1915. Its criticisms of this public servant were often couched in vague descriptive analyses of the alleged propensity of the Jewish mind for disruptive politics and economics. It said in July 1913, for example, that "by birth, education and parental tendency Brandeis represents the type of which Emma Goldman is our most distinguished example. Emma Goldman and her companion Alexander Berkman... are butters-in, outsiders, who agitate, vex, annoy and stir up strife and discontent. Samuel Gompers, kin by racial blood-ties and social sentiment, represents the same type."[33] *Life* magazine also extrapolated a generalization from a specific. Referring to Rose Pastor Stokes, the Russian-born Jewish wife of patrician Socialist J.G. Phelps Stokes, who was one of the most noteworthy women convicted under the Espionage Act, it remarked: "The radical, reformatory Jewish mind is a very obstreperous quantity. It has no political or national tradition, and usually regards government as an obstacle to improvement, and sails in promptly either to capture it or upset it."[34] J.G. Phelps Stokes apparently agreed for he decided to support the war, divorced Rose, quit the Socialist party, and turned anti-Semitic. Several weeks later on June 20, 1918, *Life* further developed this theme.

We have cherished and honored in this country during the last twenty years a type of mind totally different from any of the types to which our government owes the organization, our commercial system its development, our country its growth. It is the most destructive mind in the world, the most grasping and unabashed.... The Russian Jews... have no real national feeling. They are loyal to Socialism, to Internationalism, to whatever untried ideal of human welfare may be floating in their heads at a given moment, but are not bound by more than the loosest ties to any country or form of government....[35]

The *World's Work* suggested in a 1919 editorial, entitled "A Cure for American Bolshevism," that the only way to eradicate the "Red" cancer was to expunge from the Jews and their fellow travelers their instinctual penchant for the politics of agitation and to instill "a proper spirit of courage, initiative, and independence into these groups so that they can become a healthy part of our life."[36] If not accomplished, the Jew's weakness for corrosive extremism would continue to pose a threat to the American system of government.

The Jew, then, was viewed by some during the war years as one of the most concrete symbols of foreign radicalism. The Red Scare and the A. Mitchell Palmer raids in the postwar period increasingly served to sensitize the public to the "perils" of revolution. In a sense, the overreaction to the Bolsheviks was a sacrificial offering to an intense nativism generated the passions of war and was initiated by certain high priests of repression. Both events served to stoke the fires of the nation's latent xenophobia and lower the threshold of America's tolerance. It succeeded, for the disturbing figure of the Bolshevik Jew became a major feature of American anti-Semitism, bridging the years from Sarajevo to the 1920s.

A Justice Department report, for example, covering the summer of 1917 in New York City, wrote:

Practically all of the newspaper translations contained in this file are of a Socialistic pro-German type. While not as bitter as the out and out German papers, the Yiddish press plainly shows that they are against the draft, the war and many of the other governmental movements to forward the cause of the European battlefields.... According to unofficial reports within the past month, all of the New York Yiddish papers are in the danger class.[37]

Or there is the case of anti-Semite Russell Dunn, a former clergyman, who became fervently anti-Socialist and held numerous street meetings in Brooklyn and Manhattan during the war. At one gathering, held on June 6, 1917, he said in part:

All the Socialists were Cohens and Ginzbergs and Weinbergers and Moskowitzs and the gefilte fish crowd and the stinking onion crowd,... the crowd that have no respect for their mothers and sell their daughters for the highest price; you know the race... who are preaching this birth control thing for their own benefit, so that they can have lots of children and we won't have any, and they will outnumber us.[38]

Dunn's railings were not an isolated occurrence. Ostensibly reputable forums drew similar conclusions. The *Manufacturers Record,* a conservative business newspaper published in Baltimore, stated in August 1917:

Have you observed the great danger of socialism or anarchism (which it really is), that is steadily growing in this country, due to the immigration of the Russian Jew...? These people do not know how to treat liberty when they get it, nor can they... ever be made good American citizens.... They are secretly organizing, and when they are strong enough, unless something is done to put a stop to this immigration, will ultimately cause the most terrible of all wars or revolutions.[39]

An editorial in the *New York Exporters Review,* in June 1918, concurred with this assessment of "fact."

We have asserted all along, and we still assert, that the majority of East Side (New York) Jews are "bolshevists," that they still support the aims of the "bolshevik" government in Russia, which they largely helped to establish.... The "hoi polloi" of the East Side in the early days of the draft spent a large part of its time holding incendiary meetings, addressed by the "intelligent" Jew socialists—anarchists, denouncing the Government and the draft.... Even before the war this class of Jews had become a nuisance through the "mouthings" of their Emma Goldmans, Berkmans,... etc. They practically all supported and advocated the aims of the I.W.W. anarchists as well as those of their own crack-brained criminal "socialists."[40]

Because of positive public reaction to charges of this kind, patriotic organizations like the American Defense Society (ADS) and the American Protective League enjoyed considerable success in their campaign to organize Americans to combat the "unclean" foreign influences and to fight for "100 Percent Americanism." Over two hundred thousand citizens enlisted in the American Protective League, for example, a sort of quasi-legal, volunteer army designed to ferret out pacifists, Huns, and radicals. One of the major targets of these two groups, a focal point of their interest, was the Bolshevik Jew. Nativist William T. Hornaday's *Awake! America! Object Lessons and Warnings* (1918), a book sponsored by the ADS, used much of its space exposing this theme. Who are the socialists who present such a dangerous threat to the United States during this national crisis, Hornaday queried?

Up to this date the worst cobras that ever found shelter under the American hearthstone were the Russian-Jew anarchists long fed, housed and protected by American hospitality in the East Side of New York City. Safe in the shadow of the American flag,... they waited and fattened. They lived by agitation and by fomenting labor troubles here, until poor Russia was so weakened by war and internal strife that they dared to come out and strike her.... Wake up, Americans.... You are surrounded by snakes that in your folly you have taken in out of the cold, warmed at your fireside, and that now are all ready to strike you and your children.[41]

In stark metaphoric images, Hornaday gave the public much to fantasy about.[42] The obsession with "wild-eyed and bearded Russian radicals" seeking to overthrow American society reached the political arena. Congressman Victor Berger, leader of Milwaukee socialism, was refused his seat in the United States House of Representatives, and five Socialist New York State assemblymen, three of them Jewish, were excluded from that legislative body.

The key themes of the attack on the Jew as Bolshevik received further exposure during the well-publicized hearings of a special subcommittee of the Senate Judiciary Committee that met in February and March 1919 to deal with Bolshevism in Russia and the United States. Chaired by Senator Lee Overman of North Carolina, the subcommittee heard a parade of experts, among them Dr. George S. Simons, superintendent since 1907 of the Methodist Episcopal Church in Russia and Finland. He told the senators and the press that not only were Russian Jews leaders of the Marxists, but that their fellow malcontents were largely transplanted Jews from New York's lower East Side.

A number of us were impressed with the strong Yiddish element in this thing right from the start, and it soon became evident that more than half of the agitators in the so-called Bolshevik movement were Yiddish.... I do not think the Bolshevik movement in Russia would have been a success if it had not been for the support it got from certain elements in New York, the so-called East Side.... After the revolution they swarmed in.... I do not want to be unfair to them, but I usually know a Jew when I see one.[43]

Louis Marshall protested publicly in the pages of the *New York Times* and in a letter to the chairman, concerning the inaccuracies and outrageous innuendoes contained in Dr. Simon's testimony, but his comments fell on deaf ears.[44] Senator Overman was satisfied that Dr. Simon's evidence was impartial and that the minister "tried to be just. He only spoke of the apostate Jews who went over to Russia from this country."[45]

Other witnesses made negative and generally unsubstantiated accusations concerning the extent of Jewish participation in the revolution. William Chapin Huntington, a commercial attaché of the Department of Commerce assigned to the American embassy in Petrograd, estimated that "the leaders of the movement,... are about two-thirds Russian Jews." William W. Welsh, a representative of the National City Bank in Russia, raised the percentages. "It is well known that three-fourths of the Bolshevik leaders are Jewish." R.B. Dennis, an organizer for the YMCA, conceded Jewish participation at the highest levels, but went one step further. He placed the onus for the atrocities that were visited upon the opposition on American Jews who returned to Russia during the revolution. "These men [East Side Jews] were the most bitter and implacable men in Russia on the program of extermination, if necessary, of the bourgeoisie class."[46]

The Jew-Marxist image, menacing and fearful, was seized upon by the nativists. In Brooklyn, New York, anti-Semites set up the *Anti-Bolshevist,* "A Monthly Magazine Devoted to the Defense of American Institutions against the Jewish Bolshevist Doctrines of Morris Hillquit and Leon Trotsky." Every issue was replete with baseless accusations. The magazine stated categorically in 1919, for example, that "Bolshevism is Judaism pure and simple. The Bolshevist Jew aims at universal domination, and to accomplish this aim he is ready to deluge a world in blood. The Bolshevist in America is own brother to the Bolshevist tiger who has destroyed Russia and slaughtered millions of her people." They are both "madmen, fanatics, dreamers, etc., but there is a method in their madness, for they murder only Christians and ravish and torture only Christian women.''[47]

The Committee of American Citizens of Polish Birth and Descent, an anti-Communist group, charged the Jews with subverting both Poland and America for their own racial purposes.[48] The Russian National Society, a counterpart organization, agreed. It argued in 1921 that Jews hold "the most responsible positions in the Soviet regime" because they have a basic affinity with revolutionary politics. "There is much in the fact of Bolshevism itself," it asserted, "in the fact that so many Jews are Bolsheviks, in the fact that the ideals of Bolshevism at many points are consonant with the finest ideals of Judaism" to account for their gravitation towards radicalism, both here and abroad.[49]

General Count Cherep-Spiridovich, a White Russian who adopted this title after he emigrated to the United States, continued the attack. He issued the *Gentile's Review* in Chicago, which he advertised as the only publication not afraid to tell the truth.[50] The "truth" is that most Marxist leaders and ideologues are Jews. In a circular addressed to "all Aryans," and entitled "Confidential Communication" (do not let this fall in the hands of the enemy), he described in a semiliterate and conspiratorial style whom the enemy is.[51]

The Jews, pure Asiatics not White, don't like the "expose" by the "Spirit of '76" [Cherep-Spiridovich] of the Hidden Operations of their Judeo-Mongol Secret World Government which... through its control of Bolshevist Propaganda simultaneously Foments Strikes, Riots and Rebellion among workers and men of color. This Jew Government, through its "Minister of War" (Trotzky) Ordered the Destruction of the United States.... The Judeo-Mongols are all "het up" [?] about it and are pulling the usual "Bunk" of crying "Gewalt." They think the Truth should be Muffled..., so that their plans to Disrupt the United States, Destroy our Christian Civilization, Enslave the White Race and Attain to World Domination can succeed.... You and "we of the Spirit of '76" may be "Goys," brother, but we got to pull together if we want to keep this Judeo-Mongol Bolshevist Crowd from walking off with the Washington Monument and the Statue of Liberty.[52]

In 1920 Small, Maynard & Company of Boston published a translation of the *Protocols of the Elders of Zion* entitled *The Protocols and World Revolution,* which sold quite well and which further projected this image. In a lengthy introduction, the publishers attempted to delineate the parallels between the policies of the Marxists and the blueprint outlined in the *Protocols*. They first averred that "the Bolshevist revolution was from the beginning almost entirely led and controlled by Jews." They then went on to claim that there "is a remarkable similarity between the policies of destruction outlined in the Protocols and the actual measures of destruction put into effect by the Bolshevist regime in Russia." Specifically, "the strategy of stirring up class hatred in Christian nations, and the encouragement of revolutionary radicalism to that end, which has such a prominent place in the Protocols, finds corroboration in the very prominent part which... the Jews have been taking in the radical and revolutionary movements in many parts of the world." It is hardly surprising then that "the radical labor movement is largely controlled by Jewish internationalists," and that "recently several rabbis have taken a definite stand in support of the Red movement" [presumably they mean Rabbis Judah Magnes and Maxwell Silver, although they certainly were not communist sympathizers], or that "powerful Jewish bankers were instrumental in spreading Bolshevism."[53] Radicalism is just part of a broad plan, merely one tactic in the campaign to establish Jewish control.

The stereotype was also prevalent among more responsible individuals, who were also influenced by it. Labor difficulties, for example, were attributed by some to the radicalism of the Russian Jew type. Edward S. Beach, chairman of the Legal Advisory Board, Local 156 in New York City, argued in 1919 that it is in the ranks of the unpatriotic Jews "that the great majority of the IWW and Bolshevik thugs are to be found.... If reports are to be believed, the walking delegates of the IWW and the Bolsheviki are busy daily... in various and extensive parts of the country; and unless we are a nation of fools, this kind of mental disease has got to be stamped out as vigorously as leprosy."[54] New York State's famous Red hunter Clayton R. Lusk was still urging Jewish labor leaders like Morris Hillquit in 1921 to denounce "the present Bolshevistically inclined and largely led Socialist party."[55] Interestingly enough, two of the leaders of the "Red hunt" in New York were Assemblyman Simon Adler of Rochester and Deputy Attorney General Berger, both Jews. The Better American Lecture Service, which supplied material for lectures on world affairs, captioned its slides with comments on the Jewish role in the revolution, offering statistics such as "sixty-eight Russian Hebrews and 264 Hebrews from the Bowery district of New York" were in the Soviet government.[56]

The American Red Cross called Bolshevism a Jewish plot to control the national economy. H.T. Wright, secretary of the Hollywood, California, Board of Trade, was certain that "Bolshevism was largely fathered along by Russian Jews."[57] Congressman Albert Johnson, chairman of the House Committee on Immigration and Naturalization, warned that these subversives were now coming to the United States. "There are a large number of people designated as 'Russian Jews,' who have come here, who are not of the religious type, but are just exactly of the Trotski type." Because of their influx, they present a major argument for "the suspension of immigration."[58] Speakers of the Greater Iowa Association, an influential conservative businessmen's organization, warned against these same "Jewish Bolsheviks" at the Rotary Club meetings they addressed in 1919–20 in most every town and municipality of Iowa.[59]

It should not be surprising, given a postwar American environment steeped in Red baiting and alerted by anti-Communist roundups, deportations, and government propaganda to the "perils" of radicalism, that the Jew would be so victimized. Certainly decades of stereotyping facilitated this overgeneralized identification. A generation that sat silently back and watched Sacco and Vanzetti sacrificed in the name of democracy was equally capable of misjudging the Jew. It was as if the Jew-revolutionary image had became part of the conventional wisdom of the day. Journalist Arthur Brisbane reporded that "more than half the wily minds in Russia are Jewish."[60] Former Harvard University English professor and educator Ralph Boas argued that there is enough evidence "to give the popular impression that Jews and Bolsheviki have something in common."[61] The press frequently discussed Trotsky's role in the revolution, and on one occasion *Current Opinion* described his features as "sallow, mephistophelian and distinctly Jewish."[62] Henry Emery, chairman of the United States Tariff Board from 1909 to 1913, remarked in 1919 after returning from Russia that the movement generally "takes on the color of a revolt of the Jews against the Russians."[63] John Dyneley Prince, president of the New Jersey Civil Service Commission and professor of Slavonic languages at Columbia University, interpreted this phenomenon as a function of Jewish racial allegiance. "Their race feeling," he asserted in 1919, "prevents them from doing anything but offering support to Jewish 'red' leaders, simply because these people are Jews."[64]

John Dos Passos, in his novel *Airways, Inc.* (1928), outlined the forces that move these Jews toward radicalism. A work that deals with the drudgery, purposelessness, and materialism of middle-class suburban American living, it introduces an alien force, the Communist party labor organizer Walter Goldberg, who unsettles the otherwise boringly complacent life of the other characters in the novel. Walter describes the factors that have made him a Communist.

There's something in it. You'd have to be a Jew like me to understand. You've heard of the Pale. Everyone of us has something fenced up way down in us. We've been in prison for two thousand years. I have the mind of a jailbird, that's why prison can't hurt me. That's why we throw ourselves into every movement of freedom. That's why I feel the slavery of the workers, I feel it as a worker and I feel it as a Jew.[65]

Ultimately, Goldberg's agitation becomes so annoying and so "bad for business" that he is indicted on fraudulent charges of murder, convicted, and executed.

It should also be noted that there was a strong antipathy to Jews in the American Left. August Spies, who died on the gallows for the Hay Market Affair in 1887, was violently anti-Semitic. Jack London wrote vituperative anti-Semitic articles in the *International Socialist Review* between 1910 and 1916, linking Jews with oppressive capitalism as well as cowardly pacifism. He also revealed mild anti-Semitism when he accused the "Ghetto Socialists" of New York City of weak revolutionary ardor and pacifism. He was referring to people like Meyer London and Morris Hillquit who were Jews and the Eastern wing of the party, which was dominated by Jews. This disturbed his forthright Anglo-Saxon supremacism. In London's later years, anti-Jewish stereotypes were introduced into his novels. Elam Harnish is cheated by the Guggenheims in *Burning Daylight* (1910). Simon Nishikanta, an Armenian Jew, is described as "a bulking colossal bodied, greasy seeming grossness of flesh—the... San Francisco Pawnbroker," in *Michael, Brother of Jerry* (1919). William H. Henry, the national secretary of the Socialist party in the 1920s, was involved in nativist, anti-New York and anti-Semitic activities in a party that, rhetoric notwithstanding, had a substantial amount of midwestern, nativist sentiment. The American Communist party, despite significant Jewish participation in the movement, was also replete with anti-Semitism at the highest level, including

Earl Browder. Even Norman Thomas in 1932 was involved in a basically anti-Semitic maneuver to oust Morris Hillquit as national chairman of the Socialist party at the party's national convention. These examples of anti-Semitism in the American Left were essentially based on stereotypical perceptions of the Jews—not unlike Karl Marx's in *Zur Judenfrage*.[66]

Nevertheless, it is apparent that the image of the Jew as radical and Marxist was an important part of the anti-Semitic rhetoric abounding in American society. Despite the occasional outbursts of hysteria over anarchists and radical labor that resounded from the Gilded Age to the eve of World War I, the deluge primarily came after 1917. The emotional shock of the conflict, in addition to the failure of progressivism to deliver on its idealistic promises, led many Americans to blame first the international bankers and Wall Street and then the Russian Bolsheviks, often portrayed as Jews, for the frustrations, disturbing dissensions, and innovations of the modern era.

The years from 1917 to the mid-1920s are probably unmatched in American history for xenophobia and paranoid suspicion. "It is sad for those of us who have hitherto been proud of our fine American traditions," wrote Louis Marshall, to note what a change has occurred since the armistice."[67] The psychological impact of becoming involved in a futile crusade abroad and the "100 percent Americanism" generated by the passions of war, created a mood of fervent nationalism and suspicion that erupted in the Red Scare of 1919–20, the Henry Ford mania, and in anti-radicalism generally. This was aggravated by the stunning news that Marxist revolutionaries had overthrown the exemplar of governmental autocratic authority. Who would be next to fall? The older image of labor activists and parlor socialists was now easily merged with new fears of foreign subversion often couched in terms of Jewish influences. Traditional enmities acquired new meaning in the light of an appallingly destructive war that had not only failed to make the world safe for democracy, but had also apparently unleashed a sinister force that was driven by an evil desire to dismantle society and resurrect it in its own image. Shylock, Fagin, and the anti-Christian pawnbroker were transformed into wild-eyed radicals with "gnashing teeth and scraggly beard and dripping dagger" who stalked through "noisome alleys in the imaginary East Side."[68] The Bolshevik Revolution and the creation of the Communist International haunted Americans and intensified fears of an encroaching influence dedicated to the destruction of Western democratic life. In their search for a single, comprehensive explanation for these developments and in their desire to weed out the "Red" from the "true blue," they converged upon the Jew, that symbol of ancient, hidden enemies.

NOTES

1. *Chicago Tribune,* November 12, 1917.

2. *Mount Angel Magazine,* March 7, 1919.

3. *Judge,* Vol. 78, No. 2009 (May 1, 1920).

4. Robert Wistrich, *Revolutionary Jews from Marx to Trotsky* (New York: Barnes & Noble, 1976).

5. See Irving Howe, *World of Our Fathers* (New York: Harcourt Brace Jovanovich, 1976).

6. Zosa Szajkowski, *Jews, Wars, and Communism* (New York: KTAV Publishing House, 1972), p. 416.

7. Edward King, *The Gentle Savage* (Boston: James R. Osgood and Co., 1883), pp. 138, 309, 321. See Louis Harap, *The Image of the Jew in American Literature* (Philadelphia: The Jewish Publication Society of America, 1974), pp. 479–84.

8. Gregory Weinstein, *Ardent Eighties* (New York: International Press, 1947), pp. 40–42, 77–78.

9. Edward King, *Joseph Zalmonah* (Boston: Lee and Shepard Publishers, 1970), pp. 70, 111, 265, 356.

10. Moses Rischin, *The Promised City: New York's Jews, 1870–1914* (Cambridge: Harvard University Press, 1970), pp. 179, 185–86, 192–93.

11. King, *Joseph Zalmonah,* p. 64.

12. Ibid., p. 31.

13. *Puck,* Vol. 20, No. 516 (January 26, 1887), p. 358.

14. *Puck,* Vol. 63, No. 1624 (April 15, 1908), n.p.

15. *The New York Times,* August 21, 23, 1893.

16. Reverend A.W. Miller, *The Restoration of the Jews* (Atlanta: Constitution Publishing Co., 1887), pp. 42, 52.

17. Arthur Houghton Hyde, "The Foreign Element in American Civilization," *The Popular Science Monthly,* Vol. 52 (January, 1898), p. 397.

18. John Higham, *Strangers in the Land: Patterns of American Nativism 1860–1925* (New York: Atheneum, 1971), p. 175.

19. Arthur A. Ekirch, Jr., *The Decline of American Liberalism* (New York: Atheneum, 1971), pp. 195–242; John Chamberlain, *Farewell to Reform* (Chicago: Quadrangle Books, 1965).

20. Joseph G. Rayback, *A History of American Labor* (New York: The Free Press, 1966).

21. See also Prescott F. Hall, *Immigration; and Its Effects Upon the United States* (New York: Henry Holt & Co., 1908), p. 156.

22. John Foster Fraser, *Red Russia* (New York: The John Lane Co., 1907), p. 82.

23. Walter B. Rideout, "O Workers' Revolution... The True Messiah: The Jew as Author and Subject in the American Novel," *American Jewish Archives,* Vol. 2, No. 2 (October, 1959), p. 188.

24. See Isaac Kahn Friedman's *Lucky Number* (Chicago: Way and Williams, 1896) and *Poor People* (Boston: Houghton, Mifflin and Co., 1900).

25. Isaac Kahn Friedman, *By Bread Alone* (New York: McClure, Phillips & Co., 1901).

26. Upton Sinclair, *The Jungle* (New York: New American Library, 1962), p. 308.

27. John Corbin, *Husband* (New York: Houghton, Mifflin and Co., 1910), pp. 131, 215.

28. Florence Converse, *The Children of Light* (Boston: Houghton, Mifflin and Co., 1912), pp. 149, 268.

29. Rischin, p. 247.

30. Albert Edwards [Arthur Bullard], *Comrade Yetta* (New York: The Macmillan Co., 1913), p. 263.

31. Rischin, pp. 171 – 94; Arthur A. Goren, *New York Jews and the Quest for Community* (New York: Columbia University Press, 1970), pp. 186 – 214; Howe, *World of our Fathers.*

32. Higham, pp. 218 – 19.

33. *The Philistine,* Vol. 37, No. 2 (July, 1913), p. 53.

34. *Life,* Vol. 71, No. 1858 (June 6, 1918), p. 913.

35. Ibid., Vol. 71, No. 1860 (June 20, 1918), p. 983.

36. "A Cure for American Bolshevism," *World's Work,* Vol. 34 (November, 1919), pp. 115 – 16.

37. Special Report by J.V. Foster, September 26, 1917, National Archives, RG-60, 9-12-8-338, Washington, D.C.

38. American Jewish Committee Archival Materials, General Correspondence 1906 – 32, Discrimination H-Foundations, Russell Dunn Folder, New York.

39. American Jewish Committee Archival Materials, General Correspondence 1906 – 32, Anti-A Z, Anti-Jewish Manifestations 1917 – 22, Newspapers Folder.

40. Louis Marshall Collection, Box 130, American Jewish Archives, Cincinnati, Ohio.

41. William T. Hornaday, *Awake! America! Object Lessons and Warnings* (New York: Moffat, Yard & Co., 1918), pp. 124, 185.

42. The extent of Hornaday's irrationality on this question is underscored by the individuals he accused of being dangerous radicals. These included Dr. Max Goldfarb, Morris Hillquit, and Max Eastman.

43. U.S. Congress, Senate, Subcommittee on the Judiciary, *Brewing and Liquor Interests and German and Bolshevik Propaganda,* S. Doc. 62, 66th Cong., 1st sess., 1919, pp. 112 – 113, 116; see Morton Rosenstock, *Louis Marshall, Defender of Jewish Rights* (Detroit: Wayne State University Press, 1965); Naomi W. Cohen, *Not Free to Desist: The American Jewish Committee 1906 – 1966* (Philadelphia: The Jewish Publication Society of America, 1972).

44. *New York Times,* February 15, 1919.

45. Letter, Senator Lee Overman to Louis Marshall, February 21, 1919, Louis Marshall Papers, American Jewish Committee Archives, xerox, Box 3.

46. U.S. Congress, Senate, Subcommittee on the Judiciary, pp. 69, 269, 179.

47. *The Anti-Bolshevist,* Vol. 1, No. 7 (July, 1919), p. 3; Vol. 1, No. 6 (June, 1919), p. 7.

48. Louis Marshall Papers, American Jewish Committee Archives, xerox, p/Minority Rights Folder; Cohen, pp. 124, 127 – 28.

49. *Russian National Society Bulletin,* No. 5 (March 3, 1921), n.p.

50. American Jewish Committee Archival Materials, General Correspondence 1906 – 32, Anti-A Z, General Count Cherep-Spiridovich file.

51. Similar statements can be found in Cherep-Spiridovich's *The Secret World Government or "The Hidden Hand"* (New York: The Anti-Bolshevist Publishing Association, 1926).

52. American Jewish Committee Archival Materials, Cherep-Spiridovich file.

53. *The Protocols and World Revolution* (Boston: Small, Maynard & Co., 1920), pp. 3, 8, 130, 139, 141.

54. Letter, Edward S. Beach to Congressman Isaac Siegel, January 5, 1919, Louis Marshall Collection, Box 52.

55. Letter, Clayton R. Lusk to H. Schneiderman, January 29, 1921, American Jewish Committee Archival Materials, General Correspondence 1906 – 32, Poland A—Protocols.

56. Letter, James A. Whitemore to Harry Cutler, May 26, 1920; June 3, 1920; Cutler to Whitemore, June 2, 1920; June 7, 1920, Louis Marshall Collection.

57. Letter, H.T. Wright to H. Schneiderman, January 28, 1921, in American Jewish Committee Archival Materials, Poland A—Protocols.

58. Copy of Committee on Immigration and Naturalization Hearings, January 26, 1922, Louis Marshall Papers, xerox, Box 2.

59. Letters, Herbert Hirsch to Louis Rosenwald, October 28, 1919; Hirsch to H. Schneiderman, December 23, 1919; Woodworth Clum to H. Schneiderman, December 26, 1919, American Jewish Committee Archival Materials, General Correspondence 1906 – 32, H-Immigration, Herbert Hirsch Folder 1919 – 20.

60. Letter, A.J. Sack to Louis Marshall, June 10, 1922, Louis Marshall Collection.

61. Ralph P. Boas, "Jew-Baiting in America," *The Atlantic Monthly* (May, 1921), p. 660.

62. *Current Opinion*, Vol. 69, No. 6 (December, 1920), p. 844.

63. Henry C. Emery, "Bolshevism; An Analysis of a World Movement after Personal Experiences in Russia during the Revolution," *The Yale Review* (July, 1919), p. 6.

64. Letter, John Dyneley Prince to Prescott Hall, September 8, 1919, Prescott Hall Collection, The Houghton Library, Harvard University, Cambridge, Massachusetts.

65. John Dos Passos, *Airways, Inc.* (New York: The Macaulay Co., 1928), pp. 53 – 54.

66. Philip S. Foner, *The Autobiographies of the Haymarket Martyrs* (New York: Humanities Press, 1969), pp. 59 – 71; Henry Demarest Lloyd Papers, Correspondence, General, March 31, 1870-December 30, 1890, reels 2 – 3, The State Historical Society of Wisconsin, Madison, Wisconsin; Foner, ed., *Jack London: American Rebel* (New York: The Citadel Press, 1947), p. 404; Jack London, *Burning Delight* (New York: The Macmillan Co., 1910), pp. 142 – 43; *Michael, Brother of Jerry* (New York: The Macmillan Co., 1917), p. 63; Frederic Cople Jaher, *Doubters and Dissenters; Cataclysmic Thought in America, 1885 – 1918* (London: Collier-Macmillan, 1964), p. 219; Bernard Johnpoll, *Pacifist's Progress* (Chicago: The Quadrangle Books, 1970), pp. 59 – 60; Hayim Fineman, "Jew-Baiting and the 'New Masses,'" *Jewish Frontier*, vol. 2 (January, 1935), pp. 7 – 9.

67. Charles Reznikoff, ed., *Louis Marshall, Champion of Liberty: Selected Papers and Addresses* (Philadelphia: The Jewish Publication Society of America, 1957), p. 203.

68. Letter, Louis Marshall to Lee Overman, February 15, 1919, American Jewish Committee Archival Materials, General Correspondence 1906 – 32, Chronological File 1906 – 30, 1919 – 20 Folder.

I do not like you, Dr. Fell,
The reason why I cannot tell;
But only this I know right well
I do not like you, Dr. Fell.

SIDNEY REID[1]

This is the man who bore his shoulders
hunched
And arched his backbone like an angry
cat;
He also wore, derisively, a hat,
A low black Jewish hat battered and
punched
Out of all argument, with his ears
conched
Beneath it, small and strangely
disparate;
His lips skimmed back upon a smile
that
Spat between his toothpick and a
tooth. He scrunched
Along the pathway toward us and
without
Lifting his feet went past us with the
smile
Still pinned there by the toothpick and
Just at that moment turned.
Semitic snout
Returned and upturned eyes came
back, and while
I stared there speechless bent and
kissed your hand.

JOHN PEAL BISHOP[2]

Conclusion

What then can be said about the perplexing problem of American
anti-Semitism? I have attempted to demonstrate that negative imagery

and stereotyping was a significant factor in the development of American anti-Semitism, that these perceptions invaded a cross-section of American intellectual and cultural life, and that their use increased significantly in the Gilded Age and lasted well into the Progressive era. At least three groups harbored anti-Jewish feelings of an ideological nature: some of the agrarian radicals in the Populist movement; certain patrician intellectuals in the East; and many of the poorest classes in the cities, often of ethnic derivation, like Mme. Zénaide Ragozin or Telemachus Timayenis. Different as they each were, each of these groups found itself at a special disadvantage in the turmoil of an industrial age—the poor because it exploited them, the patricians because it displaced them.

Without minimizing the importance of social conflict brought to our attention by John Higham, I contend that the availability and near consensus of the anti-Jewish cosmology precipitated the pattern of social discrimination that enveloped American Jews in the late nineteenth century. Negative imagery, rather than serving as a rationalization for prejudice after the fact, can thus be seen as a catalyst for the proliferation of anti-Jewish manifestations in America. I believe it can be argued with some degree of confidence that stereotyping, developed in all its elaborate detail and color in literature, and oftentimes presented in the spirit of logic and impartiality by influential individuals and by respectable periodicals, created a climate of opinion that facilitated the growth of anti-Semitism within the general confines of a free and open American society. Ideology thus drove a wedge between Jews and gentiles simply by sharpening negative stereotypes. This is especially germane because there were few countervailing images to balance the barrage of ideological anti-Semitism that permeated American culture.[3]

I have come to this conclusion through an examination of a wide cross-sample of popular and high culture. Admittedly, there is still much research to be done on this question. In fact, we do not even have a full history of anti-Semitism in the United States. Political rhetoric, discrimination, quota systems, labor journals, church periodicals, and newspapers are only a few of the fruitful fields and sources that beckon the scholar's eye. Clearly, I have not touched everything, but no student of American culture can be totally exhaustive. Nevertheless, the evidence I examined is so overwhelming and consistent that I am prepared to argue that these stereotypes indicate there *was* a substantial amount of anti-Semitism in American society. Traditional prejudice is implanted in language as an index of popular attitudes. Persistence of a stereotype over time is indicative of a significant societal appeal, to say nothing of what it reveals about the author's bigotry. The data, although not definitive, thus tell us enough to conclude that a reinterpretation is warranted. Historians have left this aspect of American anti-Semitism relatively untouched; it is a serious omission.

As I examined these major anti-Semitic traditions, I discovered that over the fifty-year period under study they had not changed conceptually as much as historians might suppose. Except on the subjects of conspiracy and radicalism, the kinds of accusations that anti-Semites and others leveled against Jews remained relatively constant. Stereotypes and negative imagery broached in the twentieth century sounded much like those bruted in the nineteenth. The big changes were not so much intellectual or conceptual, but emotional and a matter of degree. The same characterization might be mildly innocuous in the latter period and charged with crude, ugly feelings in the earlier. For the history of American anti-Semitism, therefore, emotional intensity provided the significant barometer of change. If anti-Semitism is an ideological disease, as I contend, perhaps one might best diagnose it by noting when the feverish symptoms surfaced and when they subsided.

At the most basic level of comparison, it is evident that many immigrant groups underwent attack during this period. Here it must be said that Jews met neither as much hostility nor as much acceptance as certain other minorities. Rapid social and economic advancement, although exposing Jews to more social discrimination, also left them in a better position to deal with it. Once they emerged from the ghettos into the suburbs in the second generation, their newly attained economic positions, educational levels, and their emerging defense organizations served as cushions, deflating raw prejudice. In fact, their remarkable success in America, a source of mixed admiration and envy, weakened the potential impact of anti-Semitism. Jews did not fall victim to as much violence as did the Italians or Chinese; they were not subject to as much discrimination as were the blacks; and there was no organized anti-Semitic movement comparable to the anti-Catholic American Protective Association. The relative mildness of American, as compared with European, anti-Semitism must be attributed not only to the more tolerant traditions of the United States, the separation of Church and State, our emphasis on individual rights and freedom, a result of Orthodox Christian tolerance, America's role as a haven for the oppressed, democratic pluralism, and our celebration of the capitalistic way of life (hence sympathy for Jews who made it in this system), but also to the presence within the country of a great variety of ethnic and racial targets. Still, a good deal of distinctly anti-Semitic sentiment also emerged. This calls our attention to a fact of utmost importance—that anti-Semitism formed an integral part of the larger wave of antiforeign feeling.

A general look over the panorama of anti-Semitism in the United States and Western Europe during the late nineteenth and early twentieth centuries reveals two periods of special intensity. On both sides of the Atlantic ideological agitation against Jews intensified more or less simultaneously. It reached a first crest in the 1880s and 1890s and a second in the years during and immediately after World War I. The first period saw the emergence of Adolf Stoecker and Karl Lueger in Germany and Austria, Edouard Drumont and the Dreyfus case in France, anti-Jewish immigration sentiment in England, the May Laws and pogroms in Russia, and Populist anti-Semitism, social discrimination, and immigration-restriction sentiment in the United States. The second, from 1914 to 1923, brought the circulation of the *Protocols,* the assassination of Walter Rathenau, the emergence of the National Socialist party in Germany, Bolshevik anti-Semitism, and, in America, the Leo Frank case, the Henry Ford campaign, university quotas, and immigration restriction.

American anti-Semitism, although virulent and always present, was not organized on the basis of a clearly enunciated program providing what ought to be done about Jews. This is something quite different from anti-Semitism that was primarily political in vision. Modern European anti-Semitism was characterized from the beginning by large and active political aims and it included among other far-reaching social revisions precise provisions for making the Jews second-class citizens, expelling them, or exterminating them. In comparison, American anti-Semitism remained an ideological, sociological, and cultural phenomenon. The differences of intensity between Europe and America should not obscure a common rhythm.

How is this cyclical rhythm to be explained? Both periods of anti-

Semitic agitation were characterized by economic difficulties. The years from 1873 to 1896 unleashed severe class conflicts and a general unrest that was revived during the postwar disorganization and disillusionment after a war that had failed to make the world safe for democracy. There was good cause to believe that the whole social system was disintegrating. In response, each of the crisis periods unleashed a powerful display of nationalism channeled into agitation against foreign influences. Anti-Semitism was part of the more general tendency to defend the nation from various imagined foreign perils. As symbolically the quintessence of the alien, Jews were singled out. In an America experiencing mass strikes, wide social chasms, and economic hardships, the Jews were fortunate to have suffered as little as they did.[4] This is no reason to underestimate the potential.

The role of group image in human relations has been emphasized by writers, social scientists, and psychologists who see in them and in their acceptance a most potent source of misunderstanding, injustice, and social waste.[5] Whether it is the ancient Shylock canard or the more modern versions of the hunched, aggressive student, the comic opera peddler, the garment center wheeler-dealer, or the verbose, hirsute radical, the fact remains that these stereotypes have the advantage of simplicity. Ascribing an intrinsic trait to a whole group is convenient; it allows an individual, as well as a society, either to dismiss the group, to rationalize its prejudices, or at the very least, to behave on the basis of a blanket reaction without due consideration to individual variations. This process can be dangerously appealing to a nation that is as complex and fluid as the United States.

\There are those who would challenge the view that a writer, social commentator, or intellectual who introduces a Jewish stereotype is thereby manifesting anti-Semitism, whether consciously or unconsciously. Are the pejorative portraits merely literary conventions, figures of speech, or idioms that have esthetic but not necessarily social import? Would it not be more accurate to surmise that the recurrence of the stereotype is itself one index of the continued presence of anti-Semitism in a society? Does not its use by the writer and thinker and apparent acceptance by the reader presuppose certain attitudes? Lest the charge of parochialism be hurled at this suggestion, it should be emphasized that anti-Semitism is not a sharply defined phenomenon that can be measured scientifically on a Richter scale of human prejudices. It is rather a combination of often vague opinions and actions that occur within a continuous range of intensity encompassing the poles of passive acquiescence to articulate, committed belief in the convention.

In any case, the stereotype itself implies an anti-Semitic posture because in its origins and most of its uses, it was generated by hostility toward Jews. In its perpetuation, that hostility is carried forward to the populace, for the image is so overwhelmingly unfavorable. There are almost no literary treatments in this period that portray the Jew positively and realistically as a full-dimensional character. There are hardly any works that touch on this subject that are not tainted by the stock, vaudevillian images.

One encounters instead a barrage of untruths and half-truths that seriously compromise the Jew's collective personality, question his behavior, and undermine his role in society. They suggest that all Jews at least share some of these quite unpleasant or antisocial traits. Jews are not given credit for being a people like any other—some good, some evil—with a range of qualities and a variety of characteristics and experiences. Stereotyping did not do justice to the broad spectrum of Jewish identities in American life. This is the umbilical cord that connects negative imagery with anti-Semitism, for in the denial of an individual nature to Jews, American society denied that Jews were equal members of the human family. Few in the world had learned that Jews are a group of people like any other and not an abstract type, a figment of a universal imagination, a caricatured "Ikey" who is thereby made somewhat less of an individual.

The opponents of nationalism saw Jews as uncompromising nationalists, with a nationalist God and a nationalist Torah; the nationalists saw Jews as internationalists with allegiance to no country. Political liberals denounced the Jew as an instrument of reaction and pharisaic authority; political reactionaries denounced him as a threat to the stability and order of the state. Religious Christians expressed their disfavor with Jewish pedantry, science, and atheism; and the free thinkers among them never tired of accusing Jews of superstition, ignorance, and religious fanaticism. Some writers and patricians saw Jews as the root of anarchy, Bolshevism, amorality, and subversion, and some radicals and social reformers described the Jew, resentfully, as bursting with self-interest and egoism, the capitalist par excellence who is the bearer of the biblical civilization that is based on slavery, oppression, and parasitism.

Men of wealth and bearing have found in the impoverished urban Jew a threat to the rights of private property and the genteel life; but men living in poverty, whether real or a state of mind, have found in him a dark symbol of untold riches, the source of their exploitation. To the fastidious, the Jew became the epitome of vulgarity and human filth; but by the less fastidious he has been inevitably condemned as overrefined, affected, and sterile. Officialdom charged Jews with circumventing the laws of the land. Even their merits are turned into detractions. Few are murderers, they advised, because killing does not pay and essentially Jews are cowards. For the living, the Jew is a dead race with no future; for the natives, an unassimilable alien; for property holders, a radical who would dismantle society; for the poor, an exploiter and international millionaire; for patriots, a man without a country; for all classes, a potential rival.

The historiography of American anti-Semitism, although acknowledging in varying degrees the significance of ideology, has not adequately analyzed its import. Stereotyping, because of the weight of consensus and because of its permeation throughout all the written forms of communication, cannot be disposed of casually as insignificant. People's minds are shaped by what they hear, see, and experience, and in terms of the Jew in the Gilded Age through the Progressive era, this was preponderantly negative. This viewpoint challenges Oscar Handlin's contention that "there was no advance of anti-Semitism in the last two decades of the nineteenth century,"[6] and that by 1900 the favorable prevailing temper of tolerance had produced a great willingness to accept the Jew as a desirable and equal participant in the emerging culture of the nation.[7] Handlin errs in minimizing major wellsprings of Judeophobia that were proliferating rather than decreasing in the period under discussion. The Jewish question was so refractory and deep-seated and so complicated by centuries of prejudice and misunderstanding that it generated a maze of emotional reactions in many people. It became so extensive that even those who were sincerely dedicated to correcting the ills of society were susceptible to be overcome by its debilitating presence.

Herein lies the danger. Anti-Semitism erupted even in those sectors of American society that were reformist and libertarian. The democratic impulse was not and may not always be resolute enough to overcome the psychological and social momentum of anti-Semitic stereotyping. It is true that America never visited mass physical oppression upon its Jews. But there are more subtle types of oppression—the economic, the social and the cultural—that are also damaging and painful. Furthermore, the experiences of the 1930s, as well as public opinion polls, have shown how stereotyping reinforced insensitivity and misunderstanding and contributed to governmental inertia in the face of an unprecedented human tragedy.[8] During the critical decade of the 1930s, which witnessed the rise of Nazism in Europe, there was a high degree of acceptance and approval of anti-Semitism in America. (See the *Fortune Magazine* public opinion polls.[9]) This sentiment undoubtedly reinforced the isolationist sentiment in the Congress, making it extremely difficult to liberalize the immigration quota laws so more Jewish refugees could be admitted. The roots of this apathy and hostility may indeed have been nurtured in the anti-Semitic milieu that characterized the preceding decades. It is hoped that this book, in some small way, will alert us, historically, to this situation and will lay to rest the euphoric view of the Jew in pre-1920s America to which scholars have given currency. Our most impregnable defense against prejudice does not lie in uncritical national self-congratulation.

NOTES

1. Sidney Reid, "Because You're a Jew," *The Independent,* Vol. 65, No. 3130 (November 26, 1908), p. 217.

2. John Peale Bishop, "This is the Man," in Bishop, *Now with His Love* (New York: Charles Scribner's Sons, 1933), p. 36.

3. For philo-Semitic treatments see Edward Tullidge's play, *Ben Israel* (Salt Lake City, 1875); Johanna von Bohne, *Jew and Gentile* (New York: The Judge Publishing Co., 1889); Madison Peters, *The Jews in America* (Philadelphia: The J.C. Winston Co., 1905); William Dean Howells, *Impressions and Experiences* (New York: Harper & Brothers, 1896); Myra Kelly, *Little Citizens* (New York: McClure Phillips & Co., 1904); and Hutchins Hapgood, *The Spirit of the Ghetto* (New York: Funk & Wagnalls Co., 1902).

4. John Higham, *Strangers in the Land: Patterns of American Nativism 1860–1925* (New York: Atheneum, 1971), pp. 26–27, 66–67, 92–94; Higham, *Send These to Me: Jews and Other Immigrants in Urban America* (New York: Atheneum, 1975), pp. 126–32.

5. See Charles Y. Glock and Rodney Stark, *Christian Beliefs and Anti-Semitism* (New York: Harper & Row, 1966); Charles Herbert Stember, ed.,

Jews in the Mind of America (New York: Basic Books, 1966); Herbert M. McLuhan, *From Cliché to Archetype* (New York: Viking Press, 1970); Lauriat Lane, Jr., "The Literary Archetype: Some Reconsiderations," *Journal of Aesthetics and Art Criticism,* Vol. 13, No. 2 (December, 1954); C.G. Jung, *Psyche and Symbol* (New York: Doubleday Anchor Books, 1958).

6. Oscar Handlin, "Reconsidering the Populists," *Agricultural History,* Vol. 39, No. 2 (April, 1965), p. 69.

7. Oscar Handlin, "American Views of the Jew at the Opening of the Twentieth Century," *Publications of the American Jewish Historical Society,* No. 40, Part 4 (June, 1951).

8. For a discussion of American public reaction to German anti-Semitism and of American complicity in the Holocaust, see the following: Henry L. Feingold, *The Politics of Rescue* (New Brunswick, New Jersey: Rutgers University Press, 1970); Saul Friedman, *No Haven for the Oppressed* (Detroit: Wayne State University Press, 1973); Arthur D. Morse, *While Six Million Died* (New York: Hart Publishing Co., 1967); David S. Wyman, *Paper Walls* (Boston: University of Massachusetts Press, 1968).

9. See *Fortune*, January 1936, July 1938, April 1939. In the April 1939 poll, *Fortune* posed the following question: "If you were a member of Congress would you vote yes or no on a bill to open the doors of the United States to a larger number of European refugees than now admitted under our immigration quotas?" Only 8.7 percent said yes and 83 percent said no. In the July 1938 survey, only 4 percent of the population favored raising immigration quotas to let in more refugees, and 18.2 percent declared for letting them in only under the present stringent quota restrictions. The vote for keeping refugees out completely was 67.4 percent.

Bibliography

Manuscript and Archival Sources

Adams, Brooks. Papers. The Houghton Library. Harvard University. Cambridge, Massachusetts.

The Adams Papers. Letters Received and Other Loose Papers. Microfilm nos. 595–601. Massachusetts Historical Society, Boston, Massachusetts.

Adams, Henry. Papers. Box 1890-June 1891, Boxes 1905–11. Massachusetts Historical Society.

Adams, Henry. Papers. The Houghton Library.

American Jewish Archives, Anti-Semitism II, Correspondence and Miscellany. Cincinnati, Ohio.

American Jewish Committee Archives, General Correspondence, 1906–32, Chronological File, 1906–30. New York.

Board of Delegates of American Israelites Papers. American Jewish Historical Society. Waltham, Massachusetts.

Bowker, Richard Rogers. Collection. New York Public Library Annex. New York.

Butler, Nicholas Murray. Papers. Columbia University Archives. New York.

Chapman, John Jay. Papers. The Houghton Library.

Cowen, Philip. Papers. American Jewish Historical Society.

Finley, John Huston. Papers. New York Public Library.

Frank, Leo M. Clippings, Microfilm, Miscellaneous, American Jewish Archives.

Hall, Prescott F. Collection. The Houghton Library.

Hart, Albert Bushnell. Papers. Harvard University Archives.

Harvard University Menorah Society. Minutes, Constitution, Correspondence, 1906–15. Microfilm. American Jewish Archives.

Heller, Rabbi Max. Papers 1884–1925. American Jewish Archives.

The Henry Hurwitz Menorah Association Collection. American Jewish Archives.

Jordan, David Starr. Papers. Correspondence. Stanford University Archives. Stanford, California.

Leeser, Isaac. Papers. American Jewish Historical Society.

Lloyd, Henry Demarest. Papers. The State Historical Society of Wisconsin, Madison, Wisconsin.

Lodge, Henry Cabot. Papers. Massachusetts Historical Society.

Loeb, Jacques. Papers. Library of Congress. Washington, D.C.

Marcus, Jacob R. Private Collection on Anti-Semitism and Rejection, Cincinnati, Ohio.

Marshall, Louis. Collection. American Jewish Archives.

————. Papers. Correspondence and Miscellaneous American Jewish Committee Archives.

————. Papers. Xerox copies. American Jewish Committee Archives.

Morse, John Torrey. Papers. Massachusetts Historical Society.

The National Archives of the United States of America, Washington, D.C., Records of the Department of State.

Schiff, Jacob. Collection. Correspondence. American Jewish Archives.

Schwimmer, Rosika, and Lloyd, Lola Maverick. Collection. New York Public Library.

Smith, Goldwin. Papers. Microfilm. American Jewish Archives.

Sulzberger, Mayer. Correspondence 1907–12. American Jewish Committee Archives.

Warburg, Felix. Papers. American Jewish Archives.

Williams, William. Papers. New York Public Library.

Wolf, Simon. Papers. American Jewish Historical Society.

Periodicals and Newspapers*

The American Citizen, Vols. 1–4, 1912–14.

The American Hebrew, 1877–1917.

The American Israelite, 1877–1900.

The American Standard, Vols. 1-2, April 15, 1924-December 15, 1925.

The Anti-Bolshevist, 1918–19.

The Arena.

The Catholic Record.

The Catholic Telegraph.

The Century Magazine.

*Unless otherwise indicated, periodicals were examined for the entire period, 1877–1927.

The Chicago Record-Herald, August 28, 1901-October 16, 1901.
Fame and Fortune Weekly, 1908 – 1922.
Frank Leslie's Illustrated Newspaper.
Hosteller's Illustrated.
The Illustrated American, 1890 – 1927.
The Independent.
The Jeffersonian, October 1914-August 1915.
The Judge, 1882 – 1922.
Lend a Hand: A Record of Progress, 1886 – 97.
Life Magazine, 1883 – 1922.
McClure's Magazine.
M'lle. New York, 1895 – 99.
The Mail and Express, 1895 – 1900.
The National Police Gazette, 1879 – 97.
New York University Alumnus, 1920 – 24.
New York University Daily News, 1922 – 24.
The New Yorker: The New York University Weekly, 1907 – 22.
The Philistine, 1908 – 15.
Puck, 1882 – 1918.
Texas Siftings, 1887 – 91.
Tid-Bits, 1884 – 90.
Washington Square Dealer of New York University, 1914 – 18.
Watson's Magazine, 1914 – 15.

Primary Material: Articles

Abbott, Lawrence F. "Some Remarks on the Jews." *The Outlook,* Vol. 146, No. 14 (August 3, 1927), pp. 436 – 37.

Allemann, Albert. "Immigration and the Future American Race." *The Popular Science Monthly,* Vol. 75, No. 6 (December, 1909), pp. 586 – 97.

Asbury, Herbert. "When New York Was Really Wicked." *The New Yorker,* Vol. 3 (January 7, 1928), pp. 22 – 24.

Baker, Ray Stannard. "The Rise of the Tailors." *McClure's Magazine,* Vol. 24, No. 1 (November, 1904), pp. 126 – 39.

Balch, Emily Greene. "Slav Emigration at Its Source." *Charities and the Commons,* Vol. 40, No. 21 (February 24, 1906), pp. 832 – 40.

Bard, Joseph. "Why Europe Dislikes the Jew." *Harper's Magazine,* Vol. 154 (March, 1927), pp. 498 – 506.

Bercovici, Konrad. "The Greatest Jewish City in the World." *The Nation,* Vol. 117, No. 3036 (September 12, 1923), pp. 259 – 61.

Bigelow, Poultney. "The Russian and His Jew." *Harper's New Monthly Magazine,* Vol. 88, No. 526 (March, 1894), pp. 603 – 14.

Billings, John S. "Vital Statistics of the Jews." *The North American Review,* No. 410 (January, 1891), pp. 70 – 84.

Bingham, Theodore A. "Foreign Criminals in New York." *The North American Review,* No. 634 (September, 1908), pp. 383 – 94.

————. "How to Give New York the Best Police Force in the World." *The North American Review,* No. 630 (May, 1908), pp. 702 – 11.

"A Birdseye View of Jewish Civic Activity and Patriotism All Over the World During Our Civil War." Publication of the American Jewish Historical Society. No. 29 (1925), pp. 117–28.

Boas, Ralph Philip. "Jew Baiting in America." *The Atlantic Monthly* (May, 1921), pp. 658 – 65.

————. "The Problem of American Judaism." *The Atlantic Monthly* (February, 1917), pp. 144 – 52.

————. "Who Shall Go to College." *The Atlantic Monthly* (October, 1922), pp. 441 – 48.

Botkine, Pierre. "A Voice for Russia." *The Century Magazine,* Vol. 45, No. 4 (February, 1893), pp. 611 – 15.

Bouton, S. Miles. "The Persecution of Jews in Europe." *The Forum,* Vol. 75, No. 6 (June, 1926), pp. 820 – 28.

Bronsdon, E.T. "The Mysterious Case of 'K of K'." *Popular Mechanics Magazine,* Vol. 31, No. 3 (March, 1919), p. 381 – 84.

Brown, Philip Marshall. "Zionism and Anti-Semitism." *The North American Review,* Vol. 210 (November, 1919), pp. 656 – 62.

Brudno, Ezra S. "The Russian Jew Americanized." *The World's Work,* Vol. 7, No. 56 (March, 1904), pp. 4555 – 57.

————. "Status of the Modern Hebrew: The Secret of His Immortality." *The Arena,* Vol. 24, No. 3 (September, 1900), pp. 421 – 32.

Bryant, William Cullen. "Bryant's Criticism on Shylock as Portrayed by Edwin Booth." *American Israelite,* Vol. 12, No. 52 (June 29, 1866), n.p.

Bunner, H.C. "The Bowery and Bohemia." *Scribner's Magazine,* Vol. 15, No. 4 (April, 1894), pp. 452 – 62.

Casson, Herbert N. "The Jew in America." *Munsey's Magazine,* Vol. 34, No. 4 (January, 1906), pp. 381 – 95.

Chapman, John Jay. "America The Backslider." *The Spectator,* No. 4, 922 (October 28, 1922), p. 589.

————. Review of *The Cause of World Unrest,* by H.A. Gwynne. *The Literary Review,* Vol. 1, No. 12 (November 27, 1920), p. 4.

————. "The Passing of a Great Bogey." *Vanity Fair,* Vol. 11, No. 2 (October, 1918), pp. 65, 108.

Clark, Francis Edward. "Our Dearest Antipathies." *The Atlantic Monthly,* Vol. 127 (February, 1921), pp. 239–42.

Commons, John. "Immigrants During the Nineteenth Century." *The Chautauquan,* Vol. 31 (January, 1904), pp. 433–43.

"Conversations with Mr. Lowell." *The Atlantic Monthly,* Vol. 79, No. 471 (January, 1897), pp. 127–28.

Creelman, James. "Israel Unbound." *Pearson's Magazine,* Vol. 17, No. 2 (February, 1907), pp. 123–39.

Dougherty, George S. "A Word About Criminals." *The Outlook* (October 4, 1916), pp. 269–75.

Drachman, Bernard. "Anti-Jewish Prejudice in America." *The Forum,* Vol. 52 (July, 1914), pp. 31–40.

Edman, Irwin. "Reuben Cohen Considers Anti-Semitism." *The Menorah Journal,* Vol. 15, No. 1 (January, 1929), pp. 24–31.

Eliot, Charles W. "The Potency of the Jewish Race," *The Menorah Journal,* Vol. 1, No. 3 (June, 1915), pp. 141–44.

Emery, Henry C. "Bolshevism; An Analysis of a World Movement after Personal Experiences in Russia during the Revolution." *The Yale Review* (July, 1919), pp. 3–23.

Fox, Samuel F. Darwin. "Judaism and Anti-Semitism." *The Forum,* Vol. 75, Nos. 4 and 5 (April, May, 1926), pp. 503–9, 684–90.

Gannett, Lewis S. "Is America Anti-Semitic?" *The Nation,* Vol. 116, No. 3011 (March 21, 1923), pp. 330–31.

Gibbons, Herbert Adams. "The Jewish Problem." *The Century Magazine,* Vol. 102, No. 5 (September, 1921), pp. 785–92.

Gleason, Arthur. "Jews in American Colleges." *Hearsts International* (March–May, 1923), pp. 15–17.

Gracey, J.T. "The Jew in the Nineteenth Century." *The Missionary Review of the World,* Vol. 13, No. 3 (March, 1890), pp. 181–87.

Grant, Madison. "Discussion of Article on Democracy and Heredity." *The Journal of Heredity,* Vol. 10, No. 4 (April, 1919), pp. 164–65.

Haldane, J.B.S. "Nationality and Research." *The Forum,* Vol. 75, No. 5 (May, 1926), pp. 718–23.

Hall, G. Stanley. "Yankee and Jew." *The Menorah Journal,* Vol. 1, No. 2 (April, 1915), pp. 87–90.

Hall, Prescott F. "Immigration and the Educational Test." *North American Review,* No. 491 (October, 1897), pp. 393–402.

Ham, William T. "Harvard Student Opinion on the Jewish Question." *The Nation,* Vol. 115, No. 2983 (September 6, 1922), p. 225.

Hapgood, Norman. "The Jews and American Democracy." *The Menorah Journal,* Vol. 2, No. 4 (October, 1916), pp. 201–5.

Hendrick, Burton J. "The Great Jewish Invasion." *McClure's Magazine,* Vol. 28, No. 3 (January, 1907), pp. 307–21.

————. "The Jewish Invasion of America." *McClure's Magazine,* Vol. 40, No. 5 (March, 1913), pp. 125 – 65.

————. "The Jews in America; Do The Jews Dominate American Finance?" *The World's Work,* Vol. 45, No. 3 (January, 1923), pp. 266 – 86.

————. "The Jews in America; How They Came to This Country." *The World's Work,* Vol. 45, No. 2 (December, 1922), pp. 145 – 61.

————. "The Jews in America; The 'Menace' of the Polish Jew." *The World's Work,* Vol. 45, No. 4 (February, 1923), pp. 366 – 77.

————. "Radicalism Among the Polish Jews." *The World's Work,* Vol. 45, No. 6 (April, 1923), pp. 591 – 601.

Hoffman, Katherine. "In the New York Ghetto." *Munsey's Magazine,* Vol. 23, No. 5 (August, 1900), pp. 608 – 19.

Hubbard, Elbert. "Mayer A. Rothschild." *Little Journeys to the Homes of Great Business Men,* Vol. 24, No. 4 (April, 1909), pp. 111 – 12.

Hyde, Arthur Houghton. "The Foreign Element in American Civilization." *The Popular Science Monthly,* Vol. 52 (January, 1898), pp. 387 – 400.

Jordan, David Starr. "Jean De Block and the Future of War." *The Menorah Journal,* Vol. 2, No. 3 (June, 1916), pp. 132 – 38.

————. "Problems That Must Be Faced." *The Menorah Journal,* Vol. 4, No. 4 (August, 1918), pp. 228 – 31.

Josephus. "The Jewish Question." *The Century Magazine,* Vol. 43, No. 3 (January, 1892), pp. 395 – 98.

Kennan, George. "The Fight for Reform in San Francisco." *McClure's Magazine,* Vol. 29, No. 5 (September, 1907), pp. 546 – 48.

Kuh, Edwin J. "The Social Disability of the Jew." *Atlantic Monthly,* Vol. 101, No. 4 (April, 1908), pp. 433 – 39.

Landfield, Jerome. "Lenin's Lying Legion." *The Review,* Vol. 1, No. 18, pp. 380 – 81.

Lecky, W.E.H. "Israel Among the Nations." *The Forum,* Vol. 16 (December, 1893), pp. 442 – 51.

Levy, M.S. "A Rabbi's Reply to Mark Twain." *Overland Monthly,* Vol. 34, No. 202 (October, 1899), pp. 364 – 67.

Lodge, Henry Cabot. "The Restriction of Immigration." *North American Review,* No. 410 (January, 1891), pp. 27 – 36.

Lowell, James Russell. Review of *Tancred or the New Crusade,* by Benjamin Disraeli. *North American Review,* No. 65 (1847), pp. 212 – 14.

McClure, S.S. "The Tammanyizing of a Civilization." *McClure's Magazine,* Vol. 34, No. 1 (November, 1909), pp. 117 – 28.

McLaughlin, Dr. Allan. "The Bright Side of Russian Immigration." *The Popular Science Monthly,* Vol. 64 (November, 1903), pp. 66 – 70.

———. "Hebrew, Magyar and Levantine Immigration." *The Popular Science Monthly,* Vol. 65 (September, 1904), pp. 432 – 42.

———. "Immigration." *The Popular Science Monthly,* Vol. 65 (May, 1904), pp. 164 – 69.

———. "Immigration and the Public Health." *The Popular Science Monthly,* Vol. 64 (January, 1904), pp. 232 – 38.

———. "The Slavic Immigrant." *The Popular Science Monthly,* Vol. 63 (May to October, 1903), pp. 25 – 32.

MacQueen, Reverend Peter. "Russia's Terrible Persecution of the Jews." *Leslie's Weekly,* Vol. 46, No. 2473 (January 29, 1903), pp. 102 – 4.

Markham, Edwin. "The Sweat-Shop Inferno." *Cosmopolitan,* Vol. 42 (1906), pp. 327 – 33.

Mitchell, Roger. "Recent Jewish Immigration to the United States." *The Popular Science Monthly,* Vol. 62 (February, 1903), pp. 334 – 43.

Moody, John, and Turner, George Kibbe. "The Masters of Capital in America: Morgan: The Great Trustee." *McClure's Magazine,* Vol. 36, No. 1 (November, 1910), pp. 3 – 24.

Morais, Nina. "Jewish Ostracism in America." *The North American Review,* No. 248 (September, 1881), pp. 265 – 75.

Mowrer, Paul Scott. "The Assimilation of Israel." *The Atlantic Monthly* (July, 1921), pp. 101 – 10.

Oppenheimer, Francis J. "Jewish Criminality." *The Independent,* Vol. 65, No. 3120 (September 17, 1908), pp. 640 – 42.

Peck, Emelyn Foster. "The Russian Jew in Southern New England." *New England Magazine,* Vol. 31, No. 1 (September, 1904), pp. 24 – 33.

Peters, John Punnett. "Zionism and the Jewish Problem." *The Sewanee Review,* Vol. 29, No. 1 (January, 1921), pp. 268 – 94.

Peters, Madison C. "Why the Prejudice Against the Jew?" *The Trend,* Vol. 6 (February, 1914), pp. 831 – 37.

Phillips, David Graham. "The Empire of Rothschild." *Cosmopolitan,* Vol. 38, No. 5 (March, 1905), pp. 501 – 15.

Powell, E. Alexander. "Masters of Europe." *The Saturday Evening Post,* Vol. 181, No. 51 (June 19, 1909), pp. 16 – 17, 45 – 46.

Pritchett, Henry S. "Observations in Egypt, Palestine, and Greece." *International Conciliation,* No. 225 (December, 1926), pp. 501 – 41.

Ragozin, Mme. Z. "Russian Jews and Gentiles." *The Century Magazine,* Vol. 23, No. 6 (April, 1882), pp. 905 – 20.

Reid, Sidney. "Because You're a Jew." *The Independent,* Vol. 65, No. 3130 (November 26, 1908), pp. 1212 – 17.

Rhine, Alice H. "Race Prejudice at Summer Resorts." *The Forum,* Vol. 3 (July, 1887), pp. 523 – 31.

Ridpath, John Clark. "Plutocracy and War." *The Arena,* Vol. 19, No. 98 (January, 1898), pp. 97 – 103.

Ripley, William Z. "Race Factors in Labor Unions." *The Atlantic Monthly,* Vol. 93, No. 557 (March, 1904), pp. 299 – 308.

Ross, Edward A. "The Causes of Race Superiority." *Annals of the American Academy of Political and Social Science* (July, 1901), pp. 67 – 89.

————. "The Hebrews of Eastern Europe in America." *The Century Magazine,* Vol. 88, No. 5 (September, 1914), pp. 785 – 92.

Royce, Josiah. "Race Questions and Prejudices." *International Journal of Ethics,* Vol. 16, No. 3 (April, 1906), pp. 265 – 88.

Schauffer, Henry A. "The Foreign Population in Our Cities." *The Independent,* Vol. 45, No. 2301 (January 5, 1893), p. 7.

Seitz, Don C. "Jews, Catholics, and Protestants." *The Outlook,* Vol. 141, No. 13 (November 25, 1925), pp. 478 – 84.

Shively, Dr. Henry L. "Immigration a Factor in the Spread of Tuberculosis in New York City." *The New York Medical Journal,* Vol. 77, No. 6 (February 7, 1903), pp. 222 – 23.

Smertenko, Johan J. "What America Has Done for the Jew." *The Nation,* Vol. 116, No. 3014 (April 11, 1923), pp. 409 – 11.

Smith, Bertha H. "The Unique Fish Market of the Ghetto." *Leslie's Weekly,* No. 2536 (April 14, 1904), pp. 348, 358.

Smith, Charles Stewart. "Our National Dumping Ground." *The North American Review,* No. 425 (April, 1892), pp. 432 – 38.

Smith, Goldwin. "Can Jews Be Patriots." *The Nineteenth Century,* No. 15 (May, 1878), pp. 875 – 87.

————. "England's Abandonment of the Protectorate of Turkey." *The Contemporary Review,* Vol. 31 (February, 1878), pp. 603 – 19.

————. "Is It Religious Persecution?" *The Independent,* Vol. 60, No. 3003 (June 21, 1906), pp. 1474 – 78.

————. "The Jewish Question." *The Nineteenth Century,* No. 56 (October, 1881), pp. 494 – 515.

————. "The Jews." *The Nineteenth Century,* No. 69 (November, 1882), pp. 687 – 709.

————. "New Light on the Jewish Question." *The North American Review,* No. 417 (August, 1891), pp. 129 – 43.

Snyder, Reverend John. "The Problem of the Jew." *The American Citizen,* Vol. 3, No. 6 (December, 1913), p. 381.

Speranza, Gino. "The Immigration Peril." *World's Work* (November, December, 1924; April, 1925).

Starr, Harry. "The Affair at Harvard; What the Students Did." *The Menorah Journal,* Vol. 8, No. 5 (October, 1922), pp. 263 – 76.

Stearns, Harold E. "A Gentile's Picture of the Jew." *The Menorah Journal,* Vol. 2, No. 4 (October, 1916), pp. 224–30.

Steffens, Lincoln. "It: An Exposition of the Sovereign Political Power of Organized Business." *Everybody's Magazine,* Vol. 23, No. 4 (October, 1910), pp. 149–460.

Stewart, William M. "The Great Slave Power." *The Arena,* Vol. 19, No. 102 (May, 1898), pp. 577–82.

Stone, J. Turner. "The Wandering Jew." *Methodist Review,* Vol. 96 (March, 1914), pp. 267–70.

Stone, Lee Alexander. "Pacifists and Reds." *The Chicago Medical Recorder,* Vol. 46, No. 5 (June, 1921), pp. 177–86.

Thompson, Vance. "The Rothschilds of France." *Everybody's Magazine,* Vol. 13, No. 5 (November, 1905), pp. 579–88.

Tolman, Albert H. "Some Songs Traditional in the United States." *The Journal of American Folk-Lore,* Vol. 29 (April-June, 1916), pp. 155–97.

Trant, William. "Jew and Chinaman." *The North American Review,* No. 675 (February, 1912), pp. 249–60.

Turner, George Kibbe. "The City of Chicago: A Study of the Great Immoralities." *McClure's Magazine,* Vol. 28, No. 6 (April, 1907), pp. 575–92.

———. "The Daughters of the Poor." *McClure's Magazine,* Vol. 34, No. 1 (November, 1909), pp. 45–61.

———. "Tammany's Control of New York by Professional Criminals." *McClure's Magazine,* Vol. 33, No. 2 (June, 1909), pp. 117–34.

Tuttle, A.H. "Anti-Semitism in America." *The Methodist Review,* Vol. 76 (January, 1894), pp. 90–98.

Twain, Mark. "Concerning the Jews." *Harper's New Monthly Magazine,* Vol. 99, No. 592 (September, 1899), pp. 527–35.

Valesh, Eva M. "The Tenement House Problem in New York." *The Arena,* Vol. 7, No. 41 (April, 1893), pp. 580–86.

Ward, Robert Dec. "The Immigration Problem." *Charities,* Vol. 12, No. 6 (February 6, 1904), pp. 138–51.

———. "The Restriction of Immigration." *The North American Review,* No. 573 (August, 1904), pp. 226–37.

White, Arnold. "Kishineff—and After." *The Living Age,* Vol. 238, No. 3087 (September 5, 1903), pp. 805–11.

———. "The Truth About the Russian Jew." *The Contemporary Review,* Vol. 61 (May, 1892), pp. 695–708.

Whitman, Sidney. "The Anti-Semitic Movement." *The Contemporary Review,* Vol. 63 (June, 1893), pp. 699–714.

Wilson, Dr. J.G. "The Crossing of the Races." *The Popular Science Monthly,* Vol. 79 (November, 1911), pp. 486–95.

Wood, Charles W. "If I Were President. Henry Ford Tells Where He Stands on All of the Great Issues of the Day." *Collier's* (August 4, 1923), pp. 5–6.

Primary Material: Books and Pamphlets

Adams, Brooks. *The Emancipation of Massachusetts.* Boston: Houghton Mifflin Co., 1919.

———. *The Law of Civilization and Decay.* New York: The Macmillan Co., 1896.

Adams, Hannah. *The History of the Jews from the Destruction of Jerusalem to the Nineteenth Century.* Boston: J. Eliot, Jr., 1812.

Adams, Henry. *The Degradation of the Democratic Dogma.* New York: Harper & Row, 1969.

———. *The Education of Henry Adams.* Boston: Houghton Mifflin Co., 1918.

———. *Mont-Saint-Michel and Chartres.* Boston: Houghton Mifflin Co., 1933.

Adler, Cyrus, and Margalith, Aaron. *With Firmness in the Right.* New York: The American Jewish Committee, 1946.

Anthony, Alfred Williams. *The Jewish Problem,* 1924.

Armstrong, George W. *The Crime of '20.* Dallas: Press of the Venney Co., 1922.

———. *The Story of the Dynasty of the Money Trust in America.* Fort Worth, Texas, 1923.

Bell, William A. *New Tracks in North America.* London: Chapman and Hall, 1869.

Bercovici, Konrad. *Dust of New York.* New York: Boni & Liveright, 1919.

Bohne, Johanna von. *Jew and Gentile: A Commentary on 'The Original Mr. Jacobs' and 'The American Jew.'* New York: The Judge Publishing Co., 1889.

Bostwick, Arthur E. *The Different West.* Chicago: A.C. McClury & Co., 1913.

Brown, Henry Collins. *New York of Yesterday.* New York: Gracie Mansion, 1924.

Bryant, Elizabeth. *Types of Mankind as Affecting the Financial History of the World,* 1879.

Burr, Clinton Stoddard. *America's Race Heritage.* New York: The National Historical Society, 1922.

Burton, Sir Richard F. *The Jew, the Gypsy and El Islam.* London: Hutchinson & Co., 1890.

Butler, Benjamin F. *Butler's Book.* Boston: A.M. Thayer & Co., 1892.

Byrnes, Thomas. *Professional Criminals of America.* New York: Cassell & Co., 1886.

Cabot, Richard C. *Social Service and the Art of Healing.* New York: Dodd, Mead & Co., 1928.

Campbell, Helen. *Darkness and Daylight; or Lights and Shadows of New York Life.* Hartford: The Hartford Publishing Co., 1897.

Carlson, Lewis H., and Colburn, George A. *In Their Place: White America Defines Her Minorities 1850 – 1950.* New York: John Wiley & Sons, 1972.

Carter, Harold Dean., ed. *Henry Adams and His Friends: A Collection of His Unpublished Letters.* New York: Octagon Books, 1970.

Chamberlain, Houston Stewart. *Foundations of the Nineteenth Century.* New York: John Lane Co., 1912.

Chapman, John Jay. *Notes on Religion.* New York: Laurence J. Gomme, 1915.

Cherep-Spiridovich, Count. *The Secret World Government or 'The Hidden Hand.'* New York: The Anti-Bolshevist Publishing Association, 1926.

Clark, Gordon. *Shylock as Banker, Bondholder, Corruptionist, Conspirator.* Washington, D.C.: American Bimetallic League, 1894.

Columbia University Bulletin of Information, New York City, 1916– 17, and 1921 – 22.

Commons, John R. *Races and Immigrants in America.* New York: The Macmillan Co., 1907.

Coney Island and the Jews. New York: G.W. Carleton & Co., 1879.

Connolly, C.P. *The Truth About the Frank Case.* New York: Vail-Ballou Co., 1915.

Cook, William W. *American Institutions and Their Preservation.* Norwood, Massachusetts: Norwood Press, 1927.

Davenport, Charles Benedict. *Heredity in Relation to Eugenics.* New York: Henry Holt & Co., 1911.

Davis, David Brian., ed. *The Fear of Conspiracy: Images of Un-American Subversion from the Revolution to the Present.* Ithaca: Cornell University Press, 1971.

Dawes, Anna Laurens. *The Modern Jew.* Boston: D. Lothrop and Co., 1886.

Edel, Leon, ed. *The Selected Letters of Henry James.* New York: Farrar, Straus and Cudahy, 1955.

Elias, Robert H., ed. *Letters of Theodore Dreiser*. Philadelphia: University of Pennsylvania Press, 1959.

Emery, Sarah E.V. *Seven Financial Conspiracies which Have Enslaved the American People*. Lansing, Michigan: R. Smith & Co., 1892.

Fairchild, Henry Pratt. *The Melting-Pot Mistake*. Boston: Little, Brown and Co., 1926.

Ford, Worthington Chauncey, ed. *Letters of Henry Adams*. 2 vols. Boston: Houghton Mifflin Co., 1930, 1938.

Fraser, John Foster. *The Conquering Jew*. New York: Cassel and Co., Ltd., 1915.

————. *Red Russia*. New York: The John Lane Co., 1907.

Goode, James B. *The Modern Banker*. Chicago: Charles H. Kerr & Co., 1896.

Goricar, Joseph, and Stowe, Lyman Beecher. *The Inside Story of Austro-German Intrigue*. New York: Doubleday, Page & Co., 1920.

Grant, Madison. *The Passing of the Great Race*. New York: Charles Scribner's Sons, 1916.

Grose, Howard B. *Aliens or Americans?* New York: Young People's Missionary Movement, 1906.

Hall, Prescott F. *Immigration; and Its Effects Upon the United States*. New York: Henry Holt & Co., 1908.

Hapgood, Hutchins. *The Spirit of the Ghetto*. New York: Funk & Wagnalls Co., 1902.

————. *Types from City Streets*. New York: Funk & Wagnalls Co., 1912.

Haskin, Frederic. *The Immigrant*. New York: Fleming H. Revell Co., 1913.

Hearn, Lafcadio. *The Japanese Letters of Lafcadio Hearn*. Edited by Elizabeth Bisland. Boston: Houghton Mifflin Co., 1910.

————. *Occidental Gleanings*. Edited by Albert Mordell. New York: Dodd, Mead & Co., 1925.

Hendrick, Burton J. *The Jews in America*. New York: Doubleday, Page & Co., 1923.

Hilleary, Albert A. *The Jew and the Klan*. Harrisburg, Pennsylvania: The Evangelical Press, 1925.

Hobart, Mary E. *The Secret of the Rothschilds*. Chicago: Charles H. Kerr & Co., 1898.

Holst, H. von. *The Constitutional and Political History of the United States*. Chicago: Callaghan and Co., 1881.

Hornaday, William T. *Awake! America! Object Lessons and Warnings*. New York: Moffat, Yard & Co., 1918.

Hosmer, James K. *The Last Leaf*. New York: G.P. Putnam's Sons, 1912.

————. *The Story of the Jews*. New York: G.P. Putnam's Sons, 1893.

The Household Book of Wit and Humor. Philadelphia: Crawford & Co., 1883.

Howe, M.A. DeWolfe, ed. *Barrett Wendell and His Letters.* Boston: The Atlantic Monthly Press, 1924.

————, ed. *New Letters of James Russell Lowell.* New York: Harper & Brothers, 1932

Hughes, Rupert. *The Real New York.* New York: The Smart Set Publishing Co., 1904.

Huneker, James Gibbons. *New Cosmopolis.* New York: Charles Scribner's Sons, 1915.

Hurt, Walter. *Truth About the Jews Told by a Gentile.* Chicago: Horton & Co., 1922.

The International Jew: Aspects of Jewish Power in the United States. Dearborn, Michigan: The Dearborn Publishing Co., 1922.

The International Jew: Jewish Activities in the United States. Dearborn, Michigan: The Dearborn Publishing Co., 1921.

The International Jew: Jewish Influences in American Life. Dearborn, Michigan: The Dearborn Publishing Co., 1921.

The International Jew: The World's Foremost Problem. Dearborn, Michigan: The Dearborn Publishing Co., 1920.

Jack, Guy. *Captain Guy Jack's Iconoclast: Being an Exposure of Hypocritical Christians and Corrupt Jews.* New Orleans: Louisiana Printing Co., 1919.

Jordan, David Starr. *The Human Harvest: A Study of the Decay of Races Through the Survival of the Unfit.* Boston: American Unitarian Association, 1912.

————. *Unseen Empire.* Boston: American Unitarian Association, 1912.

Kallen, Horace M. *Culture and Democracy in the United States.* New York: Boni & Liveright, 1924.

Lease, Mary E. *The Problem of Civilization Solved.* Chicago: Laird & Lee, 1895.

Lee, Joseph. *Constructive and Preventive Philanthropy.* New York: The Macmillan Co., 1912.

Lowell, A. Lawrence. *Public Opinion and Popular Government.* New York: Longmans, Green and Co., 1913.

Lydston, G. Frank. *That Bogey Man the Jew.* Kansas City: Burton Publishing Co., 1921.

McCartney, Richard Hayes. *Jewish Title to Asia Minor.* New York: Fleming H. Revell Co., n.d.

————. *That Jew!* New York: Fleming H. Revell Co., 1905.

McGuffey, Wm. H. *McGuffey's New Fifth Eclectic Reader.* Cincinnati: Winthrop B. Smith & Co., 1885.

MacKeever, Samuel A. *Glimpses of Gotham.* New York: National Police Gazette Office, 1880.

Marcus, Jacob R. *American Jewry Documents, Eighteenth Century*. Cincinnati: Hebrew Union College Press, 1959.

Matthiessen, F.O., and Murdock, Kenneth B., ed. *The Notebooks of Henry James*. New York: George Braziller, 1953.

Mencken, H.L. *Prejudices First Series, Prejudices Third Series, Prejudices Fourth Series*. New York: Alfred A. Knopf, 1919, 1922, 1924.

Miller, A.W. *The Restoration of the Jews*. Atlantic: Constitution Publishing Co., 1887.

Mogyorosi, A.J. *The Reprobation of Yisróel*. Allegany, New York, 1886.

Morgan, W. Scott. *History of the Wheel and Alliance and the Impending Revolution*. St. Louis: C.B. Woodward Co., 1891.

Moss, Frank. *The American Metropolis*. 3 vols. New York: Peter Fenelon Collier, Publisher, 1897.

Norton, Sarah, and Howe, M.A. DeWolfe. *Letters of Charles Eliot Norton*. Boston: Houghton Mifflin Co., 1913.

Nott, Josiah C. *The Physical History of the Jewish Race*. Charleston, South Carolina: Press of Walker & James, 1850.

Olmsted, Frederick Law. *Journeys and Explorations in the Cotton Kingdom*. London: Sampson, Low, Son & Co., 1861.

Orth, Samuel P. *Our Foreigners*. New Haven: Yale University Press, 1920.

Park, Robert E. *The Immigrant Press and Its Control*. Westport, Conn.: Greenwood Press, 1970.

————, and Miller, Herbert A. *Old World Traits Transplanted*. New York: Harper & Brothers, 1921.

Parker, Richard G., and Watson, J. Madison. *The National Pronouncing Speller*. New York: A.S. Barnes & Co., 1869.

Parton, James. *General Butler in New Orleans*. New York: Mason Brothers, 1864.

Pennell, Joseph. *The Jew at Home; Impressions of a Summer and Autumn Spent with Him*. New York: D. Appleton and Co., 1892.

Potter, Bishop Henry C. *The Gates of the East*. New York: E.P. Dutton & Co., 1877.

The Protocols and World Revolution. Boston: Small, Maynard & Co., 1920.

Publications of the Immigration Restriction League, nos. 1, 3, 4, 166. 1894–95.

Riis, Jacob. *The Battle with the Slum*. New York: The Macmillan Co., 1902.

————. *Children of the Tenements*. New York: The Macmillan Co., 1905.

————. *How the Other Half Lives*. New York: Hill and Wang, 1957.

Ripley, William Z. *The Races of Europe*. New York: D. Appleton and Co., 1899.

Roberts, Kenneth L. *Why Europe Leaves Home*. New York: The Bobbs-Merrill Co., 1922.

Ross, Edward A. *The Old World in the New*. New York: The Century Co., 1914.

————. *The Russian Bolshevik Revolution*. New York: The Century Co., 1921.

————. *Sin and Society; An Analysis of Latter-Day Iniquity*. New York: Harper & Row, 1973.

Schappes, Morris U., ed. *A Documentary History of the Jews in the United States 1654 – 1875. New York: The Citadel Press, 1950.*

Selzer, Michael. "Kike!": A Documentary History of Anti-Semitism in America. New York: World Publishing Co., 1972.

Shaler, Nathaniel S. *The Neighbor*. Boston: Houghton, Mifflin and Co., 1904.

Sherwood, Robert. *This Is New York*. New York: Charles Scribner's Sons, 1931.

Singer, Michael. *Contribution to the History of Antisemitism*. Pamphlet-Library no. 1, January, 1900.

Smith, Goldwin. *Essays on Questions of the Day*. Edited by Arnold Haultain. New York: Macmillan and Co., 1893.

————. *Reminiscences*. New York: The Macmillan Co., 1910.

Smith, Reed. *South Carolina Ballads*. Cambridge: Harvard University Press, 1928.

Sombart, Werner. *The Jews and Modern Capitalism*. Glencoe, Illinois: The Free Press, 1951.

Speranza, Gino. *Race or Nation*. Indianapolis: The Bobbs-Merrill Co., 1923.

Stewart, William M. *Bondholders' Conspiracy to Demonetize Silver*. San Francisco: G. Spaulding & Co., 1885.

Stoddard, Lothrop. *Re-Forging America*. New York: Charles Scribner's Sons, 1927.

————. *The Rising Tide of Color*. New York: Charles Scribner's Sons, 1927.

Sumner, William Graham. *Folkways*. Boston: Ginn and Co., 1940.

Sylvanus, Pal. *Tit for Tat*. Chicago: The Satirical Historical Association, 1895.

Taft, William Howard. *Anti-Semitism in the United States*. Chicago: Anti-Defamation League, 1920.

Thayer, William Roscoe, ed. *The Life and Letters of John Hay*. Boston: Houghton Mifflin Co., 1915.

Thorpe, Thomas May. *What Is Money*. New York: J.S. Ogilvie Publishing Co., 1894.

Timayenis, Telemachus T. *The American Jew; An Exposé of His Career*. New York: The Minerva Publishing Co., 1888.

————. *Judas Iscariot: An Old Type in a New Form*. New York: The Minerva Publishing Co., 1889.

————. *The Original Mr. Jacobs: A Startling Exposé*. New York: The Minerva Publishing Co., 1888.

Van Dyke, John C. *The Money God.* New York: Charles Scribner's Sons, 1908.

Vance, Zebulon B. *The Scattered Nation.* New York: The Rational Publishing Co., 1904.

Veritas, Semper [Allan McBoden]. *An Appeal to the Jews.* San Francisco: Francis & Valentine, 1878.

Wakeley, Ebenezer. *The Gentile Ass and the Judean Monetary Establishment.* Chicago: The Mighty Price Quotient Series, 1895.

Warne, Frank Julian. *The Immigrant Invasion.* New York: Dodd, Mead & Co., 1913.

Warner, George H. *The Jewish Spectre.* New York: Doubleday, Page & Co., 1905.

Watson, Thomas E. *The People's Party Campaign Book, 1892.* Washington: National Watchman Publishing Co., 1892.

Wellman, Francis L. *Gentlemen of the Jury.* New York: The Macmillan Co., 1924.

Woods, Robert A., ed. *Americans in Process: A Settlement Study.* Boston: Houghton Mifflin and Co., 1902.

————. *The City Wilderness, A Settlement Study.* Boston: Houghton, Mifflin and Co., 1898.

Worthington, H.P.C. *Hell for the Jews.* New York: J. Haney & Co., 1879.

York, Hamilton. *The Dawes Report and Control of World Gold.* New York: The Beckwith Press, 1925.

Primary Material: Novels and Drama

Abbot, George, and Gleason, James. *The Fall Guy.* New York: Samuel French, 1928.

Adams, Henry. *Democracy and Esther: Two Novels.* Gloucester, Massachusetts: Peter Smith, 1965.

Aiken, Albert W. *The California Detective.* Beadle's Dime Library, no. 42 (New York, 1878).

————. *Dick Talbot, the Ranch King.* Beadle's Dime Library, no. 733 (New York, 1892).

————. *The Genteel Spotter; or The Night Hawks of New York.* Beadle's Dime Library, no. 320 (New York, 1884).

————. *Lone Hand the Shadow.* Beadle's Dime Library, no. 562 (New York, 1889).

————. *The Lone Hand in Texas.* Beadle's Dime Library, no. 490 (New York, 1888).

————. *The New York 'Sharp'; or The Flash of Lightning.* Beadle's Dime Library, no. 31 (New York, 1878).

————. *Old Benzine the Hard Case Detective.* Beadle's Dime Library, no. 607 (New York, 1890).

————. *The Phantom Hand.* Beadle and Adams Twenty Cent Novels, no. 23 (New York, 1877).

————. *The Spotter-Detective; or The Girls of New York.* Beadle's Dime Library, no. 27 (New York, 1878).

————. *The White Witch or, The League of Three.* New York: Beadle and Adams, 1871.

————. *The Wolves of New York.* Beadle's Dime Library, no. 161 (New York, 1881).

Akins, Zoe. *Déclassée.* New York: Boni & Liveright, 1924.

Alfriend, Edward M., and Wheeler, A.C. "The Great Diamond Robbery." *Favorite American Plays of the Nineteenth Century.* Edited by Barrett H. Clark. Princeton: Princeton University Press, 1943.

Alger, Horatio, Jr. *Adrift in New York.* Cleveland: The World Syndicate Publishing Co., n.d.

————. *Ben, the Luggage Boy; or Among the Wharves.* Boston: Loring, Publishers, 1870.

————. *Dan, the Newsboy.* New York: A.L. Burt Co., 1893.

————. *Paul, the Peddler.* New York: A.L. Burt Co., n.d.

————. *Sam's Chance; and How He Improved It.* Philadelphia: Henry T. Coates & Co., 1876.

Anderson, Maxwell, and Hickerson, Harold. *Gods of the Lightning.* New York: Longmans, Green and Co., 1928.

————, and Stallings, Laurence. "What Price Glory." *Twentieth Century Plays.* Edited by Frank W. Chandler and Richard A. Cordell. New York: Thomas Nelson and Sons, 1934.

Appleton, Horace. "Billy, the Broker's Boy or, the Wire Tappers of Wall Street." *Fame and Fortune Weekly,* no. 336 (New York, 1912).

Bailey, Grace Helen. "The Jew! A Tale of San Francisco." *Overland Monthly,* Vol. 45 (March, 1905), pp. 191–95.

Baker, Henriette N. *Lost but Found; or, The Jewish Home.* Boston: H.A. Young & Co., 1866.

————. *Rebecca the Jewess.* Boston: I. Bradley, 1879.

Baring-Gould, S. *Noémi.* New York: D. Appleton and Co., 1895.

Bates, Arlo. *Mr. Jacobs.* Boston: W.B. Clarke & Corruth, 1883.

Berry, Edmund. *Leah of Jerusalem: A Story of the Time of Paul.* New York, 1890.

Bishop, John Peale. *Now with His Love.* New York: Charles Scribner's Sons, 1933.

Bixby, Frank L. *The Little Boss*. Boston: Walter H. Baker & Co., 1901.

Blaney, Charles E. *Old Isaacs from the Bowery*. New York: J.S. Ogilvie Publishing Co., 1900.

Bolton, Guy. *The Light of the World*. New York: Henry Holt & Co., 1920.

———. *Polly Preferred*. New York: Samuel French, 1923.

Boucicault, Dion. *After Dark: A Drama of London Life in 1868*. Chicago: Dramatic Publishing Co., n.d.

———. *Flying Scud; or, A Fourlegged Fortune*. New York: Photostatic Reproduction of Original Typescript, New York Public Library, 1867.

Boyesen, H. H. *A Daughter of the Philistines*. Boston: Roberts Brothers, 1883.

Brooks, Elbridge Streeter. *A Son of Issachar: A Romance of the Days of Messias*. London: G.P. Putnam's Sons, 1890.

Brougham, John. *The Irish Yankee; or The Birthday of Freedom*. New York: T.H. French, n.d.

———. *The Lottery of Life*. New York: Samuel French, 1867.

———. *Much Ado About a Merchant of Venice*. New York: Samuel French, 1868.

Browne, J. Ross. *Crusoe's Island*. New York: Harper & Brothers, 1864.

Burned to Death or The Great Insurance Swindles. Nick Carter Weekly, no. 103 (New York, 1898).

Burnett, Dana, and Abbott, George. *Four Walls*. New York: Samuel French, 1928.

Burr, Dangerfield [Prentiss Ingraham]. *The Phantom Mazeppa; or, The Hyena of the Chaparrals*. Beadle's Dime Library, no. 188 (New York, 1882).

Burr, Enoch. *Aleph, the Chaldean*. New York: W.B. Ketcham, 1891.

Caine, Hall. *The Scapegoat*. New York: Lovell, Coryell & Co., 1891.

Carb, David. *The Voice of the People*. Boston: The Four Seas Company, 1912.

Carpenter, Edward Childs. *The Tongues of Men*. New York: Samuel French, 1913.

Chambers, Robert W. *Cardigan*. New York: Harper & Brothers, 1901.

Clarke, James Freeman. *The Legend of Thomas Didymus the Jewish Sceptic*. Boston: Lee and Shepard, Publishers, 1881.

Cobb, Sylvanus. *Orion, the Gold Beater*. New York: Cassell & Co., 1888.

Coleman, William Macon. *The Wandering Jew in America*. Washington, D.C.: J.G. Hester, Publisher, 1875.

Converse, Florence. *The Children of Light*. Boston: Houghton Mifflin and Co., 1912.

Conway, Moncure Daniel. *The Wandering Jew*. London: Chatto and Windus, Picadilly, 1881.

Cooper, James Fenimore. *The Bravo: A Tale*. Philadelphia: Carey & Lea, 1831.

Corbin, John. *Husband*. New York: Houghton Mifflin Co., 1910.

Cormack, Bartlett. *The Racket*. New York: Samuel French, 1927.

Coryell, J.R. *Among the Fire-Bugs; or, Nick Carter's Bravest Deed*. Nick Carter Library, no. 110 (New York, 1893).

————. *The Book-Maker's Crime; or, Nick Carter's Accidental Clue*. Nick Carter Library, no. 99 (New York, 1893).

Cowdrick, J.C. *Cibuta John; The Prickly Pear from Cactus Plains*. Beadle's Half Dime Library, no. 424 (New York, 1885).

————. *The Detective's Apprentice; or, A Boy Without a Name*. Beadle's Half Dime Library, no. 420 (New York, 1885).

Craig, Alexander. *Ionia: Land of Wise Men and Fair Women*. Chicago: E.A. Weeks, 1898.

Crawford, F. Marion. *A Cigarette-Maker's Romance*. New York: Macmillan and Co., 1893.

————. *A Roman Singer*. Boston: Houghton, Mifflin and Co., 1884.

————. *The Witch of Prague*. London: Macmillan and Co., 1891.

Crothers, Rachel. *A Little Journey*. New York: Samuel French, 1923.

Cumberland, Stuart C. *The Rabbi's Spell. A Russo-Jewish Romance*. New York: International Book Co., n.d.

Daly, Augustin. *The Last Word*. By the Author, 1891.

————. *Leah: The Forsaken*. By the Author, 1863.

Davis, Allan. *The Promised Land*. Cambridge: The Harvard Dramatic Club, 1908.

Davis, Elmer. *Show Window*. New York: The John Day Co., 1927.

Davis, Owen. *The Detour*. Boston: Little, Brown and Co., 1922.

Denver Dan and the Counterfeiters. The Five Cent Wide Awake Library, no. 439 (New York, 1881).

Donnelly, Ignatius. *Caesar's Column*. Cambridge: The Belknap Press of Harvard University Press, 1960.

————. *The Golden Bottle*. New York: Johnson Reprint Corp., 1968.

Dos Passos, John. *Airways, Inc*. New York: The Macaulay Co., 1928.

————. *Three Soldiers*. New York: The Modern Library, 1932.

Dreiser, Theodore. *The Hand of the Potter*. New York: Boni & Liveright, 1918.

Dunbar, Noel [Prentiss Ingraham]. *The Detective in Rags*. Beadle's Dime Library, no. 604 (New York, 1890).

————. *Duke Despard the Gambler Duellist*. Beadle's Dime Library, no. 730 (New York, 1892).

Dunne, Finley Peter. *Mr. Dooley in the Hearts of His Countrymen*. Boston: Small, Maynard & Co., 1899.

Dunning, Philip. *Night Hostess*. New York: Samuel French, 1928.

Edel, Leon, ed. *The Complete Tales of Henry James*. Vols. 3, 7, 9, 10, 11. Philadelphia: J.B. Lippincott Co., 1962 – 64.

Edwards, Albert [Arthur Bullard]. *Comrade Yetta*. New York: The Macmillan Co., 1913.

Egan, Maurice Francis. *The Disappearance of John Longworthy*. Notre Dame, Indiana: Office of the Ave Maria, 1890.

————. *The Ivy Hedge*. New York: Bennziger Brothers, 1914.

Eliot, T.S. *The Complete Poems and Plays 1909 – 1950*. New York: Harcourt, Brace and Co., 1952.

Ellis, J. Breckenridge. *Dread and Fear of Kings*. Chicago: A.C. McClurg & Co., 1900.

Farjeon, B.L. *Solomon Isaacs*. New York: G.W. Carleton & Co., 1877.

Faulkner, William. *Mosquitos*. New York: Boni & Liveright, 1927.

Fawcett, Edgar. *New York*. New York: F. Tennyson Neely, 1898.

Fay, Theodore S. *The Countess Ida, A Tale of Berlin*. 2 vols. New York: Harper & Brothers, 1840.

————. *Sidney Clifton*. 2 vols. New York: Harper & Brothers, 1839.

Fitch, Clyde. *Beau Brummel*. New York: John Lane Co., 1908.

————. "The City." *Representative American Dramas*. Edited by Montrose J. Moses. Boston: Little, Brown and Co., 1933.

Fitzgerald, F. Scott. *The Beautiful and Damned*. New York: Charles Scribner's Sons, 1950.

————. *The Crack-Up*. Edited by Edmund Wilson. New York: New Directions Paperback, 1956.

————. *The Great Gatsby*. New York: Charles Scribner's Sons, 1953.

Flavin, Martin. *The Criminal Code*. New York: Horace Liveright, 1929.

————. *Lady of the Rose*. New York: Samuel French, 1925.

Forbes, James. *The Show Shop*. New York: Samuel French, 1920.

Ford, Paul Leicester. *Janice Meredith*. New York: Dodd, Mead & Co., 1899.

Franco, Harry [Charles F. Briggs]. *Bankrupt Stories*. New York: J. Allen, 1844.

Frankel, A.H. *In Gold We Trust*. Philadelphia, 1898.

Frederic, Harold. *Gloria Mundi*. Chicago: Herbert S. Stone & Co., 1898.

————. *The Market Place*. New York, Grosset & Dunlap, 1899.

Friedman, Isaac Kahn. *By Bread Alone*. New York: McClure, Phillips & Co., 1901.

Friendly, Aunt [Sarah S. Baker]. *The Jewish Twins*. New York: Robert Carter & Brothers, 1860.

Garland, Hamlin. *Crumbling Idols*. Chicago: Stone & Kimball, 1894.

————. *Rose of Dutcher's Coolly*. New York: Harper & Brothers, 1899.

Garne, Gaston. *Bob Baxter the Young Stamp Collector or, A Thousand Dollars from One.* Fame and Fortune Weekly, no. 372 (New York, 1912).

Gillman, Henry. *Hassan: A Fellah.* Boston: Little, Brown and Co., 1898.

Glass, Montague. *Potash & Perlmutter.* New York: Grosset & Dunlap, 1911.

Gossip, George H. *The Jew of Chamant; or, The Modern Monte Cristo: A Romance of Crime.* New York: G.M. Hausauer, 1898.

Gratacap, L.P. *Benjamin the Jew.* New York: Thomas Benton, 1913.

Griffin, G.W. *"Shylock," a Burlesque.* New York: Samuel French, 1876.

Gwendolen, A Sequel to George Eliot's Danial Deronda. Boston: Ira Bradley and Co., 1878.

The Gypsy of the Highlands; or, The Jew and the Heir, no publisher, n.d. New York Public Library.

Hammond, William A. *The Son of Perdition.* Chicago: Herbert S. Stone & Co., 1898.

Harkaway and His Son Homeward Bound. The Five Cent Wide Awake Library, no. 120 (New York, 1879).

Harland, Henry. *The Cardinal's Snuff-Box.* London: John Lane: The Bodley Head, 1900.

Harvey, William H. *A Tale of Two Nations.* Chicago: Coin Publishing Co., 1894.

Hatton, Frederic and Fanny. *Lombardi, LTD.* New York: Samuel French, 1928.

Hawthorne, Julian. *Beatrix Randolph.* Boston: James R. Osgood and Co., 1884.

———. *Sebastian Strome.* New York: D. Appleton and Co., 1880.

Hawthorne, Nathaniel. *The English Notebooks.* Edited by Randall Steward. London: Oxford University Press, 1941.

Hemingway, Ernest. *The Sun Also Rises.* New York: Charles Scribner's Sons, 1970.

———. *Today Is Friday.* Englewood, New Jersey: The As Stable Publications, 1926.

Herrick, Robert. *The Real World.* New York: The Macmillan Co., 1901.

Hilton, George S. *The Funny Side of Politics.* New York: G.W. Dillingham Co., 1899.

Hobart, George V. *Buddies.* Typed Prompt Book, 1919. New York Public Library.

———. *Easy Payments.* New York: Samuel French, 1926.

———. *Ikey's Letters to His Father.* New York: G.W. Dillingham, 1907.

Hoffe, Monckton. *Christilinda.* New York: Samuel French, 1926.

Hoffman, Aaron. *Two Blocks Away.* New York: Samuel French, 1925.

————. *Welcome Stranger*. New York: Samuel French, 1926.

Howard, Sidney. "Lucky Sam McCarver." *Representative American Dramas*. Edited by Montrose J. Moses. Boston: Little, Brown and Co., 1933.

Howe, Julia Ward. *The World's Own*. Boston: Ticknor and Fields, 1857.

Hudson, William C. *On The Rack*. New York: Cassell Publishing Co., 1892.

Huneker, James. *Painted Veils*. New York: The Modern Library, 1920.

Ingraham, Joseph H. *Moloch, the Money-Lender*. New York: Robert M. DeWitt, 1869.

————. *The Pillar of Fire; or Israel in Bondage*. Boston: Roberts Brothers, 1888.

————. *The Prince of the House of David*. Philadelphia: Henry Altemus, 1897.

————. *Ramero; or The Prince and the Prisoner*. New York: Robert M. DeWitt, 1869.

————. *The Throne of David*. Boston: Roberts Brothers, 1896.

Ingraham, Prentiss. *The Cowboy Clan; or, The Tigress of Texas*. Beadle Dime Library, no. 658 (New York, 1891).

————. *The Fatal Frigate*. Beadle's Dime Library, no. 430 (New York, 1887).

————. *Gold Plume, the Boy Bandit; or, the Kid-Glove Sport*. Beadle's Half Dime Library, no. 204 (New York, 1881).

————. *The Jew Detective; or, The Beautiful Convict*. Beadle's Dime Library, no. 662 (New York, 1891).

————. *The Mad Mariner; or Dishonored and Discovered*. Beadle's Dime Library, no. 162 (New York, 1881).

————. *The New Monte Cristo; or, The Wandering Jew of the Sea*. Beadle's Dime Library, no. 399 (New York, 1886).

Irwin, Wallace. *At the Sign of the Dollar*. New York: Fox, Duffield & Co., 1905.

Jack Harkaway and His Son's Adventures Round the World. The Five Cent Wide Awake Library, no. 119 (New York, 1879).

Jackson, George Anson. *The Son of a Prophet*. New York: Houghton, Mifflin and Co., 1893.

James, Henry, *The American Scene*. Bloomington: Indiana University Press, 1968.

————. *The Awkward Age*. New York: Harper & Brothers, 1899.

————. *Embarrassments*. New York: The Macmillan Co., 1896.

————. *The Golden Bowl*. London: Methuen & Co., 1905.

————. *The Tragic Muse*. Boston: Houghton Mifflin and Co., 1918.

————. *Watch and Ward...* London: Macmillan and Co., 1923.

————. *What Maisie Knew*. New York: Herbert S. Stone & Co., 1897.

James, W.I. *Heller's Pupil; or Seligman, the Second-Sight Detective.* Old Cap. Collier Library, no. 4 (New York, 1883).

Jennings, Mary Elizabeth. *Asa of Bethlehem and His Household.* New York: A.D.F. Randolph and Co., 1895.

Jerome, Gilbert. *Dominick Squeek, the Bow Street Runner.* Old Cap. Collier, no. 80 (New York, 1884).

———. *Isaac Lazarus; The Egyptian Detective.* Old Cap. Collier, no. 114 (New York, 1884).

———. *Old Subtle; or, The Willing Victim.* Old Cap. Collier, no. 125 (New York, 1885).

———. *Young Weasel, the Detective; or "Piping" a Beautiful Friend.* Old Cap. Collier, no. 134 (New York, 1885).

Johnson, Evelyn. *An Errand Girl: A Romance of New York Life.* New York: G.W. Dillingham, 1889.

Johnston, Annie Fellows. *In League With Israel.* New York: Easton & Mains, 1896.

Jones, J.B. *Border War; A Tale of Disunion.* New York: Rudd & Carleton, 1859.

Judge, James P. *Square Crooks.* New York: Longmans, Green and Co., 1929.

Judson, E.Z.C. *Morgan; or, The Knight of the Black Flag.* New York: F.A. Brady, 1861.

Kelly, Myra. *Little Aliens.* New York: Grosset & Dunlap, 1910.

———. *Wards of Liberty.* New York: The McClure Co., 1907.

Kennedy, Margaret, and Dean, Basil. *The Constant Nymph.* New York: Doubleday, Page & Co., 1926.

Kenton, Edna, ed. *Eight Uncollected Tales of Henry James.* Freeport, New York: Books for Libraries Press, 1950.

Kester, Paul. *Beverly's Balance.* New York: Longmans, Green and Co., 1928.

King, Edward. *The Gentle Savage.* Boston: James R. Osgood and Co., 1883.

———. *The Golden Spike.* Boston: Ticknor and Co., 1886.

———. *Joseph Zalmonah.* Boston: Lee and Shepard Publishers, 1894.

Kingsley, Florence M. *The Cross Triumphant.* New York: Grosset & Dunlap, 1898.

———. *Paul, A Herald of the Cross.* New York: Grosset & Dunlap, 1897.

———. *Stephen, a Soldier of the Cross.* New York: Grosset & Dunlap, 1896.

Kirkpatrick, John. *Charm.* New York: Samuel French, 1926.

Klein, Charles. *Maggie Pepper.* New York: Samuel French, 1916.

———. *The Third Degree.* New York: Samuel French, 1908.

Lawson, John Howard. *Processional: A Jazz Symphony of American Life in Four Acts.* New York: Thomas Seltzer, 1925.

Lee, Eliza. *Parthenia: or, The Last Days of Paganism.* Boston: Ticknor and Fields, 1858.

Lewis, Alfred Henry. *Peggy O' Neil.* New York: Fenno & Co., 1903.

Lippard, George. *The Quaker City; or, The Monks of Monk Hall.* Philadelphia: Leary, Stuart & Co., 1876.

Little, C. *Jack Bruce.* "The Boys of New York" Pocket Library, no. 173 (New York, 1884).

London, Jack. *Michael Brother of Jerry.* New York: The Macmillan Co., 1917.

Loos, Anita, and Jon Emerson. *Gentlemen Prefer Blondes.* Typewritten Prompt Book, 1926. New York Public Library.

Lowell, James Russell. *The Complete Poetical Works of James Russell Lowell.* New York: Grosset & Dunlap, 1896.

———. *Latest Literary Essays and Addresses.* New York: Houghton, Mifflin and Co., 1892.

———. *Prose Works.* Boston: Houghton, Mifflin and Co., 1890.

Ludlow, James Meeker. *A King of Tyre: A Tale of the Times of Ezra and Nehemiah.* New York: Harper & Brothers, 1891.

Luska, Sidney [Henry Harland]. *As It Was Written: A Jewish Musician's Story.* New York: Cassell & Co., 1885.

———. *Mrs. Peixada.* New York: Cassell & Co., 1886.

———. *The Yoke of the Torah.* New York: Cassell & Co., 1887.

Lust, Adelina. *A Tent of Grace.* Boston: Houghton, Mifflin and Co., 1899.

McArthur, Alexander. *The Leveller.* New York: C.H. Doscher & Co., 1908.

Mackaye, Steele. *Money-Mad.* Typewritten prompt book, n.d., Harvard College Library.

McLaren, Amy. *With the Merry Austrians.* New York: G.P. Putnam's Sons, 1912.

Malloch, W.H. *Tristram Lacy or the Individualist.* New York: The Macmillan Co., 1899.

Manners, J. Hartley. *The House Next Door.* Boston: Walter H. Baker & Co., 1912.

Mantle, Burns, and Sherwood, G.P. *The Best Plays of 1899 – 1909.* New York: Dodd, Mead & Co., 1944.

———. *The Best Plays of 1909 – 1919.* New York: Dodd, Mead & Co., 1933.

———. *The Best Plays of 1919 – 20, 1920 – 21, 1921 – 22, 1922 – 23, 1923 – 24.* Boston: Small, Maynard & Co., 1920–24.

———. *The Best Plays of 1924 – 25, 1925 – 26, 1926 – 27.* New York: Dodd, Mead, & Co., 1925 – 32.

March, E.S. *A Stumbler in Wide Shoes.* New York: Henry Holt & Co., 1896.

Marcin, Max. *Cheating Cheaters.* New York: Samuel French, 1916.

Mason, Caroline Atwater. *The Quiet King: A Story of Christ.* Philadelphia: American Baptist Publishing Society, 1896.

Matthews, Brander. *Vignettes of Manhattan*. New York: Harper & Brothers, 1894.

Matthews, Brander, and Jessop, George H. *A Tale of Twenty-Five Hours*. New York: D. Appleton and Co., 1892.

Melville, Herman. *Redburn*. New York: Harper & Brothers, 1849.

Montgomery, James. *Ready Money*. New York: Samuel French, 1920.

Mumford, Edward. *Bargain Day at Bloomsteins*. Philadelphia: The Penn Publishing Co., 1913.

Myers, Peter Hamilton. *The Miser's Heir; or, The Young Millionaire*. Philadelphia: T.B. Peterson, 1854.

Newberry, Fannie E. *The Wrestler of Philippi: A Tale of the Early Christians*. Elgin, Illinois: David C. Cook Publishing Co., 1897.

Newton, Harry L., and Hoffman, A.S. *All About Goldstein: A Hebrew Monologue*. Chicago: The Dramatic Publishing Co., 1902.

Nichols, Anne. *Abie's Irish Rose*. New York: Harper & Brothers, 1927.

————. *Abie's Irish Rose*. New York: Samuel French, 1937.

Nobles, Milton. *The Phoenix*. Chicago: The Dramatic Publishing Co., 1900.

Norris, Frank. *McTeague*. New York: New American Library, 1964.

Norton, Franklin P. "Financier of New York." *Six Dramas of American Romance and History*. New York: The Schulte Press, 1915.

O'Brien, Fitz James. *The Diamond Lens*. New York: The Happy Hour Library, 1925.

Odell, George C.D. *Annals of the New York Stage*. 15 vols. New York: Columbia University Press, 1927–49.

Ogden, C.A. *Into the Light or the Jewess*. Boston: Lee and Shepard, 1899.

O'Meara, Kathleen. *Narka, the Nihilist*. New York: Harper & Brothers, 1887.

Page, Thomas Nelson. "John Marvel, Assistant." *Scribner's Magazine*, Vol. 15, Nos. 1–6 (January-June, 1909), pp. 25–41.

Parker, Louis N. *Disraeli*. New York: John Lane Co., 1911.

Peple, Edward Henry. *The Jury of Our Peers*. New York: Samuel French, 1925.

Pierson, Jane. *The Coming of the Dawn*. Cincinnati: The Standard Publishing Co., 1917.

Pollock, Channing. *The Fool*. New York: Samuel French, 1922.

Pritchard, Martin J. *Without Sin*. Chicago: Herbert S. Stone & Co., 1896.

Ralph, Julian. *The Millionairess*. Boston: Lothrop Publishing Co., 1902.

————. *People We Pass*. New York: Harper & Brothers, 1896.

Rice, Elmer C. *Street Scene*. New York: Samuel French, 1929.

Ridge, Lola. *The Ghetto and Other Poems*. New York: B.W. Huebsch, 1918.

Rolfe, Maro O. *Diamond Dan, the Brooklyn Divorce Detective; or, The Crimes of a Wicked Woman*. Old Cap. Collier, no. 93 (New York, 1884).

Rollin, Horace J. *Yetta Segal*. New York: G.W. Dillingham Co., 1898.

Roof, Katharine Metcalf. *The Stranger at the Hearth*. Boston: Small, Maynard & Co., 1916.

Rose, Edward Everett. *Rose of the Ghetto*. New York: Samuel French, 1927.

Rutherford, Mark [William Hale White]. *Clara Hapgood*. New York: Dodd, Mead & Co., 1896.

Saltus, Edgar. *Mary Magdalen: A Chronicle*. New York: Belford Co., 1891.

Savage, Richard Henry. *Delilah of Harlem*. New York: The American News Co., 1893.

———. *An Exile from London*. New York: The Home Publishing Co., 1896.

———. *In the Shadow of the Pyramids*. Chicago: Rand, McNally & Co., 1897.

———. *A Modern Corsair: A Story of the Levant*. Chicago: Rand, McNally & Co., 1897.

———. *My Official Wife*. New York: The Home Publishing Co., 1891.

———. *The White Lady of Khaminavatka*. Chicago: Rand, McNally & Co., 1898.

Scoville, Joseph A. [William Barrett]. *Vigor*. New York: Carleton, 1864.

Selwyn, Edgar. *The Country Boy*. New York: Samuel French, 1917.

Sharron, Trafford. *A Jew's Christian*. New York: J.S. Ogilvie Publishing Co., 1904.

Sifton, Paul. *The Belt*. New York: The Macaulay Co., 1927.

Sinclair, Upton. *Jimmie Higgins*. Racine, Wisconsin: Western Printing & Lithographing Co., 1919.

Sleuth, Old [H.P. Halsey]. *Lights and Shades of New York*. Old Sleuth Library, no. 101 (New York, 1905).

———. *Mephisto; or, The Razzle-Dazzle Detective*. Old Sleuth Library, no. 84 (New York, 1899).

———. *Monte-Cristo Ben, the Ever-Ready Detective*. Old Sleuth Library, no. 63 (New York, 1893).

———. *Night Scenes in New York: In Darkness and by Gaslight*. Old Sleuth Library, no. 5 (New York, 1885).

———. *On Their Tracks Being the Continuation of "The American Monte-Cristo."* Old Sleuth Library, no. 95 (New York, 1903).

Smith, Henry James. *A Tailor-Made Man*. New York: Samuel French, 1919.

Southworth, E.D.E.N. *Allworth Abbey*. Philadelphia: T.B. Peterson & Brothers, 1865.

———. *The Bridal Eve*. Philadelphia: T.B. Peterson & Brothers, 1864.

Sterner, Lawrence. *The Un-Christian Jew*. New York: The Neale Publishing Co., 1917.

Steve, Shadow [Robert C. Brown]. *The Frozen Face; or Dick Dobbs Among the Smugglers.* Dick Dobbs Detective Weekly, no. 7 (New York, 1909).

Stevenson, Robert Louis. *Across the Plains.* New York: Charles Scribner's Sons, 1895.

Stocking, Charles F. *Thou Israel.* Chicago: The Maestro Co., 1921.

Stoddard, William O. *The Swordmaker's Son.* New York: The Century Co., 1896.

————. *Ulric the Jarl.* New York: Eaton & Mains, 1899.

Sullivan, J.W. *Tenement Tales of New York.* New York: Henry Holt & Co., 1895.

Tarkington, Booth, and Wilson, Harry Leon. *The Gibson Upright.* New York: Doubleday, Page & Co., 1919.

Taylor, Tom. *The Ticket-of-Leave Man.* New York: Samuel French, 1864.

Teaser, Tom. *Mulligan's Boy.* The Five Cent Wide Awake Library, no. 68 (New York, 1879).

Thomas, Augustus. *As a Man Thinks.* New York: Duffield & Co., 1911.

Thurston, E. Temple. *The Wandering Jew.* New York: G.P. Putnam's Sons, 1925.

Tilton, Dwight. *Meyer & Son.* Boston: C.M. Clark Publishing Co., 1908.

Townsend, Edward W. *A Daughter of the Tenements.* New York: Lovell, Coryell & Co., 1895.

————. *Near a Whole City Full.* New York: G.W. Dillingham Co., 1897.

Twain, Mark. *Life on the Mississippi.* New York: Harper & Brothers, 1904.

Tyler, Robert. *Ahasuerus; A Poem.* New York: Harper & Brothers, 1842.

Wallace, Lew. *Ben-Hur, A Tale of Christ.* New York: Signet Books, 1962.

————. *The Prince of India.* New York: Harper & Brothers, 1893.

Ward, Elizabeth S.P. *The Story of Jesus Christ, An Interpretation.* Boston: Houghton, Mifflin and Co., 1898.

Ward, Mrs. Humphry. *Sir George Tressady.* New York: The Macmillan Co., 1896.

Wellman, Rita. *The Gentile Wife.* New York: Moffat, Yard & Co., 1919.

Wharton, Edith. *The House of Mirth.* New York: New American Library, 1964.

Wheeler, Edward L. *Apollo Bill, the Trail Tornado.* Beadle's Half Dime Library, no. 236 (New York, 1882).

————. *Boss Bob the King of Bootblacks; or, The Pawnbrokers Plot.* Beadle's Pocket Library, no. 111 (New York, 1886).

————. *Canada Chet, the Counterfeiter Chief.* The Deadwood Dick Library, no. 22 (Cleveland, 1899).

————. *Deadwood Dick of Deadwood*. The Deadwood Dick Library, no. 17 (Cleveland, 1899).

————. *Deadwood Dick in Leadville*. The Deadwood Dick Library, no. 23 (Cleveland, 1899).

————. *Death-Face, the Detective; or, Life and Love in New York*. Beadle's Pocket Library, no. 18 (New York, 1884).

————. *Jim Bludsoe, Jr., the Boy Phenix; or, Through to Death*. Beadle's Half Dime Library, no 53 (New York, 1878).

————. *Wild Ivan, the Boy Claude Duval*. The Deadwood Dick Library, no. 5 (Cleveland, 1899).

Whittaker, Fred. *Alligator Ike; or, The Secret of the Everglade*. Beadle's Dime Library, no. 427 (New York, 1883).

Wilcox, Constance G. *Egypt's Eyes*. New York: Samuel French, 1924.

Wilson, Anna May. *The Days of Mohammed*. Chicago: D.C. Cook, 1897.

Woods, Katherine. *John: A Tale of King Messiah*. New York: Dodd, Mead & Co., 1896.

————. *The Son of Ingar*. New York: Dodd, Mead & Co., 1897.

Young, Rida J., and Coleman, Gilbert P. *Brown of Harvard*. New York: G.P. Putnam's Sons, 1907.

Public Documents

Annual Report of the Commissioner-General of Immigration, 1899 – 1914. Washington: Government Printing Office.

U.S. Congress, House. *Temporary Suspension of Immigration*. House Report 1109, 66th Cong., 3rd sess., 1920.

U.S. Congress, Senate, Subcommittee on the Judiciary. *Brewing and Liquor Interests and German and Bolshevik Propaganda*. S. Doc. 62, 66th Cong. 1st sess., 1919.

U.S. Congress, Senate, *Changes in Bodily Form of Descendants of Immigrants*. S. Doc. 208, 61st Cong., 2nd sess., 1910.

U.S. Congress, Senate, *Importing Women for Immoral Purposes*, S. Doc. 196, 61st Cong., 2nd sess., 1909.

U.S. Department of State. *Dispatches from United States Ministers to Russia 1808 – 1906*. Microfilm. National Archives Microfilm Publications.

U.S. Immigration Commission. *Letter from the Secretary of the Treasury, Transmitting a Report of the Commissioners of Immigration upon the Causes Which Incite Immigration to the United States*. Vol. 1. Washington: Government Printing Office, 1892.

U.S. Immigration Commission. *Reports of the Immigration Commission.*
Abstracts of Reports of the Immigration Commission. S. Doc. 747,
61st Cong., 3rd sess., 1911.

U.S. Immigration Commission. *Reports of the Immigration Commission.*
Immigrants in Industries. Vols. 21 – 22. Washington: Government
Printing Office, 1911.

U.S. Immigration Commission. *Reports of the Immigration Commission.*
Immigration and Crime. Vol. 36. Washington: Government Printing
Office, 1911.

Unpublished Theses and Dissertations

Bloom, Steven. "Interactions Between Blacks and Jews in New York City,
1900 – 1930, as Reflected in the Black Press." Ph.D. dissertation,
New York University, 1973.

Bloore, John Stephen. "The Jew in American Dramatic Literature, 1794 –
1930." Ph.D. dissertation, New York University, 1950.

Davis, Leona. "A Certain Blindness in Henry James: A Study of the Treatment
of Jewish Characters in His Fiction." M.A. thesis, University of
Pittsburgh, 1961.

Dell, Robert M. "The Representation of the Immigrant on the New York
Stage—1881 to 1916." Ph.D. dissertation, New York University,
1960.

Fine, David Martin. "The Immigrant Ghetto in American Fiction, 1885 –
1917." Ph.D. dissertation, University of California, L.A., 1969.

Flowers, Edward. "Anti-Semitism in the Free Silver and Populist Movements
and the Election of 1896." M.A. thesis, Columbia University, 1952.

Gan, Robert T. "A Documentary Source Book for Jewish-Christian Relations
in the United States, 1865 – 1914." M.A. thesis, Hebrew Union College, 1967.

Goldberg, Mark Franklin. "The Representation of Love and Romance in
American Fiction About East European Jews in New York City:
1894 – 1917." Ph.D. dissertation, New York University, 1970.

Grant, Curtis Robert. "The Social Gospel and Race." Ph.D. dissertation,
Stanford University, 1968.

Grover, Janice Zita. "Luxury and Leisure in Early Nineteenth Century America: Saratoga Springs and the Rise of a Resort." Ph.D. dissertation,
University of California, Davis, 1973.

Haller, John Samuel "Science and American Concepts of Race, 1859 – 1900."
Ph.D. dissertation, University of Maryland, 1969.

Halpern, Rose A. "The American Reaction to the Dreyfus Case." M.A. thesis, Columbia University, 1941.

Heald, Morrell. "Business Attitudes Towards European Immigration." Ph.D. dissertation, Yale University, 1951.

Hellwig, David Johns. "The Afro-American and the Immigrant, 1880–1930: A Study of Black Social Thought." Ph.D. dissertation, Syracuse University, 1973.

Herzog, Joseph P. "The Emergence of the Anti-Jewish Stereotype in the United States," Rabbinic thesis, Hebrew Union College, 1953.

Kachuck, Rhoda S. "The Portrayal of the Jew in American Drama Since 1920." Ph.D. dissertation, University of Southern California, 1970.

Lichliter, William F. "Political Reflections of an Age: The New York Graphic Weeklies During the 1880's." Ph.D. dissertation, Brandeis University, 1970.

Mayo, Louise. "The Ambivalent Image: The Perception of the Jew in Nineteenth Century America." Ph.D. dissertation, City University of New York, 1977.

Neuringer, Sheldon Morris. "American Jewry and United States Immigration Policy, 1881–1953." Ph.D. dissertation, University of Wisconsin, 1969.

Passi, Michael Matthew. "Mandarins and Immigrants: The Irony of Ethnic Studies in America Since Turner." Ph.D. dissertation, University of Minnesota, 1972.

Raphael, Marc Lee. "Intra-Jewish Conflict in the United States, 1869–1915." Ph.D. dissertation, University of California, L.A., 1972.

Sable, Jacob M. "Some American Jewish Organizational Efforts to Combat Anti-Semitism, 1906–30." Ph.D. dissertation, Yeshiva University, 1964.

Steinberg, Abraham H. "Jewish Characters in the American Novel to 1900." Ph.D. dissertation, New York University, 1956.

Urquhart, Ronald A. "The American Reaction to the Dreyfus Affair. A Study of Anti-Semitism in the 1890's." Ph.D. dissertation, Columbia University, 1972.

Walsh, Joseph Howard. "Protestant Response to Materialism in American Life, 1865–1900." Ed.D. dissertation, Columbia University, 1974.

Yodfat, Aryeh. "The Jewish Question in American-Russian Relations 1875–1917." Ph.D. dissertation, The American University, 1963.

York, Lawrence Francis. "The Image of the Jew in Modern American Fiction." Ph.D. dissertation, University of Connecticut, 1966.

Secondary Material: Articles

The following abbreviations are used:

AJA   (American Jewish Archives)

AJHQ   (American Jewish Historical Quarterly)

PAJHS   (Publications of the American Jewish Historical Society)

YIVO   (YIVO Institute for Jewish Research, Annual of Jewish Social Science.

Adams, Harold E. "Minority Caricatures on the American Stage." *Studies in the Science of Society*. Edited by G.P. Murdock. New Haven: Yale University Press, 1937.

Adler, Selig. "The United States and the Holocaust." *AJHQ,* Vol. 64, No. 1 (September, 1974), pp. 14 – 23.

Arms, George, and Gibson, William M. "'Silas Lapham,' 'Daisey Miller,' and the Jews." *The New England Quarterly,* Vol. 16, No. 1 (March, 1943), pp. 118 – 22.

Auerbach, Jerold S. "From Rags to Robes: The Legal Profession, Social Mobility and the American Jewish Experience." *AJHQ,* Vol. 66 (December, 1976), pp. 249 – 84.

Baskin, Stuart. "Raising the Ivy Covered Walls: Jews and the Universities, 1916 – 23." *Stanford Quarterly Review* (Winter, 1972), pp. 20 – 29.

Billington, Ray Allen. "Frederick Jackson Turner Visits New England." *The New England Quarterly,* Vol. 41, No. 3 (September, 1968) pp. 409 – 36.

Bitton, Livia E. "The Jewess as a Fictional Sex Symbol." *Bucknell Review,* Vol. 21, No. 1 (Spring, 1973), pp. 63 – 86.

Blinderman, Abraham. "Henry Adams and the Jews." *The Chicago Jewish Forum,* Vol. 25, No. 1 (Fall, 1966), pp. 3 – 8.

Bloore, Stephen. "The Jew in American Dramatic Literature (1794 – 1930)." *PAJHS,* No. 50, Part 4 (June, 1951), pp. 345 – 60.

Byrnes, Robert F. "Edouard Drumont and La France Juive." *Jewish Social Studies,* Vol. 10, No. 2 (April, 1948), pp. 165 – 84.

Cahalan, Don, and Trager, Frank N. "Free Answer Stereotypes and Anti-Semitism." *The Public Opinion Quarterly,* Vol. 13 (Spring, 1949), pp. 97 – 102.

Chyet, Stanley F. "The Political Rights of the Jews in the U.S., 1776 – 1840." *American Jewish Archives,* Vol. 11 (April, 1958), pp. 14 – 75.

Clymer, Kenton J. "Anti-Semitism in the Late Nineteenth Century: The Case of John Hay." *AJHQ,* Vol. 60, No. 4 (June, 1971), pp. 344 – 54.

Cohen, Naomi. "Pioneers of American Jewish Defense." *American Jewish Archives* (November, 1977), pp. 116– 50.

Cohn, Norman. "The Myth of the Jewish World-Conspiracy." *Commentary*, Vol. 41, No. 6 (June, 1966), pp. 35– 42.

Coleman, Edward D. "Jewish Prototypes in American and English Romans and Drames à Clef." *PAJHS*, No. 35 (1939), pp. 227– 80.

———. "Plays of Jewish Interest on the American Stage, 1752– 1821." *PAJHS*, No. 33 (1934), pp. 171– 98.

De Voto, Bernard. "Mark Twain About the Jews." *Jewish Frontier*, Vol. 6, No. 5 (May, 1939), pp. 7– 9.

Dinnerstein, Leonard. "A Note on Southern Attitudes Toward Jews." *Jewish Social Studies*, Vol. 32, No. 1 (January, 1970), pp. 93– 99.

Dobkowski, Michael N. "The Jew in 19th Century French Literature: Shylock up to Date." *Patterns of Prejudice*, Vol. 8, No. 1 (January-February, 1974), pp. 17– 23.

Fein, Isaac M. "Niles Weekly Register on the Jews." *PAJHS*, Vol. 50, No. 1 (September, 1960), pp. 3– 22.

Feldman, Egal. "The Social Gospel and the Jews." *AJHQ*, Vol. 58, No. 3 (March, 1969), pp. 308– 22.

Ferkiss, Victor C. "Populist Influences on American Fascism." *The American Past*. Edited by Sidney Fine and Gerald S. Brown. New York: The Macmillan Co., 1961.

Fiermann, Floyd. "The Jew and the Problem of Church and State in America Prior to 1881." *The Educational Forum*, Vol. 15, No. 2 (January, 1951), pp. 335– 41.

Fineman, Irving. "The Image of the Jew in our Fiction." *Tradition*, Vol. 8, No. 4 (Winter, 1966), pp. 19– 47.

Forrey, Robert. "The 'Jew' in Norris' The Octopus." *Western States Jewish Historical Quarterly*, Vol. 7 (April, 1975), pp. 201– 9.

Frank, Florence Kiper. "The Presentment of the Jew in American Fiction." *The Bookman*, Vol. 71, No. 3 (June, 1930), pp. 270– 75.

Friedenberg, Albert M. "The Jews and the American Sunday Laws." *PAJHS*, No. 11 (1903), pp. 101– 15.

Friedman, Lee M. "The Problems of Nineteenth Century American Jewish Peddlers." *PAJHS*, Vol. 44 (September 1954-June 1955), pp. 1– 7.

Glanz, Rudolf. "German Jews in New York City in the 19th Century." *YIVO Annual of Jewish Social Science*, Vol. 11, 1957, pp. 9– 38.

———. "Jewish Social Conditions as Seen by the Muckrakers." *YIVO Annual of Jewish Social Science*, Vol. 9, 1954, pp. 308– 31.

———. "Jews and Chinese in America." *Jewish Social Studies*, Vol. 16, No. 3 (July, 1954), pp. 219– 34.

————. "Notes on Early Jewish Peddling in America." *Jewish Social Studies,* Vol. 7, No. 2 (April, 1945), pp. 119–36.

————. "The Rothschild Legend in America." *Jewish Social Studies,* Vol. 19 (1957), pp. 3–28.

Glicksberg, Charles I. "Anti-Semitism in American Literature." *The Chicago Jewish Forum,* Vol. 5, No. 3 (Spring, 1947), pp. 159–63.

Goldhurst, William. "Literary Anti-Semitism in the 20's." *Congress Bi-Weekly,* Vol. 29, No. 18 (December 24, 1962), pp. 10–12.

Gorenstein, Arthur. "The Commissioner and the Community: The Beginnings of the New York City 'Kehillah' (1908–1909)." *YIVO Annual of Jewish Social Science,* Vol. 13 (1965), pp. 87–212.

Graeber, Isacque A. "Immigrants All, Americans All." *Judaism,* Vol. 2, No. 2 (April, 1953), pp. 140–47.

Greenberg, Hayim. "The Myth of Jewish Parasitism." *Jewish Frontier,* Vol. 9, No. 3 (March, 1942), pp. 19–22.

Gutman, Herbert G. "The Knights of Labor and Patrician Anti-Semitism: 1891." *Labor History,* Vol. 13, No. 1 (Winter, 1972), pp. 63–67.

Handlin, Oscar. "American Views of the Jew at the Opening of the Twentieth Century." *PAJHS,* No. 40 (June, 1951), pp. 323–45.

————. "How U.S. Anti-Semitism Really Began: Its Grass-Roots Source in the '90's." *Commentary,* Vol. 2, No. 6 (June, 1951), pp. 541–48.

————. "Reconsidering the Populists." *Agricultural History,* Vol. 39, No. 2 (April, 1965), pp. 68–74.

Hapgood, Hutchins. "Is Dreiser Anti-Semitic?" *The Nation,* (April 17, 1935), pp. 436–38.

Hellman, George S. "Joseph Seligman, American Jew." *PAJHS,* Vol. 41 (September 1951, June 1952), pp. 27–40.

Hertzberg, Steven. "The Jewish Community of Atlanta from the End of the Civil War Until the Eve of the Frank Case." *AJHQ,* Vol. 62 (March, 1973), pp. 250–85.

Higham, John. "Another Look at Nativism." *The Catholic Historical Review,* Vol. 44, No. 2 (July, 1958), pp. 147–58.

————. "Anti-Semitism in the Gilded Age: A Reinterpretation." *Mississippi Valley Historical Review,* Vol. 43, No. 4 (March, 1957), pp. 559–78.

————. "The Cult of the 'American Consensus': Homogenizing our History." *Commentary,* Vol. 27 (February, 1959), pp. 93–100.

————. "Social Discrimination Against Jews in America, 1830–1930." *PAJHS,* Vol. 47 (September 1957-June 1958), pp. 1–33.

Hindus, Milton. "F. Scott Fitzgerald and Literary Anti-Semitism." *Commentary,* Vol. 3, No. 6 (June, 1947), pp. 508–16.

Holmes, Colin. "Goldwin Smith: A 'Liberal' Antisemite." *Patterns of Prejudice,* Vol. 6, No. 5 (September-October, 1972), pp. 25–30.

Holmes, William F. "Whitecapping: Anti-Semitism in the Populist Era." *AJHA,* Vol. 63, No. 3 (March, 1974), pp. 244–61.

Howe, Irving. "The Stranger and the Victim: The Two Jewish Stereotypes of American Fiction." *Commentary,* Vol. 8, No. 2 (August, 1949), pp. 147–56.

Isaacs, Joakim. "Candidate Grant and the Jews." *American Jewish Archives,* (April, 1965), pp. 3–16.

Karp, Abraham J. "New York Chooses a Chief Rabbi." *PAJHS,* Vol. 44 (September 1954-June 1955), pp. 129–98.

Kopf, Josephine Z. "Meyer Wolfsheim and Robert Cohn: A Study of a Jewish Type and Stereotype." *Tradition,* Vol. 10, No. 3 (Spring, 1969), pp. 93–104.

Kutzik, Alfred. "Faulkner and the Jews." *YIVO Annual of Jewish Social Science,* Vol. 13, 1965, pp. 213–26.

Lane, Lauriat, Jr. "The Literary Archetype: Some Reconsiderations." *Journal of Aesthetics and Art Criticism,* Vol. 13, No. 2 (December, 1954), pp. 226–32.

Leonard, Henry B. "Louis Marshall and Immigration Restriction, 1906–1924." *American Jewish Archives,* Vol. 24, No. 1 (April, 1972), pp. 6–26.

Levy, Leo B. "Henry James and the Jews." *Commentary,* Vol. 26, No. 3 (September, 1958), pp. 243–49.

Lifschutz, E. "Jewish Immigrant Life in American Memoir Literature." *YIVO Annual of Jewish Social Science,* Vol. 5 (1950), pp. 216–31.

Maccoby, Hyam. "The Anti-Semitism of T.S. Eliot." *Midstream,* Vol. 19, No. 5 (May, 1973), pp. 68–74.

MacIver, R.M. "Group Images and Group Realities." *Group Relations and Group Antagonisms.* Edited by R.M. MacIver. New York: Harper & Brothers, 1944.

Maller, Allen S. "Anti-Semitism and Jewish Historiography." *Judaism,* Vol. 21 (Fall, 1972), pp. 490–96.

Munson, Gorham. "Anti-Semitism: A Poverty Problem." *The Christian Century,* Vol. 56, No. 40 (October 4, 1939), pp. 119–20.

Murphy, Paul L. "Sources and Nature of Intolerance in the 1920's." *The Journal of American History,* Vol. 51 (June, 1964), pp. 60–76.

Nichols, Jeannette P. "Bryan's Benefactor: Coin Harvey and His World." *Ohio Historical Quarterly,* Vol. 67, No. 4 (October, 1958), pp. 315–16.

O'Grady, Joseph P. "Religion and American Diplomacy: An Incident in

Austro-American Relations.'' *AJHQ,* Vol. 59, No. 4 (June, 1970), pp. 407 – 23.

Panitz, Esther. "In Defense of the Jewish Immigrant 1891 – 1924.'' *AJHQ,* Vol. 55, Nos. 1-4 (September, 1965-June, 1966), pp. 57 – 97.

Peskin, Allan. "The Origins of Southern Anti-Semitism.'' *The Chicago Jewish Forum,* Vol. 14, No. 2 (Winter, 1955 – 56), pp. 83 – 87.

Pollack, Norman. "Fear of Man: Populism, Authoritarianism, and the Historians.'' *Agricultural History,* Vol. 39, No. 2 (April, 1965), pp. 59 – 67.

―――. "Handlin on Anti-Semitism: A Critique of 'American Views of the Jew.''' *Journal of American History* (December, 1964), pp. 391 – 403.

―――. "Ignatius Donnelly on Human Rights: A Study of Two Novels.'' *Mid-America,* Vol. 47, No. 2 (April, 1965), pp. 99 – 112.

―――. "The Myth of Populist Anti-Semitism.'' *The American Historical Review,* Vol. 68, No. 1 (October, 1962), pp. 76 – 86.

Polos, Nicholas C. "Black Anti-Semitism in Twentieth-Century America: Historical Myth or Reality.'' *AJA,* Vol. 27, No. 1 (April, 1975), pp. 8 – 31.

Ribalow, Harold U. "Of Jews and Thomas Wolfe.'' *The Chicago Jewish Forum,* Vol. 13, No. 2 (Winter, 1954 – 55), pp. 89 – 98.

Richards, Bernard G. "The Melville Dewey Affair.'' *Congress Weekly,* Vol. 21, No. 16 (April 20, 1954), pp. 12 – 16.

Rideout, Walter B. "O Workers' Revolution.... The True Messiah: The Jew as Author and Subject in the American Novel.'' *AJA,* Vol. 2, No. 2 (October, 1959), pp. 157 – 75.

Rieff, Susan. "Henry Harland: The Philo-Semite as Anti-Semite.'' *The Chicago Jewish Forum,* Vol. 10, No. 3 (Spring, 1952), pp. 199 – 205.

Rockaway, Robert A. "Anti-Semitism in an American City: Detroit, 1850 – 1914.'' *AJHQ,* Vol. 64, No. 1 (September, 1974), pp. 42 – 54.

Rose, Arnold. "Anti-Semitism's Root in City-Hatred.'' *Commentary,* Vol. 6, No. 4 (October, 1948), pp. 374 – 78.

Rubin, Philip. "H.L. Mencken and Jews.'' *Congress Weekly,* Vol. 23, No. 8 (February 20, 1956), pp. 6 – 8.

Russell, Francis. "The Coming of the Jews.'' *The Antioch Review* (Spring, 1955), pp. 19 – 38.

Saunders, Robert M. "The Transformation of Tom Watson, 1894 – 1895.'' *The Georgia Historical Quarterly,* Vol. 54, No. 3 (Fall, 1970), pp. 339 – 54.

Saveth, Edward N. "Henry Adams' Norman Ancestors.'' *Contemporary Jewish Record,* Vol. 8, No. 3 (June, 1945), pp. 250 – 61.

Schoenberg, Philip Ernest. "The American Reaction to the Kishinev Program of 1903." *AJHQ,* Vol. 63, no. 3 (March, 1974), pp. 262 – 83.

Seitz, Don C. "A Prince of Best Sellers." *Publisher's Weekly,* Vol. 119 (February 21, 1931), p. 940.

Shapiro, Leo. "The Anti-Semitism of T.S. Eliot." *The Chicago Jewish Forum,* Vol. 1, No. 3 (Spring, 1943), pp. 23 – 30.

Slemovitz, Philip. "Recalling the 'Harvard Scandal'; Lowell's False Prophecy 20 Years Ago." *Congress Weekly,* Vol. 10, No. 9 (February 26, 1943), pp. 12 – 13.

Snyder, Franklyn Bliss. "Leo Frank and Mary Phagan." *Journal of American Folk-Lore,* Vol. 31 (1918), pp. 264 – 66.

Stein, Norton B., and Kramer, William M. "Anti-Semitism in the Jewish Image in the Early West." *Western States Jewish Historical Quarterly,* Vol. 6, No. 2 (January, 1974).

Steinberg, Stephen. "How Jewish Quotas Began." *Commentary,* Vol. 52, No. 3 (September, 1971), pp. 67 – 76.

Stewart, Omer C. "Rural Anti-Semitism." *Frontier,* Vol. 2 (August, 1914), pp. 18 – 20.

Unger, Irwin. "Critique of Norman Pollack's 'Fear of Man.'" *Agricultural History,* Vol. 39, No. 2 (April, 1965), pp. 75 – 80.

Weinstein, Jacob J. "Popular Superstitions About Jews." *Jewish Frontier,* Vol. 8, No. 5 (May, 1941), pp. 6 – 11.

Secondary Material: Books

Arendt, Hannah. *The Origins of Totalitarianism.* New York: World Publishing Co., 1951.

Baltzell, E. Digby. *The Protestant Establishment: Aristocracy and Caste in America.* New York: Vintage Books, 1964.

Bell, Leland V. *In Hitler's Shadow; the Anatomy of American Nazism.* Port Washington, New York: Kennikat Press, 1973.

Billington, Ray Allen. *Frederick Jackson Turner.* New York: Oxford University Press, 1973.

Blau, Joseph L.; Friedman, Philip; Hertzberg, Arthur; and Mendelsohn, Isaac. *Essays on Jewish Life and Thought.* New York: Columbia University Press, 1959.

Brandes, Joseph. *Immigrants to Freedom.* Philadelphia: The Jewish Publication Society of America, 1971.

Bridges, Horace James. *Jew-Baiting: An Old Evil Newly Camouflaged.* New York: International Press, 1923.

Brown, Heywood, and Britt, George. *Christians Only: A Study in Prejudice.* New York: The Vanguard Press, 1931.

Byrnes, Robert A. *Antisemitism in Modern France: The Prologue to the Dreyfus Affair.* New Brunswick, New Jersey: Rutgers University Press, 1950.

Cohen, Naomi W. *Not Free to Desist: The American Jewish Committee 1906 – 1966.* Philadelphia: The Jewish Publication Society of America, 1972.

Davies, Rosemary Reeves. *The Rosenbluth Case: Federal Justice on Trial.* Iowa: The Iowa State University Press, 1970.

Debŕe, Moses. *The Image of the Jew in French Literature from 1800 to 1908.* Translated by Gertrude Hirschler. New York: KTAV Publishing House, 1970.

Diamond, Sander A. *The Nazi Movement in the United States 1924 – 1941.* Ithaca: Cornell University Press, 1974.

Dinnerstein, Leonard, ed. *Anti-Semitism in the United States.* New York: Holt, Rinehart & Winston, 1971.

————. *The Leo Frank Case.* New York: Columbia University Press, 1968.

Elson, Ruth Miller. *Guardians of Tradition.* Lincoln: University of Nebraska Press, 1964.

Epstein, Benjamin R., and Forster, Arnold. *Some of My Best Friends....* New York: Farrar, Straus and Cudahy, 1962.

Fiedler, Leslie A. *The Jew in the American Novel.* New York: Herzl Institute Pamphlet No. 10, 1959.

Fisch, Harold. *The Duel Image.* New York: KTAV Publishing House, 1971.

Flannery, Edward H. *The Anguish of the Jews.* The Macmillan Co., 1965.

Friedman, Lee Max. *Jewish Pioneers and Patriots.* Philadelphia: The Jewish Publication Society of America, 1942.

Gilbert, Douglas. *American Vaudeville, Its Life and Times.* New York: McGraw-Hill Book Co., 1940.

Glanz, Rudolf. *The Jew in Early American Wit and Graphic Humor.* New York: KTAV Publishing House, 1973.

————. *Jew and Italian.* New York: Shilsinger Bros., 1971.

————. *The Jew in the Old American Folklore.* New York, 1960.

Glock, Charles Y., and Stark, Rodney. *Christian Beliefs and Anti-Semitism.* New York: Harper & Row, 1966.

Goren, Arthur A. *New York Jews and the Quest for Community.* New York: Columbia University Press, 1970.

Graeber, Isacque, and Britt, Stewart Henderson. *Jews in a Gentile World.* New York: The Macmillan Co., 1942.

Handlin, Oscar. *Adventure in Freedom: Three Hundred Years of Jewish Life in America.* New York: McGraw-Hill Book Co., 1954.

———, and Handlin, Mary. *Danger in Discord: Origins of Anti-Semitism in the United States.* New York: Anti-Defamation League of B'nai B'rith, 1948.

———. *Race and Nationality in American Life.* New York: Little, Brown and Co., 1957.

Harap, Louis. *The Image of the Jew in American Literature.* Philadelphia: The Jewish Publication Society of America, 1974.

Hertzberg, Arthur. *The French Enlightenment and the Jews.* New York: Columbia University Press, 1968.

Higham, John. *Send These to Me: Jews and Other Immigrants in Urban America.* New York: Atheneum, 1975.

———. *Strangers in the Land: Patterns of American Nativism 1860 – 1925.* New York: Atheneum, 1971.

Hofstadter, Richard. *The Age of Reform; from Bryan to F.D.R.* New York: Alfred A. Knopf, 1956.

Hovey, Richard B. *John Jay Chapman—An American Mind.* New York: Columbia University Press, 1959.

Hudson, Winthrop S. *Religion in America.* New York: Charles Scribner's Sons, 1973.

Isaac, Jules. *The Teaching of Contempt: Christian Roots of Anti-Semitism.* New York: Holt, Rinehart & Winston, 1964.

Jackson, Kenneth T. *The Ku Klux Klan in the City 1915 – 1930.* New York: Oxford University Press, 1967.

Jaher, Frederic Cople. *Doubters and Dissenters; Cataclysmic Thought in America, 1885 – 1918.* London: Collier-Macmillan, 1964.

Johannsen, Albert. *The House of Beadle and Adams.* Norman, Oklahoma: University of Oklahoma Press, 1950.

Johnpoll, Bernard. *Pacifist's Progress.* Chicago: Quadrangle Books, 1970.

Jung, C.G. *Psyche and Symbol.* New York: Doubleday Anchor Books, 1958.

Korn, Bertram W. *American Jewry and the Civil War.* New York: Atheneum, 1970.

Landa, M.J. *The Jew in Drama.* Port Washington, New York: Kennikat Press, 1926.

Landman, Isaac, ed. *Christian and Jew; A Symposium for Better Understanding.* New York: Horace Liveright, 1929.

Lasch, Christopher. *The New Radicalism in America.* New York: Alfred A. Knopf, 1966.

Lehrmann, Charles C. *The Jewish Element in French Literature.* Translated by George Klin. Rutherford, New Jersey: Fairleigh Dickinson University Press, 1971.

Leschnitzer, Adolf. *The Magic Background of Modern Anti-Semitism: An Analysis of the German-Jewish Relationship.* New York: International Universities Press, 1956.

Levinger, Lee J. *Anti-Semitism in the United States; Its History and Causes.* New York: Bloch Publishing Co., 1925.

Lippman, Walter. *Public Opinion.* New York: Penguin Books, 1946.

Liptzin, Sol. *The Jew in American Literature.* New York: Bloch Publishing Co., 1966.

Livingston, Sigmund. *Must Men Hate?* New York: Harper & Brothers, 1944.

MacLeish, Archibald. *Jews in America.* New York: Random House, 1936.

McWilliams, Cary. *A Mask for Privilege: Anti-Semitism in America.* Boston: Little, Brown and Co., 1948.

Manners, Ande. *Poor Cousins.* New York: Coward, McCann & Geoghegan, 1974.

Marrus, Michael R. *The Politics of Assimilation.* Oxford: At the Clarendon Press, 1971.

Mersand, Joseph. *Traditions in American Literature.* New York: The Modern Chapbook, 1939.

Myers, Gustavus. *History of Bigotry in the United States.* New York: Random House, 1943.

Noble, David W. *The Progressive Mind, 1890–1917.* Chicago: Rand McNally & Co., 1970.

Nugent, Walter T.K. *The Tolerant Populists.* Chicago: The University of Chicago Press, 1963.

Olson, Bernhard E. *Faith and Prejudice.* New Haven: Yale University Press, 1963.

Parkes, James. *Anti-Semitism.* Chicago: Quadrangle Books, 1963.

———. *An Enemy of the People—Anti-Semitism.* New York: Penguin Books, 1946.

Pickens, Donald. *Eugenics and the Progressives.* Nashville: Vanderbilt University Press, 1968.

Poliakov, Leon. *The History of Anti-Semitism.* Translated by Richard Howard. New York: Schocken Books, 1974.

Pollack, Norman. *The Populist Response to Industrial America.* New York: W.W. Norton & Co., 1966.

Randall, Earle Stanley. *The Jewish Character in the French Novel.* Menasha, Wisconsin: By the Author, 1941.

Rideout, Walter B. *The Radical Novel in the United States, 1900–1954.* Cambridge: Harvard University Press, 1956.

Ridge, Martin. *Ignatius Donnelly, the Portrait of a Politician.* Chicago: University of Chicago Press, 1962.

Rischin, Moses. *The Promised City: New York's Jews, 1870–1914.* Cambridge: Harvard University Press, 1970.

Roche, John P. *The Quest for the Dream, the Development of Civil Rights and Human Relations in Modern America.* New York: Macmillan, 1963.

Rose, Peter, ed. *The Ghetto and Beyond: Essays on Jewish Life in America.* New York: Random House, 1969.

Rosenberg, Edgar. *From Shylock to Svengali: Jewish Stereotypes in English Fiction.* Stanford: Stanford University Press, 1960.

Rosenberg, Stuart. *The Jewish Community in Rochester, 1843 – 1925.* New York: Columbia University Press, 1954.

Rosenstock, Morton. *Louis Marshall, Defender of Jewish Rights.* Detroit: Wayne State University Press, 1965.

St. John, Robert. *Jews, Justice and Judaism.* New York: Doubleday & Co., 1969.

Samuels, Ernest. *Henry Adams, the Major Phase.* Cambridge: Harvard University Press, 1964.

———. *Henry Adams, the Middle Years.* Cambridge: Harvard University Press, 1958.

———. *The Young Henry Adams.* Cambridge: Harvard University Press, 1965.

Sandmel, Samuel. *The First Christian Century in Judaism and Christianity: Certainties and Uncertainties.* New York: Oxford University Press, 1969.

Sartre, Jean-Paul. *Anti-Semite and Jew.* New York: Schocken Books, 1965.

Saveth, Edward N. *American Historians and European Immigrants, 1875 – 1925.* New York: Columbia University Press, 1948.

Seiden, Morton Irving. *The Paradox of Hate: A Study in Ritual Murder.* South Brunswick: A.S. Barnes & Co., 1967.

Simmell, Ernst, ed. *Anti-Semitism: A Social Disease.* New York: International Universities Press, 1946.

Solomon, Barbara Miller. *Ancestors and Immigrants.* Chicago: The University of Chicago Press, 1972.

Spiller, Robert E., et al., ed. *Literary History of the United States.* New York: Macmillan, 1974.

Starr, Rabbi Earl S. *How a Minority Was Viewed Through the Eyes of the Theatre in the Critical Years of 1925 – 1937.* Wyoming, Pennsylvania: Cro Woods Publishing, 1969.

Stember, Charles Herbert, ed. *Jews in the Mind of America.* New York: Basic Books, 1966.

Stocking, George W., Jr. *Race, Culture and Evolution: Essays in the History of Anthropology.* New York: The Free Press, 1968.

Strong, Donald S. *Organized Anti-Semitism in America.* Washington, D.C.: American Council on Public Affairs, 1941.

Sward, Keith. *The Legend of Henry Ford*. New York: Russell & Russell, 1968.

Szajkowski, Zosa. *Jews, Wars, and Communism*. New York: KTAV Publishing House, 1972.

Teller, Judd L. *Scapegoat of Revolution*. New York: Charles Scribner's Sons, 1954.

―――. *Strangers and Natives*. New York: Dell Publishing Co., 1968.

Trachtenberg, Joshua. *The Devil and the Jews*. New Haven: Yale University Press, 1943.

Unger, Irwin. *The Greenback Era*. Princeton: Princeton University Press, 1968.

Weinstein, Gregory. *Ardent Eighties*. New York: International Press, 1947.

Weisbord, Robert G., and Stein, Arthur. *Bitter-Sweet Encounter: The Afro American and the American Jew*. New York: Schocken Books, 1972.

White, Morton and Lucia. *The Intellectual Versus the City*. New York: New American Library, 1962.

Wilson, Edmund. *A Piece of My Mind; Reflections of Sixty*. New York: Farrar, Straus and Cudahy, 1956.

Young, James. *The Toadstool Millionaires*. Princeton: Princeton University Press, 1961.

Zborowski, Mark, and Herzog, Elizabeth. *Life Is with People*. New York: Schocken Books, 1962.

Ziff, Larzer. *The American 1890's: Life and Times of a Lost Generation*. New York: The Viking Press, 1966.

Index

About the Author
Michael N. Dobkowski is assistant professor of religious studies at
Hobart and William Smith Colleges in Geneva, New York. He is a
specialist in modern Jewish and American Jewish history, and his arti-
cles have appeared in the *American Quarterly of Judaism* and the
Markham Review.